AF622920

FOUNDATION®
BOOKS

Foundation Books is an imprint of Cambridge University Press India Pvt. Ltd.

Cambridge House, 4381/4 Ansari Road, Daryaganj, New Delhi 110 002

www.cambridgeindia.org

© Cambridge University Press India Pvt. Ltd. 2014

This publication is in copyright. Subject to statutory exception and to the provisions of relevant collective licensing agreements, no reproduction of any part may take place without the written permission of Cambridge University Press India Pvt. Ltd.

First published 2014

Printed in India at Bhavish Graphics, Chennai

ISBN 978-93-82993-06-3 Hardback

Cambridge University Press India Pvt. Ltd. has no responsibility for the persistence or accuracy of URLs for external or third-party internet websites referred to in this publication, and does not guarantee that any content on such websites is, or will remain, accurate or appropriate.

A Struggle for Identity

Muslim Women in the United Provinces

Firdous Azmat Siddiqui

FOUNDATION®
BOOKS

Contents

Acknowledgements *v*

Introduction *vii*

1. Social Stratification of Muslim Women in the United Provinces 1
2. Socio-religious Movement and the Muslim Women's Issue 18
3. British Perception of Muslim Women: Questions of Fecundity and Health 35
4. Crises in the Social and Economic Identity of Muslim Women: The Great Uprising of 1857 55
5. Changing Profile of Muslim Women through Education 76
6. Patriarchy and Social Obligation of Indian Muslim Women 109
7. Cultural Clash: From *Tawaif* to *Kasbi* 155
8. Law, Land and Muslim Women: The Economic Situation 180
9. Muslim Women's Response to the New Judicial System 197

Conclusion 219

Glossary 221

Bibliography 228

Index 237

Acknowledgements

I am indebted to many people, among whom only a few names can be mentioned in this limited space. Before I name others, I express my sincere gratitude to Professor Sushil Srivastava who taught me and shared his learning environment and lives. His understanding of minority issues provided a foundation of this title. Academically, I have benefited from scholarly insights of many friends and colleagues. I pay my sincere thanks to Professor Imtiaz Ahmad who constantly encouraged me to get this work published. I greatly value his detailed and constructive comments and his important support throughout this work. I would also like to express my special gratitude to my teacher Professor N.R. Farooqui for his suggestion and views about the Muslim society in India.

I am grateful to my colleagues at the University of Allahabad – Dr Vinita Mishra, Dr Alok Prasad, Dr Asutosh Tiwari, Sanjai Rai, Dr Amit Singh, Dr Meraj Uddin, Dr Zeba Naqvi, Rais Khan, Dr Refaque and Dr Ismat Usmani who supported and facilitated this research with their critical and constructive comments. Also, I am thankful to all staff members at the libraries where I collected material for this research. My special thanks to Rahmat Ullah who made me aware about a number of Urdu sources.

My family has been a constant source of support especially my parents, late Azmat Ullaha Siddiqui and Rehana Zahoor Jafri, who have both inspired this work throughout my study. From an early age, they nurtured within me a keen appreciation for disciplined study and intellectual curiosity. It is with all my love and respect that I dedicate this book to my parents and also to all marginalized Muslim women. In particular, I also acknowledge my husband Shah Abul Faiz and my brothers, Ehtesham, Mohtesim, Atique and Aftab for their constant moral support. My mother-in-law Nafees Bano was always very supportive over the years of my research.

Others to whom I am most grateful are my colleagues and the former Director, Professor Janaki Rajan at Sarojini Naidu Centre for Women's Studies, who created an environment of intellectual rigor and disciplined practice that nurtured my studies. Professor Nishat Zaidi is gratefully acknowledged for translating the Urdu poems into English. Finally, I express my sincere thanks to Cambridge University Press, India and the editor Suvadip Bhattacharjee for giving the book its final shape.

The original research for this project was generously funded by the Indian Council for Historical Research. Some portions of this book appeared elsewhere in different forms. However, I revised them substantially for the book version. Chapter 1 was previously published as 'Social stratification of Muslim women in United Province', *Journal of Women Studies*, ed. Sumita Parmar, Vol. IV, No. 1, March, 2011, 75–96. Chapter 3 is based on my paper 'Colonial report on census and its reflection on Indian Muslim women in United *Province*', *Islam and Muslim Societies: A Social Science Journal*, ed. Nadeem Husnain, Serial Publication, New Delhi, Vol.1, No.1, 2005, 155. A section of Chapter 5 is taken from my article 'Muslim female education in United Province: A case study of Allahabad University', *Muslims of Uttar Pradesh*, ed. Abdul Waheed, CEPECAMI, Aligarh Muslim University Press, Aligarh, 2007. Chapter 6 is based on a part of my article '*Unnisavai Sadi ke Utrardh me Muslim Vidhvaon ki Isthiti* (in Hindi) published in *U.P History Congress Proceeding*, ed. A.K Sinha, Anamika Publisher, New Delhi. Chapter 9 is based on another article 'Legal position of Indian Muslim women with special reference to United Province', *Facets of Indian History*, ed., A.K. Sinha, Anamika Publisher, New Delhi and 'A long journey of Muslim child wives: Age of consent bill to Sharda Act, in *Islam and Muslim societies*, Vol. 3, 2006.

Introduction: Making the Invisible Visible

> Social changes in the 19th century focused primarily on women, whose independence had been completely eroded by socio-religious customs which regulated the age of marriage, education, widow re-marriage, inheritance, etc. By and large there was a general acceptance of the need for change but due to the politicization of group solidarity and the need to maintain identity, the debate on reform was between those who opted for covert change with no open rejection of past customs and practices which would make community solidarity in political and economic terms more difficult and those who felt social change to be necessary prerequisite for the desired political and economic changes in the community. The reaction was fairly widespread as it was a response not to social reform, but to the all-pervasive political changes underway.[1]
>
> Shaheeda Lateef

This book attempts to understand the social and economic profile of women, particularly the Muslim women of the United Provinces. The first question that lay before me while starting this book was: Why choose the United Provinces (UP) and not those regions where Muslims live in sizeable numbers? The Sachar Committee Report of November 2006 states that Indian Muslims lag behind others in development indices, and that the condition of Indian Muslim women is worse than that of Dalit women. The report's data and analysis highlights the pathetic condition of their education and socio-economic status in UP.[2] However, this was not always the case. Francis Robinson's data

---

[1] Lateef, Shaheeda K., *Muslim Women in India: Political and Private Realities (1890–1980)* (New Delhi: Kali for Women, 1990), 17.

[2] Sachar, Justice Rajinder, 'High level Report on Social, Economic and Educational Status of Muslims', November 2006.

for the colonial period post-1857 shows that their socio-economic condition was better a century ago.[3] At the same time, he is of the opinion that the UP Muslims were separatists. Was this due to their better socio-economic condition? Was the 1857 mutiny responsible for Hindu-Muslim polarisation and the creation of community identity?[4] If so, then how do these issues influence women's status? This complex issue of the socio-economic condition of the Muslims of UP and its direct link with their political position is intriguing, especially when it seen in light of their steady decline in socio-economic terms. The problem becomes even more complex when we narrow our focus on the Muslim women of this region.

The second question that arose was: Why Muslim women? The tendency to see them as a collective or monolithic entity integrated by their adherence to Islam and its traditions (a flawed approach that unfortunately extends to the treatment of Muslim men also) is a primary cause behind their invisibility in historical and socio-economic perspectives, and should be given up in favour of an approach that seeks to view them in segregated terms—that is, social class, caste and regions.[5] This work proceeds with an awareness of the social stratification within Muslim society and aims to examine the status of Muslim women in terms of their specificity, situatedness and context. Second, my approach emphasises an inherent tendency that arises from the political orientation of Hindus and Muslims to view themselves as parallel communities. This tendency needs to be given up in favour of an approach that seeks to view Muslim women on their own terms. Efforts should be made to explore the realities of Muslim women's lives without carrying the burden of trying to decide how comparable, similar or better-off they are in comparison to Hindu women. It is only after a baseline picture of the realities of Muslim women's lives on their own terms is made available that meaningful comparison with women in other communities, including Hindu women, will become possible. Therefore, this book attempts to understand the status of Indian Muslims, particularly women, from the perspective of its own social stratification.

The situation of women in contemporary times is largely a by-product of the past, and it is in this context that a historical enquiry into the changing

---

[3] Robinson, Francis, *Separatism among Indian Muslims: The politics of the United Provinces Muslims 1860–1923* (New Delhi: Oxford University Press, 1997), 22–23, 39, 46.

[4] Robinson, *Separatism among Indian Muslims*, 84–132.

[5] Jeffery, Patricia, *Frogs in a Well: Indian Women in Purdah* (New Delhi: Manohar, 2000), ix.

social and economic profile of women in the nineteenth century becomes significant. As Azra Asghar Ali says, the impact of feminism in South Asia must be understood in the cultural context of colonialism and the particular concerns of social reformers.[6] The situation of Indian Muslim women was and is determined by several social biases, economic deprivation and traditions. Hence, I have also tried to examine the status of the most marginalised section among the Muslim lower socio-economic stratum, the *arzal* class. It is very difficult to find any literature on the status of lower-caste Muslim women, and repeated suggestions to keep a distance from non-*ashraf* women in *adab* literature indicate the hostility against this marginalised section. My experience in dealing with archival sources has taught me that those interested in a baseline study on *kamin/paji/arzal* women have to depend only on oral and folk tradition, or to some extent on census reports. Therefore, I have tried to look at this section from a new perspective, and hope that it will fill the lacuna that exists on this subject.

Women constitute half the population of any society, and within the context of the Indian subcontinent, any study related to the situation of women becomes all the more significant because of the patriarchal attitudes that traditionally prevail. I also explore how the colonial presence influenced the status of Muslims in India. Contemporary Indian women are products of the past, and it is here that colonial biases play an extremely significant role. While one may accept that traditions determined biases, it cannot be denied that dominant determinants also contributed to changing these biases. The colonial outlook was influenced largely by Victorian ideas about nineteenth-century British society, where women were subordinate to the dominant position held by men. Women were understood as dependent personalities, and this bias was transferred by the ruling power to the colonial society in India.[7] This book proposes that a peculiar relationship between the ruler and the ruled emerged with the coming of the Europeans to India, one that was apparent particularly in the early nineteenth century. It was in this context that all Indian women were viewed as subjects meant to secure the interest of the ruler. Edward Said rightly observed that the East-West relationship is one of power and domination, of varying degrees in a complex hegemony.[8]

---

[6] Ali, Azra Asghar, *The Emergence of Feminism among Indian Muslim Women (1920–1947)* (New Delhi: Oxford University Press, 2000), 4.

[7] Pearce, Charles E., 'Love Beseiged,' ed. Ralph Crane (New Delhi: Oxford University Press, 2003), xiii. See also Said, Edward, *Orientalism: Western Conception of the Orient* (London: Penguin Books, 2001), 6.

[8] Said. *Orientalism*, 5.

Also significant is exploring how the colonial presence influenced the status of Indian Muslim women. What was the role of Muslim social reformers vis-à-vis their womenfolk? Colonial critics used the condition of Muslim women to highlight the backwardness of their society, and it is perhaps because of this that the Muslim intelligentsia sought a change in the position of women; this change being symbolic of their desire for change in the entire social order. What was the educational status of Muslim women, and to what extent did Western thought influence their curriculum? What was the Western perception of Indian Muslim women? Can we consider 1857 a turning point for the gender debate in India? This book looks critically at how the colonial judicial system destroyed traditional custom, and whether this legal system was beneficial to women, or if it merely enhanced the complexitie of their lives. An attempt is also made to see the impact of the law of primogeniture on women's rights.

In the nineteenth century, the British were occupied with the question of becoming socially acceptable, as they had already established political and military sway in major tracts of India. It was in this context that the servants of the East India Company, merchants, adventurers and missionaries who arrived in India from Europe attempted to enter the '*zennana*', in much the same manner as the ruling Indian elite. These foreigners adopted the ways of the ruling class, and thus demonstrated a preference for the Muslim section of Indian society. In a way, we can assume that it was an easier and a natural way of intervening. The Europeans established themselves as the dominant group by the early nineteenth century, and consequently adopted certain habits peculiar to Islamic society.

In this way, the Europeans began a social dialogue with the old Muslim households and adopted a Muslim way of life. The first dialogues that the British established were with the Muslim ruling class, evident in their attempt to identify more closely with the ruling families. This could have been easy because of their common food habits (both Muslims and Europeans were non-vegetarians)[9] and because Muslims and Christians both belong to Semitic religions (*ahl-e kitab*). Besides Islam sanctioned marriages between Muslims and those communities that believe in the other three revealed Books—Injeel, Tauret and Jaboor. This frequent intermingling led to European

[9] Dalrymple, William, *The White Mughals* (New Delhi: Penguin, 2002), 9–10, 64, 66–67, 73, 77, 85. See also Malcolm Speirs, '*The Wasikadars of Oudh*' (New Delhi: Rupa & Co., 2008).

entry into the '*zenana*', and a few European men even married Indian Muslim women.[10] As these Europeans were either unmarried, or came to India without their spouses, the declaration of their marriages with Muslim ladies of status was all the more celebrated.[11]

Therefore, the early part of the nineteenth century witnessed a definite East-West intermingling.[12] As Patricia Jeffery emphasises, the essence of Islam has long been, and continues to be, a matter of considerable dispute and contestation among Indian Muslims themselves: ranging from debates on why the Mughal Empire collapsed to how Indian Muslims should have engaged with the British and forces of modernity in the nineteenth century.[13] In an attempt to further extend their interest in India, the British had to penetrate the Indian social structure, and it was in this context that some European women did a commendable job of entering the *zenana.*[14] The Muslim zenana was an object of curiosity for them. Since no man was allowed to enter the *zenana*, it was European women who could cross the threshold (barring a few rare instances of marriage between European men and royal Muslim women; in fact, in the beginning European women, whose influence was considered pernicious, were also refused admission into the *zenana*).[15] It was in this environment that a fruitful interaction began between women of the East and the West. What is interesting is that these European women left behind a rich account of Indian

[10] It is very interesting to observe that before 1857, it was common to find marriages between European women and influential Muslim men. In this regard, the examples of Mrs Meer Hasan (a European woman who travelled extensively throughout India in the early nineteenth century; she married a Westernised Muslim man, but their marriage failed because of the cultural differences between their communities) and Vilaeti Begum (a British lady who married into the royal family of Oudh and adopted Islam) are significant. As it was rare to find European women in the Muslim *zenana*, these women's accounts are important insofar as they wrote about the *zenana* not merely as observers, but as residents. Col. Gardner's marriage to a Muslim girl is well-celebrated in writings.

[11] Speirs, Malcolm, *The Wasikadars of Oudh.*

[12] 'Oh East is East, West is West, and never the twain shall meet': this famous line from Rudyard Kipling only serves to enlarge the gulf between the East and the West.

[13] Jeffery, *Frogs in Well,* ix.

[14] De Souza, Eunice, *Pardah: An Anthology* (New Delhi: Oxford University Press, 2004), 3–165.

[15] Dalrymple, *The Last Mughal: The Fall of a Dynasty, Delhi, 1857* (UK: Bloomsbury, 2006), 467.

women, which provides us with an understanding of them.[16] Indian men did not consider it appropriate for their women to be known through the process of discursive writing. Muslim men considered it a form of unveiling if their women so much as wrote their names on paper. It is only official records and European travelogues that present us with a one-sided picture. Muslim women remained otherwise invisible in discursive writings.

It is also hoped that this book will lead to a discussion on why Muslim women remained invisible in academic discourse, and how we can make them visible. Although I have gone though all government records, private papers and letters, literature, newspapers, travelogues and memoirs, I found a very general/stereotyped picture of Muslim women that made it necessary to think beyond the archive, which says little on common women. A few example of such history came through as I was writing Chapter 4 on 1857: mutiny papers say very little about the involvement of common women in the revolt except for presenting them as victims of a great uprising, the only exceptions being a few recent works on Dalit and other marginalised women.[17] However, when I talked with people of western UP, I found that they still cherish the memory of brave *gujar* women like Habibi and the *Rajput* Rahimi. No archival evidence, though, is available to support these claims. Likewise, in Allahabad, a research scholar working on the 1857 uprising in Allahabad had interviewed a descendant of Maulvi Liaqat Ali, who boasted that it was not only men but also women of their family who had taken part; women assisted their male counterparts by making *roti*s and sending them to neighbouring villages. The *roti*, it must be remembered, had become the symbol of revolt.[18] While history as text may not be available, history as memory is almost organic to human society, as the Allahabad school historian Lal Bahadur Verma says in his popular book, *Understanding History*. He would often quote Rahul Sankratayan, saying, '*Ek kankar ka bhee itihaas hota hai*' (every particle has its history).

> History is all pervasive. The past leaves its relics everywhere. It is up to the historian to hunt for them and use them as construction of material. So the sources of history are there in archeology, oral traditions, myths, legends, folklore, all kind of documents official and private archives, newspaper and magazine, private papers and what not.

[16] See Indira Ghosh, *Memsahib Abroad: Writings by Women Travellers in Nineteenth-Century India* (New Delhi: Oxford University Press, 1998).

[17] Narayan, Badri, *Women heroes and dalit assertion in North India: Culture, Identity and Politics* (New Delhi: Sage Publications, 2006).

[18] Margaret MacMillan, *Women of the Raj* (London: Thames and Hudson, 1988), 104.

Like all literature, originally, all history must have been oral history. Of course, then there was not much differences between history and myth or legends, all of them constituting the core of folklore.[19]

Most of the written sources, from literary to archival, are individualistic. They may be a product of societal energy, but they are coloured by individual authorship. Oral traditions are oriented through collective authorship. Anthony Seldon states that most social sciences are not social because they do not take into consideration the limitations under which man works. And when one tries to know them only through written sources, the limitations increase. According to him, in such a situation oral sources provide that environment and colour that is unavailable in other sources.[20] In this way, oral evidence is more relevant and imperative, especially in areas where written documents are inadequate.

My *Nani* (maternal grandmother) Aliya Khatoon helped me to understand and bridge the gap of three generations and provided an insight into the existing oral traditions, which I have presented in this book in the form of folk songs and family tradition. I feel that this constitutes new research into the subject, particularly my *nani*'s memories about her own initial education and her father's bias against women's writing. She shared with me her father's anguish when she started learning to write, an act which made him slap her for the first time in her life. She loved talking about her in-laws, because it was her brothers-in-law who had taught her how to read and write in Urdu. She always used to say: '*Hamka admi banae deen*' (They made me human). And when one talked to her about education and her father, she expressed her anguish by saying: '*bahut haramjada*[21] *the hamare abba, hamka parhe nahi diye. Ham chup-chpke apni chachi*

[19] Verma, Lal Bahadur, *Understanding History* (Allahabad: Abhiveyakti Prakashan, 1995), 54.

[20] Verma, *Understanding History*, 77.

[21] The word *haramzada* seems abusive, but one should take into account her situation and age; she is an old, weak and octogenarian matriarch in a big house, with five daughters and one son and many grandchildren. She is often unclear about what she is saying, and about whom. But it is true that I have always heard her praise her in-laws. She remains aware of contemporary politics, and can talk extensively on politics, the Partition and religion. I often heard her murmuring, 'Boli bi amma beta khilafat pe jaan de dena.' I think she must have been born after the Khilafat movement, but look how memory and oral tradition passes from one generation to another. Another significant issue that I heard her speak of is, '*Marenge mar jaenge seene pe goli khaenge, Pakistan banaenge*'. She revealed that this was the slogan of children born in the late 1930s, as her elder daughter, Najma, used to shout this out

se sikhe.'[22] She told me that one of her *chachis* (aunt) was considered educated enough; however, when my *nani* wanted to learn from her, she was forbidden to do so, as it was undesirable for an *ashraf* girl to learn to write.

Both my *nani* and my *dadi* (paternal grandmother) were very interesting figures in my life when it came to gender construction. My *dadi,* the late Safi-un Nisa, who had received only traditional education at home, was the big matriarch of our household, and it was she who gave me an insight into how powerful women could influence male decision. It is not true that Muslim women were always oppressed; rather, they played a very significant role in family matters and in the neighborhood, much like my *dadi* did. All of us, young and old, fondly called her *baji.* She also preferred staying in the village of her choice instead of her husband's home, since she considered that place backward. It is also noteworthy that while she had the choice of staying in her natal village (as she was also the inheritor of her father's property), she rejected both options and convinced her husband to live with her in a village of her choice, despite his being the only son of a landholding family.

Although most of the women who travelled in the early nineteenth century did so with a missionary intent, there were a few who left a mark in Muslim women's early colonial historiography. Most remarkable amongst them were Fanny Park and Mrs Meer Hasan, who travelled to north India during this period. Fanny Park, who showed a clear interest in the royal *zenana*, left a detailed and lively account of royal families. She was also a close friend of Colonel Gardner, who had married into a royal family of India, thereby making it easy for Park to gain access to the royal *zenana.*[23] At that time, one often found a European lady in the Muslim *zenana.* A fine example of such a marriage was that of Mrs. Meer Hasan, who married into the influential Shia Saiyid family of Lucknow, where she lived for twelve years (1816–28). She then returned to

often at home. My maternal grandfather, Saiyid Zahoor Alam Jafri, was a supporter of the Pakistan movement, and an active member of Anjuman-e Rafatiya in Etawa. When she talks about Gandhi, it almost seems as though she was his childhood friend.

22 One striking observation of mine is that the Saiyids used to be very liberal towards female education, while Sheikhs were less flexible. Also, my Nani came from Mirzapur district, where higher-caste Muslims had a very conservative attitude vis-à-vis women. However, she was married to a family living in the small town of Allahabad, where Muslims were very liberal with regard to female education, as is discussed in detail in Chapter 5.

23 De Souza, *Purdah: An Anthology,* 22.

England and wrote a book on Indian Muslims. Mrs. Hasan's account is reliable because she had been an intimate part of this society, instead of remaining an outside observer. Her own experience with the Muslim women of Oudh is very interesting.

Hence, this Introduction will try to understand the significance of 1857: Why was 1857 so important for both the ruler and the ruled? An attempt is also made to explore why earlier encounters of Europeans with Indian Muslim women were different from those in the late nineteenth century. What was different about their post-mutiny perception, and why had it changed towards Muslims? Is it reasonable to view this period as a turning point in the gender history of India? This work is primarily concerned with evaluating the condition of Muslim women, particularly after 1857, when Muslim society was going through a socio-economic transition and the Mughal dynasty seemed ruined forever. Therefore, it was only natural that their condition worsened afterwards.[24] While the deterioration affected the entire Muslim community, the worst affected were the women. The great Urdu Poet Ghalib drew a pathetic picture of Delhi in a letter dated January 1862 to his friend:

> Alas my dear boy; this is not the Delhi in which you were born, not the Delhi in which you got the schooling, not the Delhi in which you used to come to your lessons with me, not in Delhi in which I have passed fifty-one years of my life.
>
> It is a camp. The only Muslims here are artisans or servants of the British authorities. All the rest are Hindus. The male descendants of the deposed king—such as survived the sword—draw allowances of five rupees a month. The female descendants, if old, are bawds; if young, are prostitutes ....[25]

Making the Invisible Visible: Mrs Meer Hasan's Account of 'Zenana'

Since the social structure of north India was hierarchical, the women of this region were also subjected to the upper-class patriarchal system. For as long as they did not come in the way of their male counterparts, they could avail of the freedom and rights given to them in Islam. Yet, there was a widely-held belief that women should be confined within their homes.[26] However, in the case of

---

[24] Dalrymple, *The Last Mughal*, 462.

[25] Dalrymple, *The Last Mughal*, 462.

[26] Hasan, Meer, *An Observation on Musalmans of India*, Vol. 1 (London: Oxford University Press, 1974 [1832]).

the royal women and *begums* of the princely states, the confinement was not as rigid, as can be gauged from observing the Begums of Oudh and Bhopal, who broke all barriers in achieving their political ambitions.[27] There were also the wives of many *talluqdars*, who managed their big estates very well.[28] Indeed, not only did the Begums of Oudh interfere in political activities, but they also played the role of king-maker. They received a monthly allowance in the name of *'jam-e bahu'*.[29] Thus, they were very strong financially, which was why the British could not overlook their significance in the East India Company's relations with the state of Oudh.

European women considered the zenana a prison and often referred to Muslim women as caged birds or tigers. In their accounts, women were imagined as prisoners, deprived of all rights. It is this context that Patricia Jeffery termed them 'frogs in a well', completely ignorant of the outside world.[30] She states:

> The historical and ethnographic record indicates that seclusion practices are feature of societies marked by economic inequalities. Typically, the women who are most systematically secluded are from the social and economic elites, whose family can forego any contribution that women might make through economic activities outside their home—whether as unpaid workers on the family farms or as paid employees.[31]

Mrs Meer Hasan's observations on the Indian Musalman throws light on several unknown aspects of Muslim women. She was not only an eyewitness in Oudh society, but she also became a part of this society. She interacted with many Muslim women in the *zenana*. Interestingly, she depicted the Indian Muslim woman neither as an oppressed and exploited creature nor as a broad-minded revolutionary, but as a self-satisfied and prosperous *zenana*. In her account, she states that the houses of Indian Muslims were divided into two sections—the *zenana* and the *mardana*. Since both the major Indian communities practised

---

27 Nawab Sikandar Jahan Begum and her daughter Nawab Shajahan Begum are among the most significant names; they not only contributed politically, but their socio-cultural contribution also remains unforgettable.

28 Bhatnagar, G. D., *Audh under Wajid Ali Shah* (Varanasi: Bharatiya Vidya Prakashan, 1968), 64.

29 Bhatnagar, *Audh under Wajid Ali Shah*, 3.

30 Jeffery, *Frogs in a Well*, vii.

31 Jeffery, *Frogs in a Well*, xii.

the segregation of sexes, the *zenana* was a part of the society of both upper-caste Muslims and Hindus. Mrs Hasan describes the *zenana*

> as a tolerably sized quadrangle, three sides of which is occupied by habitable buildings, and the fourth by kitchens, office, lumber rooms leaning in the centre on open courtyard. As they have neither doors nor windows to the halls, warmth or privacy is secured by means of thick wadded curtains. The wadded curtains are called 'purdah'. Besides the purdah, the opening between the pillars have blinds neatly made of bamboo strips, wove together [sic] with coloured cords, these are called jhilmils or cheeks. These blinds constitutes a real comfort to everyone in India, as they admit air when let down and at the same time shutout flies and other annoying insects.[32]

Purdah was observed by both communities. The crucial characteristic of the *purdah* system was the restriction it imposed on interactions between men and women outside of certain well-defined categories, which differ among Muslims and Hindus. The Muslim *purdah* restriction did not apply within the immediate kinship unit but only outside it, while for Hindus, *purdah* was based on a set of avoidance rules between a woman and her male affines. Muslim seclusion begins at puberty; Hindu seclusion, strictly speaking, begins with marriage.[33]

In spite of their strict confinement, Muslim women were very creative, in both their literature and their handicrafts. Since this was a period of rapid change, several new states were replacing those of the weak Mughals. There was also a change in the linguistic make-up of the region. Urdu replaced Persian, and many Muslim women contributed to its spread.[34] These were not common women, but either elite zenana women such as Mughal princess and begums of princely states, or the *tawa'ifs*. Court culture shifted from Delhi to Lucknow and the *tawa'ifs* of Lucknow emerged as the chief connoisseurs of literature, contributing vastly in establishing the Oudhi culture of *tahzeeb* and *tameez*. Indeed, the latter part of the eighteenth century and first part of the nineteenth is considered a period of emergence of *tawa'if* culture, as a number of princely

---

[32] Hasan, *An Observation*, 304–6.

[33] Papanek, Hanna and Gail Minault (eds), *Separate World: Studies of Purda in South Asia* (New Delhi: Chanakya Publications, 1982), 3.

[34] Petievich, Carla, 'Feminine Authorship and Urdu Poetic Tradition: Bahristan-I Naz vs Tazkira-I Rekhti,' in *A Wilderness of Possibilities: Urdu Studies in Transnational Perspective,* eds Kathryn Hansen and Devid Lelyveld (New Delhi: Oxford University Press, 2005), 223–50.

states that emerged in the eighteenth century provided them with space. These states played a significant role in patronising them. Perhaps this can explain why Hyderabad, Lucknow and Benares became big centres for these *tawa'ifs*.

Famous Muslim Women of the Early Nineteenth Century

Bibi Allah Bandi was the daughter of Haji Ahmadullah and the mother of Mufti Ubaidullah. She was a well-educated and pious Urdu poetess, who died in AD 1830 at Gopamau. Her *takhallus* was '*bibi*'.[35] Another prominent Muslim lady of that time was Saiyidat-un nisa Hirman, an Urdu poetess who belonged to Khairabad but lived in Delhi. Hirman was her *takhallus*. She studied logic and acquired a vast knowledge about the Islamic religion.[36] Shams-un Nisa Sharm was another Urdu poetess and daughter of Qamaruddin Kaleem, a pupil of Khawaja Wazir, the celebrated poet of the time. She was born in Benares. Most of her life was spent in Lucknow. She had compiled a lot of lyrics in Urdu, which are now available in printed form. We know that she lived around AD 1855.[37] It is interesting to see how women of that time would compose ghazals in male costume; as Carla Petievich says, they chose a masculine voice instead of a feminine one. This could either be because they wanted to confuse readers about their gender identities, or because the strict *purdah* system forced them to conceal their true identities, since *shareef* women in those days were not allowed to participate in public discourse. I quote a few lines from one of Shams-un Nisa's verses:

> Pahle sabit Karen is vahshi ki taqsiren do
> Phir mujhe shauq se pahnae zanzeeren do
> Ek busa liya kis din hoven taqsiren do
> Kyun mere paun me pahnate ho zanzeeren do
> Ae musawwir tujhe dunga main bahut sa inam
> Meri aur uski baham khainch de tasweeren do[38]

> First prove a couple of mistakes of this soul humble
> Thereafter you may happily put me in the manacle.

[35] Singh, Nagendra (ed.), *Encyclopaedia of Women Biography: India, Pakistan, Bangladesh*, Vol. I (A. P. H. Pub. Corp., 2001), 40.

[36] Singh, *Encyclopaedia of Women Biography*, Vol. II, 244. See also Petievich, 'Feminine Authorship and Urdu Poetic Tradition', 240–41, for details.

[37] Singh, *Encyclopaedia of Women Biography*, Vol. II, 267.

[38] Petievich, 'Feminine Authorship and Urdu Poetic Tradition', 240.

Just a kiss it was, not offenses twin
Why at all my feet do you shackle?
If only you could portray us together in a picture,
O painter I will honour thee with rewards several.
(*Translated by Nishat Zaidi*)

These *ashraf* women were also politically aware. In this regard, the role of the begums of princely states cannot be overlooked. Begum Shams Tajdar, the royal lady from Rampur state and a very capable princess, claimed the rulership of Rampur after her father's death in AD 1840, and persisted with this claim all through her life. The East India Company's government, however, declined to honour her wish. She was married to Saiyid Mehndi Ali Khan, who was imprisoned by the British in Calcutta on charges of participating in the great uprising of AD 1857. He was later released, largely through the efforts made by his wife.[39]

While the elite women had several opportunities to make themselves visible, the common Muslim women remained invisible in patriarchal historiography as they had no glorious family history that could make them popular. Hence, they were ignored in European accounts as well. Also, both *swarn*[40] Hindu and *ashraf* Muslims did not allow European women inside their *zenana*, as they feared this intermingling would lead to the undesirable influence of Western culture on their women. The Europeans, however, had easy access to common women belonging to a lower social order. This led to their creating a generalised and incomplete picture of Indian society. As a result, women were projected as either backward (as the lower-class/caste Muslim women were), or according to the imaginations of and perceptions held by Europeans, gleaned mostly through second-hand accounts of the few European women allowed access to the *zenana*, or those of the royal Muslim women who married British men.

As stated earlier, Mrs Meer Hasan has presented a mixed picture—and one that is very different from European missionary accounts—of Muslim women as being both oppressed and satisfied; she has even highlighted a powerful zenana presence in Muslim households. On several occasions, she even witnessed women taking part in social gatherings.[41] We have sufficient

---

[39] Petievich, 'Feminine Authorship and Urdu Poetic Tradition', 240.

[40] Brahmin, Kshatriya and Vaishya are the three upper castes among Hindus, in descending order of their social hierarchy.

[41] In my own family, my mother tells me that her grandmother was a very impressive and bold lady. She had six sons, three daughters, and many granddaughters. Every

evidence showing that Muslim women would socialise and participate in male gatherings from behind the *purdah*, and even influenced male decisions.[42] Aziz-un Nisa Begum, the mother of Sir Saiyid Ahmed Khan had an inborn talent. Although she had read only the Quran and some Persian books, she wielded tremendous power. Sir Saiyid used to say that 5 per cent of her income was always kept aside for charity, and that many young girls were married only by her grace. She secretly helped veiled women who were also financially weak. She advised young widows from poor families to remarry, and detested those who considered widow remarriage an undesirable practice. She helped poor relatives secretly, and did not desist from visiting those in her family who had married women considered unworthy. Their children were always greeted cordially.[43]

In this way, despite being veiled, Muslim women participated in both social and political activities. There was a custom among landlords and *talluqdars* to arrange big occasions at home for leisure, so a number of female attendants would stand ready to offer their services to their ladies. These attendants performed all the household chores, besides arranging parties and receiving guests, and helping the rich Muslim women with their hair and attire, as well as caring for their children. They were also considered a source of amusement in their solitude.[44] At that time, the *mujra* was considered a great source of entertainment at marriage ceremonies and other festive occasions. Sir Saiyid and Mrs Meer Hasan both described a *Basant* festival, where a famous *tawa'if* of that time was invited for *mujra*. Sir Saiyid, too, was once present on such an occasion, and he admired both Jinna and Sheerin Jaan, two famous *tawa'ifs* of

night she would call a *sabha*, where women from the other branches of the Jafri family (my maternal family name) would gather for a meeting. One by one they would organise the *Milad shareef*. Till the 1960s, this was a regular occurrence. I remember that in my village, too, women would gather in our *dalan* where, under the leadership of my grandmother, they discussed family matters and other issues. It appeared to work like a female panchayat.

42 I have rarely seen a Muslim family where women's voices were overlooked in family matters, particularly in joint families, where the matriarch played a very important role in all matters.

43 Hali, Altaf Husain, *Hayat-e Javed* (New Delhi: Taraqqiie Urdu Board, 1979), 41–42.

44 Hasan, *An Observation on Musalmans of* India, 323. Some ladies of rank had between two to ten companions, independent of slaves and domestics; some royal families of Lucknow had in their service 200–300 female dependents of all classes. A well-filled *zenana* was considered a mark of gentility, and even the poorest lady in the country would retain a number of slaves and domestics, if she could not afford companions.

Delhi.[45] In fact, Mrs Hasan's account details a number of festivals celebrated in the *zenana*. The women dressed themselves very well on such occasions, as did their attendants.[46] Each *zenana* was controlled by a head. This head, or mistress, was easily distinguished by her specific seat in the hall, a *musnad*, which was not allowed to anyone other than the lady of the mansion.[47]

The women living in the *zenana* seemed happy on the whole, probably because they were used to it from infancy, and regarded it as an obligation to follow the customs and values of the *khandan*. Indeed, women were supposed to be the protectors of *khandani* values and tradition. According to Mrs Hasan:

> They are happy in their confinement; and never having felt the sweets of liberty, could not know how to use the boon if it were to be granted them. As the bird from the nest immured in a cage is both cheerful and contended, so are these females. They have not, it is true many intellectual resources, but they have naturally good understanding and having learned their duty they strive to fulfill it.[48]

The ideal women would be affectionate mothers, kind mistresses, sincere friends and liberal benefactresses to the distressed poor. These were their moral qualifications, and in their religious duties, they were zealous in performing the several ordinances that they had been instructed by their parents or husbands to observe. Mrs Hasan was very surprised at the self-restraint of the women in the *zenana:*

> It is very strange thing about them that they were so customary to follow such routine from infancy to old age and never felt any problem to perform it. Here they had their own engagement and entertainment. They are entirely satisfied with their social structure and never felt need of any kind of freedom and their health did not affected from that confinement as it was made a general notion among many European travelers .... They are educated from infancy for retirement, and they have no wish that the custom should be changed, which keeps them apart from the society of men, who are not very nearly related to them. Female society is unlimited and that they enjoyed without restraint.[49]

---

[45] Hali, *Hayat-e Javed*, 54–55.

[46] Hasan, *An Observation on Musalmans of India*, 312. In her memoirs are detailed, lively accounts of *Eid, Eid-ul zoha, Shab-e Barat* and *Nauroj.*

[47] Hasan, *An Observation on Musalmans of India*, 309.

[48] Hasan, *An Observation on Musalmans of India*, 313.

[49] Hasan, *An Observation on Musalmans of India*, 314–15.

A peculiar custom often connected with Muslim society is polygamy. It was generally assumed that a Muslim man could marry four women at a time because of the provision cited in the Qur'an. *Adal*, however, was never reflected in discursive writing, viz., the conditions for marrying twice, thrice and four times. It is clearly stated in the Qur'an that if one cannot treat all wives equally, he should not marry more than once. This provision is called *adal*, and has often deterred common Muslim men from marrying more than once. Indeed, polygamy, as Mrs Hasan saw it, was considered a plague by *ashraf* Muslims of that time.[50] It was certainly practised amongst some high-ranking men, both Hindu and Muslim, who considered it a social honour to keep a full-fledged *zenana*.[51] Common/middle-class Muslims rarely practised it, although Muslims from a lower social order did do so. Also, even in polygamous families, priority was often given to the first marriage,[52] with the first wife being regarded the head of the female establishment. Although high-ranking Muslims had several co-wives, each had separate habitations, if possible.[53] It is quite surprising how these co-wives lived together cordially. It seems that they had to compromise with circumstances with the passage of time, probably due to a fear of divorce. Protest was often considered a disgrace in *ashraf* families, and a man had the right to divorce his wife if she displayed signs of a violent temper. An interesting picture is available in Mrs Hasan's account:

> I may here add to praise of a good wife among these people, that she never utters a reproach, nor gives evidence by word or manner in her husbands presence that she has any cause for regret, she receives him with undisguised pleasure, although she has just before learned that another member has been added to his well peopled harem. The good and forbearing wife, by this line of conduct, secure to herself the confidence of her husband; who feeling assured that the amiable woman has an interest in his happiness, will consult her and take her advice in the domestic affairs of his children by other wives.[54]

At that time, the marriageable age for girls was eighteen among the higher castes and fourteen among the lower castes. Many girls were willingly given in

---

[50] Hasan, *An Observation on Musalmans of India*, 342. The social and religious reformer Saiyid Ahmed Barelvi had protested against bigamy.

[51] Hasan, *An Observation on Musalmans of India*, 342.

[52] Hasan, *An Observation on Musalmans of India*, 342

[53] Hasan, *An Observation on Musalmans of India*, 340.

[54] Hasan, *An Observation on Musalmans of India*, 342–43.

marriage by impoverished parents as *dhollie* (second or third) wives. It should be noted that extravagant marriage ceremonies were common in those days. Priority was given to brides of sixteen or seventeen, and even poor peasants objected to marrying an 18-year-old girl.[55] The social structures of Hindu and Muslim societies were similar, and it was quite surprising to see the birth of a girl child being greeted with gloom even in Muslim families,[56] despite the several instructions in the Qur'an in favour of a girl child.

Women from rural areas were very superstitious, compared to urban women. It is a fact that Muslims in rural areas were closer to their Hindu counterparts, while urban Muslims tried to maintain a distinct identity of their own. That is why superstitious was often considered *shirq* by *ashraf* Muslims, who were mostly urbanised.[57] Mrs Meer Hasan had this to say about rural life in India:

> .... In village where there are a greater portion of Hindus than Musalman the female of the two people mixed more generally than is usually allowed in cities or large towns; and it is amongst this mingled population that we find the spirit of superstition influencing the female character in a more marked manner than it does in more populous places.[58]

Muslim women from *ashraf* families were financially self-reliant. Their inheritance came not only from the property of their parents, but also that of their husbands. Indeed, there was a custom among some elite families to have the groom contract an *iqrarnama* prior to the marriage. The groom was supposed to make sure that his wife was financially taken care of. Contrary to traditional Indian society, a groom was supposed to live with his wife's family as a *khanadamad*. The father of Sir Saiyid Ahmed Khan, Mir Mutaqqi,[59] and that of Maulvi Nazir[60] were both *khanadamads*. It seems, though, that the girl's relatives, especially the men, could not accept a girl as a co-sharer, which was why the *khanadamads* often had to leave their in-laws' homes.[61] Mrs Hasan,

---

[55] Hasan, *An Observation on Musalmans of India*, 349.

[56] Hasan, *An Observation on Musalmans of India*, 349.

[57] Hali, *Hayat-e Javed*, 42. Aziz-un Nisa considered it *shirq*.

[58] Hasan, *An Observation on Musalmans of India*. In an interesting example, she described how a village Mullah was supposed to tie a *narah in moosul* by his wife for the welfare of her daughter.

[59] Hali, *Hayat-e Javed*, 39.

[60] Bashir, Zeenat, *Nazir ke Navilon me Nusvaee Kirdar* (Hyderabad: Iliyas Traders and Publisher, 1991), 21.

[61] Bashir, *Nazir ke Navilon*.

too, had accepted that financially, Muslim women in India were stronger than in other places.[62]

While the uprising of 1857 smashed the Mughal dynasty forever, Lord Dalhousie's doctrine of lapse marginalised the princely states. Consequently, the British policy of destruction affected the Muslims more because they happened to reside in those areas that were most affected during the uprising. Also, the mutiny had forced the British to rethink their alignment with Muslims, and it also changed their earlier perception of Muslims living in India. Now they needed to prove them barbaric; and this is why we do not find any true depiction of Muslims in British discursive writings, other than Mrs Meer Hasan's *An Observation on Musalmans of India*. It is an interesting exercise to reevaluate this book from an earlier Western perspective. We find no detailed account of the author; even her name goes unmentioned on the cover page. Instead, she bears her husband's name, indicating that she had merged completely with Muslim society. It was said that she never allowed her husband to take another wife; however, she suddenly left India for Britain to live a quiet life, and then produced this precious academic work. One explanation could be that since she did not bear a child, she left him in order to give him space for a second marriage, which he contracted subsequently. Her writing makes it clear that she disliked the polygamous nature of elite Muslims, but otherwise accepted the *zenana* as a powerful presence in Muslim households. Later British accounts, though, portray the *zenana* in a derogatory manner.[63]

So far, studies conducted on Indian Muslim women present them as caged, imprisoned and deprived of all happiness.[64] This attitude, present in colonial historiography, is still evident. Also, this period was often overlooked by feminists, although studies of women in Bengal and Bombay in the late nineteenth century indicate that in comparison, the condition of Bengali and Marathi Hindu women was far better than that of Muslim women.[65] In this

---

[62] Hasan, *An Observation on Musalmans of India*, 370.

[63] For details, see Mrs Marcus Fuller's account of the *zenana* in '*Purdah:* An Anthology', ed. Eunice de Souza (New Delhi: Oxford University Press, 2004), 66–77.

[64] Papanek, Hanna and Gail Minault (eds), *Separate World: Studies of Parda in South Asia* (New Delhi: Chanakya Publications, 1982). See also de Souza, *Pardah*.

[65] Sarkar, Mahua, *Visible Histories and Invisible Womens: Producing Muslim Womanhood in late colonial Bengal* (New Delhi: Zubaan, 2008). See Uma Chakarvarti and Priti Gill (eds), *Shadow Lives: Writings on Widowhood* (New Delhi: Kali for Women, 2001). This book reveals how Hindu women were becoming conscious of the deteriorating condition of Hindu widows, even writing several articles on this issue. It appears that enforced widowhood was common only amongst upper-caste Hindus.

way, a generalisation was made with regard to Muslim women of the United Province. By considering Muslims as a monolithic bloc, Muslim women living in the United Province, too, fell victim to this generalisation. However, a few books did focus on north Indian Muslim women to some extent, and Barbara Metcalf, Gail Minault and Hanna Papanek did try to focus on this province. They, however, had their own limitations, of period, region and issues. Metcalf views Muslim women through a religious lens, through which women seemed to hold a subordinate position. It must be mentioned, though, that all religions, be it Islam, Christianity or Hinduism, discriminated against women. Barbara Metcalf looks at the several religious dogmas Muslim women were subjected to, as well as the way they were projected by their own religious reformers, and this becomes her main focus.[66] However, Gail Minault's approach seems broader, as she tried to destroy several misconceptions about Muslim women by projecting them as educated and literate.[67] It seems, though, that her focus remained centred round the Aligarh movement, which is why her work remains within the confines of Abdullah College, where 1906 was apparently viewed as a turning point in the educational advancement of Muslim women. Also, the educational status of Muslim women cannot be understood without comprehending their socio-economic status; and therefore this book will complement the many previous works on Muslim women. This book will show how Muslim women emerged from the shackles of confinement, and I hope it will throw light on the different socio-religious, cultural and economic aspects of Muslim society. In contrast to other works, it also takes into consideration oral and folk traditions, thereby revealing many socio-cultural and emotional aspects of Muslim women rarely found in archival works, and therefore neglected by modern scholars of the nineteenth century.

The discussion above is what inspired me to study how the late nineteenth century became a crucial period for a gender discourse on Muslim women. I have tried to penetrate some significant issues hitherto denied by social reformers. Muslim women were considered free from social evils like the prohibition of widow remarriage, child marriage, sati and infanticide. This book will reveal some striking aspects of Muslim society, and will show that the condition of, and problems faced by, Muslim women were the same as their counterparts in other communities. It also insists on a composite social order of Indian society,

---

[66] Barbara Metcalf (trans. And ed.), *Perfecting Women: Maulana Ashraf Ali Thanawi's Bihishti Zevar* (Berkeley: University of California Press, 1982).

[67] Minault, Gail, *Secluded Scholar: Women's Education and Muslim Social Reform in Colonial India* (New Delhi: Oxford University Press, 1998).

that is, the *Ganga-jamuni tahzeeb* developed through an amalgamation of Hindu and Muslim culture.

Chapters 1 and 2 will introduce a general profile of Muslim society and contests the prevalent idea of a uniform category of Muslims. Chapter One argues that Muslim society followed the same social stratification as the Hindus. It presents an anthropological survey of Muslim society, and provides space for the author's own observations of society in constructing a gender historiography. This chapter also looks at the social hierarchy within Muslim society, and how the status of women was influenced by caste and regional variations. Chapter Two focuses on the role of the social reform movement. It argues against several misconceptions about the Muslim social reform movement, specifically that it was confined solely to female education. From the nineteenth century, the role of social reformers was considered very significant in gender issues, especially since it was Indian social reformers who raised their voices against age-old customs. A common belief is that Muslim women remained ignored in the social reform agenda, since their male counterparts had never accepted their degraded position in Islam. They did deal with gender issues since all issues are indirectly connected to religion, and they believed that all solutions were available in the shariat law. Given this attitude, they did not consider change necessary, believing that all evil customs currently practised in society were due to the influence of Hindu culture. The example of the prohibition of widow remarriage was offered by many Muslim reformers; however, it was also accepted that the restriction on widow remarriage is as rampant amongst Muslims as it is among Hindus. And since this is not prohibited in religion, it is only religion that can bring them back on track by following the true nature of Islam.

Chapter 3 focuses on the condition of Muslims in that period, and how the colonial perception of Indian Muslims as a whole and Muslin women in particular complicated the social order. Moreover, the basic question is: What was the condition of Indian Muslim women under patriarchy and caste hierarchy? To what extent had they been influenced by the colonial presence? Why did the British project Indian Muslim women as backward in their discursive writing? This chapter also attempts to understand the problems faced by Indian Muslim women, and to that extent, it examines the positive and negative impacts of the British colonial system.

The great uprising of 1857 had warned the British that interference in social and religious matters could lead to tension; as such, they decided to stay away from such issues. As a result, they discouraged social intermingling between Indians and Europeans. Hence, British officers and soldiers began arriving in large numbers along with their spouses. Eventually, a large number of European ladies arrived as well, sometimes in search of appropriate husbands and sometimes for missionary work. All of this led to an attack on Indian society as a whole, and the *zennana* in particular. British women considered native women their sexual rivals, which is one reason for the colonialists' rejecting interracial marriages. They, too, enforced the white '*memsahib*' burden onto themselves. *Ashraf* Muslims soon began keeping their women away from the European gaze, in the process turning them into objects of curiosity for the latter, who projected them according to their own imaginations and perceptions.

Chapter 4 centres round Muslim women's consciousness, their motherland, womanhood, and ultimately their community. It also reflects how aware they were about what was happening around them. It reveals how the mutiny had jeopardised the lives of the common people. This chapter raises several questions: Were common Muslim women too connected with the mutiny? Why was prostitution considered problematic just after 1857? Did colonial presence make it more challenging? Why were all prostitutes registered under Muslim sects? I have tried to look into the conviction records of Port Blair and every other mutiny papers and file, which only strengthens the question: Why were Muslim women sentenced to life imprisonment in large numbers? Why did they need to prove themselves loyal to the British? The theme of this chapter is to reevaluate the impact of the revolt from a gender perspective, and show how it became a turning point in the gender history of Muslim society.

This book also attempts to understand the mental trauma of Muslims, and the way they reacted to the new power. It throws light on several untouched sources that highlights the role of Muslim women in the uprising, popularly considered the first war of Independence, and tries to discover why a large chunk of these Muslim women hailed from the western United Province. This chapter also focuses on the increasing political consciousness among Muslim women during the course of time, as well as challenges the conventional and colonial notion that Muslim women were a backward lot, and were not even aware of events around them. On the contrary, they took part in large numbers in the great revolt of 1857, and even martyred themselves for their motherland.

Chapter 5 focuses on the educational and literary activity of Muslim women, and also brings to light the role played by the British government and missionaries. An attempt is made to review the state of education among women, particularly Muslim women in the United Province. This chapter accepts that education among Muslim women—like that among Hindu women—was determined by the social and economic class they came from.

Chapter 6 focuses on the civil condition of Muslim women, that is, the role of customs and practices, childhood, marriage, child marriage, widowhood, issues of re-marriage and divorce. In Chapter Seven, I attempt to revive the lost culture of Muslim society—like *shair-shairee* and *ghazal*—which used to be an integral part of Muslim society. This chapter also focuses on the declining culture of the courtesan, and how this highly esteemed culture was reduced to the level of flesh trade. Why was prostitution viewed as a threat by Europeans? Why did the British implement double standards vis-à-vis these women? Why were they so eager to keep them under control? Why did the Census report place all of them under Islamic sects?

The last two chapters throw light on the changing economic scenario of India. How have Indian Muslims faced these increasingly changing circumstances? Did they avail of all the rights related to property guaranteed under Islamic law? How did the colonial system affect their position in the traditional socio-economic set-up? How did the law of primogeniture affect their inheritance rights? Was Sir Saiyid right in saying that the economic condition of Indian Muslim women was better than that of contemporary Christian, Jew and Hindu women? Chapter Nine also looks at the impact of industrialisation. Is it right to say that the new legal system had secured the position of Indian Muslim women?

Before we move forward, let us place the United Provinces on the map, as it were. The United Province lies at the heart of the Indian subcontinent, midway between the Hindukush, to the north. It was separated from Tibet by the great Himalayan range; to the south, it was separated from the Deccan by the Vindhyan mountain range.[68] The Province had been formed gradually through conquest and annexation.[69] The area administered by the Lt. Governor

[68] See map.

[69] *The Imperial Gazetteer of India*, 'Provincial Series: United Provinces of Agra and Oudh', Vol. 1, ed. Usha Jain (Usha Publication, 1984), 1–2, 30–31. At the beginning of the nineteenth century, the British held only the present Benares division and the fort of Allahabad. In 1801, Wellesley acquired the lower Doab, Rohilkhand and Gorakhpur. In 1803, the Anglo-Maratha war led to the annexation of the upper Doab and Bundelkhand. In 1815, after the Anglo-Nepalese wars, most of Kumao was added to it. Other small enclaves were absorbed within it, and finally, in 1856, the last major territorial acquisition was made with the annexation of Oudh. The period immediately after the mutiny was in fact the period of modern state formation: the Delhi territories were added to the Panjab Province, while the Rohilkhand part of the tarai north of Oudh was given to the Nepalese, and a few villages in Bareilly and Moradabad were granted to the Nawab of Rampur. In 1877, the two provinces were

of Agra and Oudh lies between 23°52′ and 31°18′ N and 84°39′ E. The area of the two provinces was given in square miles: Agra, 83,198, and Oudh, 23,966; this makes for 107,164 square miles, including some riverbeds which form district boundaries and are excluded from the district details. The total area amounts to 107,494 square miles. The area covered by the two native states in the provinces Rampur and Tehri was 5,079 square miles more.[70]

The entire Province could be divided into three natural divisions, according to its specific cultural, linguistic and geographical peculiarities, as the Western, Central and Eastern United Provinces. This has been one of India's most densely populated provinces, as it is situated at the confluence of two of its biggest rivers—the Ganges and the Yamuna.[71] The total population was 47,691,782, of which Muslims constitute 14.19 per cent.[72] A big chunk of its people—66 per cent—depended on hired labour for agriculture, and the women's share in the labour market was 44 per cent, 80 per cent of which was in agriculture labour.

brought together under the Lt. Governor of the North-Western Provinces and the chief commissioner of Oudh, and in 1902, the name of the province was changed and the title of chief commissioner dropped.

70 *The Imperial Gazetteer of India*, 'Provincial Series: United Provinces of Agra and Oudh', 1.

71 The significance of this province was due to its political and economic importance. A number of wars were fought to occupy its several fertile and politically important cities, such as Agra, Oudh, Jaunpur, Rampur, Allahabad and Benares.

72 *Census Report of India*, North Western Province of Agra and Oudh, 1901, Part 1, Vol. XVI, R. Burn, Superintendent (Allahabad: Government Press, 1902), 63.

CHAPTER 1

Social Stratification of Muslim Women in the United Provinces

Ek hi saf me khare ho gae sab Mahmud-o Ayaaz
Na koi banda raha aur na koi banda nawaaz.'

Mahmood and Ayaz stood together in the same flank
The ruler and the ruled forgot the difference in their rank.

Banda O sahib-o Muhtaj-o ghani ek hue,
Teri sarkar me pahunche to sabhi ek hue.

The rich and poor, lord and slave, all were leveled down,
All became brethren in love, with thy grace crowned.[1]

Can all Muslims be referred to as a monolithic bloc? Although all the women who can be classified as 'Muslim' adhere to Islam and its customs, is it an adequate basis for referring to them as a collective entity, or placing them within an undifferentiated category? Are there no differences of caste, social class or region among them? Is it not true that in culturally, socially and economically progressive regions, the status of Muslim women is better than in the regions that have experienced no such development historically? Is it not time for researchers to explore how these differences affect these women's status—within the same or different regions of India?[2]

[1] Iqbal, Allama, '*Shiqwa*'.

[2] The most significant work on Indian Muslims has been done by Rafiuddin Ahmad on the Muslims of Bengal, which breaks the myth of homogeneity in Muslim society. He, however, classified Muslims into only two major categories, *ashraf* (foreign origin) and *atrap* (converted from within the Hindu castes). Rafiuddin Ahmed, *The Bengal Muslims 1871–1900: A Quest for Identity in India's Muslims* (New Delhi: Oxford University Press, 2008).

The answer to these questions lies in comprehending the significance of social stratification amongst the Muslims. The first question that comes to mind is, 'Who is the Indian Muslim/Musalman?' The definition provided in colonial deliberations and census reports is: 'One who eats cow, who hates pork, who believes in one God and does not believe in idol worship; whose men keep beards and wear skull-sized caps, and whose women wear a *burqa*.' The general perceptions that form Muslim identity state that Muslim women are veiled, as opposed to the unveiled Hindu women, as Muslims always do the opposite of what Hindus do.

The next question that arises is: What is the true picture of a Muslim in India? Are there any differences on the basis of caste, class or region? Indeed, the late nineteenth century had witnessed debates on the various terms used for believers of Islam: the Arabic 'Muslim', the Persian 'Musalman', and the English 'Mohammedan'. As De Tassy writes, in the latter half of the nineteenth century, the term 'Mohammedan' was revived to refer particularly to the educated and 'respectable' class within the community; this English construction, though, was not acceptable to the faithful, since they believed—a fact repeated by De Tassy—that Prophet Muhammad did not start a new religion as Christ had.[3] In this connection, Norman Daniel correctly pointed out that Christian thinkers tried to understand Islam as analogical: since Christ was at the basis of Christian faith, it was assumed quite incorrectly that Muhammad was to Islam what Christ was to Christianity. Hence the polemic name 'Mohammedanism', which was given to Islam.[4] It is for this reason that a section of Muslims did not want to use the term 'Mohammedan' in 'Mohammedan Anglo Oriental College', and a few years after the establishment of the All India Muslim League in 1906, the college was renamed the Aligarh Muslim University. The Arabic term 'Muslim' superseded the Persian 'Musalman', hence quotations pertaining to identity are many; but Indian Muslims continued to call themselves 'Musalmans'.

[3] De Tassy, Garcin (ed.), *Muslim Festivals in India and Other Essays*, M. Waseem (trans. and ed.), (Oxford: Oxford University Press, 2006 [1997]), 10. See also Edward W. Said, *Orientalism: Western Conception of the Orient* (New Delhi: Penguin Books, 2001), 60

[4] Said, *Orientalism*, 60.

The Social Milieu of Muslims

The United Province was the hub of Islamic culture. C. A. Bayly notes that the four main religious families of India, which influenced both Muslim society and politics throughout the colonial period, were from this province, viz., the *Deobandi* from Saharanpur, *Barelvi* from Bareilly, *Shahjahani Sufi* from Allahabad, and *Firangi Mahal* from Lucknow.[5] On the whole, the two important sects of Islam were Sunni and Shia (comprising 97 and 3 per cent, respectively, of the total Muslim population).[6] Despite being negligible in numbers, the Shia influence was very significant in the United Province, since they had ruled two of its old regions, Oudh and Jaunpur, for a considerable period of time.[7] The Shia Muslims appeared to be an undivided category, whereas the Sunnis were divided further into two sub-groups: *ashraf* and *ajlaf*.[8] Medieval *ashraf* monarchs traced their origins to Arabia and other Middle Eastern countries,[9] while the British claimed that the *ajlaf* were originally Hindus belonging to the lower castes.[10] The British are wrongly accused of being the first to differentiate between Muslims on the basis of origin, as there are several references to the same from medieval times. For instance, the famous court historian Zia Uddin Barni had expressed his dislike of 'low-born' Muslims on several occasions, as during that period only Muslims who came from Arabia or other Islamic

---

[5] Bayly, C. A., *Rulers, Townsmen and Bazars: North Indian Society in the Age of British Expansion: 1770–1870* (New Delhi: Oxford University Press, 2009), 190.

[6] Census Report of India, 1901, 152.

[7] For the Shia influence in Oudh, see Madhu Trivedi, *Making of Awadh Culture* (New Delhi: Primus Books, 2010), 41–61.

[8] Rasum-e Hind, Sir Rishta-e Panjab, 1868, 260. At that time, Ashraf Ali Thanvi also emphasised birth, instead of occupation.

[9] Rasum-e Hind, Sir Rishta-e Panjab; *The Imperial Gazetteer of India*, Vol. 1, 329. Also see Francis Robinson, *Separatism Among Indian Muslims: The Politics of the United Provinces' Muslims, 1860–1923*, Cambridge South Asian Studies (Cambridge: Cambridge University Press, 2007).

[10] William Crook, *The North Western Provinces of India: Their History Ethnology and Administration* (New Delhi: Low Price Publication, 2003), 262. Crook's emphasis was on the conversion of lower-caste Hindus to Islam. This conclusion appears to have been arrived at on the basis of some outward differences; it was illogical to conclude that they converted or came from the outside, especially given the multiethnic society they had been living in for a long time.

countries were considered 'pure Muslims'.[11] Qateel differentiates between *ashraf* and *ajlaf* Muslims as 'old' or 'original' Muslims (conquerors and other migrants) and 'new' (*nau*) Muslims (recent converts), respectively. The 'new' Muslims were allowed to have relationships only with each other.

The poet Meer has written about the days when the 'low-born', or the *ajlaf*, were not allowed access to poetry, and when masters instructed only the *ashraf*.[12] This was not the first attempt to claim the *ashraf* as 'noble born'; in the medieval period, too, *nasbi* birth was boasted of. However, it was the British who systematically differentiated between upper-caste and lower-caste Muslims. Their economic interests, which remained their main concern, might perhaps have compelled them to identify people from professional castes, since these were what most *ajlaf* groups belonged to.[13] This was probably why the British Gazetteer and the Census Report persistently insisted on this issue. The same has been authenticated by colonial reports.

Indeed, 'keeping their control' over Indian society appeared to be a big problem for the British. It was perhaps necessary for them to classify the people of India into categories for easy governance. Since Hindus and Muslims formed the two major constituents of the Indian population, it was natural for them to categorise Indians as per their own requirements.[14] Indians were divided not only on the basis of religion, creed and race, but also on the basis of caste, sex and profession. All Muslims were relegated to one of four groups in the colonial census report,[15] a division based on both birth and profession. The *ashraf* were in Group I, owing to their foreign origin, and were consequently considered the highest Muslim class. This group was further divided into four

---

[11] De Tassy, *Muslim Festivals in India*, 17.

[12] ibid.

[13] Rasum-e Hind, Sir Rishta-e Panjab, 260.

[14] As Gail Omvedt argues, it was during the colonial period that the question of a community identity was crystallised, and became relevant. Earlier, in the later part of the eighteenth century, the British had begun looking at the people living in the Indian subcontinent as a uniform category. See Gail Omvedt, 'Muslim-Dalit Reflections', 22 May 2005, available at countercurrent.org.

[15] Census Report of 1901, 96. This was a time when the British had begun dividing people in the name of religion, and they deliberately incited communal feelings among Hindus and Muslims on trivial issues. See Crook, *The North-Western Provinces of India*, 187.

sub-categories,[16] viz., Saiyid, Sheikh,[17] Pathan[18] and Mughal,[19] in descending order of 'superiority'.

There are several debates on this sub-division; some perceive the groups as different castes, and some as categories. Sociologist Imtiaz Ahmad suggests that the four are not castes at all but categories, somewhat similar to the earlier Hindu categories of Brahmin and Kshatriya, which were based solely on the criterion of profession.[20] Terminologically, Saiyid means chief or *sardar*, and they trace their lineage to the Prophet. Although they constitute only 3.8 per cent of the Muslim population in the United Province, their religious and spiritual importance is considerable. Amongst Saiyids, there are numerous sub-divisions like *Hashmi, Jafri, Zaidi, Ansari, Naqvi, Alvi, Bukhari, Husaini, Qazmi*, etc. Sheikh etymologically means an elder or reputed saint, and they constitute 19.9 per cent of all Muslims. With the passage of time, they too developed nine sub-castes or categories: *Abidi, Abbasi, Farooqui, Bani Israeeli, Quraishi, Usmani* and *Siddiqui*. Siddiquis comprised the largest chunk of all Sheikhs (7.9 per cent).[21] The list of sub-castes amongst the *ashraf* is indeed a long one.

As M. Waseem argues, the division into four 'classes' (de Tassy), 'categories' (Schimel), and 'groups' (Herklots) is rather misleading, and definitely not

---

[16] These four categories claim a non-Indian descent: Saiyids trace their ancestry to the Prophet's family; and Sheikhs from the families of his companions, Siddique, Umar Farooque and Usman. Hence, they claim their Arabic origins confer upon them the most superior status. Mughals and Pathans are from Central Asia, from the Timurid family and of Afghan origin.

[17] Barbara Metcalf states that the term 'Sheikh' in India is used for a Sufi master and for those regarded as descendants of the companions of the Prophet. See 'Islamic Revival in British India, Deoband, 1860–1900', in *India's Muslims: An Omnibus*, by Mushirul Hasan, Barbara Daly Metcalf and Rafiuddin Ahmed (New Delhi: Oxford University Press, 2008), 29.

[18] Mushirul Hasan et al., *India's Muslims*. Pathans comprised 11.4 per cent of the entire Muslim population. They were divided into different sub-castes—*Afridi, Bangash, Dilazak, Ghilzai, Ghori, Kakar, Khatak, Lodi, Muhammadzai, Rohilla, Tarin, Warkzai, Yusufzai*, and others.

[19] Mushirul Hasan et al., *India's Muslims*. They comprised only 1.2 per cent of the entire Muslim population and were divided into four sub-castes—*Chagtai, Qizilbash, Turkman*, and others.

[20] Gupta, Dipankar (ed.), *Social Stratification* (New Delhi: Oxford University Press, 2008), 214.

[21] Census Report of 1901, 254–55.

comprehensive.[22] The *ashraf* comprised 36.3 per cent of the Muslim population of this province in Group I.[23] Saiyids were often considered the highest and most significant category of all, although they only comprised 3.8 per cent of the Muslim population. According to Barbara Metcalf, these four hierarchically ordered groups or *qaum* formed the social elite, and they guarded this status not merely through *qaum* endogamy, but by keeping marriage within the family itself.[24]

Group II comprises those Muslims who were believed to have converted from Hinduism. Conversion took into account the Hindu caste they originally belonged to, like Brahmin, Rajput and Bhumihar. Then, of course, there was a long list of low-born Dalit castes, like Pasi, Teli, Tharu, Tamboli, Taga, Nat, Nai, Mushar, Mallah, Mochi, Kewat, Mali, Chamar, Gujar, Dhobi, Dom, Bhangi, Bhand, Bhil, Bind and Gaderiya, Bharbhunja, Banjara, Khatik and Rangar. Indeed, census reports enumerate almost 96 sub-castes that had converted, from both touchable and untouchable Hindu castes. The crowd of new converts, hardly distinguishable from their Hindu brethren, was termed *ajlaf*, and formed 33.2 per cent of the entire Muslim population. *Ajlaf* comprised those people engaged in lowly professions, and there is reason to believe that in the countryside, Muslim converts continued to pursue their hereditary professions. The Muslim *dhobi*, for example, did the same work among the Muslims that his Hindu brothers did in their community, just like the *nai*, *mehtar*, *bhishti*, *mirasi*, etc.

Profession was the criterion for recognising Muslims in Group III; for example, *Atashbaz* (fireworks maker), *Bhatyara* (innkeeper), *Bhishti* (water carrier), *Bisati* (haberdasher), *Churihar* (bangle maker), *Dafali* (drummer), *Faqir* (mendicant), *Halwai* (confectioner), *Hurkiya* (singer), *Julaha* (weaver), *Kabariya* (costermonger), *Kingriya* (gipsy), *Kunjra* (market gardener), *Manihar* (bangle maker), *Mirasi* (musician), *Nalband* (farrier), *Nanbai* (baker), *Qalaigarh* (tin smith), *Qassab* (butcher), *Rajgeer* (mason), *Rangrej* (dyer and painter), *Saiqalgarh* (cutter) and *Tawaif* (prostitute).[25] They comprised 28.1 per cent of the entire population.[26] It is very interesting to see prostitution being recognised

---

[22] de Tassy, *Muslim Festivals in India*, 17.

[23] *Census Report of 1901*, 254–55.

[24] Barbara Daly Metcalf, 'Islamic Revival in British India: Deoband, 1860–1900', 239.

[25] *Census Report, 1901*, Subsidiary Table I, 254–55.

[26] There was an XXIII sub-caste in this group, *Atashbaj, Bhatiyara, Bhishti, Bisati, Churihar, Dafali, Faqir, Halwai, Hurkiya, Julaha, Kabariya, Kingriya, Kunjra, Manihar, Mirasi, Nalband, Nanbai, Qalaigar, Qassab, Raj, Rangrej, Saiqalgar* and *Tawaif*. *Julahas* formed the major caste in this group, comprising 13.3 per cent of the whole.

as a profession. By registering them in the census report, it appears that the British had recognised sex workers as being part of the regular workforce. Prostitutes comprised 0.3 per cent of the Muslim population,[27] and interestingly, a considerable portion of income tax was collected from them at the time.[28]

In Group IV were Muslims identified as foreigners, although their numbers were negligible (almost 2.3 per cent of the whole population).[29] It appears contradictory that while Groups I and IV also trace their origins from foreign lands, this particular group was excluded from the *ashraf* caste. It appears—as their names suggest—that they were neo-Muslims who had migrated to India and established their identities based on the regions they came from, for instance Biloch (born in Bilochistan), Habshi (born in Africa), and Turk (born in Turkistan).[30] With the passage of time, they became integrated within the local society.

Theoretically, Islam does not believe in the caste system; instead, it believes in the unity of the collective body of believers called *umma*. All umma are equal, and therefore there must be no caste-like division among Muslims. However, in practice the caste system was as rampant as it is in Hinduism, although unlike Hindus, Muslims seemed a little more flexible. But this flexibility was confined only to the mosque or other religious pilgrimages where everyone stood together without any social differences whatsoever; where all other relationships were concerned, though, a strict hierarchy prevailed, wherein no *Mehtar* Muslim dared to sit with a Saiyid or any other *ashraf*. In fact, women seemed more conscious of caste than men. For example, a *Mehtarani* who cleaned houses had to use a separate passage to approach the toilet. She could not touch a water tap or use a well to wash her hands or drink water; someone would pour water from a distance for her. A separate cup and plate was kept outside on a *tak* for her use. Her wages were placed in her outstretched *pallu* to prevent her unclean hands from coming into contact with her upper-caste *malkin*'s.[31]

---

27 *Census Report*, 1901, Subsidiary Table I, 254–55.

28 Ibid. Veena Talwar Oldenberg, Rosie Llewellyn-Jones and Abdul Halim Sharar, *The Lucknow Omnibus* (New York: Oxford University Press, 2001), 131–43.

29 *Census Report*, 1901, Subsidiary Table I, 254–55; Oldenberg et al., *The Lucknow Omnibus*. *Biloch, Dogar, Gara, Habshi, Iraqi, Jhajha, Meo, Mewati, Pankhia* and *Turk*.

30 *Census Report*, 1901, Subsidiary Table I, 254–55.

31 This practice has been continuing since time immemorial. Although the increasing urbanisation of India has improved their status, this change is taking place slowly. In villages, untouchables continue to exist, amongst both Muslims and Hindus. However, it is very difficult to find literature on *arzal* Muslims.

According to the practice in *ashraf* households, no lower-caste woman was allowed to sit on a cot; all women from the *praja*[32] class had to sit on the ground. Some women had to visit the homes of others on a daily basis, for example the *Dhobin, Naeen, Mehtarani, Faqiran, Panbharan* and *Churihain*. Amongst them, only the *Mehtarani* was considered untouchable, although the others were not supposed to visit frequently or sit anywhere but on the ground. The lower castes could not give their children names considered good or honourable. In addition, lower-caste women could not bear their own names; they were identified by the names of their husbands, who were in turn identified by their masters.[33]

Even *adab* literature advised women to keep a distance from lower-caste women, and the castes of the women with whom *sharif* women should or should not interact was clearly mentioned. It is interesting to read how the great 'liberal' Urdu writers, for instance Maulvi Nazir and many others, had internalised the notions of caste. Nazir, in the very first chapter of *Mirat-ul Uroos*, warned his female readers about lower-caste women, stating that their company was extremely undesirable and could even bring disgrace to one's family. Maulvi Nazir's essays construct the ideal 'sharif *bibi*', the only 'perfect women' who can have relations with women from the *ashraf* class alone. This raises serious questions about the humanitarianism practised in Islam, and the concept of umma. If all umma are equal in Nazir's eyes, then why should it be wrong to interact with lower-caste women?

In the book, Akbari has an argument with her husband, where she states that it is only the heart that matters in friendship, and not caste or class:

> Her husband said, '[I]n all of your squabbles with my mother and sisters, which I have happened to overhear, it is you who have been wrong. Whatever people

[32] In India, a few lower castes could serve the upper castes; they were called *praja*. Even to this day, this custom is in practice in many villages. Generally a few castes which come into daily contact with people are considered *praja*, for example, the *Dhobi, Naee, Faqir, Churihain, mehtar*. Each caste had their regular master to whom they provide their service, in return for which they there are given a fixed share of the yearly crop, known as *jewra*. Indeed, *jewra* is considered the right of all *praja* working in the household.

[33] In my family, the name of our *dhobin* name was Guddi, that of the *Nain* was Sajjan bahu; the Panbharan's name was Saptain, the Faqiran's name was Tadau bahu, and the Mehtarani's name was Nanka bahu. Normally, their names include Kalua, Nanka, Jannu, Dattu, Mannu, Chedi, Bachai, Dhakelu, Khaderu, Bhageru, Pachai, etc., while *ashraf* names would include Meer Raushan Ali Jafri, Syed Neamat Ali, Sheikh Mohiuddin, Sheikh Mansab Ali, Mirza Altaf Husain, Dilawar Khan, etc.

> there are of the commonest sort living in the *mohalla*, you treat their daughters as if they were your sisters. Chunia, the daughter of Bhondu the sutler, Zulfan, the daughter of Bakhshu the tinker, Sulmati, the daughter of Kimmu the water carrier, ... and you take no account of the fact that these people are not of our family. The *mohalla* is talking about it and saying, 'what sort of bride has come here now?' After all, there are people living in the *mohalla* too, like Kazi Imam Ali, Halim Shifa-uddaula, Munshi Mumtaz Ahmad, Maulvi Ruhullah, and Mir Hasan Riza, whose daughters and daughters-in-law are in the habit of visiting us. You don't vouchsafe a word to any of them. If my honoured mother warned you against associating with girls of low-bred and vulgar people, what was there improper in her doing so?'
>
> The silly wife replied, 'Affection and friendship depend on the union of hearts. There was a bangle seller named Basu living next door to my mother's house, whose daughter Banno was my bosom friend. I used to play with her when I was little. Yes, Banno and I made a marriage between our two dolls. Banno, poor thing, was very badly off! I used to steal things from my mother and give them to her. I would never give up my meetings with Banno, however much my mother forbade them.'
>
> Her husband replied, 'A precious idiot you were then!'[34]

This interesting conversation between a husband and wife shows how greatly Muslims were affected by ideas of caste and class—so much so that even a 'liberal' author could not disengage himself from this obsession. Indeed, it was not only common Muslims who practised the caste system; a large number of Ulema at the time were not free from it, either. For example, a leading Ulema and Sufi, Shah Wali Ullah, also seemed much attached to his noble origin (Saiyid). Shah Wali Ullaha was proud not only of being a Saiyid, but also of his mastery over the Arabic language: 'I hail from a foreign country; my forebears came India as immigrants. I am proud of my Arabic origin and my knowledge of Arabic, for both of these brings a person close to Saiyid (master), of the ancients and moderns.'[35]

Records indicate that the two classes accepted amongst Muslims at the time were old Muslims (*ashraf*) and *nau* Muslims (*ajlaf*). However, recent studies

---

[34] Maulvi Nazir Ahmad, *Mirat-ul Uroos*, G. E. Ward (trans.), (New Delhi: Permanent Black, 2004), 18–19.

[35] Ayesha Jalal, *Partisans of Allah: Jihad in South Asia* (New Delhi: Permanent Black, 2009), 41. Maulana Qasim Nanautvi also believed that religious learning should be entrusted only to the four elite qaum, that is, Saiyid, Sheikh, Mughal and Pathan. See Metcalf, 'Islamic Revival in British India: Deoband, 1860–1900', 239.

suggest that the Muslims were grouped into three classes: *ashraf* (old Muslims), *ajlaf* (converted from touchable Hindu castes), and *arzal* (converted from untouchable Hindu castes). Although broadly speaking *ashraf* and *ajlaf* were the only classes that seemed visible in Muslim society, they were as different from each other as Brahmins and Dalits.[36] So theoretically, it may appear that while many low-caste Hindus had converted to Islam in the hope of more equal treatment, they found themselves still discriminated against. As Francis Robinson rightly observes, by and large the *ashraf* were not prepared to accept low-caste Hindus who were being drawn slowly into the Islamic milieu.[37]

The census report of 1891 states,

> All the wandering caste and tribes, *nats, banjaras, Bengalis, bavariya* etc. and impure caste of sweepers and *dom* show a considerable proportion of Muslims, but it may be stated with confidence that their Islam is altogether ostensible. They are circumcised and they have ceased to intermarry with Hindus of their castes, but in all other respects they are ignorant of the Islamic creed and conform to the precepts of the Islamic social law only in refusing the use of the flesh of the pigs as food. Many of them continue to worship and sacrifice to *devi* or their formal low-caste gods, while most of them are so ignorant of Islam as to imagine that in worshiping the five *pirs* or some other Muslim saints they are conforming to Mohammadanism.[38]

As Rafiuddin Ahmad rightly observes with regard to lower-caste Muslims, conversion to Islam made almost no change in their social situation. Although

---

[36] *Census Report of 1891,* Allahabd, 1894, 175. See also Zarina Bhatty, 'Status of Muslim Women and Social Change', in *Indian Women: From Purdah to Modernity*, by B.R. Nanda (ed.), (New Delhi: Radiant Publishers, 1976), 110.

[37] Francis Robinson, *The 'Ulama of Firangi Mahal and Islamic Culture in South Asia* (London: C. Hurst and Co. Publishers, 2001), 11. Robinson emphasised that Muslim culture in India was a largely Perso-Islamic culture, which could be considered *ashraf* culture, that is, the culture of those who came from far-flung countries to rule India. They considered power their birthright. They only accepted those people who cherished the international Perso-Islamic culture, from which they hailed, for instance the upper-caste Kayastha and Kashmiri Brahmins, who joined their administration and businesses and absorbed elements of their Perso-Islamic culture. They were not, however, prepared to accept those low-caste Hindus who were gradually converting to Islam.

[38] Robinson, *The 'Ulama of Firangi Mahal'*. See also De Tassy, *Muslim Festivals in* India, 36. De Tassy believes that these *pirs* are so popular, that their names are given to the lunar months in which their feasts fall.

it is generally assumed that conversion was motivated primarily to avoid the social discrimination inherent in the hierarchical Hindu society, immigrant Muslims (*ashraf*) were not ready to admit the converts to a position of equality.[39] To some extent, it can be said that Muslims are flexible, as their social rules are not as strict as those of Hindus, especially where the old ways of life and ties of commensality were concerned; but it was also true that a line was drawn between intermingling and marriage.[40] If both *hasb* and *nasb* (a person's socio-economic condition as well as origins of birth) had to be considered in the choice of a bridegroom, it led to problems—particularly for Saiyid girls (who were supposed to marry only upper-caste Saiyid men, failing which they had to remain unmarried; Saiyid men, on the other hand, could marry Sheikh girls), many of whom remained unmarried, as noted by both Mrs. Hasan Ali and Schimmel.[41] Only under the pressure of poverty would an *ashraf* give his daughter to an *ajlaf*, or low-born Muslim.

Qateel made certain observations on Indian society:

> Among the Hindus even those who own elephants would not hesitate to get their daughters married to brokers, gram sellers, and confectioners. In Shahjahanabad there was a *khatri*, who had elephants and *palkis*, but his brother-in-law's son carried his attar jug during his rides. But among Muslims, persons engaged in low professions—domestic servants, water carriers, elephant drivers, medicine and perfume sellers, confectioners and bakers—are considered *paji* (ajlaf). Let alone rich people, even sharif persons who draw a salary of five rupees would not consider it permissible to have matrimonial relations in the family of an elephant driver who might be earning even five hundred rupees as salary; who would then consider water carriers and others engaged in business in the marketplace? As a matter of fact, many rich persons would not allow reciters of *marsiyas* to sit in their presence except during *moharram* .... If a Saiyid adopts the profession of a tailor or a Mughal becomes a baker, a vegetable seller, or a water carrier, he is not allowed to sit in the presence of his relations or other sharif people. There are two kinds of *sharafat*: nasbi (according to birth) and *hasbi* (according to status). The Hindus consider former more important, but among Muslims it is the opposite .... It is not possible for a Saiyid to give his daughter in marriage to another Saiyid who runs a medicine shop.[42]

---

[39] Ahmad, *The Bengal Muslims*, 8.

[40] Ashraf Ali Thanvi, *Behisht-e Zewar* (New Delhi: New A.S. Press, 1994), 193. See also *The Imperial Gazetteer*, Vol. 1, 329.

[41] De Tassy, *Muslim Festivals in* India, 19.

[42] ibid., 18–19. See also Ahmad, *The Bengal Muslims*, 15.

In practice, therefore, Muslims were as rigid as Hindus, particularly in marital relations, where *hasb* and *nasb* encouraged the practice of endogamy because it reduced impurity in one's race and caste. Interestingly, even the ulema maintained this attitude and condemned inter-caste marriages. Although so far only the *ashraf* and *ajlaf* had been recognised as Muslim sub-groups, there was another group of Muslims who has thus far not been mentioned separately, but erroneously included in the *ajlaf* caste: the *kamin*. These were the untouchable Muslims, against whom Ashra'f Ali Thanvi warned the upper castes repeatedly. In fact, Ashra'f Ali Thanvi gave a detailed account of why an *ashraf* should not marry a *kamin*, and whom one could marry. Here, he was talking about the *arzal*[43] Muslims of *Masawat Ki Jang*,[44] who were also termed *paji and kamin* in nineteenth-century writings. He did not approve of *nau* Muslims[45] either, and advised the *ashraf* to not give their daughters to such a groom.

Ashrafisation Amongst Muslims

The social classification of Indian Muslims was not similar to that of Muslims living in the Arab world. In Muslim society, the status of a person is gauged by

[43] For a few years, particularly after the 1990 Mandal Commission recommendations, which sought reservation in higher education and the workforce for SCs, STs and OBCs, these *arzals* claimed to be Dalits. Ali Anwar, a *kunjra* Muslim from Bihar, gave this claim further impetus by writing his book, *Masawat ki Jang*. In this revealing book, he insisted that caste oppressiveness is not the sole problem of Hindus, but is also a significant part of Muslim society, motivated by security concerns. Indeed, these upper-caste Muslims had completely ignored the social discrimination and problems faced by *arzal* Muslims; they were also against low-caste Muslims being given the status of Dalits. It is only after 1990 that backward Muslims developed an outspoken leadership of their own.

[44] Ali Anwar, *Masawat Ki Jang* (New Delhi: Vani Prakashan, 2001). Thanvi termed them *kamin*, or *Qateel paji*, while Ali Anwar popularised them as *arzal* or Dalit Muslims.

[45] The concept of *nau* Muslim is so deep-rooted amongst *ashraf* Muslims that to this day, they discriminate against them and do not inter-marry. A neighbour of mine in Colonelganj, Allahabad, was from the *Pathan* caste while another was from the *Malik* caste; Maliks claim to have converted from the Hindu Thakurs. This is what my lady neighbours had to say about the Malik family: 'You know they are *nau* Muslims'. Interestingly, my grandfather believed that a *Pathan* could not marry a Saiyid girl either, since that particular *Pathan* lady had once expressed her desire to marry an engineer. I suggested she speak with my aunt, who was also ready to consider her; however, my Saiyid grandfather refused to entertain any notion of marriage with a *Pathan*.

his or her social and economic position, and not just by birth.[46] It seems that social stratification based on both hasbi and nasbi did exist. Hence, any low-born person could move into a higher status by improving their socio-economic position. Saiyid Husain Madani is one of the finest examples of social mobility, as he improved his position from a weaver to a Saiyid. It was his learning and skill that made this possible; nobody challenged the Deoband-educated, Arabia-returned weaver's claim to being a Saiyid. Husain himself believed that only belief and behaviour mattered; however, as both were facilitated by birth, one should rejoice in being high-born as one would rejoice in having a flawless body.[47] Even Meer Taqi Meer, the famous contemporary poet, was said to have been a baker by Sauda, while Meer himself claimed to be a Saiyid.[48] Nonetheless, it was observed that amongst Muslims, an awareness of caste identity became increasingly prominent in the colonial period. Since revenue tax was a huge source of income for the colonial government, they desperately needed a loyal landed class, and as a result, a new class came into being. As landed property was the privilege of the upper castes in both communities, the British had to appease them by identifying and registering them in record books, and granting large pieces of land that were exempt from any religious law of inheritance.

Second, this class had to be distinguished from the professional caste so that a greater amount could be easily collected as tax.[49] Therefore, the British began registering them in land records. Social mobility was accelerated during the British period due to these records, and improving one's social status became an easy task. Hence, a new sort of group or caste consciousness started growing in Indian society, making people feel more secure. In the late nineteenth century, Metcalf calculated that no less than a quarter, or one-third of the Muslims of the United Provinces, reported themselves in the census as *ashraf*.[50] Surprisingly, this sort of upward mobility was increasing rapidly amongst Muslims; it seemed that the flexibility existing in Muslim society paved the way to an improvement in social status. Mushir–ul Hasan states that until the last quarter of the nineteenth

[46] This attitude was maintained by most reformers and ulema during the colonial period.

[47] Metcalf, 'Islamic Revival in British India', 247.

[48] De Tassy, *Muslim Festivals in India*, 18.

[49] *The Imperial Gazetteer of India: The Indian Empire*, Vol. 1, 1907 (Oxford: Clarendeon Press, 1907), 292. It was accepted that Madras and the United Provinces were the only provinces where professional tax formed an important part of municipal revenue, although the tax is levied in most parts of India.

[50] Metcalf, 'Islamic Revival in British India', 256.

century, most Muslims relied on their own resources without any awareness of their corporate political identity. The *ajlaf*, for example, were relegated to the humbler ranks and took up the occupations the *ashraf* eschewed.[51]

One could easily improve one's status through education, or by acquiring a government job. There is a well-known saying amongst Muslims: 'Last year I was a *julaha* (weaver); now I am a Sheikh; next year, if the prices rise, I shall become a Saiyid.'[52] It is also said about Indian Muslims: '*Shahar ashrafon se khali ho gaya, Jitne the kamin aali ho gae.*' This process of '*ashrafisation*' or 'Islamisation', which parallels the 'Sanskritisation'[53] among Hindus, has been particularly marked in modern India. In no way can it be concluded that social mobility is a new trend. The colonial presence made this mobility easier by giving these groups a permanent identity through inclusion in the Census Report and the Gazetteer, something that would have been difficult in an oral culture. Thus, this registration process encouraged brotherhood on the basis of caste, and in turn, this brotherhood paved the way for a caste identity. Caste identity imposed several new cultural values on women. The following chapters will discuss how women from the lower social strata began imitating upper-caste women and secluded themselves from the outside world (since *ashraf* culture did not allow their womenfolk to move about freely).

Gendering Caste

Despite their numerous outward differences, Indian Muslims were actually very influenced by Indian culture.[54] It was the idea of unity within diversity that made them comfortable in a composite culture of *gange-jamuni tahzeeb*. Parallel to the diverse dissimilarities found at the local level, only two classes seemed to exist in a broader perspective: *ashraf* and *ajlaf*. The status of their womenfolk can also be gauged from this classification. At the same time, a new class was being recognised by the colonial government in Group III, that is, the prostitute

[51] Mushir-ul Hasan, 'A Moral Reckoning: Muslims Intellectuals in the 19th century, (New Delhi: Oxford University Press, 2009), 33. Rafiuddin also noticed a similar upward mobility amongst the Muslims of Bengal during this period; see his *The Bengal Muslims*.

[52] *The Imperial Gazetteer of India*: The Indian Empire, Vol. I (Oxford: Clarendon Press, 1907), 329.

[53] M. N. Srinivasan, the well-known sociologist, was the one who coined this term.

[54] *Census Report of 1891*, 175–76. See also *Census Report of 1911*, 153; and the *Gazetteer of Province of Oudh*, Vol. III, N to Z, 1878, North Western Provinces and Oudh Government, 387.

and the dancing girl. This classification of womanhood posed a challenge to the male domain, as to some extent these women can be said to have believed in a matriarchal social order.[55] Since the caste hierarchy encouraged patriarchy, it affected the common women adversely, and often proved an obstacle in their lives. This work will try to analyse the condition of these three categories of women—*ashraf*, *ajlaf* and *tawaif*/dancing girl—under both patriarchal and matriarchal social orders.

Apart from caste variation, it is important to also look at regional variation.[56] It is noteworthy that two-fifths of the Muslim population resided in the Meerut and Rohilkhand Division (Western United Provinces), a very prosperous quarter of the United Province.[57] Also, it is important to understand how this region was becoming the centre of the socio-religious movement.

Ajlaf Muslims differed from *ashraf* Muslims in their living conditions and customs, in much the same manner that Dalits differed from upper-caste Hindus.[58] Therefore, it is necessary to look at the condition of Indian Muslim women across all castes, instead of viewing them as a unified whole. Colonial reports, however, neglected to do so by viewing Muslims as a monolithic bloc, thereby ignoring the local and caste variations found amongst Indian Muslims.[59]

---

[55] Mirza Hadi Ruswa, *Umrao Jan-e Ada*. It is quite surprising how this section of women had made their own way without any dependence on men, and practised an uncommon matriarchal social order where there was no discrimination on the basis of gender, in contrast to the rest of Indian society.

[56] *Lecturon ka Majmua: Maulvi Nazir Ahmad*, VIIth Lecture delivered at Anjuman-e Himayat-e Islam, 25 February 1890.

[57] *Census Report of 1901*, 63. See also Crook, *The North-Western Provinces of India*, 261–62; in Crook's opinion, Muslims were mostly found in the upper Doab, where the proximity to Delhi prompted conversion, and in Rohilkhand and northern Oudh.

[58] Although colonial reports constantly raised the issue of conversion, they never connected it with the composite culture that resulted from the intermingling of Hindu-Muslim society. Perhaps it could explain why the *Khanzada* and *Jugela Rajput* of the United Provinces could not let go of their Hindu customs (for instance, in the women's choice of the sari, their insistence on wearing *bindi*s and *sindoor*, and certain religious rituals marking important social events) even after converting to Islam (Gazetteer of the Province of Oudh, Vol. III, N to Z, 386, 388).

[59] *The Imperial Gazetteer of India: The Indian Empire*, Vol. 1, 328–29. It was assumed that with regard to social affairs, the religion of Muhammad was opposed to the Hindu scheme of a hierarchy of castes, which led to an elaborate stratification of society based upon distinctions of food, drink, dress, marriage and ceremonial usage. However, to some extent the caste system was accepted in the Gazetteer.

For instance, in some places women were held in high regard, while in regions where patriarchy and caste hierarchy was very strong, they were considered little more than commodities. Apropos Indian society, two factors seemed to influence women: patriarchy and caste hierarchy. Both complicate matters: patriarchy often views women primarily as commodities, and then as child-bearing machines and good housewives. But the basic question of what the status of Muslim women in such a patriarchal society was, remained unanswered.

It will be wrong to state that it was only patriarchy and caste hierarchy that led to the miserable condition of women; other issues of gender, class and region were also responsible for their situation. To understand this, it is necessary to trace the class, castes and regions from which they hail. Muslims from the Western United Province and the Central United Province were either from the landed class, or the service gentry. Muslims who hailed from the Eastern United Province belonged to a lower social order, which comprised mostly of artisans, peasants or agricultural labourers. Weavers were the most affected due to industrialisation, and were continuously migrating to other industrial cities.[60] Naturally, the socio-economic condition of Muslims affected their womenfolk immensely. In places where Muslims were economically strong, their women held a good position in society.[61] In any society, the woman is considered the repository of honour, and therefore a common notion is that women must be protected from strangers. This concern with honour encouraged *zenana* or the system of veiling, prevalent in both communities in India. It was considered a disgrace for women to venture out in public without veiling themselves properly. As Mrs. Marcus Fuller observed, the *purdah* system has a lot to do with the caste system and the advancement of one's social status. She rightly said:

> When we turn to the Mohammedan community we find the same conditions there. True the pious Muslim cries, 'There is but one God, Allah, and Mohammed is his prophet', but with this general creed and the Quran we find them divided and subdivided until it has passed into a proverb that there are

---

[60] *Census Report of 1891, 134*. See also *Census Report of 1901, 65*.

[61] Women of the Western United Province and the Central United Province were very advanced and conscious about their rights; this is why the women of this region were very active in the uprising of 1857, and remained politically active even later. Also, a close study of the Indian Law Report shows that women of these areas were very conscious of their legal and property rights, even filing several petition to challenge their male counterparts in this regard. They went not only to the lower and upper courts, but also to the apex court, that is, the King-in Council.

> seventy two sects of Mohemmadan. Hence it is easy to see that in speaking of the zenana, it is difficult to make general statements that would cover the whole Mohemmadan community.[62]

Thus Shahida Lateef observes that in the nineteenth century, Muslim communities in India, like other castes or religious communities, had little in common with each other; they were separated by language, cultural traditions, and sometimes even religious practices. The occupational structure of communities, whether primarily engaged in agriculture or trade or service industries, determined certain cultural and religious practices. The differences between the regional communities could also be seen in their attitude towards the role and status of women, as many socio-religious customs and beliefs pertaining to women, and families in general, tended to be localised.[63]

[62] Eunice De Souza, *Purda: An Anthology* (New Delhi: Oxford University Press, 2004), 73.

[63] Shahida Lateef, *Muslim Women in India* (New Delhi: Kali for Women, 1990), 16–17.

CHAPTER 2

Socio-religious Movement and the Muslim Women's Issue

After the revolt of 1857, Indian Muslims lost the privileges they had enjoyed for a long time.[1] Their role in the revolt meant that Muslim losses in terms of power and privileges were greater than those suffered by other communities. Unlike the Hindus, they began to feel increasingly distanced from the mainstream, and could not come to terms with their continuously deteriorating condition.[2] Holding the British responsible for their miseries,[3] an alienation of sorts from the Western way of life set in, to the extent that even English education was considered profane.[4] Maulvi Nazir revealed his father's hostility towards English education thus: 'He would rather see me die

---

[1] *Gazetteer of the Province of Oudh*, Vol. III, 53. The Hindu town looked well-to-do, but the Mohemmadan Muhallas have, for the most part, a decayed and impoverished appearance. In Shahabad tahseel, out of 1,055 houses, only 32 are made of brick.

[2] Iftikhar Alam Khan, *Sir Saiyid Ahmad Khan* (New Delhi: Urdu Academy, 2008), 29–31.

[3] Sir Saiyid Ahmed Khan, Asbab-e Baghawat-e Hind, Abu Layis Siddiqui (ed.) (Karachi: Urdu Academy, 1976), 152–58.

[4] Khan, *Asbab-e Baghawat e Hind*, 123–26. See also Shan Mohammad, Sir Syed Ahmed Khan: A Political Biography (Bombay: 1969), 35. Not only were the Muslims economically crushed, there were several obstacles in their way even where education was concerned. Persian and Arabic were no longer taught in schools; the curriculum had been so designed that for Muslims, who considered learning English 'irreligious', accepting it was impossible. They firmly believed that education had no value unless based it was on Arabic. Consequently, out of the 300 boys in the English College, Muslims made for less than 1 per cent of students. The Muslims also vehemently opposed the new system of education and considered it beneath their dignity to study English; in fact, those who studied English were no longer considered gentlemen.

than learn English'.[5] Men sought to safeguard their religion, culture and caste by confining their females within their homes. As a result, they began lagging behind in the race for progress.

The uprising of 1857 seemed to have awakened Muslims from a long slumber.[6] Fortunately, they found an outspoken leader in Sir Saiyid Ahmed Khan (1817–98), who was born in a leading Saiyid family of Delhi, and whose ancestors had served the Mughal court for generations. Sir Saiyid was the first Muslim to question every aspect of life in Muslim society, and highlight how their ignorance was leading to the deteriorating condition. He concluded that neutrality vis-à-vis the new system of education was the main cause of their backwardness.[7] Sir Saiyid Ahmad Khan sensed the significance of science in 1864 and founded a Scientific Society in Ghazipur.[8] Soon after its establishment, he found Ghazipur unsuitable and shifted the society to Aligarh in 1864.[9] It appears that Aligarh's proximity to Delhi and its sizeable Muslim population were factors that motivated this decision. Also, Aligarh was dominated largely by Muslim landlords and nawabs who, it was hoped, would offer vast tracts of land by way of donations.[10] Thus began Sir Saiyid's movement against illiteracy, ignorance, and every other evil custom that had permeated Muslim society. He also launched a journal, named *Akhbar-e Scientific Society*, to promote scientific awareness amongst the members of the community.[11] Thus, the Aligarh Movement (as it is popularly known) gave direction to the newly emerging groups of Muslim social reformers. This first generation of the Aligarh Movement was sheltered under Sir Saiyid's English umbrella.[12] But even as we

---

[5] Maulvi Nazir Ahmad, *The Brides Mirror: A Tale of Life in Delhi a Hundred Years ago*, G.E. Ward (trans.), (New Delhi: Permanent Black, 2004), 205.

[6] Andrews, xvii, 43. See also Ayesha K. Jalal, *Partisans of Allah: Jihad in South Asia* (Cambridge, MA: Harvard University Press, 2010), 144–49.

[7] Md. Saiyid Iqbal, *Saiyid Ahmed ka Safarnama –e Panjab* (New Delhi: Educational Publishing House, 1979), 141–42. In his evidence before the Hunter Commission, he accepted that neutrality towards education was the main cause for Muslims lagging behind the other communities.

[8] Khan, *Sir Saiyid Ahmad Khan*, 33. See also Altaf Husain Hali, *Hayat-e Javed* (New Delhi: Taraqqi Urdu Board, 1979), 173.

[9] Khan, *Sir Saiyid Ahmad Khan*.

[10] Hali, *Hayat-e Javed*, 189.

[11] Khan, *Sir Saiyid Ahmad Khan*, 33. See also Hali, *Hayat-e Javed*, 173.

[12] Bashir Uddin Ahmad (ed.), *Lecturon Ka Majmua*, Maulvi Nazir Ahmad, jild-1 (1918), 186–87. At the time, Maulvi Nazir was also lamenting the deteriorating condition

note its importance, we should not deny the increasing significance of Deoband and the Dar-ul Uloom.

At first glance, the Aligarh Movement seems progressive in every aspect, especially in its educational agenda. It was launched by Sir Saiyid Ahmed Khan to mobilise Muslim society and make them aware of the fast-changing world they were living in. In 1875 he established the Mohammedan Anglo Oriental College (popularly known as M.A.O. College) to impart the new education to Muslim boys, which proved a milestone in the educational history of Muslim society. As Qeam Uddin Ahmad rightly said, Sir Saiyid represented a new school of thought, which postulated that the future of the Indian Muslim lay not in staying aloof from Western ideas and education, but in accepting and adapting themselves to those very ideas.[13] In this way he provoked a *jihad* against the evil customs influencing Muslim society through *'tahzeeb-e Ekhlaq'*. As Mushir-ul Hasan explains, its objective was to enlighten and propagate social refinement or correctness of manner among its readers.[14] Sir Saiyid seemed inspired by Miskawayh's famous work on ethics, which aimed at improving the ethical life of the British. Therefore, after returning from London in 1870, he launched his journal in an attempt to emulate their achievement by encouraging a rational and critical discussion among Muslims.[15] Through this journal, he expressed his support for property rights of women, purdah,[16] and the *shariat* law.[17] He argued against several evil customs that had entered society over time, such as the prohibition of widow remarriage[18] and various superstitions; unfortunately, he attributed the latter to women's ignorance, as he firmly believed that men were superior to women.[19] It is very surprising that Sir Saiyid, who had been left a widower at a young age, never remarried, despite supporting the practice of polygamy. Shan Mohammad has written about his views on polygamy; according to Sir Saiyid, the main purpose of a family is procreation, and it is on the basis

of Muslims on several occasions at the Mohemmadan Education Conference. He raised a question about the social reform agenda of Muslims in his one of lectures held at Aligarh on 28 December 1889.

13 Qeamuddin Ahmad, *Wahabi Movement in India* (New Delhi: Manohar, 1994 [1966]), 304. See also Jalal, Partisans of Allah, 144.

14 Mushirul Hasan, *A Moral Reckoning: Muslim Intellectuals in Nineteenth-century Delhi* (USA: Oxford University Press, 2005), 8.

15 Jalal, *Partisans of Allah*, 168. See also Hali, *Hayat-e Javed*, 164–69, 193.

16 *Maqalat-e Sir Saiyid*, Vol. 13, 186.

17 *Tahzeeb-e Akhlaq*, No. 41, Jild 1, 10 Jamadi aual, 1288 H.

18 *Maqalat-e Sir Saiyid*, 31 March 1876, 200–03.

19 ibid., 14 April 1876.

of this belief that he favoured polygamy. Woman was created to carry out the divine command, 'Increase and multiply and replenish the earth'; but this is also a duty enjoined upon man.[20] Therefore, if either of them fails in this duty, it is a violation of the very purpose for which the family was created by God, and some alternative arrangement must be sought. In an article, Sir Saiyid wrote:

> When however cause, this helpmate fails to perform her natural duty, some remedy must surely have been appointed by the all wise creator to meet the exigency, and that remedy is polygamy—that act is the act of a man's marrying wither more than one wife at one and the same time or after divorcing the former one. The latter privilege is allowed to the wife in the event of the husband's in competency, with this reasonable difference only, that the man can have recourse to authorization for the act.[21]

He was neutral where issues such as child marriage was concerned, as he believed in the non-interference of the government in socio-religious matters.[22] He firmly believed that this practice was confined solely to the Hindu community (for more details, see Chapter Nine). However, *tahzeeb-e Ekhlaq* did play a vital role in awakening Muslims in India. But at the same time, a question arises with regard to his intended audience in Muslim society: For whom had this esteemed college been created?

The names of his followers indicate the social category they belong to: all of them had *ashraf* origins. Among his most prominent assistants and followers were Altaf Husain Hali (Saiyid), Maulvi Nazir Ahmed (Saiyid and Ulema), Zaqaullah (Saiyid), Mehdi Hasan (Nawab), Iftikhar Bilgrami, Mumtaz Ali (Saiyid), (Sheikh) Ismail Panipati (Saiyid), and Sheikh Abdullah (nau Muslim), who were all well known for their commitment to the cause of women's upliftment. Interestingly, all the social reformers were connected to noble Muslim families, with the exception of Sheikh Abdullah, who was a *nau* Muslim (before converting to Islam, he had been a Kashmiri Brahmin). Their social status reflected their social concerns; as most of them hailed from the *ashraf* stratum, their concerns were confined to issues related to upper-class Muslims. They remained unaware of even the basic problems faced by common Muslims, whose lot in life was very different from that of *ashraf* Muslims. Common Muslims were mostly low-born or belonged to the artisan class, and

[20] Sir Saiyid was more outspoken than other social reformers, who only believed in theories but never practised what they preached.

[21] Mohammad, *Sir Syed Ahed Khan*, 198–99.

[22] *Maqalat-e Sir Saiyid*, 12 May 1876, 514–18.

shared the same social issues and a common understanding with their Hindu counterparts. They were largely ignored by these reformers, who perceived all Muslims as an umma, or a monolithic category.

Although Sir Saiyid was considered a firebrand reformer amongst Muslim social reformers, in no way were his thoughts on women very progressive; he was even blamed to be a *naturee* (infidel) and charged with infidelity. He accorded no importance to women-centric issues like child marriage, the Age of Consent bill, and education; in fact, he was against women's education. He was convinced that all evil customs concerning women were the sole preserve of Hindu society, as he believed that the status of Muslim women was better than that of their Hindu counterparts. Perhaps, as his biographer Altaf Husain Hali believes, circumstances had forced him to shut his eyes to reality. Sir Saiyid Ahmad blamed all evil customs in Indian society on the influence of Hindu culture, which he believed should be reformed by spreading awareness about the 'true' nature of Islam, and not through government policies.[23] He considered his mother, Begum Aziz-un Nisa, his role model. While she had no formal education, she was an impressive lady who left a deep impact on her son's mind; unfortunately, this led him to believe that traditional education at home was enough, as it made a woman competent to run her home and family. He thus saw no need to impart Western education to girls; the traditional education *ashraf* girls received at home was deemed sufficient. He believed that with the passage of time, Muslim women would automatically be educated by their male counterparts, provided the education was given and received in a 'proper' way. Therefore, he considered it essential to educate boys instead of girls. Sir Saiyid also supported the purdah system,[24] and this perhaps prevented him from including women in his educational institute. However, many of his close associates were staunch supporters of female education, which might possibly explain why a women's section was set up in his institute in 1896, well before his death.

A close associate of his, Nawab Mehdi Ali Hasan Mohsin ul Mulk (1837–1907) from the Etawah branch of the Barah Saiyid family, contributed to *Tahzeeb-e Akhlaq* and *The Aligarh Institute Gazette*.[25] He wrote a number of articles related to women's issues and supported the cause of female education,[26] a directive achieved only after Sir Saiyid's death.

---

[23] Hali, *Hayat-e Javed*, 642–47.

[24] ibid., 646

[25] Francis Robinson, *Separatism among Indian Muslims: The Politics of the United Provinces' Muslims, 1860–1923*, Cambridge South Asian Studies (Cambridge: Cambridge University Press, 2007), 397–98.

[26] Haji Mohammad and Md. Wahid Uddin Salim (eds), *Maroof*, 1 May 1899, 347.

Indeed, the late nineteenth century was the period of social reform . For Hindus, the mission was to emancipate women from age-old customs, by focusing on issues like widow remarriage and female education, and banning child marriage, *sati* and female infanticide. Muslims, however, believed these issues to be restricted to Hindus, a misconception they were alerted to in only the last decade of the nineteenth century. In this context, the names of Altaf Husain Hali and Maulvi Nazir Ahmad are unforgettable, for they exposed the social evils in Muslim society through their discursive writing. Urdu literature effectively played its part by reflecting the true face of society.

By this time, Urdu had emerged as a common language in north India.[27] Its contribution can be discerned by the increased circulation of Urdu newspapers. Gail Minault believed that the lithographic proceedings of the emerging madrasas had contributed to the expansion of Urdu as a medium of public discourse,[28] and therefore the circulation of newspapers increased speedily.[29] Since the common language in most households was the *Hindustani zubaan*, which women were more fluent in,[30] the opportunity to acquire literary knowledge evaded them. Urdu opened up the outside world for women, a world that had remained closed so far because of the use of the classical Persian in educational discourse. Besides, Maulvi Nazir and Altaf Husain Hali popularised the language among common Muslim women. As a result, Muslims found it easier to re-assess their condition through the newly acquired medium of a common language.

Altaf Husain Hali (1837–1914) was born in Panipat, and his ancestors were from Herat.[31] Hali was born into a family known for its piety and learning, long established in the *qasba* of Panipat, some 50 miles north of Delhi. His ancestors had served the royal court from the very beginning of the Delhi Sultanate. Hali's father was the first in the family to render his services to the British.[32]

---

[27] C. F. Andrews, *Zaka Ullah of Delhi* (New Delhi: Oxford University Press, 2003), 38. In his opinion, Old Delhi had given birth to its youngest child, viz., the Urdu language, as a literary medium of primary historical importance.

[28] Gail Minault, *Secluded Scholar: Women's Education and Muslim Social Reform in Colonial India* (New Delhi: Oxford University Press, 1998), 60.

[29] Robinson, *Separatism Amongst Indian Muslim*, 33.

[30] Francis Robinson, *The 'Ulama of Firangi Mahal and Islamic Culture in South Asia* (London: C. Hurst and Co. Publishers, 2001), 27.

[31] ibid., 431.

[32] Gail Minault, *Voices of Silence*. English Translation of Hali's 'Majalis-un Nisa' and 'Chup ki Dad' (New Delhi: Chanakya Publications, 1986).

He was a great Urdu poet who was deeply concerned about Muslim women's ignorance and the social evils prevalent in society. His concern is visible in his poems 'Chup ki Dad' and 'Munajat-e Bewa'. In 'Munajat-e Bewa', he narrates the story of a shattered, wailing widow, disappointed with her life and seeking relief in prayer. To her, life was a living death, a burden, and she wished she could commit sati on her husband's funeral pyre like a Hindu widow. In fact, widowhood was a severe burden across all religions; for women, all chances at happiness ended with the death of their husbands.

'Chup ki Dad' is dedicated to the cause of female education, and the poet laments their ignorance in the following words:[33]

> *A maon, bahnon, Betion, Dunia Ki Zeenat tumse hai*
> *Mulkon ki basti ho tumhi, qaumon ki izzat tumse hai*
>
> Oh mothers, sisters and daughters! The honour of the world comes from you.
> Countries, populations, and the greatness of nations, come from you ...
>
> *Afsos! Duniya me bahut tum pe hue zoro zafa*
> *Haq talfiyan tumne sahi be mahriya jheli sada*
>
> Alas! The world repays your virtue by oppression.
> Deprived of rights, in truth, you endure untold transgression.

Women's ignorance is also discussed in his 'Majalis-un Nisa', a dramatic satire on uneducated women. He demonstrates how education is important for both sexes: if a parrot's ability to speak makes it more significant than other animals, then how can men keep women silent by depriving them of education?[34] Both Nazir's novel and Hali's writings were influenced by the example of Western society, and repeatedly projected Queen Victoria as a role model. Hali, in his second Majlis, tried to explain the importance of knowledge through several examples:

> Mahmooda: 'Mummy! Men certainly seem to be superior.' But she said: 'No, little woman! Never believe that! Knowledge is something that permits the woman who possessed it to have hundred of thousands of men as her subjects. You see as an example our ruler, Queen Victoria, who lives many thousands of miles away. Because she is so learned, she can rule over two countries.'[35]

[33] ibid., 141–150. See also Begum Mutaz Mirza (ed.), *Hali Panipati ki Nazmen* (Haryana: Haryana Urdu Academy, 2008), 62–69.

[34] Khwaja Altaf Husain Hali, *Majalis-un Nisa* (Delhi: Art Press, 1971), 98.

[35] Minault, *Voices of Silence*, 54.

Maulvi Nazir Ahmad (1836–1912), another Delhi School alumnus, was a good representative of the Urdu-speaking elite. A resident of Bijnour, he was connected by marriage to a learned, religious family of Delhi. Indeed, Maulvi Nazir's marriage was a contract marriage, the best example of Islamic marriages that used to be made in favour of the wife, unlike other traditional marriages that are akin to business deals, with the woman being considered a commodity. Maulvi Nazir had to sign an agreement before the *nikah* ceremony stating that he would live in his marital home and would never remarry.[36] Both conditions are interesting, particularly in a society where the bride is supposed to move to her husband's home, and where polygamy was very much in practice among both Hindus and Muslims. It is believed that Maulvi Nazir's mother had never approved of his first marriage, as the bride did not belong to their kin. She insisted on his marrying a girl of her choice, as at that time it was considered desirable for an *ashraf* to marry within his family. Since Maulvi Nazir's first marriage was a love marriage (although it is not clear whether the woman reciprocated Nazir's love), his mother never accepted it. Interestingly enough, he married a second time, though this did not succeed either.[37] Ironically, this marriage took place five years after writing his famous novel *Fasana-Mubtala* (1877), which dealt with the various bad habits of *ashraf* Muslims, among them gambling, alcoholism, prostitution and polygamy. The author lamented the increasing poverty levels amongst Muslim; however, his humanitarian, reformist credentials come under question in the light of his later actions: Were all his beliefs theoretical, or did he ever practice any of them in his day-to-day life?

Yet another important personal belief was his conviction that a woman's purpose—indeed, her only use—lay in her fertility. Therefore, a barren wife must be replaced by one who could bear her husband children. This was perhaps why he compelled his son, Maulvi Bashir Ahmad, to remarry.[38] It thus seems clear that despite the content of his novels, he did not consider any of what he wrote to be of practical significance. On one occasion he states that a man has only one heart, which cannot be shared by two women. Given this statement, how he himself remarried and compelled his son to do so while their wives were living, remains unexplained. Clearly these so-called social reformers had double standards; they did not practice what they preached.

---

[36] Zeenat Bashir, *Nazeer Ah med ke Navilon me Nusvae Kirdar*, (Hyderabad: Iliyas Traders Publishers & Book Sellers, 1991), 31.

[37] ibid., 38.

[38] ibid., 39.

Maulvi Nazir was a follower of Sir Saiyid Ahmad Khan, and projected himself as the true champion for the cause of women's upliftment. He was aware that only education could raise one's status, and that it was necessary for both the sexes. He felt a dire need for relevant books that could work towards building 'better' women. While his first novel advocated the education of his daughters, its popularity forced him to think about a vast number of issues related to women. He was among the first writers to become popular with female readers, and this might have dictated his choice to write on various social issues. But it was *Mirat-ul Uroos* and *Banat-ul Nas* that earned him renown amongst his readers as '*akbari-Asghari begum vale maulvi sahib*'.[39] *Mirat-ul Uroos*, along with *Banat-ul Nas* and *Taubat-un Nasooh*, form a syllabus of instruction for women, *Mirat* for teaching the household arts, *Banat* for teaching useful facts, and *Taubat* for teaching piety.[40] Maulvi Nazir himself describes its popularity in his Preface thus:

> In accordance with the family custom, my daughters also were taught by the elder ladies of the house to read such small vernacular tracts as 'The Holy Quran and its teaching', 'A Letter on the Last Day', 'The Way of Salvation', etc. It was a house in which reading and writing formed a constant topic of conversation at all times. I noticed that even my little daughter, taking her cue from us men, had quite a longing of her own for the acquisition of knowledge. At the same time, however, I became convinced that purely religious subjects of study are not suited to the capacities of children, and that the literature to which my children's attention was restricted had the effect of depressing their spirits, of checking their natural instincts, and of blunting their intelligence.
>
> I then tried to find some kind of book, well stored, of course, with moral instruction, and which should improve their ideas and correct their habits in respect of those affairs which a woman encounters in her daily life, and in which, by reason of their romantic notions, or through ignorance or perversity, so many women are overtaken by disaster and sorrow, and yet which should be in a form sufficiently attractive to prevent their being discouraged or dismayed by its perusal. But though I searched and searched for such a book through a whole library of volumes, not a trace of one could I find.
>
> It was then that I formed the design of the present tale. The story of Akbari was put into shape three years ago, when I was at Jhansi. My daughters made it their daily task to read it, and they began pestering me everyday to complete the book, until, a year and half a later, the story of Asghari was also written. By degrees the book came to be talked of in the mohalla. A few women came in to

[39] Hasan, *A Moral Reckoning*, 160.

[40] ibid.

> listen when it was being read, and all who listened were charmed with it. The manuscript was borrowed for perusal in some great houses. Applications were made for permission to take copies of it. In the meanwhile my eldest daughter's marriage took place. I included the manuscript in her dowry, as a jewel of great price, and it achieved no less a reputation in her new home.[41]

This novel received so much attention from both the public and the government that it won a prize of Rs 1,000, and for decades remained part of the curriculum in several schools. It was considered the first Urdu bestseller. First published in 1869, it had, within twenty years, gone into several editions totalling over 100,000 copies. It had also been translated into Bengali, Braj, Kashmiri, Punjabi and Gujarati.[42]

Although the author was patriarchal in his tone and deeply influenced by caste, it cannot be denied that this work was unparalleled. He was perhaps the first Muslim social reformer to connect widowhood with child marriage. As Hindus and Muslims regularly gave female children in marriage to relatively older grooms (who were sometimes three times older than their prospective brides), such marriages resulted in early widowhood.[43] Maulvi Nazir was aware of the declining fortunes of the British in India, and therefore considered it necessary for Muslims to assess their situation and make adjustments vis-à-vis the new power, instead of alienating themselves from it completely. He was against a blind imitation of Western practices, but all through his novel, tried to familiarise his reader with the significance of British rule, and how benevolent they were with regard to Indians.

Both Altaf Husain Hali and Maulvi Nazir lamented the deterioration among Muslims and tried to convince their readers that, being alone responsible for their own plight, they should refrain from blaming the British. Both felt the need for a new educational system and realised that it was only ignorance that crippled Muslims. Hali's *Musaddas* is a great contribution towards making his fellow Muslim citizens aware of their existing reality. *Musaddas*, as Francis Robinson says, 'recited aloud at political and educational conferences, featured

---

[41] Maulvi Nazir Ahmad, *The Brides Mirror: A Tale of Life in Delhi a Hundred Years Ago*, G. E. Ward (trans.), (New Delhi: Permanent Black, 2004), 1–2. See also Hasan, Moral Reckoning, 160.

[42] Ahmad, *The Brides Mirror*, 204–05.

[43] Hali depicts a child-bride in his famous poem, 'Chup Ki Daad':
Married before you knew, the meaning of the word.
Bound for a lifetime, by this straitening cord. (Minault, *Voices of Silence*, 146).

on the front page of journals and learnt by most young Muslims, summed up for generations what Muslim revivalism was about'.[44] A common trait among all Muslim reformers was their concern with *ashraf* society. They never talked about the majority of Muslims, who belonged to the lower social orders. A great poet of his time, Hali laments the deterioration of *ashraf* Muslims in the following verse:

Shareefon ki aulaad be-tarbiat hai
Taubah unki halat buri unki gat hai
Kisi ko kabootar udane ki lat hai
Kisi ko baterein ladane kid hat hai
Charas aur ganje pe shaida hai koi
Madak aur chandu ka rasiya hai koi

Sons of noble parents are bereft of upbringing
Their ravaged condition sinks deeper in ruin
Some live for cock fights, life carelessly flinging
Some stake all they have for quails and for pigeons
On hemp and cannabis they are often hooked
For opiates and liquor their existence is booked.

Sada garm anfaar se unki sobat
Har ek rind-o-bash se unki millat
Parhe likhe ke saaye se unko vehshat
Madaris se unko nafrat
Kameenon ke jirge mein umrein ganwaani
Unhein gaaliyaan deni aur aap khaani

They are often found lingering in company vile
Their best friends are junkies and ruffians and crooks
From shadow of wisdom they run a straight mile
Schools and instruction they truly despise
Among measly and mean they fritter their lives
Hurling curses at others and being cursed alike.[45]

Zaka Ullah (1832–1910), son of Sana Ullah, was born to a family that had for several generations served as tutors of the royal family. His descent can be traced back to Abu Bakr, the first successor of the Prophet. He was much influenced

[44] Robinson, *Separatism Amongst Muslims*, 431.

[45] Altaf Husain Hali, Musaddaas, Saiyeda Saiyidain Hameed (trans.), (New Delhi: Harper Collins, 2003), 216–17.

by his grandfather, Baka Ullah, and it was from him that he inherited the deep religious thoughts that permeated his whole life. Interestingly, most of the first generation of Aligarh's social reformers, who were also the first graduates of MAO College and involved in the Aligarh movement, had connections with the Delhi College, and had been somewhat influenced by the 1857 uprising and its aftermath. When they lost everything in the mutiny, it was his mother who sold all her jewellery and household goods, and used part of the money to purchase books for her children. Zaka Ullah was also a close friend of Nazir Ahmed's at the Delhi College.

Zaka Ullah was one of the few reformers with a modern outlook towards education. However, instead of blindly supporting English, he advocated adherence to vernacular languages and remained in favour of the mother tongue, which he believed was a more potent medium of instruction. He was also amongst the first to back female education, and work for the upliftment of socially marginalised widows.[46] even opening a school for widows in Bulandshahar.[47] This appears to have taken place during his tenure as Deputy Inspector of Scholars School (1869–72), in Bulandshahar,[48] but unfortunately it has not been documented in the archives. It is surprising to observe how such credible work has gone unnoticed by scholars.

Another, less well-known name is not that of a reformer, but of a legal practitioner who was well-versed in diverse languages and legal matters. This was Justice Mahmood (1850–1900), the son of Sir Saiyid Ahmed Khan. He was educated at Christ College, Cambridge, where he studied Oriental and classical languages.[49] He joined the Allahabad Bar in 1879, and the ICS as a district judge in 1882. He went on to become the first Indian Judge (1884–93), and then a Judge of the Allahabad High Court in 1893.[50]

Justice Mahmood supported his father's work in Aligarh wholeheartedly.[51] Although not as popular as his great father, Sir Saiyid Ahmed, Justice Mahmood can be credited with helping both the British and Indians understand the true nature of the *shariat*. He was one of the few Indian Muslims who dared to say that the real *shariat* was not being followed by the British court in matters related to Muslims. He commented that the 'Hedaya' (a significant book on

[46] Andrews, Zaka Ullah of Delhi, 80.

[47] Aligarh Magazine, Khawateen Number, 32.

[48] Robinson, *Separatism Amongst Muslims*, 434.

[49] Hali, *Hayat-e Javed*, 176.

[50] Robinson, *Separatism Amongst Muslims*, 433.

[51] Hali, *Hayat-e Javed*, 174.

Islamic law) was a much distorted translation of previous translations—written in Arabic in the twelfth century, it was translated into Persian during the Mughal period, and then into English during the colonial era. He believed there was an urgent need to understand the proper meaning of the Quran and its Prophetic tradition. With his commendable expertise in both Arabic and English, he was probably the first judge to deliver almost all his judgements after going through the real scripture of Islam, written in Arabic. English was required to carry out legal proceedings in the British court, and Arabic for understanding the true nature of Islam and the *shariat*.[52]

Justice Mahmood delivered a number of judgements related to women's right to property, conjugal rights, and maintenance rights. Indeed, he provided a space where rationalism could interact with religious laws, in the light of the Quran and the Hadith.[53] Had he lived longer, he could have brought about revolutionary changes in the personal laws of Muslims, the misinterpretation of which he often lamented.

An important question that comes to mind is: How, and to what extent, had the social reform movement influenced Muslim women in India? Indian Muslims were influenced by two major reform movements—the Aligarh Movement and the Wahabi Movement, both active in the Western United Provinces. One was progressive and the other, regressive. The Wahabi movement demanded religious reformation in Islam, while the Aligarh movement was launched to bring about social reforms. Wahabis asserted that Indian Muslims had deviated from an Islamic path and therefore become miserable; to counteract this, they needed to bring 'pure' Islam back to India.[54] They declared that all local customs and traditions not validated by the Holy Quran were un-Islamic.[55] Shah Wali Ullah termed all customs in India *Turk's (ajam)* custom, and recommended abolishing them.[56]

Saiyid Ahmad Shaheed's social activities focused on the problems facing the popular reform of customs and practices. According to him, there was a dire need to explain the harmful effects of customs and practices linked with

---

52 Aligarh Law Journal, V: Mahmood Number, Md. Anees Ansari and Arshad Masood (eds), (AMU: Faculty of Law, 1973), 22–23.

53 *The Indian Law Report*, Allahabad, 1883–93, suggests this. For further details, see Chapter Nine.

54 Qeamuddin Ahmad, *The Wahabi Movement in India*, 21–27.

55 Ashraf Ali Thanvi, *Behisht-e Zewar* (New Delhi: New A. S. Press, 1994), 50–51, 299. See also Jalal, *Partisans of Allah*.

56 Jalal, *Partisans of Allah*, 41.

birth, circumcision, marriage, death, visits to tombs, and the celebrations of *urs* (death of saints) in his famous religious commentary *Sirat-ul Mustaqeem.* They tried to open people's eyes to the wasteful expenditure incurred during pompous circumcision ceremonies; in fact, lack of money often led less well-off people to delay it beyond a reasonable time. A similar problem affected the elaborate marriages, for both girls and for boys, which were also accompanied by a great deal of indulgence in sinful activities.[57] The Wahabis' main assertion was to get people to read religious texts in their original form and understand them, instead of enlisting the help of the *ulema.* They advocated *tauhid* and rejected *bidat* in everyday life. They categorised all local customs as *bidat*, which had to be abolished.[58]

Women, in general, were given to several superstitions. They therefore became the focus of concern for the Wahabis. They advocated widow remarriage and several other women's rights already given in the *shariat*, which they remained deprived of partly due to their own ignorance, and partly due to local customs and tradition.[59] Widowhood forced many unfortunate women to live lives of isolation, drudgery and humiliation. Condemning this custom, many Wahabis, including Saiyid Ahmad Barelvi himself, set an example by marrying widows.[60] The Urdu translation of the Quran by Shah Abdul Qadir and some *Risala* of Shah Ismail were distributed amongst members of their gatherings, which also included some women.[61]

Almost 6 per cent of the donors to the Deoband School were women, implying that the movement had attracted women's attention as much as it had men's. The low percentage of women donors is explained by the fact that women were excluded from ownership or control over the assets of their homes. It is also noteworthy that most donors hailed from the Western United Province—particularly from Saharanpur, Muzaffarnagar and Merutt divisions.[62] The agenda of the Deoband School was very clear, although it did seem somewhat orthodox—to reform society, even if it was through religious initiatives. Indeed, they considered religion a weapon with which to attack the

[57] Ahmad, *Wahabi Movement in India*, 15.

[58] ibid., 84, 309–10.

[59] Qeamuddin Ahmed, *Wahabi Movement* (Calcutta: Manohar, 1966), 29. See also Thanvi, *Behisht-e Zewar*, 338.

[60] Ahmad, *Wahabi Movement in India*, 309–10.

[61] ibid., 84.

[62] Barbara Daly Metcalf, 'Islamic Revival in British India: Deoband 1860–1900', in *India's Muslims* (New Delhi: Oxford University Press, 2008), 262.

evil customs that had entered society. The issues of widow remarriage, reform in marriage customs, the advocation of female education, along with lessons on how to be a perfect wife, were the main points in their agenda.

Maulana Muhammad Ahsan of the Nanautah family was its most prominent campaigner. He wrote a number of articles in Urdu to spread awareness among common people, the most notable of which was on the *Hanafi* definition of categories of marriageable women. He personally taught the Quran to the women in his family. At the request of Marry Kempson, Director of Public Instruction, he wrote a number of Urdu schoolbooks. His finest works were on versification, and in favour of female education.[63]

It is generally believed that the movement for women's rights was launched by reformers who had been exposed to Western influence and education. Surprisingly, however, one comes across Maulvi Mumtaz Ali (1860–1935), who had been educated in Dar-ul Uloom Deoband and yet had revolutionary ideas regarding women's rights,[64] some of which even English-educated Muslim social reformers did not dare articulate. Despite the many challenges that faced him, he advocated gender equality in the light of Quranic precepts. Like other social reformers, he too was a close associate of Sir Saiyid Ahmed Khan; Sir Saiyid, though, disagreed with many of his views, particularly those concerning women's issues. Although Gail Minault has criticised Saiyid Ahmed Khan for his views, it was—as suggested earlier—the compulsion of the times that forced Sir Saiyid to take a neutral stance. Maulvi, however, proved that every argument curtailing women's rights was flawed, supporting his contentions by citing the Quran, even to the extent of claiming the possibility of a woman Prophet. He believed that since there were only a few dozen names of Prophets available in the Quran, one could not prove that Prophet-hood was restricted only to men.

Huquq-e Nuswa is like a charter of rights for Muslim women. Mumtaz Ali provided a rational interpretation of the Quran with regard to women's issues, and claimed that contrary to what Muslims believed, men and women had equal rights and men have no authority over women. However, because of the strong support it extended to women's rights, this book was rejected by traditional Muslim society. This was perhaps why no second edition of this significant work was ever printed. It threatened patriarchal society by seeking to confer upon women the same status and rights enjoyed by men, both in worldly and religious

[63] Metcalf, 'Islamic Revival in British India', 242–43.

[64] Gail Minault, 'Saiyid Mumtaz Ali and Tahzeeb-e Niswa', in *Women and Social Reform in Modern India: A Reader*, by Sumit Sarkar and Tanikar Sarkar (eds), (New Delhi: Permanent Black, 2007), 70–95.

matters. In 1898, he launched a weekly newspaper with his wife, Muhammadi Begum. He wanted to name the paper after his wife, but Sir Saiyid forbade it, suggesting *Tahzeeb-e Niswa* instead. Sir Saiyid strongly believed in the complete confinement of women, and disapproved of even their names being unveiled in print. The magzine, as Gail Minault says, changed the lives of thousands of *purdah*-observing women over the years by providing them with a platform to express their thoughts. It focused on ideas related to housekeeping and child-rearing and encouraged creative writing amongst its female readers, advocated women's rights in Islam, and prepared them to play responsible roles as good wives and good mothers. Female readers also sent in their suggestions in their letters. This journal proved a milestone in the reformation of Muslim society.[65] Within a short span of time, his journal became popular among Muslim women. It drew the attention of women writers, who discovered a platform on which they could express their ideas.[66]

Apart from believing in women's right to property, considering women on par with men when it came to being witnesses and prophets, as well as his pro-women stance on the issue of polygamy, Maulvi Mumtaz Ali was a true champion of female education. He realised that only education could change the power equation between the sexes, since men's authority over women came from their knowledge and education. Women were considered ignorant of all worldly proceedings. It is interesting to see how passionate he was regarding the education of his illiterate wife. After her death, he married Muhammadi Begum, and tried to mould her according to the model provided by Asghari Begum, the heroine of Maulvi Nazir Ahmed's novel, who was an educated, well-mannered, good housewife. He made every possible arrangement for her education at home.

Almost all the social reform movements in India focused on education. Educational institutions were built, and reform movements initiated to safeguard the right to property and fix the appropriate age of marriage.[67] Indian Muslims were apparently not too influenced by these movements, as they already enjoyed the rights to property as per Islamic law. Social reformers also raised issues related to divorce,[68] polygamy,[69] widow remarriage,[70] and the lavish marriage

---

65 Minault, 'Saiyid Mumtaz Ali and Tahzeeb-e Niswa', 71.

66 ibid., 70–98.

67 *Maqalat-e Sir Saiyid*, Hissa XIII (Aligarh: Aligarh Scientific Society, 12 May 1876), 514.

68 ibid., 266.

69 Islah, V, Jild I, Gulam Husain (ed.), *Syed Ali Haider*, 1315 H, 139–40.

70 *Maqalat-e Sir Saiyid*, 31 March 1876.

ceremonies.[71] However, they never sought government aid to introduce social reforms, as the government presence would lead to religious interference, as all social issues are connected directly to religion. Also, these problems were to some extent prevalent only amongst low-born Muslims. Therefore, any other problems that women faced (beyond the ones listed above) did not become apparent at their own socio-economic level, and thus remained unaddressed. The Aligarh School considered the spread of education the solution to all problems related to Muslim women. It appears that they were either not concerned about common Muslims, or were completely ignorant of their culture.

Moreover, the Aligarh school had advocated imparting new education to both Muslim men and women.[72] Consequently, the Muslims of the Western United Province were more advanced, compared to those in the Eastern United Province. It appears that Muslims of the Eastern United Province did not show much interest in either social or religious reform movements. Most of the Muslims in this region hailed from either the lower class or the professional class, and therefore could not gauge the significance of such movements; the men were not educated, so how much thought could they spare to the condition of their women? Women merely assisted the men in earning a living.

---

71 *Majmua Lecture va Speech*, Nawab Mohsin-ul Mulk, 22 October 1883 (Lahore: Nawal Kishor Printing Press, 1904), 28.

72 Haji Ismail Khan, Karamat Husain, Iftikhar Bilgrami, Sheikh Abdullah, and Mumtaz Ali were the true champions of female education.

CHAPTER 3

British Perception of Muslim Women: Questions of Fecundity and Health

The Indian Muslim faced several problems because according to the British perception, all Muslims of the world formed a monolithic category;[1] they assumed that Indian Muslims were no different from the Muslims they had come into contact with in Europe or other Islamic countries. The connection of Indian Muslims with those in other Islamic countries can be better understood in Edward Said's concept of Orientalism:

> Yet at certain moments of that general European history of interest in the East, particular part of the Orient like Egypt, Syria, and Arabia can not be discussed without also studying Europe's involvement in the more distant parts, of which Persia and India are the most important; a notable case in point is the connection between Egypt and India so far as eighteenth and nineteenth century Britain was concerned.[2]

The British needed to provide a moral basis to their rule, and therefore projected Indian society as uncivilised and backward. Muslims, as part of

---

1 *Census Report of 1901*, 92. To the Musalman of every stratum, however, the Quran bears a definite meaning and is the ultimate source of all inspired knowledge, although there may be disagreements on the authority of other writings, to which some classes attribute almost equal validity. This shows the tendency towards uniformity in essential beliefs in Islam, which is lacking in Hinduism. See also *Imperial Gazzetteer of India: The Indian Empire*, Vol. 1 (Oxford: Clarendon Press, 1907), 329. As sociologist Imtiaz Ahmad argued, disadvantaged groups within the community have begun to question the representation of Muslims as a monolithic community. See Ahmad, 'Community of Differences', *Legal News and Views*, December (2006), 18.

2 Edward Said, *Orientalism: Western Conception of the Europe* (London: Penguin, 1995), 17.

that society, were placed in the same category. According to the British, their purpose was to introduce rationality in what they assumed was the irrationality inherent in Islam.

This chapter explores British remarks about and observations on Indian Muslim women, and argue how and why the British projected them in a derogatory manner in their discursive writings. The revolt of 1857 alarmed the British, making them review ways to control Indian society, and future policies to be adopted towards Muslims. This incident also served as a lesson in maintaining a distance from Indians where administration was concerned. As a result, recruitment became restricted to the upper-class service gentry of European origin. British men began arriving in large numbers with their families, followed by many unmarried women, who came for missionary work (and sometimes in search of appropriate husbands).[3] The sudden influx of Europeans made it even more vital for the British to establish a racial hierarchy and condemn Indians as morally and racially inferior.[4] Concurrently, European women undertook the duty of penetrating the zenana[5] to seek information about women in society, and like their male counterparts, tried to enforce 'the white woman's burden' on native women. Also, the event of 1857 increased hostility towards Muslims; the British now perceived Muslim customs or culture as

---

[3] Indrani Sen, *Women and Empire: Representation in the Writing of British India (1858–1900)* (New Delhi: Orient BlackSwan, 2002), 4, 9, 10. At the time, the female to male ratio in England was very high as most men had migrated to the colonies, resulting in a dearth of suitable grooms for unmarried girls. See also Margaret MacMillan, *Women of the Raj* (London: Thames and Hudson, 1988), 110–24.

[4] The white race was located at the apex, Asians occupied the middle spot, and Africans were relegated to the bottom. These nineteenth-century 'race theories' were deployed to establish the inferiority of all coloured races. Women possessed 'faculties, characteristic of lower races ... and of a past and lower state of civilization'. See Charles Darwin, *The Descent of Man and Selection in relation to Sex*, 1871, quoted in Sen, *Women and Empire*, 6, 7, 19. See also William Crook, *The North Western Provinces of India: Their History, Ethnology and Administration* (New Delhi: Low Price Publications, 2003 [1897]), 191.

[5] Indira Ghosh, *Women Travellers in Colonial India: The Power of the Female Gaze* (New Delhi: Oxford University Press, 1998), 53–68, and Charles E. Spearce, *Love Besieged*, Ralph Crane (ed.), (New Delhi: Oxford University Press, 2003), xiii. Fany Park, who married a royal prince, wrote about the *zenana*, but her account was limited to the upper-class/royal households. In contrast to Mrs Park and other European women travellers, Mary Francis Billington wrote explicitly about the daily routines of common women from both Muslim and Hindu communities.

unequivocally barbaric. They were termed 'butchers' and 'savages', while the British soldiers who had taken part were remembered as 'brave martyrs'.[6] It became necessary for them to divide India on the basis of religion, hence their depiction of Muslim as invaders, and of their rule as the 'dark period'. They glorified the ancient period when women were free of all restrictions, as opposed to the enforcement of the zenana system with the coming of Islamic rule.

Sir Lepel Grifin, who served British India as superintendent of Maharaja Jagjeet Singh of Kapoorthala, cited examples from Hindu myths and literature (for example, Kalidas, Ramayana, Mahabharata, etc.), where women seemed to hold a very high status. In these accounts, women were equal participants in all social and religious gatherings and their age of marriage was relatively high—they married only after attaining maturity.[7] He also praised those Sikh, Maratha and Muslim women who made their mark in Indian history by marrying relatively late.[8]

There was an increasing trend to project Muslims as lustful, and their zenanas as filled with beautiful Hindu women.[9] It was claimed that Hindu men began confining their women indoors and veiling them only in fear of Muslim abductors,[10] thereby laying the blame for purdah squarely at the Muslims' door. Everything retrogressive was connected with the arrival of Muslims in India.

This negative representation of Muslims made Ashraf Muslims even more hostile, which resulted in an imposition of new forms of religious and cultural restrictions on Ashraf women. In their attempt to keep their women away from

---

[6] MacMillan, *Women of the Raj*, 98–99.

[7] Eunice De Souza (ed.), *Pardah: An Anthology* (New Delhi: Oxford University Press, 2004), 62.

[8] ibid., 63.

[9] MacMillan, *Women of the Raj*, 104–05.

[10] De Souza, *Pardah*, 69. The British author tried to defame Islam by stating that the Prophet's zenana contained eleven wives, including two slave girls. It needs to be pointed out that all the Prophet's marriages were with widows or divorcees; his first wife, Khadiza, was in her forties and a widow at the time of their marriage, while Prophet Muhammad was barely twenty-two years pld. Only Ayesha was a virgin. Second, his marriages were justified by the circumstances prevailing in contemporary Arab countries, which were in the throes of war, as many pre-Islamic and Islamic poets have depicted (see the poems and Muallaqaats of Imrul Qais, Zuhair Bin Salma, Alkhansa, Hisham Bin Sabit and Abu Sufiyan). In Islamic countries, women always outnumbered men, and so Islamic scholars always justified the earlier polygamous societies as supporting destitute women. See Ismail Kurban Husein Poonawala (revised and annotated), *Pillars of Islam*, Vol. II (New Delhi: Oxford University Press, 2008).

Western influence, they confined them within the home. This led to Muslim women becoming the object of curiosity for many European scholars, who consequently imagined them in accordance with their Western notions. Fuller noticed that the purdah system prevailed wherever Muslims were the strongest, namely in Bengal, north and northwest India, and in Muslim capitals and states.[11] However, she believed that these new impositions were not obligatory for poor Muslims, whose wives were forced into labour, and who often had only one room for the entire family to live in.

The veil or purdah led to the institution of the harem, or zenana. According to Fuller, 'harem' is an Arabic term meaning 'something forbidden or not to be touched'. The word 'zenana', confined in its usage to India, is of Persian origin. '*Zan*' means 'woman'; hence zenana was explained as pertaining to the domain of women. Zenana is an apartment devoted exclusively to the women of the household of an Indian gentleman. It was also used for those women who lived in seclusion.[12] The British were clearly forming several stereotypes of Indian Muslim women. Census Reports play a very significant role here; it was the British who began making accounts of the living conditions of women in their reports. Before these colonial reports, women had found virtually no space in government records.

The Census Report and its Objective

The apparent objective behind the Census Report (henceforth referred to as CR) was to count the Indian people and record their social statuses. As Bernard Cohn emphasises, the history of the Indian census must be seen in the context of the colonial government's efforts to collect systematic information about the many aspects of Indian society and economy.[13] It seems that they wanted to create a rift amongst Indians on the basis of caste and religion.[14] The CR constantly expressed great apprehension about the increasing growth rate of Muslims.[15] Whether this was an appropriate time to alarm people about the

[11] De Souza, *Pardah*, 69.

[12] ibid.

[13] Bernard Cohn, *An Anthropologist among the Historians and other Essays*, in *The Bernard Cohn Omnibus* (New Delhi: Oxford University Press, 2009), 231.

[14] ibid., 242. In the mid-nineteenth century, many British officials considered caste and religion the sociological keys to understanding the Indian people.

[15] It is interesting to observe that while the British were propagating the myth of the Muslim growth rate, they were actively pursuing the multiplication of the white race. The images of the affectionate wife and tender mother were encouraged over

growth rate is debatable; also, the CR was unable to explain this increasing growth in rational terms. Illogically, they considered Muslims more fertile than Hindus.[16]

These reports, condoned by the government, were heavily centralised, and their approach towards space and people was, like many other reports, dominated by a concern for centralisation. The CR reduced numerous variables into uniform categories. Thus, all Indian Muslim women were treated as part of a general phenomenon, and the several reflections on their condition were dealt with in a general way. The Census made observations that were derogatory and humiliating to Indian Muslims women; while the report of 1901 provided a comprehensive table, it could not supply any basic reason for the growth rate. It was later Census reports, of 1911 and 1921, that accepted diversities across provinces, and put forth scientific reasons about how the growth rate was higher in those periods that experienced no significant natural calamity. A serious error can be noticed in the 1901 report regarding the high population figures attributed to Indian Muslims.

The greatest problem facing the British government appeared to be maintaining a hold over Indian society, for which commissions were instituted whenever disruptions arose. The *Gazetteer* and the CR were probably compiled by government officials whose intention was to demonstrate their moral superiority. Nevertheless, in the process the government undertook a peculiar system-building exercise, which resulted in the social engineering of Indian society. They classified Hindus and Muslims into two groups: those who ate cows were to be considered Muslim, and those performing idol worship, Hindu. Although child marriage was rare among Muslims, widow remarriage and polygamy were considered common.[17] As such, numerous authors of government reports concluded that a liberal diet and propensity for marriage resulted in making them more fertile.

Although certain observations on social customs and behaviour might have been correct, one cannot overlook the hidden intention behind projecting Indian Muslims as more sexually vibrant. It was in this environment that a debate on

that of the career-oriented white woman (MacMillan, *Women of the Raj*, 125).

[16] CR of 1901, 63. See also CR of 1891, 181–82. See also Firdous Azmat Siddiqui, *Colonial Report on Census and Its Reflection on Indian Muslim Women' in Islam and Muslim Societies*, Nadeem Hasnain (ed.), Vol. I (New Delhi: Serial Publications, 2005), 155–62.

[17] Mary Francis Billington, *Women in India*, 1895 (New Delhi: National Archives of India), 120. All other Census Reports of the United Provinces displays this tendency.

the fertility and fecundity of Indian Muslim women was begun in the early twentieth century.[18]

The British began attacking the diversity they found at the provincial level.[19] Not only did they divide Indian society on the basis of religion and caste, but they also provided permanency to the identities of people through the *Gazetteer* and the CR.[20] In this way, they reduced the numerous flexible identities normally found in Indian society. The different statements and statistics provided by the CR demonstrated an attempt by its authors to undermine the very subject the report dealt with. The next sections reflect upon such numerous misunderstandings and misstatements introduced by the government reports.

Muslim Women vs. the Fertility Rate

Can Muslim women be considered more fertile than those in other communities, as the CR claimed? Would it be logical to connect fertility with race, religion or community? Were Muslims bound by religion to reproduce more? If not, then why were Muslim women projected as objects of pleasure and child-bearing machines? My second and major problem is: How can the growth rate of any country be defined rationally? The British felt the need to control India in much the same way that a husband would want to control his sensual wife. They attributed femininity to India,[21] automatically making Indian women commodities in the hands of their new master. Indian women—particularly Muslim women—were perceived to be meek, submissive wives.[22]

They believed that Indian women were uneducated, superstitious, and very sensual in nature, and this attitude was upheld by their female counterparts,

---

[18] Charu Gupta, 'Hindu Womb, Muslim Progeny', in Sarah Hodge (ed.), *Reproductive Health in India: History, Politics, Controversies*(Hyderabad: Orient BlackSwan, 2006). In this revealing article, Gupta shows how the propaganda of the growing Muslim population alarmed the Hindus, and became one of the major causes of the increasing communal riots, particularly after the 1920s.

[19] As C. A. Bayly shows, there were great regional differences in late eighteenth-century north India, so it would be inappropriate to issue any generalisations (See Bayly, *Rulers, Townsmen and Bazaars: North Indian Society in the Age of British Expansion, 1770–1780* (Cambridge: Cambridge University Press, 1983), 193.

[20] CR of 1901, 254–55. This report divides the Muslim community into four groups, and 130 sub-castes.

[21] Sen, *Women and Empire*, 40, 41, 43.

[22] ibid., 43–44.

too, who attacked the morality of Indian women.[23] Muslims became even more victimised because of the purdah system, the provision of widow remarriage, and the widespread acceptance of Islam amongst prostitutes, which convinced the British that Muslim women were more active sexually. It The Muslim involvement in the 1857 rebellion[24] made the British feel the need to keep this 'barbaric' and 'uncivilised' group under surveillance, and their policies towards the Muslim community also changed from time to time. They enforced their political and moral superiority by taking away several privileges that Muslims had long since enjoyed.[25] The British began questioning every aspect of their lives, while white women expressed great consternation over the wretched condition of the women, and began talking about their rights.[26] It is interesting to see how Europeans, who themselves denied their women several basic rights at home in England, felt perfectly justified in raising issues pertaining to women's rights in India.[27] Even Darwin proposed a scientific explanation

---

[23] Indira Ghosh, *Memsahib Abroad* (New Delhi: Oxford University Press, 1998), 174–75, 192. See also Ghosh, *Women Travellers in Colonial India*), 56–60. Mary Francis Billington attacked the purdah system, considering it a hurdle in the path of feminism. A few other travellers, however, expressed their fear of the supposed viciousness of the servants (see Crook, *The North Western Provinces*, 152–53, 56; Billington, *Women in India*, 122). The common view is that a vast amount of immorality and intrigue is fostered by the zenana system.

[24] Shan Mohammad, *Sir Syed Ahmad Khan: A Political Biography* (Meerut: Meenakshi Prakashan, 1969), 32. See also Ayesha Jalal, *Partisans of Allah* (New Delhi: Permanent Black, 2008), 115.

[25] Jalal, *Partisans of Allah*. While Muslim intellectuals at the time lamented the deterioration among Muslims, they appear to have been comparing the status of Muslims in their time to that of the Mughals. In the same period, another picture emerges: Muslims of the United Provinces were far more advanced than the Hindus. *The Mirat-ul Hind* (Lucknow), 1882, 553.

[26] See the issues raised by European women travellers during this period, and the way they focused on the deprived section of women instead of elite women, as travellers in the early nineteenth century had done. Since the condition of women from the lower socio-economic strata is always worse, be it with reference to conjugal or legal rights, their propaganda about women's condition seemed to be borne by the facts. Ghosh, *Women Travellers in India*, 62–63.

[27] Mohemmadan Social Reformer, *Tahzee-e Akhlaq*, No. 41, Jild 1, 1288 (H), 87. In an article, Sir Saiyid defended Muslim women's rights against those of Christian women, and expressed his satisfaction over *shariat* law. John Stuart Mill, *Strion ki Paradheenta* (New Delhi: Rajkamal, 2002 [1867]). This book raises questions about

for the idea of women's inferiority by stating that since a man's brain is bigger than a woman's, women are obviously less intelligent.[28] It is intriguing to note, though, that British barrack wives were leading miserable lives, with domestic violence and child marriage being common phenomena.[29] But it is also true that most of these barrack wives were either Indian, or hailed from the lower British classes.[30] This shows that despite the claims of equality in Christianity, Europe believes no less in race, class, gender and ethnicity. It is noteworthy that women of Eurasian origin were never given the same status as Europeans.

It would be unjust to say that the British were only critical of Indian society; indeed, on occasion they also praised the Indian way of life. While they criticised the purdah system, in a few cases they accepted the 'powerful purdah government', as they termed those instances where royal women, despite their *purdah*, ruled as capably as their male counterparts. Notable in this regard is the Begum of Bhopal. Grifin admired Begum Shah Jahan and her social and political achievements. In fact, he seemed disappointed in the Western notion of womanhood and praised the influence that Eastern women had. He hoped that Indian women would never go the way of their Western sisters.[31]

Despite being such staunch critics of Muslims, why did European men choose to marry Muslim women?[32] One logical reason could be that since women are the repositories of honour for communities, 'owning' the women of a community could win half the battle for the colonial rulers. Perhaps they considered Muslims their political rival, necessitating the subjugation of their womenfolk. The fact that Islam and Christianity are both Semitic religions,

---

gender equality among Europeans. See also Ghosh, *Women Travellers in India*, 67. It was found that among the 'downtrodden' Indian women were hard-headed businesswomen, at a time when English women were still not allowed to own property in their own right after marriage!

[28] George John Romanes, 'Mental Difference Between Men and Women', in S. T. Joshi (ed.), *A Documentary history of Prejudice against Women: In Her Place* (New Delhi: Prometheus Books, 2006), 127–28.

[29] Sen, *Women and Empire*, 12–16.

[30] ibid.

[31] De Souza, *Pardah*, 61.

[32] Several examples of interracial marriages follow this trend. It is almost as if the British were trying to take the Mughals' place and raise their own social status by marrying harem women. By the beginning of the nineteenth century, though, interracial marriages gradually came to an end, although the native concubine or bibi continued to be widely prevalent (Sen, *Women and Empire*), 43–46.

with similar food habits, might have made it easier for European men to marry Muslim women, instead of the idol worshipping Hindu women. However, they tended to depict them as commodities in their discursive writings. Till then, the relationship between co-wives was considered amicable, especially since Muslims were supposed to be polygamous. They appeared to be convinced that only Muslim women could tolerate co-wives peaceably (the reality, however, was that, being sexual rivals, they could all rarely live together peacefully under one roof), and so chose them when it came to legitimising their multi-partner relationships, including those outside wedlock.

The British connected sexuality and sensuality to the provision of widow remarriage. Flora Annie Steel, in her story 'Firoza', drew a picture of a contemporary Muslim family in her collection *Flower of Forgiveness*. Firoza,[33] the heroine, makes several attempts to attract the attentions of her husband, to the extent of discarding her traditional Muslim apparel, but in vain; her husband, despite having lived in London for many years, was very conservative and preferred Indian simplicity. Eventually he falls in love with his younger brother's widow, Karima, who leads a life of simplicity, as befits a widow. Driven nearly insane with jealousy, Firoza kills herself. The author's attempt is clearly to highlight the sensuality of women, as well as the mental anguish suffered by widows. However, in her portrayal of a Muslim family, Steel's focus remained on the prevalence of polygamy and widow remarriage, both of which were absent among Hindus.[34]

The British thus distinguished between Indians on the basis of religion in this simplistic fashion, despite the customs and traditions of both communities remaining largely the same. In fact, geographical location was a better determining factor than religion, but, as stated earlier, all Muslims were lumped into a monolithic bloc by the British government. Naturally, the CR aimed to do the same, and in the process overlooked several logical reasons for the high fertility rate. They neglected the socio-economic factors of the growth rate, focusing instead on the sexual behaviour of Muslims.[35] The CR asserted that Muslims had a greater tendency to reproduce than other communities; however, the statistics provided in the report do not support that contention, and their explanations run contrary to those held by medical science to explain the causes

[33] Flora Annie Steel, *Flowers of Forgiveness*, quoted in Sen, *Women and Empire,* 146.

[34] Crook, *The North Western Provinces,* 135.

[35] Firdous Azmat Siddiqui, 'Colonial Report on Census and its Reflection on Indian Muslim Women', in Nadim Husnain (ed.), *Islam and Muslim Societies*, Vol. 1 (New Delhi: Serial Publications, 2005), 155.

of fertility. Clinical reports state that fertility among women is determined by health and living conditions, which includes education, age at marriage, and the environment. The reports further elaborate that the rate of reproduction in a community is determined by the number of women of child-bearing age, the sex ratio, death rate and infant mortality rate, along with socio-economic conditions.

Taking the clinical reports into consideration, we find that in the United Province, the composition of the urban population was 36 per cent Muslim and 62 per cent Hindu. In the rural areas, 11 per cent were Muslim and 88 per cent Hindu.[36] Again, the economic condition of Muslims can be assessed from the fact that in the countryside, they held one-fifth of the total land area in 1882.[37] Muslims also held 35 per cent of government jobs, where their share in the un-covenanted services was high, and as much as 45 per cent of the positions in the subordinate judicial services were held by Muslims.[38] These statistics clearly indicate that the general condition of Muslims was satisfactory, although this is not to deny the existence of poverty.

As far as education was concerned, Muslim women were better educated than their Hindu counterparts.[39] The CR clearly shows a dense concentration of Muslims in the Western United Provinces.[40] In this area, Muslims were economically better-off as they held both land and government jobs. A large chunk of the Muslim population was urban, and so the women tended to be educated. It can be assumed that the age of marriage increased with the spread of education. Also, child marriage was virtually unknown among Muslims.[41]

However, despite a better economic and educational status, the CR assumed that Muslims reproduced more.[42] It contended that Muslim women were sexually more active and fornicated frequently. Such derogatory remarks dominate the CR analysis, which attempts to establish a relationship between the age of marriage, fertility and fecundity of women. Table 3.1 provides statistics with regard to women belonging to Hindu and Muslim communities, along with their respective ages. Child marriage was common and socially accepted among

---

36 CR of 1901, 63.

37 Francis Robinson, *Separatism among Muslims of India* (New Delhi: Oxford University Press, 1993), 254–55.

38 ibid., 63.

39 CR of 1901, 154. See also CR of 1881 and 1891.

40 Robinson, *Separatism among Muslims of India*, 63.

41 CR of 1881, 78. See also CR of 1891 and 1901.

42 All Census Reports from 1881 to 1901 claimed this.

Hindus,[43] because of which death in childbirth was a common phenomenon, too.[44] It can also be observed that the Hindu community lacked proper medical facilities, and that death rate was the highest in the 0–5 age group.[45] It can also be observed that as a corollary, the number of married Hindu women declined gradually. As a result, in the age group of 20–40, the number of Hindu married women declined considerably, while the figure for Muslim women remained constant.

Table 3.1: Marriageable Age in the 0–10 Age Group of Females per 1,000

Age	*All Religion*					*Hindu*					*Muslim*				
	1921	*1911*	*1901*	*1891*	*1881*	*1*	*2*	*3*	*4*	*5*	*1*	*2*	*3*	*4*	*5*
00–5	7	10	9	6	51	7	10	9	6	53	6	8	8	6	35
50–10	102	101	110	99	11	106	106	115	104	-	72	77	82	73	-

Source: CR of 1921

Table 3.2: Number of Married Women per 1,000 Women

Age	*Hindu*					*Muslim*				
	1921	*1911*	*1901*	*1891*	*1881*	*1921*	*1911*	*1901*	*1891*	*1881*
10–15	520	541	562	594	569	379	419	419	456	428
15–20	882	896	881	920	907	812	840	830	867	849

Source: CR of 1921

The CR also comments on sanitary conditions and the death rate among women; it maintains that midwives were unaware of antiseptics, which led to several deaths among women and infants. Also, in some cases surgery was required to deliver a child, and as it was usually performed late, this contributed to physical deformities and death among infants.[46] The CR reported that Muslim women who practised purdah were prone to such situations. However, it is hard to imagine that urban women would be subjected to the same crude methods of delivery. A greater number of Muslim women resided in cities,

43 In later reports, it was accepted that Muslim women were healthier than their Hindu counterparts, and that late marriages was probably responsible. Consequently, infant and maternal mortality rates were less among them. CR of 1911, 192.

44 The ratio of death of females to males was 1,081 during 1891–1900. This varied between 1,008 and 1,176 per 1,000 males.

45 CR of 1901, 129.

46 ibid., 96.

and therefore it can be safely assumed that they had access to better medical facilities.[47] Statistics demonstrate that the infant mortality rate, particularly in the age group 0–5, was less among Muslims.[48] So Muslim women seemed more aware where their health was concerned.

The CR tried to establish a peculiar—and erroneous—relationship between widow remarriage and the high birth rate. It is hard to believe that Muslim widows reproduced more in the 1880s.[49] The figures for widows among Hindus and Muslims were approximately the same, and the suffering associated with widowhood was the same for both too.[50] It would be wrong to assume that till the end of the nineteenth century, widow remarriage was common among Muslims (for more details, see Chapter Five). Taking into consideration the reproductive age, that is, between 15–40, 15.88 per cent of Hindus and 13.80 per cent of Muslims in this age group were widows.[51] Again, the CR made an interesting observation: that Hindu widows lived longer because of their enforced widowhood, while Muslim widows died early in childbirth. However, statistics do not support this contention because the number of widows among high-caste Hindus and Muslims remained constant, clearly showing that both high-caste Hindus and Muslims considered widow remarriage socially degrading.[52]

Table 3.3: Sex Ratio as per 1,000 Males

All Religion			*Hindu*			*Muslim*		
1901	*1911*	*1921*	*1901*	*1911*	*1921*	*1901*	*1911*	*1921*
937	917	911	935	915	909	957	921	912

Source: CR of 1921, 101

The CR established a connection between the mean age of women and sex ratio with fertility. It was assumed that as the mean age in the sex ratio for

[47] The Annual Report of the Female Dufferin Fund showed that Muslim women made more use of hospitals than Hindus, their percentage being 22.5 per cent of all outgoing patients.

[48] CR of 1911, 172.

[49] Davis Kingsley, *The Population of India and Pakistan* (New Jersey: Princeton University Press, 1951), 80.

[50] *Azad* (Lukhnow), 30 March 1886.

[51] CR of 1881, 81.

[52] Maulvi Nazir Ahmed, *Aiyama*, and Altaf Husain Hali, *Munajat-e Bewa*, both highlight the pitiable condition of widows.

women was greater among Muslims, it pointed towards more prolific sexual activity and a consequent rise in the birth rate. However, figures do not support this contention; the CR also contends that the death rate among adult women was greater. The mean age of Hindu women was 3.7 months more than Muslim women in 1901.[53] It may be added that there was a higher ratio of girl children among Muslims than Hindus, testifying to the fact that unlike the Hindus, Muslims did not greet the birth of daughters with dismay.[54]

The CR blamed polygamy for the high birth rates.[55] Polygamy in India was not a religious, but a social phenomenon. It was common amongst the ruling and wealthy classes, regardless of religion. However, polygamy was practised by only a small number of Indians.[56]

The CR also argues that Hindu prostitutes converted to Islam.[57] They did do so; but they embraced Islam to safeguard their property for their children, as under Hindu law, women were not allowed property rights.[58] Government statistics also considered all prostitutes Muslims, who could be registered as property owners and taxed.[59]

Yet another strange observation of the CR was that the liberal diet of Muslims, and their abstinence from *ganja* (marijuana), alcohol, and other intoxicants led to their being sexually more prolific.[60] Interestingly, at about the same time a number of Muslim women demonstrated against *chandu* smoking and drinking, both of which were widely prevalent among Muslims.[61] The most prominent Urdu poet of the time, Altaf Husain Hali, lamented how the 'evil custom' had crippled Muslims and led to their losing their glory.[62]

---

[53] CR of 1911, 165.

[54] ibid., 190.

[55] All CRs blamed polygamy for the high birth rate among Muslims.

[56] Shaheeda K. Lateef, *Muslim Women in India: Political and Private Realities: 1890–1980s* (New Delhi: Kali for Women, 1990), 10.

[57] CR of 1881, 80. This propaganda led to Hindu fundamentalists launching a movement to bring such women back into their fold. However, it was difficult to conclude that inter-religious marriages had affected the growth rate. In fact, this was one of the main causes behind the increasing communal violence in north India.

[58] Only Islam recognised maternity rights over illegitimate children, too.

[59] CR of 1901, 254–55.

[60] ibid., 63.

[61] *Dabdaba-I Qaisari*, Bareilly, 28 November 1891.

[62] '*Charas aur ganje ka saida hai koi, madak aur chandu ka rasia hai koi*' (Altaf Husain Hali, *Hali's Musaddas: A Story in Verse of the Ebb and Tide of Islam*, Sayeda Saiyidain

The mis-statements and distortions developed through the CR damaged the reputation of Muslim women. As the government considered the entire Muslim population a uniform and monolithic bloc, they did not take into account the educational and economic status of Muslim women.[63] Table 3.4 provides the population figures from 1881–1921, which are not very high where Muslims are concerned. It is reasonable, though, to connect the living conditions of women with their caste and region. Two-fifths of the Muslim population resided in the Western United Province, a large number of whom were of Ashraf origin. The question that comes to mind is: Where, and in which group, did this growth occur? What was the average decennial growth rate, which had been neglected in earlier reports?

Table 3.4: Net Growth Rate

Religion	*% of variation increase (+) decrease (-)*				*Net Variation*	
	1911–21	*1901–11*	*1891–1901*	*1881–91*	*1881–1901*	*1901–21*
Hindu	-3.5	-1.4	+.77	+6.11	+6.9	-4.9
Muslim	-2.6	-1.1	+6.06	+7.5	+13.11*	-3.7

Source: CR of 1921
Note: *in the CR, it was stated 13.66
% age have been drawn by me

The net population growth from 1881–1921[64] was 802,081, and the average growth rate per decade was 2.35 per cent, much less than had been propagated. In reality, this growth occurred during 1881–1901; after 1901, it decreased rapidly because of an increase in the death rate, which was true for the entire province. In fact, the growth rate was visible in only four regions out of eight,

Hameed [trans.], [New Delhi: Harper Collins, 2003], 216).

[63] CR of 1901, 63. Muslims, taken as a whole, are better-off than Hindus as they do not include so large a proportion of the very poor. At the best of times, the agricultural labourer was probably the worst-paid in India, and it is certain that in proportion to the total population, there were more Hindu labourers than Muslim.

[64] In this section, I extend the period to 1921 to continue the important debate surrounding the fertility of Muslims. This study takes 1901 as the dividing line for the growth rate among Muslims. The CR of 1911 and 1921 provides very different reasons for the fertility and fecundity of Muslim women; the 1901 report is not as explicit in providing reasons for this concern—however, it does discuss the great increase in population figures related to Indian Muslims. In later reports, the British began accepting provincial diversities and provided more reasonable causes of fertility.

which accounted for 71.18 per cent of the total Muslim population. These reports were clearly politically motivated on the part of the British, who were alarmed at the growing Indian nationalism.

Lady Dufferin Medical Fund

The issue of health is directly connected to the growth rate. Would it be correct to say, as the CR had suggested, that better sanitary conditions improved health among the Muslims, thereby leading to a higher birth rate?[65] European missionaries in this period were penetrating remote villages, and attacking the Indian social order and education system. Their next target was the traditional medical system, through which they sought to approach the masses. However, three types of medicine had been in practice in India for a long time: *ayurveda*, *unani*, and a third kind that was especially popular among women, *tantrik* or *jhar-phunk*. As Indian women were of the belief that pain or illness were often caused by malign spirits, they sought a cure for ailments through charms, incantations, or amulets.[66] Barren women often visited shrines in order to conceive.[67]

Sir Saiyid painted an interesting picture of a superstitious family in India:

> In their day to day lives and routine, they considered it better to practice their old customs. And they were under the impression if they change any usual custom, difficulties would befall them. Illnesses were considered the effect of ghosts and charms. Therefore, they tried to cure illness by casting out evil spirits and/or making an offering to deities. In medical emergencies, they would take vows and create a hullabaloo, and neglect the real cause in the process. For example, rather than calling a doctor or *hakim* to assist in the delivery of a pregnant woman, they would encircle her and indulge in their nonsensical practices .... Even the death of ill people failed to change their thinking.[68]

---

[65] The CR of 1911 stated that better sanitary conditions among Muslims was one of major causes behind the population growth in this community. See also Firdous Azmat Siddiqui, *Islam and Muslim Society*, Vol. I (New Delhi: Serial Publications, 2005), 99.

[66] Hali, *Hayat-e Javed*; see also Ashraf Ali Thanvi, *Behisht-e Zewar* (New Delhi: New A.S. Press, 1994), 299.

[67] CR of 1901, 94. The shrine of Saiyid Salar Masood at Bahraich was frequented by both Hindus and Muslims if a woman was childless, or if family quarrels could not be settled amicably. Diseases were supposed to be cured by a visit to the shrine of Sheikh Saddo at Amroha in Moradabad, while Shah Mina's dargah at Lukhnow is renowned for help in legal difficulties.

[68] Panipati, *Maqalat-e Sir Saiyid*, 14 April 1876, 189–90.

Evil customs were widespread in India; for instance, if childbirth was delayed, women would make loud noises and burst crackers around the pregnant woman, as the general belief was that the child had captured the intestines of the mother, and would leave her only upon hearing the loud sounds.[69]

For centuries, unani medicine remained popular amongst Indian Muslims, chiefly due to the presence of several renowned as well as petty *hakims*. Lucknow, Aligarh and Allahabad were emerging as the chief centres of unani medicine. In the absence of further evidence, it is difficult to ascertain how many Muslim women relied on hakimi medicine; but several Urdu sources reveal that a large number of Muslim women did not take any medicines without the advice of hakims. Some women were experts at dispensing prescriptions at home for minor illnesses; there were even magazines and books for women dealing with such matters. Thanvi wrote several prescriptions for major and minor diseases, aiding women to learn about their health. He also warned them to not take medicines without the advice of a hakim, especially during serious illnesses,[70] and further advised them to avoid medicines as far as possible. Hence, Muslims were not unfamiliar with issues of health before the advent of Western medicine. It is this awareness that led to the acceptance of the Dufferin Medical Mission.

European women took a generalised view of Indian women; they assumed that Indian women had no access to medical facilities, and were hostile to Western medicine because of their ignorance and lack of education. This ignorance had caused them 'torment', which the Europeans wanted to 'relieve' them of. Furthermore, a Home Department report also revealed widespread death in childbirth due to the dearth of skilled midwives and doctors. Since both Hindus and Muslims practiced purdah, male doctors were not allowed into the zenanas,[71] creating a desperate need for female doctors and midwives. European missionaries saw in this a golden opportunity to penetrate the zenana and propagate their religion. Perhaps this can explain why a large number of European women and missionaries made their careers in teaching and medicine, as these professions enabled them to maintain a close contact with the common people.

A nation-wide debate soon began over the necessity of the Female Dufferin Medical Fund. One group considered it a blessing for Indian women, while another viewed it as a danger. The former argued that the Lady Dufferin Fund

---

[69] ibid. This misconception had been reported by a European woman, who assisted in the delivery of a native women named Rani.

[70] Thanvi, *Behisht-e Zewar*, 363.

[71] Home Department: Sanitary, September 1890, Nos 24–25.

had come as a Godsend to the country and would not only alleviate the suffering of women, but would also appeal to the well-off classes to come forward with liberal subscriptions.[72] Additionally, they argued that thousands of women died every year in the absence of female medical aid, and therefore it would be better to train women in midwifery.[73] *Rafi-ul Akhbar* saw this as an excellent opportunity for screened women.[74] The Bareilly Medical Report accepted that this arrangement would provide *purdanashin* women in the country with skilled professional advice, which had earlier been unavailable to them as only men occupied the medical field.[75]

Another section protested that these missionary groups would try to propagate their religion in the guise of medical aid. A few incidents in eastern India supported this contention, especially the cases of Bibi Nasir-un Nisa and Kusum Kumari. In both cases, it was suspected that the medical officer in charge of the hospital was responsible for allowing Christian missionaries free access to the women, and surrendering them to their care. Therefore, they warned people to remain alert and think twice before sending their women to hospitals.[76] It cannot be denied, though, that these female mission dispensaries did a commendable job; despite this, the women were often criticised and condemned for reciting passages from sacred books before dispensing medical aid to patients. A female doctor of a Lucknow Zenana Hospital, who was in the habit of doing so, was even reported about in newspapers.[77]

Thus, a number of zenana hospitals flourished in the United Province with financial assistance from the Female Dufferin Fund. Besides, a female Medical College was also established in Agra. The main factor behind its success was that its staff, which comprised European, Eurasian and native women,[78] who in turn planned to train their daughters in nursing and midwifery.[79] Vernacular newspapers also played a very significant role in spreading awareness amongst people and argued, 'When thousands of women have become prostitutes and

[72] *Oudh Akhbar* (Lucknow), 1February 1886; see also 3 February 1886.

[73] *The Sajjan Kirti Sudhakar*, 8 February 1886.

[74] *The Rafi-ul Akhbar* (Benares), 29 March 1886.

[75] Fifth Annual Report, Countess of Dufferin Medical Fund, 1889, 163.

[76] *The Jam-e Ulum* (Moradabad), 28 February 1897.

[77] *The Roznamah* (Lucknow), 27 January 1886.

[78] Fifth Annual Report, Countess of Dufferin Medical Fund, 1889.

[79] At the time, there were seven and eight Hindu and Muslim nurses, respectively, out of a total of nineteen in training (ibid., 157, 160). At Lady Lyall Hospital, this number was fourteen and two, respectively, out of forty-four pupils.

dancing girls, will women not be forthcoming to learn such an honourable profession?'[80]

However, female Indian doctors were yet to be found. Apparently, no native girls fulfilled the essential eligibility criteria for admission.[81] However, provincial governments had encouraged female students, providing them with fellowships based on certain conditions.[82]

Zenana medical colleges became gradually popular with Indians. The increasing number of nurses and midwives of Indian origin perhaps helped to inspire confidence.[83] The British seemed keen to provide separate accommodation to Hindus and Muslims in the colleges,[84] perhaps in an attempt to attract common people by guaranteeing their religious freedom; or perhaps to sow the seeds of communal disharmony among women. However, it is significant that no separate cooking or accommodation demands were made by the people themselves. The Agra Medical College followed the recommendations of the Handford Report of 1868, which claimed that Hindus did not want to send their daughters to the same schools as Muslims.[85]

However, the report of 1889 on the Female Dufferin Fund expressed its satisfaction over the increasing number of female patients in zenana hospitals, attributing its success to female doctors and native nurses and midwives. Although skilled native women were still few in number, their contribution was considerable.[86] However, Indians had to overcome the prevalent misconceptions about this profession,[87] as respectable families from both communities considered it dirty and worthy only of the lower castes. The Female Dufferin Fund soon felt the need to attract more high-caste girls, and turned their attention towards high-caste widows.[88] This is perhaps why the Agra Medical College provided separate cooking rooms for Hindu and Muslim patients, to avoid inconveniencing them.

---

80 *The Rafi-ul Akhbar*, 29 March 1886.

81 Billington, *Women in India*, 100.

82 Depart: Judicial, Sub.: Female Medical Education, 1889, Bundle-161, Box No. 224, Sl No. 13, File No. 166.

83 Bibi Kunwar Singh's efforts were appreciated in the Fifth Annual Report.

84 Vth Annual Report, 152.

85 Home: Education, 1868.

86 It was accepted in the Fifth Annual Report.

87 A native Brahmin nurse, Shama, had been killed by her father and brother just because she had adopted this profession.

88 Billington, *Women in India*, 120. Also see the Fifth Annual Report.

Despite several demonstrations, Indian women continued visiting zenana hospitals. The building was created keeping in mind the needs of screened women; therefore, it had many verandahs, surrounded by an enclosing wall. In Allahabad, female hospitals contained a reception room for out-patients, a compounding room, a room for the nurses on duty, a ward (37 ft., 7 inches by 22 ft.) for eight general patients, a room (19 ft. by 22 ft.) for Eurasians, and three rooms: one 19 ft. by 22 ft and two 21 ft. by 22 ft., all for confinement cases. The two latter rooms were for the purdanashin women. In the Bareilly hospital (which had been constructed with indigenous people in mind), in addition to the main building, there were seven private houses to accommodate purdanashin women. Each house was equipped with a separate bathroom and cooking space, in order to provide them with complete privacy. Female servants occupied the houses formerly tenanted by male employees, and these too were within the enclosure walls.[89]

In the beginning, the Agra Medical College had only outdoor patients, but indoor patients soon increased, to the extent that the zenana hospital found it difficult to accommodate them all with ease. As a result, several patients had to be put up on the verandah. However, charges for a bed were very high; patients had to pay over Rs 200 for accommodation and treatment. Interestingly, a greater number of paying patients comprised purdanashin Muslim women, who had come from distant places for surgery. The major operations such as ovariotomy, the removal of stones, and cataract surgeries were performed by civil surgeons.[90]

In every part of the United Province, out-patients greatly outnumbered in-patients. However, there were very few Hindu and Muslim in-patients; only one Muslim woman and three Hindu women were hospitalised out of the twelve confinement cases at Allahabad Zenana hospital. At the same time, twenty-four Muslim women (22.6 per cent of all patients) had been registered as out-patients out of a 106 cases.[91] Apparently, both communities were hesitant when it came to admission in hospitals. But Muslim women visited hospitals more frequently than Hindu women. In Kanpur, they constituted 200 out of 1,600 patients, while in Bijnor, they made up 30.3 per cent of all patients.[92] Most of them were affected by diseases of the digestive system, malaria, eyes, skin, generative system, respiratory system, rheumatism and diarrhoea.

---

[89] Fifth Annual Report, 152.

[90] ibid., 162.

[91] ibid., 164.

[92] ibid., 164–65.

It is surprising that despite there being facilities for women who practised purdah, Muslim women protested against male doctors when vaccinations were required. The British argued that since vaccinations were generally administered during infancy or early childhood (before Muslim women take the purdah), male doctors should not pose a problem. However, the Home Department failed to supply female vaccinators, as was the case in Madras.[93]

To sum up, sanitary conditions under which Muslim women lived were better than those of Hindu women; perhaps this could explain the higher mortality rate in the latter community. In addition, the Census Report accepted that a large number of Muslim women fell in the reproductive age period (15–40 years), proving that delivery deaths were few.[94] This might be why Muslim women were considered more fertile than Hindu women.

[93] Home Department: Sanitary, September 1890. Nos. 24–25.

[94] Siddiqui, 'Colonial Report on Census'.

CHAPTER 4

Crises in the Social and Economic Identity of Muslim Women: The Great Uprising of 1857

Bagh alam me churana tha apno se
Pahle hi sabza-e beghana banaya hota
Garch-e- manzoor na thi khana-e- Nasheeni meri
To mujhe sakin veerana banaya hota

Husain Begum, Umrao[1]

The great uprising of 1857 brought about a significant change in Indian society. This incident led to several socio-political developments in the Indian subcontinent.[2] However, the impact was greater on north Indian Muslims, both socio-culturally and politically. For centuries, Delhi remained the centre of power, and for over six centuries Muslims ruled this region. To the common people, the Mughal dynasty was very important, given their long emotional connections with the emperors,[3] irrespective of whether the emperors were strong like Akbar, Jahangir or Shah Jahan, or inconsequential like Bahadur Shah Zafar.[4] For the people, the king was their *anndata*, a divine power who would bring back their lost glory, and therefore a figure of rebellion, whether real or symbolic. This perception helped the Mughals to consolidate their presence

[1] Sughra Mehndi, *Urdu Adab men Khawateen Ka Hissa* (New Delhi: Urdu Academy, 2006), 34. Umrao's fitting reply to Bahadur Shah's famous ghazal written in exile, *Kitna badnaseeb hai zafar do gaz zameen na mili kuche yar me.*

[2] Margaret MacMillan, *Women of the Raj* (London: Thames and Hudson, 1980), 97.

[3] ibid.

[4] K. M. Ashraf, *Rebellion 1857*, C. P. Joshi (ed.), (New Delhi: National Book Trust, 2007), 93.

over a long period.[5] Although the country was fragmented into several small states after the disintegration of the Mughal Empire, these newly-formed states could not erase the memory of Mughal glory, specially after their painful experiences with regional power. The erstwhile subjects were filled with despair and frustration, which was why the spark of rebellion caught on so quickly.

The initial social reforms the British undertook were through Legislative Acts such as the Anti-Sati Act (1829), the Widow Re-marriage Act (1856), and the introduction of the Western education system in the traditional education system of India. The British had intended it as only a social reform, but it was perceived as religious interference by the Indian people, especially those who actively participated in the mutiny. At first glance, the mutineers appeared to be protesting any kind of progressive change, leading to Metcalf[6] viewing the 1857 uprising as backward-looking, while Rudranshu Mukherji considered it a collective disappointment. As Ayesha Jalal argues, Muslims were in every respect more dissatisfied than Hindus.[7] If the mutiny was backward-looking or merely a disappointment, then why did the common people, including women, participate in it actively? For both Hindus and Muslims, it was a joint attempt to overthrow the British.

The Muslims, especially Wahabis, were held more responsible for their alleged involvement, and blamed for having plotted a conspiracy against Christ.[8] Since a large section of the Muslims hailed from urban areas, their fear of being uprooted was heightened.[9] In the face of such significant change taking place

---

[5] When Qulsum Zamani Begum, daughter of Bahadur Shah Zafar, was on her Haj pilgrimage, she met a Hindu shopkeeper who expressed deep concern over the deterioration of the royal family and stated that the King was the father and teacher of all Indians (Khawaja Hasan Nizami, *1857 Ki Kahaniyan* [New Delhi: National Book Trust, 2008), 7.

[6] T. R. Metcalf, *Aftermath of Revolt: 1857-1870* (Cambridge: Cambridge University Press, 1965).

[7] Ayesha Jalal, *Partisans of Allah: Jihad in South Asia* (New Delhi: Permanent Black, 2008), 133.

[8] ibid., 85. See also, Qeamuddin Ahmad, *The Wahabi Movement* (New Delhi: Manohar, 1994), 163–225.

[9] Of the total urban population, 36 per cent were Muslim and 62 per cent Hindu, while in rural areas the figure was 11 per cent and 88 per cent, respectively (CR of 1901, 63). See also Francis Robinson, *Separatism among Indian Muslims* (New Delhi: Oxford University Press, 1993), 13; Nadim Husain (ed.), *Islam and Muslim Societies*, Vol. I (New Delhi: Serial Publications, 2005), 155–60.

in Indian society, women too had to be involved. They could not remain silent once they were aware of what was going on. Alarmed at their deteriorating condition, they had no option but to step out of their homes to attend the trials of the mutineers, who were related to them. The question that now arises is: To what extent did this mutiny influence Indian Muslim women? Were common Muslim women also connected with the uprising?

After the mutiny, the British labelled Muslims as rebellious by nature, incapable of peaceful existence.[10] It was assumed that even though this revolt was begun by a Hindu Brahmin, it was Muslims who had contributed to its spread. Therefore, Muslims began being targeted from all sides.[11] This hypothesis has created three kinds of historiographies: European historiography, nationalist historiography and Muslim historiography.[12]

This could explain why, immediately after the revolt, Sir Saiyid defended Muslims against these allegations to safeguard his *qaum*'s interest and prevent the persecution of Muslims. He tried his best to absolve the common Muslim of charges of betrayal.[13] He attributed the responsibility for the uprising to the British lack of interest in the common people.[14] Muslim scholars of the nineteenth century also endorsed this view in their writings. It is interesting to observe the way Maulvi Nazir projected his imaginary hero, *Ibn-ul waqt.*[15]

[10] Ahmad, *The Wahabi Movment*, 222. Muhammad Zafar, a mutiny convict, states that W. W. Hunter believed that if the Wahabis were released, they would consider it a favour from God, not the government, and would renew their anti-government activities. Hence, Zafar lost all hopes of his own release (Hali, *Hayat-e Javed*, 176–77).

[11] It is noteworthy that Muslim scholars dealing with this period were often defensive about colonialism, while after independence they emphasised the Muslim involvement in 'the first war of independence'. See Saiyid Ahmad Khan, *Asbab-e Baghawat Hind*, Abu Layis Siddiqui (ed.), (Karachi: Urdu Academy, 1976), Preface, 61, to see how he attempted to highlight Muslim involvement in the freedom struggle.

[12] Sir Saiyid Ahmed KHan, *Asbab-e Baghawat-I Hind*, 16. William Darlymple, *The Last Mughal* (New Delhi: Penguin, 2006), 329.

[13] Hali, *Hayat-e Javed*, 177–78.

[14] Khan, *Asbab-e Baghawat Hind*, 16.

[15] It was written in the 1880s, and surprisingly enough, this great champion of women's cause kept strangely silent about incidents of molestation of Indian Muslim women, while similar incidents vis-à-vis European women. This was a time when Europeans were writing a number of accounts of the mutiny to justify their rule. It is even said that this novel is about his own experiences of the mutiny, especially the time when he saved the life of a European lady. Some believe that Nazir based Ibn-ul Waqt, the true friend of the British, on Sir Saiyid Ahmad Khan.

He portrayed Ibnul Waqt as a true friend of the British, who offered all kinds of assistance to British men in dire need of assistance. In this way, Nazir tried to emphasise that the common Muslims was essentially peace-loving, and against rebellion. In his opinion, it was only the opportunist and deviant evil-doer who actively participated in the mutiny, and brought shame to the name of the entire community. This begs the question: Why did Muslims need to prove their loyalties towards the British much after 1857? The question of Muslim loyalty towards the Raj acquired greater significance particularly after the 1870s. This also explains why the importance of W. W. Hunter increased when he was appointed advisor to the Governor General soon after the revolt. His views were bound to influence British policy regarding Muslims, and hence it was considered strategically important to remain in his good books.[16] Hunter was instructed to analyse the causes of the mutiny, and the result of his investigations was his famous book, *The Indian Musalman*, published in 1869.

The British had restored peace by crushing the revolt and putting the mutineers on trial. Soon after that, they began analysing its root causes and the impact it might have had. While reviewing the tyrannies committed by *sepoys* during the revolt, several cases of rape and molestation of European women attracted the attention of the British government, as well as of travellers documenting facts about the mutiny.[17] Thus, these women became the subjects of their accounts, both factual and fictional.[18] Not surprisingly, these authors ignored the plight of Indian women who had suffered similar violations, choosing to focus only on the European women. Indian scholars were not comfortable addressing this issue. Censorship restrictions on printing presses played a major role in suppressing their voices. The British, on the other hand, persisted on writing on this issue. At times European women were projected as vulnerable and innocent, at times as bold heroines, who preferred death to

---

[16] Qauamuddin Ahmad, *Wahabi Movement in India* (Calcutta, 1966), 222.

[17] Christopher Hibbert, *The Great Mutiny: India 1857* (London: Penguin Books, 1980), 195. See also Indira Ghosh, *Women Travellers in Colonial India: The Power of the Female Gaze*, (New Delhi: Oxford University Press, 1998), 88–103; Indrani Sen, *Women and Empire: Representation in the Writing of British India*, (Hyderabad: Orient BlackSwan, 2002), 24–28. See also Margaret MacMillan, *Women of the Raj* (London: Thames and Hudson, 1980), 98–103.

[18] Charles E. Pearce, *Love Besieged*, Ralph Crane (ed.), (USA: Oxford University Press, 2003), Introduction. This became a trend when writing about the mutiny, particularly in the 1880s.

molestation.[19] Accounts of Indian women, on the other hand, swung between perfidy and devotion. During this period, Indian women were imagined as acquiescent and submissive to their husbands.[20] Indian women who fought against the British were treated positively in their discursive writings. This dearth of recorded information by relevant sources greatly hinders an academic's attempt to establish a gender theory based on 1857, especially with regard to Indian women.

As described, Indian women were devoted and submissive wives; and they proved this during the mutiny by fighting the British when the lives of their male relatives were in danger. Conviction records from Port Blair substantiate this truth, as a large number of Muslim women are recorded to have been sentenced to life imprisonment at this time.[21] Thus far, it seemed that only a few royal women took active part in the revolt; however, mutiny accounts belie the established belief that only those elite women whose found themselves in danger participated in the revolt. These days, we do not only speak of Zeenat Mahal,[22] Beghum Hazrat Mahal, Rani Laxmi Bai, and the conspiracy of the palaces; we have moved beyond them in relation to the revolution. Women's contribution has been accepted to a large extent, as even prostitutes stepped out of their brothels to support the cause. Sceptics, however, continue to question the authenticity of such facts.

Therefore, this chapter attempts to explore the contribution of marginalised Muslim women, that is, common women, courtesans and prostitutes, along with the royal ladies. At this juncture, one must remember that around this time, prostitutes were being registered in the census as part of the Muslim

---

19 Saul David, *The Indian Mutiny: 1857* (London: Viking, 2002). See also MacMillan, *Women of the Raj*, 99–103.

20 See how Firoza, a common Muslim woman, was depicted in Flora Annie Steel's *Flower of Forgiveness*, as merely a sex object and submissive wife. No positive interpretation was attached to the heroic deeds of Muslim women whether it be Hazrat Mahal, the Rani of Jhansi, or any other rebellious women.

21 Branch: Port Blair, Proceeding: December 1886, 158 and 159, Part B, October 1886, 147–48, Part B. Rubia, another female convict, was released from Port Blair in June 1886 (Branch: Port Blair, Proceeding: 49–50, Part B. Subject: Female Convicts, Branch: Port Blair, Proceeding: January 1990 119–20, Part B). Same file for April, 27–28, and September 168–69.

22 She wanted access to her son Dara Bakhsh, for which she compromised with the British secretly; see Khwaja Hasan Nizami, *1857 Ki Kahaniyan* (New Delhi: National Book Trust, 2008), 8.

professional caste. The British repeatedly emphasised that Hindu prostitutes had all converted to Islam,[23] especially in the Census Report of India.[24] So did Islam provide a space for all forms of promiscuity, or was there some flexibility inherent in Islam that provided a space for prostitutes, making conversion worth their while? Significantly, it is only Islam that gives maternity rights to women who have children born out of wedlock.[25]

This chapter is divided into two sections. The first explores the role of common Muslim women, including courtesans and prostitutes. The second focuses on the repercussions of the uprising on the lives of women in general. What instigated Indian Muslim women to emerge from their long slumber?

British Atrocities against Women

While the Revolt of 1857 spread to remote parts of north India, it is the Western United Province that is believed to have been the most affected. Here, the participation of common people, including women, was on a larger scale, and posed a greater threat to the British. The motives behind participation differed in various sections and regions: in Kanpur and Lucknow, where the leadership was in royal hands, it was the royalty who had vested interests, while in Faizabad, Allahabad, Benares and Azamgarh, the revolt spread to the masses. The Western United Province is also remembered for the heroic deeds of Muslim women, particularly those from the middle and lower classes. Situated close to Delhi and with a large concentration of Muslims (two-fifths of the Muslim population lived in Meerut and Ruhelkhand), this region witnessed greater disturbances compared to other parts of India.[26] The majority of the people uprooted hailed from the *ashraf* clan, and from other well-off families.[27] The fact that government jobs were available to only those who had received Western education added to the misery of the Muslim population, most of

---

23 D. C. Belly, *Census Report of India North Province of Agra and Oudh, 1891* (Allahabad: Government Press, 1894), 180.

24 Edmund White, CR 1881, Allahabad. See also Census Report of 1901, compiled by R. Burn, 1902, 254–55. In 1901, prostitutes constituted 0.3 per cent of the entire Muslim population.

25 Firdous Azmat Siddiqui, 'Legal Position of Indian Muslim Women', in A. K. Sinha (ed.), *Facet of Indian History* (New Delhi: Anamika Publications, 2006), 332.

26 Dalrymple, The White Mughal, 124–26.

27 CR of India, 1901, 63. Francis, Robinson, *Separatism among Muslims of India*, (New Delhi: Oxford University Press, 1993), 17–20.

whom had only acquired traditional knowledge and learning and were therefore unemployable. This led to Muslims perceiving the British as their enemy, and holding them responsible for their deteriorating conditions.[28] They believed that their interests had been safeguarded better under Mughal rule. This was one of the reasons why they initiated a rebellion to overthrow the British government.[29]

It has been established that, in the absence of their menfolk, the women persisted in the fight against the British government. They soon became a dangerous threat, especially in Meerut, Bulandshahar, Farukhabad, Rampur[30] and Muzaffarnagar.[31] The women from the Meerut division were praised repeatedly by V. D. Savarkar. These women, a significant number of whom were Muslims from the Gujjar and Rajput castes, not only participated in the revolt, but also gave up their lives in their quest to free their motherland. The most prominent among them was Habiba,[32] a Muslim Gujjar, and Rahimi,[33] a Muslim Rajput from Meerut, who were sentenced to death in 1858 for their role in the insurgence.[34] Viewed strategically, these regions were politically significant as the Mughals had had strong ties with the Meerut division. This could also be why Qulsm Zamani[35] and other Mughal princesses chose Meerut for shelter and protection when they were forced to leave Delhi. After the British crushed the royal Mughal family, several princesses were left orphans and, as Ghalib laments in his letter, some were even forced to move into prostitution.

---

28 Sir Saiyid stated that unemployment was the basic cause behind the mutiny (*Asbab-Baghawat-e Hind*, 152–58). In contrast to Saiyid, Robinson's analysis shows that the condition of north Indian Muslims, particularly those who hailed from the United Provinces, was much better (*Separatism Among Indian Muslims*, 46).

29 Coll-16, foll-20, 7 September 1857 (NAI): Orders have been issued to the Hindus and Muslims of Delhi to fight with the English.

30 At the time, Christopher Hibbert expressed his astonishment at two rebellious Muslim women leaders of Rampur. Hibbert, *The Great Mutiny*, 296.

31 Asghari Begum, who was born in Muzaffarnagar on 5 July 1811, participated in the struggle against the British forces. For this she was captured by the British and burnt alive in 1857. See Nagendra Kumar Singh, *Encyclopedia of Women's Biography*, Vol. I, 2001, 82. See also Kabir Qauser and Inamul Kabir, *Biographical Dictionary of Prominent Muslim Ladies* (New Delhi: Light and Life Publishers, 1982), 28.

32 Qauser and Kabir, *Biographical Dictionary of Prominent Muslim Ladies*, 111–12.

33 ibid., 279.

34 Some prominent figures executed for their involvement in the mutiny were Kasifa Sultan, Jahan Afroz Begum, Nawab Khas Mahal and Sarfraz Begum.

35 Nizami, *1857 ki Kahaniyan*, 1–8.

Nargis Nazar[36] made the mistake of seeking shelter in Ghaziabad in her *ayah's* house, where she was abused and beaten by Sikh troopers and taken prisoner. It is estimated that during the uprising, as many as 258 young women lost their lives. Women like Jamila, a young Pathan from the United Provinces who took part in the mutiny, were captured and later executed.[37]

Delhi, by virtue of its importance, had been plundered several times earlier. Before the British, the Tilangas and Gujjars had already ravaged both the area and its women. The women had also been treated badly by members of their own community.[38] During the mutiny, they were even assaulted by mutineers from outside Delhi.[39] The women fought against it all bravely and made numerous appeals to the King to extend royal help to destitute women. Widows appealing for their sons' release[40] also had to deal with the brutality of the Tilangas and the mutineers.[41] This shows that the politically conscious Indian Muslim women maintained their faith in the crown, even when the King was weak and unsure of his own position.

Incidents of rape and abduction added to women's misery. It is an age-old custom that whenever a war is fought, it is women who become the primary victims. After the uprising was suppressed, the women were sexually assaulted at the hands of the Europeans too.[42] Many such horrific incidents concerning royal ladies were narrated by Khawaja Nizami in *Begmat ke Aansu*. Nizami talks about how, having been turned away by courtiers and employees of the Mughal

---

[36] ibid., 20–27.

[37] ibid., 144.

[38] Coll-67, foll-47, 14 July 1857. Coll-70, foll-210, 13 August 1857. Coll-67, foll-141, 11 September 1857 (NAI). Qulsum Zamani Begum, Nawab Noor Mahal and Hafiz Sultan, who left Delhi in search of shelter, were robbed by the Gujjars and Jats in Korali village. Even women from these communities took part in this plunder, and snatched all the precious belongings of the royal ladies (Nizami, *1857 ki Kahaniyan*, 2, 3).

[39] K. A. Nizami, *1857 Ki Tarikhi Roznamcha*, (Delhi: Nadwat-ul Musnafeen, 1958), 169–70.

[40] Coll-71, foll-149, 1 August 1857, NAI.

[41] Coll-70, foll-27, 31 July 1857, Coll-67, foll-47, 14 July 1857, Coll-62, foll-163, 11 September 1857, NAI.

[42] Coll-60, foll-348, 20 July 1857. In her plea to the king, she complains that Ghulam Husain's troopers assaulted her and abducted her daughter. See also Coll-60, foll-349, 20 July 1857.

court, the royal refugee was left wandering in search of shelter. It was at this time that Faiz Ali, Haqeem of Ajara, sheltered Qulsum in his own house while Basti, a local zamindar, helped the others. Qulsum tells the tale of her hardship to Khawaja Nizami in these words:

> That time was one of despondency. In addition, we were scared that the British army was following us. Our condition was so bad that everyone turned away. All those who had danced to our tunes and obeyed our ever order did not want to even look at us. I thank Basti Zamindar, who helped his sister till the end. Helpless, we left Ajaara for Haiderabad. Women were sitting on Basti's bullock cart while the men accompanied them on foot. On the third day we reached a river bank where an army of the Koel's Nawab was camping. When they heard we were from the royal family, they welcomed us courteously and helped us to cross the river on his elephant. Soon after we had crossed over, the British army arrived and a fight began with the Nawab's army.
>
> My husband Mirza Sultan wished to fight, but *Risaldar* sent a message: 'He should leave along with the women. We will see to them.' We saw a field of crops in front of us, and hid there. We do not know whether the cruel people had seen us or whether it was an accident, but a bullet hit the field and set it on fire. We began running. We tripped on the grass and fell, our veils were torn and we fled bare-headed. Nawab Mahal's feet and mine were bleeding. We were thirsty, and Zeenat kept fainting. The men tried to support us, but it became difficult to handle the situation.[43]

Stories of such incidents are rare in Muslims accounts. Perhaps they did not want to accept that their women had been molested, or perhaps they feared British highhandedness. After decades, the turmoil that Muslim women had faced in that period emerged through women's writings. Zohra Segal has penned several incidents that occurred to the women of her family, who escaped to nearby forests with their children and jewellery chests, and finally took shelter in Moradabad.[44]

The consequences of the mutiny were also clearly visible in contemporary fiction, a case in point being Maulvi Nazir, the famous Urdu novelist, who talks about the fate of common Muslims in his novel *Ibn-ul Waqt.*[45]

---

[43] Nizami, *1857 Ki Kahaniyan*, 3–4.

[44] Close-up. 23–24.

[45] Maulvi Nazir Ahmed, *Ibn-ul Waqt: Qaumi Council Brae Farogh Urdu* (New Delhi: Zubaan, 2005).

Rebellious Women

These circumstances perhaps forced some members of the royal family to join the uprising, despite the emperor's indecisiveness.[46] They seemed more unhappy with their present condition, and might have hoped for a return to their splendid past. Many royal women asked for security guards at their residence,[47] and it is remarkable how some women took over the responsibility for the fort's management. One of them was *Ibrat-un Nisa*, who became very significant in the imperial palace during the revolt. She was the superintendent of stores for the heir apparent of Siraj-ud Din and Bahadur Shah Zafar.[48] The many atrocities the British had committed on Indian women had made them rebellious, particularly the Muslims, who continued their protests even long after the mutiny. Saqina Begum was one such victim-survivor: she lost her husband, her father-in-law and newborn child in the uprising. She was born in Farrukhabad and was educated at home by learned scholars. At the age of seventeen, she was married to Faulad Khan's son; he was one of the nobles of the last Mughal king, Bahadur Shah Zafar, and was killed during a battle with the British army in 1857. The day her father-in-law died, she gave birth to a child who was torn from her arms by her *ayah*. After twelve difficult years, she succeeded in finding her son. She died at her birthplace.[49]

There is no doubt that women did not remain mute spectators, but took up arms to save their families when the British launched their campaign against the rebels. It appears that initially, they fought from within the confines of their homes, but eventually had to come out of *purdah*. Women, too, soon came to the notice of the British, and many of them were executed.[50]

On the one hand, the British criticised the mutineers for being cowards and butchers who did not spare even women and children. Interestingly, though, their concern was reserved only for European women.[51] There was no one to speak on behalf of Indian women, who were kidnapped, molested, beaten and tortured

---

[46] Qauser and Kabir, *Biographical Dictionary*, 180.

[47] Nawab Anwar Mahal asked the King to not remove the present guards from her gate. Coll-100, foll-115, 16 August 1857, NAI. See also Coll-100, foll-179.

[48] Qauser and Kabir, *Biographical Dictionary*, 136.

[49] Nizami, *1857 Ki Kahaniyan*, 37–43. See also *Encyclopaedia of Indian Women*, Vol. II, 177.

[50] Quaser and Kabir, *Biographical Dictionary*, 112.

[51] David, *The Indian Mutiny*, 251–54.

not only by their own fellowmen, but also by the English troops. Keith Young's letter to his wife, describing how he had confronted an old woman lamenting over the dead body of her son in a mosque, raised a big hue and cry all across north India. He claimed to be unlike the feral people taking advantage of the times and plundering and killing; instead, he had let this old woman live. At the same time, he expressed astonishment over a female mutineer:

> Did I tell you that they took a woman prisoner the other day who they made out was leading a charge of cavalry and who killed two of our men with her own hands? I believe the great part of this is to be a fiction; and as she is old and ugly not much romance attached to her, though she is wounded.[52]

The rebelliousness of Indian women clearly astounded the British. Another instance of bravery on the part of Muslim women occurred in Rampur, and Syed Mubarak Shah applauded them by pointing out how they encouraged their men by taunting them:

> They went far in advance with naked swords, bitterly taunting the sepoys when they held back, calling them cowards and shouting to them to see how women went in front where they dared not follow .... The sepoys would excuse themselves, saying 'We go to fetch ammunition'. But the women would reply, 'You stop and fight and we will get your ammunition for you.' These women frequently did bring cartridges to the men in the batteries and walked fearlessly in perfect showers of grape.[53]

The Bibigurh incident was another concerning Indian women that attracted the attention of the British. As the name suggests, Bibigurh had originally been built for an officer's *bibi* (wife), but at the time of the uprising, it was occupied by the magistrate's babu.[54] Bibigurh, built around a central courtyard, was a single-storied building consisting of two main rooms, 10 ft. x 20 ft. with square pillars and cusped arches that looked out onto an inner veranda. All European prisoners had been imprisoned here. Since 27 June, the original number of prisoners had increased to more than 200, many of whom were children, after fugitives escaping in Vibant's boat and a second flotilla were captured. According to John Shepherd, who was being held in a separate location, the prisoners

[52] ibid.

[53] Hibbert, *The Great Mutiny*, 296.

[54] At the time it was common to find Muslim women in European households as wife or concubine, who was called 'bibi'.

received only a small quantity of *dal* and *chapatti* daily for the first few days, after which a little meat and milk was allowed for the children. They were also allowed a sweeper woman and a *bhishti*, despite which their living conditions remained pitiable, especially compared to European standards.[55]

The wretched conditions under which their women were being housed caused British authorities great anguish, and they were convinced that some women were even being raped. *The Times* reported:

> The history of the world affords no parallel to the terrible massacres which during the last few months have desolated the land. Neither age, sex nor condition has been spared. Children have been compelled to eat the quivering flesh of their murdered parents, after which they were literally torn asunder by the laughing fiends who surrounded them. Men in many instances have been mutilated and, being absolutely killed, have had to gaze upon the last dishonour of their wives and daughters previous to being put to death.[56]

Yet, according to a captive drummer, John Fitchet, they were neither ill-treated nor disgraced in any way. The daily supervision of prisoners was the responsibility of a Muslim woman named Husaini Khanam, servant of the Nana's favourite courtesan Adla. Most people called her 'Begum' on account of her imperious manner, and she is said to have made the prisoners' lives miserable. It was she who selected the women to grind gram; yet she was the one responsible for the improvement in the food and handing out 'fresh clothe', presumably on the Nana's orders.

The destiny of the prisoners was sealed by Havelock's quick response to the revolt. It was believed that were the prisoners to be left alive, they would expose everyone involved in the rebellion in Kanpur. Therefore, most of the Nana's advisors, including Bala, Baba Bhutt, Azim-ullah Khan and Tatya Tope were in favour of executing the prisoners. Half an hour later, according to John Fitchet, the begum informed the ladies of the Nana's order to execute them. In a dramatic turn of events, the sepoys deputed to carry out the order decided among themselves to not hurt a single woman, although they would kill every man. Outraged, the begum went to consult Nana and returned with Tope, who threatened to kill the sepoy if he did not carry out his orders.

A contradictory picture thus emerges vis-à-vis Indian women—while in some instances they seem oppressed, elsewhere they come across as the oppressors.

---

55 Hibbert, *The Great Mutiny*.

56 *The Times*, 17 September 1857, 9. Quoted in Charles E. Pearce, *Love Besieged*, Ralph Crane (ed.), (New Delhi: Oxford University Press, 2003), xi.

These significant incidents also demonstrate women's cruelty towards other women. Some women, though, displayed their feminist side while dealing with European women; prominent among them was Lala Rukh, a Mughal princess, who witnessed the murder of about fifty English women and children. She and her learned teacher, Maulana Azimullah, protested this brutal action, but found her father, a Prince, helpless in the hands of rustic, ruthless soldiers, who decided to put them to death.[57] Many Muslim *ayahs* came to the attention of the British government, who recognised their worthy deeds. One such *ayah* was Buboo, who saved her master's two children at considerable risk to her own life. The Benares commissioner recommended that she be granted a monthly pension of Rs 4 for her loyalty.[58] There were several other instances of *ayahs* saving the lives of European women by risking their own.[59] These examples were often used in European fiction to highlight how devotion was rooted in Indian women, in stark contrast to Indian men.

The impudent behaviour of some servants, on the other hand, shocked European women. As Mrs Sneyd said:

> My ayah would often stand before looking glass throwing herself into a variety of attitudes herself and dancing with a shawl fantastically thrown over her shoulder, like the nautch girls, instead of dressing me when I wanted her, and this she did in my presence with the taunt ... 'Ah! Your rule will soon come to an end and we shall have our own king!'[60]

Role of Courtesans: Sexuality, Prostitution and Clandestine Relations

It is also interesting that during the revolt, courtesans and prostitutes were very active in boosting the morale of both sepoys and mutineers. They acted as scouts for the rebels, and paid for their actions after the revolt, when the wrath of the British fell upon them. Nevertheless, the question arises: Why did they support the common people, who often treated them as outcasts? It was

---

[57] Qauser and Kabir, *Biographical Dictionary*, 185.

[58] No-2993, From: F. B. Outram to Government of India, Home Deprt. Fort William, No-248, 19 March 1859.

[59] Indrani Ghosh, *Mem Sahib Abroad* (New Delhi: Oxford University Press, 1998), 191.

[60] David, *The Indian Mutiny*, 262.

not merely the danger of being uprooted that forced them to join the rebels. Perhaps it was the ruthless destruction of their patronage that compelled them to revolt. This was a group that had been affected the most by British policies; at one time, they had enjoyed the patronage of many landed and royal families. Therefore, it was only natural for them to want to assist the patron to whom they were emotionally attached. It is said that the dancer Azizan inspired and incited Indian soldiers in the British army to revolt. Learned personalities like Vinayak Damodar Savarker, Shastri Bhushan Chaudhri and Balaji Hardikar have spoken highly of her organisational skills, her patriotism and self-sacrifice. After her arrest, General Havelock expressed his willingness to free her if she sought his pardon. But she refused to bow down before the British, willingly embracing death instead.[61]

The courtesans' actions during the revolt led to their properties being confiscated and their houses seized;[62] a similar fate befell the courtesans of Allahabad, particularly those from the *Dariabad mohalla*, who had also played a very active role.[63]

Was this why the British decided to suppress courtesans after 1857? Did the colonial presence make it more challenging for courtesans to earn a livelihood? Why were all courtesans/prostitutes registered under Muslim sects in the census? These issues remain relevant and debatable. It appears to be the status of prostitutes, rather than prostitution per se, that unnerved the British. These women owned land and property, and the financial security they enjoyed made them fearless and independent. It therefore became necessary to degrade their status from connoisseurs of art and music to mere peddlers of the flesh trade. Initially, when British influence had begun to spread, it was only men to came to the country. Being on their own, they naturally needed female companionship, and thus upper-class Europeans were encouraged to enter marital relations with upper-class Muslim families.[64] When their economic interests began overlapping with their political interests, they decided to avoid intermingling with the natives, especially since their political interests were predicated upon notions of racial superiority. So this necessitated clandestine

---

[61] Andrew Ward, *Our Bones are Scattered: The Cawnpore Massacres and the Indian Mutiny*, (New York: Henry Holt & Co., 1996), 148, 200, 236, 536.

[62] Coll-61, foll-550, 13 September 1857. Coll-61, foll-608, 13 September 1857; see also Coll-61, foll-551, 13 September 1857, And Coll-62, foll-91–92.

[63] Basta No-6, File No-7, Criminal Records, Regional Archive, Allahabad.

[64] B. Joardar, *Prostitutes in India*, (New Delhi: Inter India Publications, 1986), 92–96. See also Dalrymple, *The White Mughal.*

relations with Indian women, without giving them any legal status. This led to the encouraging of physical, rather than marital, relations, which subjugated the Indians automatically.

The second half of the nineteenth century witnessed the arrival of European women, who viewed Indian women as sexual rivals.[65] The few interracial marriages that did take place were often short-lived due to the enormous cultural difference between the couples. The British men would often end their marriages upon returning home, and give the women a monthly allowance.[66] These contracts seemed like a *muta* (temporary marriage), valid in among the Shias. What is truly remarkable is that the offspring born of these marriages supported the Indian rebels during the mutiny: this seems to have been the result of their mother's upbringing, or the emotional attachment they formed with their motherland.[67]

However, 1857 can also be considered a turning point in Indo-European matrimonial relations. Acquaintance with *Hindustani* has been taken as one possible cause behind the great uprising, which was perhaps why the British began discouraging interracial marriages. This led a greater number of English ladies to come to India in search of good husbands. However, only high-grade officers had European wives at home; the low-grade soldiers had to visit brothels.[68]

At this time, yet another problem related to prostitution made itself felt in England: venereal diseases made an alarming appearance, and spread to nearly all the colonies. It was soon realised that the abject poverty and enforced celibacy in cantonments had resulted in an increase in prostitution, and in an attempt to contain a potentially explosive situation, the British government decided to permit their soldiers to marry, and bring their wives along. Interestingly, though, this leeway was not extended to India,[69] as they believed that India provided a source of cheap, convenient sex as prostitution was part of Indian culture and religion. In this way, a state-sponsored flesh trade began in the second half of the nineteenth century, and interracial marriages were firmly discouraged. To control sanitary conditions in brothels, the British passed a law, which they named the Contagious Diseases Act. This act required every prostitute to undergo a weekly check-up in the lock hospitals; and these lock hospitals were clearly working to

---

[65] Sen, *Women and Empire*, 4.

[66] Dalrymple, *The White Mughal*, 73, 89, 238, 290.

[67] ibid.

[68] Sen, *Women and Empire*, 9–10.

[69] William Acton, *Prostitution Considered in its Moral, Social and Sanitary Aspects* (London: Frank CASS, 1972 [1870]), 176.

supply healthy and disease-free prostitutes to the cantonments.[70] An application was actually expected from procurers who could provide healthy *lalbibis.*[71] The British were keen to bring prostitutes under the purview of the Income Tax Act and mandatory medical check-ups, whereas all the prostitutes were looking for was an escape route.[72] What is more, the police were authorised to be present at these weekly check-ups and declare the *qasbis* disease-free.[73] Elite courtesans considered this a direct attack on their status.[74] They argued that they were not sex workers, and asked why these diseases had not occurred earlier, given that their profession was as old as time itself. Oldenberg connects this to 1857 and its repercussions; the British backlash against elite courtesans was severe because of the assistance they offered the rebels and mutineers. More European soldiers died of venereal diseases than they did in wars![75] This fact also alarmed the British enough to try and take control of the situation.

Landed Muslim Women: British Policy Towards Landowning

Muslim women of that period held land in places where the *Mahalwari* system was in vogue, since their right to land was protected under the *shariat*[76] in such areas. After peace had been instituted, particularly after 1858, the British began identifying landowners from whom they could collect a greater amount of revenue. Under this new policy, they punished the rebellious by seizing their property, while those who had remained loyal during 1857 were rewarded.[77] Since it was presumed that Muslims were rebellious by nature and could not

[70] *Oudh Akhbar*, 26 May 1868.

[71] Oudh Panch, No. 45, 10 November 1892.

[72] *Oudh Akhbar*, 26 May 1868.

[73] ibid.

[74] Veena Talwar Oldenberg, *Lifestyle as Resistance: The Case of the Courtesans of Lucknow* (New Delhi: Oxford University Press, 1990). See also Amrit Lal Nagar, *Ye Kothevaliyan*, Collected from Hindi Sahitya Sammelan Library, Allahabad.

[75] William Acton, *Prostitution, Considered in its Moral, Social and Sanitary Aspects* (London: Frank Cass).

[76] The Law of Primogeniture (male inheritance) was practised in places where the Taluqdari system was in existence; therefore under the Mahalwari system, a woman could claim her inheritance rights by virtue of being Muslim.

[77] Home Judicial, Bundle No. 35, Box No. 57, Sl. No. 6, File No. 9. Regional Archive, Allahabad (henceforth RAA).

live peacefully, they came at receiving end of British atrocities. Perhaps this can explain the large number of petitions for re-possession of land by Muslim women, particularly from areas that were most affected during the mutiny. Women applicants, by and large, were widows appealing for mercy on the grounds of their helpless and impoverished condition.[78] It is surprising to note that there were more women from the Chail *pargana*, in comparison to other areas. They were either very conscious of their rights or most deprived, particularly during the backlash that followed the revolt. Maulvi Liaqat was from a landed class of Chail *pargana*; this could explain the heightened suffering of Muslim women from this area. The Limitation Act of 1858 was a big hurdle in reclaiming their seized land, since this Act fixes the expiration period at twelve years. Their claims were very often rebuffed, and the property seized was directly related to the concerned people's involvement in the mutiny.[79] Some *parganas*, among them Chail, were declared completely confiscated. This led to the women from this *pargana* appealing to the collector on grounds of their widowhood and poverty, and attempting to disassociate themselves and their husbands from any kind of involvement in the mutiny. Also, these women approached the court after 1870, when they automatically came under the Limitation Act of 1858, which gave a person only twelve years in which to file a petition in the court.[80] In addition, the British attitude in dealing with such cases was often discouraging.

The second type of cases had to do with ceded or conquered land. In this context, Bundelkhand region was very significant. While acquiring this land, the British government used to fix compensation in the form of cash and pension.[81] The Muslim widows begun complaining about the reduction in their pensions. These women were not commoners or even from the middle class, but belonged to big landholding families.

Emergence of Muslim Women as an Entity

The year 1857 is considered a turning point for the status of Muslim women as a whole. The socio-political uproar had ingrained a sense of consciousness amongst them and provided them with an opportunity to become self-reliant,

[78] Bundle No. 36, Box No. 58, Sl. No. 14, File No. 30, RAA.

[79] Deprt.: Board of Revenue, File No. 36, Bundle No. 35, Box No. 58, Sl. No. 14, 1861, RAA.

[80] File No. 104, Bundle No. 135, Box No. 189, 1873, RAA.

[81] Home Deprt.: Public, 1862, Part B, Proceeding - 5 March, Nos 37–38, NAI.

since they now had to face the outside world, moving literally from the '*pardah* to the court'. This was perhaps why Indian Muslim women, particularly from the United Provinces, were frontrunners in the forming of several women's organisations, for example *Anjuman* and *Khawateen-e Hind*, prior to the All India Women Conference, and began raising issues related to gender, such as polygamy, child marriage, and liquor and legal issues.

Of course, 1857 also inculcated confidence in the women, since ruthless suppression had taught them how to face adversity. Their accidental political consciousness paved the way to demonstrations and protests. From then on, women were no longer meek spectators, but were becoming gradually aware of the world around them, and how to react to each other and to their new rulers. Despite adhering to strict customs of *pardah*, a number of Muslim women participated in social and charitable activities. They aided women from the lower classes—and sometimes even from their own class—to arrange a daughter's marriage, or spread awareness amongst poor young widows that widow remarriage was not anti-Islamic.[82] The events of 1857 had clearly aggravated the misery of widows. The data available in the Census Report of 1881 shows a large number of widows in the age group of 30–50.[83] Nazir Ahmad also painted a pathetic picture in his famous novel *Aiyama*, where he expressed shock at the sight of very young widows. Since widow remarriage was against tradition amongst upper-caste Hindus and Muslims,[84] several widows from respected families were forced into prostitution to earn their livelihood, or began taking up jobs. This explains why the number of *khangi's chaklakhana* increased in the late nineteenth century. A number of *ashra'f* women took to teaching as a profession,[85] imparting education to poor girls in their own homes, often without charging a fee, till their homes began resembling *madrasas*. Umme Safiya, the wife of Maulvi Nazeer, used to teach poor girls at her home, and started a collection to distribute winter clothes among the poor.[86]

---

[82] Altaf Husain Hali, *Hayat-e Javed* (New Delhi: Taraqqi Urdu Board, 1979), 42–43.

[83] Census Report of India, North Western Province of Agra and Oudh, 1881, W. White, Government Press, Allahabad, NAI, New Delhi.

[84] S. Abul Hasan Nadvi, *The Musalman* (Lucknow: Islamic Research and Publication, 1977), 53.

[85] Zeenat Basheer, *Nazeer ke Navilon me Nuswaee Kirdar* (Hyderabad: Iliyas Traders Publishers & Book Sellers, 1991), 38; see also Qausar and Kabir, *Biographical Dictionary*, 14.

[86] Basheer, *Nazeer ke Navilon*, 38.

In fact, 1857 is considered a landmark vis-à-vis changing educational patterns, too. Like the Hindus before them, Muslims began understanding the importance of Western education, and raised funds to establish the Mohammedan-Anglo Oriental College (MAO College). Their women supported them and did their bit to collect money for the MAO College Fund. Muslim women were among the first in northern India to address any male leader (Sir Saiyid Ahmed Khan), drawing his attention towards their declining educational status.[87] However, lacking the courage to speak to him publicly, they addressed him from behind the *pardah*. Sir Saiyid, though, turned down their request, insisting that the level of education was satisfactory with regard to women and stating that it was more important for men to be educated, as that would automatically improve the condition of women.[88] However, the condition of Muslim women improved only because of their own persistence; they continued to raise this issue from time to time through several platforms, and even wrote a letter to the MAO Educational Conference to appoint a leader on their behalf.[89] It is only through their efforts that a number of Muslim advocates like Haji Ismail Khan, Mumtaz Ali, Saiyid Iftikhar Bilgrami, Nawab Mohsin-ul Mulk, and the most successful educationist of his time, Shaikh Abdullah, emerged during those days.

Creativity in literature was very apparent among Muslim women, despite their sheltered existence in the *zenana*. It was a general presumption that English education would lead to the degeneration of Muslim women. Muslim women used to receive traditional education, and thus were not totally illiterate. However, the purpose of the education received differed according to their station in life. So while an *ashra'f* woman's education equipped her to manage her home, a *tawa'if* would receive the education befitting her profession But by and large, the objective of women's education was to challenge the male-dominated society through acquiring knowledge. It was through their superior knowledge that men had subjugated women. The *tawa'if's* curriculum was not confined to sewing, stitching and cooking; instead, it extended to music, dance

87 Md. Saiyid Iqbal Ali, *Saiyid Ahmed Khan ka Safarnama-e Panjab* (Delhi: Educational Publishing House, 1978), 139.

88 ibid.

89 Saiyid Iftikhar Alam Bilgrami, *Vakeel-e Nuswa* (Aligarh: Institute Press, 1907). This letter referred to a letter of the December 1899 session of the Mohammedan Educational Conference held in Calcutta.

and literature, and also to etiquette and manners.[90] A *tawa'if* always desired to break the shackles of tradition and enforced values in the name of honour, which is why several *tawa'ifs* had composed *ghazals* and *qaside* under their real names, with a *takhallus* of *jan, dilbar, ada* and *bai* instead of *shaira purda nashin* or *hijab*, as *sharif* women did.[91] Some *sharif* (noble) women began writing on women's causes by the 1890s. Muhammadi Beghum was one step ahead, launching a magazine for women, named *Tahzeeb-i Niswa.*[92] The name means 'culture of woman'; lacking the courage to launch the magazine under her own name or after the name of any other woman, it was decided to name it *Tahzeeb-i niswa*, harking back to the notion that it was a woman's duty to preserve her culture and civilisation.[93] Women were not allowed to be writers, editors, or even meet with European ladies, as these were considered forms of cultural degeneration in Muslim society.

So clearly, Sir Saiyid was not in favour of women's freedom. He was undoubtedly the true champion of the Muslim cause, but only as far as preserving male domination was concerned; he tried to impose unnecessary cultural restrictions on women in the name of *tahzeeb* and culture. It was only the women of north India who emerged as progressive despite the many hurdles they had to face; their counterparts in other regions did not dare do so. It is interesting to read their writings and see the issues they were focusing on and discussing. While their poetry was confined to romantic verse, they seemed very conscious of contemporary issues in their prose. However, nothing could match *Sultana's Dream* by Roqaiya Sakhawat Husain. She came from a conservative family, brought up in the hierarchical society of Bihar (in undivided Bengal; she was born in Darbhanga district and moved to Bengal after her marriage) in the nineteenth century, which was replete with unwanted values and customs. She dreamed of a land where the rulers were all women and the subjects men.

---

[90] Mirza Hadi Ruswa, *Umrao Jan-e Ada* (New Delhi: Lerity Art Press, 1991). See also Oldenberg, *Lifestyle as Rresistance*.

[91] See the famous nineteenth-century journal, *Payam-e Yar*, edited by Md. Nisar Husain, Lucknow.

[92] *Aligarh Magazine*, 2001, AMU, 30.

[93] ibid. When Maulvi Mumtaz Ali sought Sir Saiyid's view on naming the first magazine for women, he forbade him to name it after his wife, Muhammadi Beghum, the editor of the magazine. Instead, he suggested the name *Tahzeeb-e Niswa.* See also *Aligarh Law Journal*, V. Sir Saiyid was a staunch supporter of *pardah*; so much so that he never permitted his daughter-in-law to meet with European ladies. Even the wives of judges were not allowed to meet her.

Indeed, she was several steps ahead of her contemporaries in that she even wrote about a solar cooker and other scientific developments.[94]

During this time, Muslim women had begun attending functions organised by European ladies and exchanging ideas with them. This was unique at a time when it was considered undesirable to intermingle in European society.[95] A native newspaper reported a demonstration held by the Muslim women of Lucknow to protest the increasing trend of *chandu* smoking amongst Muslims; they demanded that the government either ban it or seize all the property of offenders, so that the men would work hard and realise that money and health were precious, and not to be squandered on tobacco and alcohol.[96]

This chapter proves that Indian Muslim women were progressive and took a firm stand on pertinent issues; however, it was Indian Muslim men who enforced several Victorian values and restrictions on women, thereby retarding their growth There is no doubt that the impact of the mutiny had reached the masses, and the role played by women in this context was truly remarkable.

---

[94] Jasbir Jain (ed.), *Women in Patriarchy: Cross Cultural Reading* (Jaipur: Rawat Publications), 47–59.

[95] Shaikh Abdullah, *Sawan-e Hayat Beghum Abdullah* (Aligarh, 1956), 8.

[96] *The Dabdaba-e Qaisari* (Bareilly), 28 November 1891.

CHAPTER 5

Changing Profile of Muslim Women through Education

Likh kar hamara nam zameen par mita Dia
Lo aaj hamne uska bhi jhagra mita Dia
Taqseer yar ki na qasoor-e ard hai kuch
Akhtar hamare dil hi ne hamko jala dia

Nawab Akhtar Mahal, Akhtar[1]

In the field of social sciences, the second half of the nineteenth century in India is generally considered a period of transition, both socially and economically. The revolt of 1857 led to significant changes, not only in British administrative policies but also in the attitudes of the subjects of the British Empire in India. The second half of the nineteenth century, according to Natrajan, was a period of social reform.[2] However, the general belief of Muslim scholars is that there was a growing consciousness among Hindus to bring about social change,[3] while the Indian Muslims chose to remain in a backward state.[4] In the second half of the nineteenth century, social awareness for reform was generally gauged

---

1 She was a Mughal princess who composed ghazals under the pen name of Akhtar. Sughra Mehndi, *Urdu Adab me Delhi ki Khawateen ka Hissa* (New Delhi: Urdu Academy), 32.

2 S. Natrajan, *A Century of Social Reform in India* (Bombay: Asia Publishing House, 1962).

3 A close analysis of contemporary vernacular literature highlights Muslim fears, and just how repeatedly they expressed their concerns.

4 Saiyid Ahmed Khan's journey to England proved a milestone in the evolution of his view regarding the religious, social, educational and political problems facing the Muslim community in India.

by the growing literacy rate amongst Hindu women, and it was assumed that educationally, Indian Muslim women lagged behind considerably.[5]

This chapter reviews the state of education among women, particularly Indian Muslim women, in the United Provinces. This chapter states that like their Hindu counterparts, Indian Muslim women, too, were educated. Again, like Hindu women, education among Indian Muslim women was determined by class demarcations in social and economic terms.[6]

The Muslim community in India underwent several divisions in the nineteenth century, and swung alternately between hope and despair. One section of Muslims still had hopes of the Empire, viewing the Empire in India as progressive and wishing to be part of it without losing their identity as Muslims.[7] This group, which sought to share the progress promised by the Empire, comprised of members of the landed class and professionals.[8] However, a vast section of people were dejected with the Empire and sought an ideal that was apparent, but unobtainable, in the circumstances that prevailed in the nineteenth century. This group of Indian Muslims projected the idea of the *Dar-ul Harb*,[9] an attractive idea that soon gained acceptance. In the nineteenth

---

[5] This was particularly true vis-à-vis the women of Bengal; they were projected as backward and uneducated in Hindu nationalist discourse. Mahua Sarkar contests conventional views on the absence of Muslim women from the written history of nineteenth-century Bengal, an absence typically explained in terms of their apparent traditionalism / backwardness. Mahua Sarkar, *Visible Histories, Disappearing Women: Producing Muslim Womanhood in Late Colonial Bengal* (New Delhi: Zubaan, 2008), 48.

[6] At the time, Muslims were divided into three groups: *ashra'f* (high born), *ajla'f* (low born) and *kamin* or *arzal* (low-born people who did the menial work). Garcin De Tassy, *Muslim Festivals in India*, M. Waseem (ed.), (New Delhi: Oxford University Press, 1997), 17–20. Particularly after 1857, the Muslim community started debates within the community to determine how to react to the British without losing their religious identity. Ayesha Jalal offers a comprehensive account of such socio-religious leaders in her chapter 'Jihad in Colonial India'; Ayesha Jalal, *Partisans of Allah* (New Delhi: Permanent Black, 2008), 114–75.

[7] Gail Minault, *Secluded Scholars: Women's Education and Muslim Social Reform in Colonial India* (New Delhi: Oxford University Press, 1998), 56–59.

[8] Francis Robinson, *Separatism Among Indian Muslims* (New Delhi: Oxford University Press, 1993), 14–24. See also Minault, 4.

[9] The idea of *Dar-ul Harb* (abode of war) was expounded by Shah Abdul Aziz. According to him, India had become a *Dar-ul Harb* because Muslims had lost sovereignty, and infidels were administering the affairs of the country. See Jalal, *Partisans of Allah*, 67.

century, the second section of Indian Muslims started on a dominant note, but soon lost out to the other section.

It was while they were in this flux of despair and hope that the Muslim community in India was confronted with issues related to the idea of progress. In the nineteenth century, progress (as understood by the Empire) meant education, particularly Western education.[10] Issues related to the education of women were also raised.[11] It is a peculiarity of present-day scholars to evaluate the state of consciousness for reforms in a community with reference to its response to education.[12] The response of women to education formed the barometer for assessing progressive consciousness. It has always been assumed that in the nineteenth century, the Indian Muslim community did not look favourably upon education. Likewise, it is also assumed that Muslim women lagged far behind in education.[13]

After 1857, a large number of European women arrived in India. However, since they were not permitted to involve themselves in the local administration, they entered the field of teaching.[14] This led to the emergence of a new *memsahib* class. Through their condemnation of the pre-British political, social, administrative and judicial system of India, the British government was persistently attempting to justify its rule. Soon after their arrival, these *memsahibs* and Christian missionaries targeted the *zenana*. They categorised Indian women into two groups: the Hindu women as sati, who burnt themselves on the funeral pyres of their husbands; and Muslim women, *purdanashin*, who were deprived of all knowledge because of their confinement to their homes. Consequently, they devised a new excuse for entering the *zenana*, by claiming that since these women were deprived of enlightenment, it was their duty to educate them.

---

[10] Mushirul Hasan, *A Moral Reckoning: Muslim Intellectuals in the Nineteenth Century* (New Delhi: Oxford University Press, 2009), 8–11.

[11] Shan Mohammad (ed.) *The Aligarh Movement: Basic Documents: 1864–98*, Vol. II (Meenakshi Prakashan, 1978), 671–72.

[12] The question of women's education became a volatile topic for debate among social reformers in the late 1870s. This was when the MAO College had produced the first generation of men who felt a dire need for an educated wife, and hence raised the issue of female education. It is clear from their writings that they were only concerned about the welfare of *ashraf* society, and never talked about *ajla'f* or *kamin* women.

[13] Mohammad, *The Aligarh Movement: Basic Documents: 1864–1894*, abstract from a letter of a European woman, 386–87. See also Aligarh Institute Gazette, 18 July 1871.

[14] Indrani Sen, *Women and Empire*, 4–5.

The latter half of the nineteenth century also witnessed the emergence of Hindu social reformers, who questioned the still prevalent age-old social customs and tried to sow the seeds of progress by borrowing heavily from Western thought. Muslims, too, were influenced by their outlook, and two groups of social reformers emerged: the Aligarh school of progressive thought, and the wahabi ulema, who were considered retrogressive. The Aligarh school, led by Sir Saiyid Ahmed Khan (whom the orthodox called a *naturee*—someone who reduces religion to worldly matters and charged with infidelity),[15] was not against female education, although they did not support it openly. At that time, the dominant concern was educating boys. The orthodox *ulema*, on the other hand, saw the path of progress as stemming only from the old social system, and declared English education 'un-Islamic'.[16] They argued that Christian missionaries were on a proselytising mission, disguised as education.[17] It was natural for Muslim women to be more affected by such thoughts. [18]

The basic question is: Were Muslim women really deprived of education? If yes, then why was this so? With regard to the first question, the first three Census Reports seemed unclear about the criteria determining literacy: Who was to be considered literate, illiterate, or in the process of learning?[19] It is surprising how people were considered illiterate, despite the general criterion of literacy being able to read and write in one language. A number of Muslim women who were educated at home might be considered literate, but were probably not included in the earlier Census Reports. Second, both Hindu and Muslim communities believed that women did not need Western education. So why was the same education system considered essential for boys deemed worthless for girls? The answer lies in the objectives of the new education system.

---

[15] *Lecturon ka Majmua: Maulvi Nazir Ahmed, Jild-1, 1918*, Bashir Ahmed (ed.), Fifth Annual Lecture held on 28 December 1889. See Jalal, *Partisans of Allah*, 169.

[16] Shan Mohammad, *Sir Saiyid Ahmed Khan*, 35.

[17] Raj Bahadur Sharma, *Christian Mission in North India: 1813–1913* (New Delhi: Mittal Publications, 1988), 43, 162.

[18] A letter written by Haji Md. Ismail Khan expressed this belief on the part of Muslims, that all missionaries were instruments of conversion, and should hence be kept away from women. In his letter, he accepted that this was 'the obstacle that lies in the way of growing desire of female education' (Aligarh Institute Gazette, Haji Mohemmad Ismail Khan, 13 March 1894). See also *The Aligarh Movement: Basic Documents: 1864-1894*, Vol-II, 671.

[19] CR of India, 1901, R. Burn, Vol. XVI (Allahabad: Government Press, 1902), 152.

Macaulay firmly believed that traditional education was irrational and based on faith and religion, while Western education, based on reason, was rational.[20] Once again, the question arises: If traditional education was irrational, why were Muslim women creative? How had India produced poets, writers, artists and painters? Did their creativity have no rationality?

The nineteenth century was the period of experimentation for English education. The Charter of 1813 had encouraged traditional education. After 1830, the British needed a class of 'black *baboos*', and so they encouraged Western education. Christian missionaries began arriving in the Indian subcontinent in large numbers and propagated Christianity in the guise of social work and education.[21] As they faced resistance from time to time, the Wood Dispatch of 1854 came into existence. So far education had been connected only with employment,[22] which meant that anyone deprived of education would lose out. Since in the Indian social system a woman's domain was considered the home and she was not expected to work outside, it was not considered necessary to extend the new education to her. It is interesting to see how Maulvi Nazir delineated an educated woman in his famous novel *Mirat-ul Urus:*

> In the world, there is a big burden placed on men's heads. Everything in the world, food, clothes and daily necessities, is obtained by rupees, and therefore all play is that of rupees. So women should be pleased that they are free from the toil of earning a livelihood and producing notes.[23]

For the Muslim community, education was linked to religion. The word 'Quran' comes from 'Qara', which means 'read'. It is obligatory for both sexes to read and seek knowledge. So a traditional system of education was prevalent amongst Muslim women, especially in the *ashraf* class, chiefly imparted through religious texts. Its objective was to impart the message of the Holy Quran. Thus, there were two streams: British education, also known as secular or formal

---

[20] Home: Education, a letter of W. Handford, 3 September 1868. Handford stated that it is one thing to force girls to go to school or use undue official influence to induce them to study, and quite another to give those who come a chance to become rational and civilised women.

[21] Geraldine Forbes, *Women in Colonial India: Essays on Politics, Medicine and Historiography* (New Delhi: Chronicle Books, 2005), 13.

[22] *Lecturon ka Majmua: Maulvi Nazir Ahmed, Satvan Lecture,* 25 February 1890, Maulvi Bashir Ahmed (ed.), 1918, 187.

[23] Maulvi Nazir Ahmed, *Mirat-ul Uroos*, 13.

education, imparted in schools, and traditional education at home. Christian missionaries played a major role in educating women in India. In the nineteenth century, education among Indian Muslims (particularly women) came into being through two agencies—the traditional agency, where the emphasis was on educating women within the confines of their homes; and the agency of the missionaries, where women were encouraged to move beyond their homes to receive education.

Traditional Education

Amongst *ashraf* Muslims, there was a custom called the *Bismillah* ceremony, where a child began his or her education at the age of four years, four months and ten days.[24] The child's education began with the '*Bughdadi Qaeda*', and the main objective was to finish reading the Quran.[25] An *ustani* was appointed to impart religious education at home.[26] Once the Quran had been read, the child's further education depended on the economic condition of the parents.

Every parent wanted their child to read the Quran and perform *namaz*, and it did not matter whether the girl child understood even a single word of the Quran; or, indeed, whether her *ustani* did so.[27] Moreover, the Holy Quran was in Arabic. At that time, Urdu was emerging as the common language in north India and by the nineteenth century, it had become part of the identity of the Muslim community.[28] Traditional education at the time was imparted in Arabic and Persian; Arabic was the language of the Quran, while Persian was used by the upper class. However, there was a break in the late nineteenth century, when even *ashraf* Muslim women showed an inclination towards a new language. They tried to learn Urdu along with the Quran,[29] and even tried

[24] Altaf Husain Hali, *Hayat-e Javed*, 54–55.

[25] Muslim fathers have always been careful in instructing their daughters in the Quran and in diverse primary Urdu books (Haji Md. Ismail Khan, 13 March 1894).

[26] Hali, *Hayat–e Javed*, 55. See also Suraiya Husain, *Sir Saiyid aur Unka Ahad* (Aligarh: Educational Book House, 1993), 354.

[27] Minault, *Secluded Scholars*, 15.

[28] Francis Robinson, *Separatism among Indian Muslims* (New Delhi: Oxford University Press, 1993), 33. Urdu and Hindi became markers of identity for both communities in India. It should be noted that at the time, the circulation of Urdu newspapers was far greater than that of Hindi newspapers.

[29] At the time, women did not feel any need for education, as they were not responsible for earning a living. Reading and writing in Urdu was considered necessary, as this

to pick up some Persian, despite the objections raised by Muslim men. The curriculum of this oral, traditional education system comprised of primary books in Arabic and Persian, such as *Amadnama, Gulistan, Bustan and Ayar Danish of Sadi, Sarf Nahu of Arabic.*[30]

As Urdu was increasingly becoming the language of the masses in north India, most women used it to express their feelings. Women were not as fortunate as men, who received formal instruction by a teacher or an *ustad.* Under these circumstances, it was easy to write in Urdu. Some women, though, managed to master both Persian and Arabic.

The traditional *ustani*, mostly widows and wives of *maulvis*, performed their duties till the 1860s. This period witnessed the emergence of an increasing number of people from the traditional service gentry class, who came to be known as *ustaniji* or *ustani sahiba.*[31] After 1860, though, it was very difficult to find a female *ustani.* The deteriorating condition of *ashraf* Muslims, who were no longer in a position to hire them, was partly responsible for their disappearance.[32] Also, it was not considered desirable to send one's womenfolk out to earn a livelihood, especially amongst *ashra'f* Muslims.

The revolt of 1857 is considered to have brought about a change in the educational system. A number of Mughal princesses and women from the *ashraf* families of Delhi had lost their homes and their protection. These destitute women had taken shelter in nearby surroundings, especially in the Western United Province. Many women from these classes adopted teaching as their profession— some to earn a livelihood, and some to spread knowledge amongst deprived girls.[33] Thus, a new cultural shift took place among Muslim women, with women working for women's causes. These women converted their houses

would help women manage their households, write letters and prepare home budgets; and so *ashraf* women only acquired knowledge of this kind, known as *haraf shanasi.* Nazir, *Mirat-ul Uroos,* 14.

30 Altaf Husain Hali provided a detail account of these books in *Majalis-un Nisa*, which was considered an essential part of the curriculum of female education at the time.

31 Husain, *Sir Saiyid Ahmad Khan aur unka Ahad*, 354.

32 Sir Saiyid, too, expressed his views on this issue before the Indian Education Commission, 1882. Sabyasachi Bhattacharya, Joseph Bara, Chinna Rao Yagati and B. M. Sankhdhar (eds), *Development of Women's Education, 1850–1920* (New Delhi: Krishna Publication and Distributors, 2001), 101.

33 Most prominent among them was Umme Safiya, wife of Maulvi Nazir Ahmed, who opened a *madrasa* of sorts for poor girls in her home.

into *madrasas*, and girls from surrounding areas would be taught vocational courses such as sewing and stitching, and how to manage a home.

The 1860s and 1870s witnessed a revolutionary change in the traditional education system. Instead of *ustanis* going from house to house to teach, aspiring students came to the houses of women to learn. These homes had taken the form of the *zenana madrasa*[34] much hyped in the British Education Report. Many social reformers and nawabs assisted in this task. The first evidence of the *zenana madrasa* can be found in the state of Rampur in July 1868, through a local newspaper established by *Wali-e Rampur.*[35] According to Zohra Segal, during his tenure as vice-president of the Regency Council and commander-in-chief in Rampur, General Azimuddin Khan, her maternal grandfather (an uncle of her mother, Natiqua Begum), introduced several reforms, setting up schools where English was taught and encouraging the education of girls.[36] These reforms were initiated in other areas of north India, too, as evidenced by Delhi's *zenana madrasas* of the 1870s. A Punjabi Muslim woman managed this *madrasa*, where almost forty girls were enrolled.[37] These girls represented every group in Muslim society. One of these *madrasas* was in Bulandshahar, and had been established for widows through the efforts of Maulvi Zaqaullah.[38]

However, the question remains: Could these *madrasas* provide the education expected in a competitive era? The biggest problem facing *zenana madrasas* was the dearth of educated Muslim women who could step out of their houses and function as professional teachers, since at the time *ashraf* Muslims refused to send their women outside their homes, neither for work nor for studies.[39] Faced with a paucity of *ustanis*, men began teaching their female relatives. Wealthy families that wanted to provide Western education along with traditional education to their daughters appointed either European female tutors, or taught them on their own.

[34] Minault, *Secluded Scholars*, 23.

[35] *Oudh Akhbar*, 28, 1868, 713.

[36] Zohra Segal, *Close-Up* (New Delhi: Women Unlimited, 2010), 19.

[37] Allahdad Fatima was an Urdu poetess and teacher of Persian in the Delhi *zenana madrasa* during the later part of the nineteenth century. Kabir Kausar and Imamul Kabir, *Biographical Dictionary of Prominent Muslim Ladies* (New Delhi: Light and Life Publisher, 1982), 14. See also Minault, *Secluded Scholars*.

[38] *Aligarh Magazine*, Aligarh Muslim University, Aligarh, 2001, 33.

[39] ibid.

In 1868, the British government established a regular *zenana* school in Lucknow, which became a milestone in the history of female education. The purpose of this school was to fulfil the demand for female teachers who could impart education to the *purdanashin* women who could otherwise not attend school. In fact, for the first time W. Handford accepted the reality of the prevailing traditional education among *ashraf* Muslims in his correspondence with the Chief Commissioner of Oudh:

> I proposed, in the first instance, to invite respectable natives to select candidates for the national schools, whom they would be willing to admit to their *zenanas* to teach their female relatives. There is reason to hope that many of the more respectable Musalman and Hindus would be willing enough to permit teachers, whom they know to visit and instruct in their house, who would not send their daughters to public school.[40]
>
> Moreover, *ashraf* Muslims had maintained their insistence that their female counterparts would not leave the house for education, whether it was religious or secular.[41] There were some people from both communities who considered it a menace to impart anything more than religious education to the women. They opined that women should only learn to read and should never be taught to write, or they would write letters to any *namahram*, and that would mar the family's honor.[42] In general, Sheikhs were considered more orthodox than Saiyids. Since a large number of Sheikhs hailed from the landed class whose social structure was based on the feudal system, the women were kept under strict control. Women who hailed from such families had to struggle to be educated. The most prominent among them were Ruqaiya Sakhawat Husain of Bengal and Begum Ashraf-un Nisa of Bijnour. Their tireless struggle strengthened their will power to be an educationist.[43]

At the time, the British attitude was to question the rationality of traditional education. However, if traditional education was irrational, then why were traditionally educated Muslim women such talented writers? In fact, Muslim

[40] Home Department: Education, 31 October 1868, From W. Handford, Esquire, M.A. Director of Public Instruction, Oudh, to the Secretary to the Chief Commissioner of Oudh, No. 678, dated Lucknow, 3 September 1868.

[41] Husain, *Sir Saiyid Ahmad Khan aur unka Ahad*, 354.

[42] Muslim fathers have always been careful while instructing their daughters in the Quran and diverse primary Urdu books. The progress of time has not been without its blessings; it has given them a little writing. Haji Mohemmad Ismail, *Aligarh Institute Gazette*, 13 March 1894.

[43] *Aligarh Magazine*, 2001.

women had not only challenged the male-dominated literary world, but they were also doing better in the field of editing. In 1896, Muhammadi Beghum edited her first journal, *Tahzeeb-e Niswa.* From its very first issue, it attracted a surprisingly large number of women writers.[44]

Since these skilled, virtuous ladies preferred to remain anonymous, they chose to be known by titles such as *purdanashin* and *mussawarat*, instead of publishing under their real names. Sometimes they even wrote under male names; it was perhaps the strict purdah system and cultural confinement that were the main hurdles in their way of attaining the fame due to them. I quote one of the finest ghazals that highlights their *gumnam* contribution:

Rahenge tumse seedhe kuj adaee dekhne vale
Vafadari karenge bevafaaee dekhne vale
Tarapne bhee dete hai vo dame qatl apne bismil ko
Uthaen lutf kea teej ajmaee dekhne vale
Idhar naaz jawaani tha udhar shauq ham agosh
Yahi vassal me the vo hatha paee dekhne vale
Janab-e shekh ko bekhauf maikhane me peene do
Nahi baithe hain unki paarsaee dekhne vale
Sar Toor-e kaleem-ullah Qaba deed laazim thi
Bane the aap agar jalva numaee dekhne vale
Museebat hashr ki ae aasman dushman ko keun milti
Ki ham kea kam the us but ki judaee dekhne vale
Hami ko jalvah gaah hai hazrat deedar laee hai
Hami hain ek jalva numaee dekhne vale[45]
Shaera Parda Nasheen Hijab Shahjahanpuri
Hashar ko den gavaahi ae qatil
Daaman va teegh vaasten na kahen
Jaan pe ban aee hai furqat me
Saath choren dil hazeen na kahen[46]

Bi Nawab Begum Sahiba Nazakat Shagirda Janab Rasheed

When, in the late nineteenth century, awareness of the need for education spread amongst Muslim women, there were a few people who tried to publish their creative writings. One of them was Abul Qasim Mohtesim, whose

[44] Devaki Jain (ed.), *Indian Women* (New Delhi: Publication Division, Ministry of Information and Broadcasting, Government of India, 1975), 204.

[45] *Payam-e Yaar*, May 1892, Jild, 10.

[46] *Payam-e Yaar*, October 1899, Jild, 14.

Bahistan-e Naz (1864; the second edition was published in 1869) is dedicated to such *purdanashin* poetesses and authors. Mohtesim claimed to have given recognition to almost eighty-two women who wrote in Persian.[47]

Hasina Begum, Mohtesim's mother, was one of the women who never sought renown for her writing skills. Although she died an anonymous writer, her son saw to it that her works were recognised in public by publishing her *Qasida*, written in Persian.[48] *Ashraf* Muslims were of the view that it was immodest to publish the names of women in books or magazines.[49] Therefore, many Muslim women composed *ghazals* and *qasidas* anonymously, or under pseudonyms like *Shaira Purdanashin* or *Hizab*.[50]

Indeed, Muslim women have shown a keen interest in literature for a long time. While it was believed that these women hailed mainly from the elite classes, the names inscribed in magazines and journals suggest that there were many middle-class women, too. The Benares-born Shams-un Nisa Sharm, daughter of Qamaruddin Kaleem, was the disciple of Khawaja Vazeer, and a famous Urdu *shaira* of her time. As Lucknow was the centre of Urdu literature, several litterateurs sought their fortunes there. Sharm, too, spent most of her time in Lucknow. A number of *ghazals* and *qaside* written by her have now been published.[51] Another famous writer was Umrao Begum Abida, who left two *diwans* after her death—one in Urdu, and the other in Persian. She used to write her ghazals under the name Abida.[52]

Women were as interested in literature as men. Men, though, had recourse to several platforms from which to expose their talent—either in *Mushaira* or under the protection of the princely states. Women were given no such opportunity to expose their hidden talents. Had they been given equal opportunities, they

---

[47] Annemarie Schimmel, 'A 19th Century Anthropology of Poetess', in *Islamic Society and Culture*, 51–57.

[48] ibid., 54.

[49] When Sir Saiyid was asked his views on naming the first magazine for Muslim women after its female editor, he suggested naming it *Tahzeeb-e Niswa* instead, as naming it after a woman would be *bepardagi* (*Aligarh Magzine*, 2001).

[50] See the volumes of the monthly journal *Payam-e Yar*, which shows that while a number of women contributed to the journal, no *sharif* (noble) woman dared to write under her real name; instead, they signed their works *shaira purdanashin* or *hizab*. Prostitutes, though, wrote under their real names, along with a pen name.

[51] Nagendra K. Singh (ed.), *Encyclopedia of Women*, Vol. III (New Delhi: A. P. H. Publishing Corporation, 2001), 267.

[52] ibid., 426.

might have achieved the greatness of Hali or Ghalib. While any woman who dared to break this tradition was considered a *tawaif*, we do find a few examples of women who had done so by participating in *Mushaira.*[53] To sum up, women's contribution to Urdu literature cannot be overlooked; yet another example is that of Zeenat Begum Ibrat, a famous *shaira* of her time who left behind a fine collection of *ghazals*.[54]

During the uprising of 1857, many Mughal princesses took shelter in the Western United Province. Since these women had inherited literary qualities, they did not lose their courage despite the several hurdles in their way, and contributed with great enthusiasm. Among the most prominent was Suraiya Barhi Begum, widow of Mirza Ali Khan, a courtier of Bahadur Shah Zafar, who sheltered in Agra during the mutiny and continued to write, despite the uprising all around.[55] This bold lady dedicated her whole life to literature.

In the late nineteenth century, the Urdu novel became increasingly popular, especially among women. It is probably Akbari Begum, the sister of Nazar Sajjad, who took the first initiative with her novel in 1898. Her second novel, *Gudri Ka Lal* (1904), became so famous that it was soon considered the most suitable gift for new brides.[56] Another famous name was that of Khadijatun Nisa, who was an expert in both languages of the literary world, Arabic and Persian. She wrote *Azkar-e Khawateen* (Sketches of Ladies), which was published in 1847. While women expressed their romantic feelings in *ghazals* and *qasidas*, in prose they expressed their real feelings and contributed to the cause of feminism (as examples, see the novels of Akbari Begum or the stories written by Mohamadi Bagum).[57]

The contribution of the Begums of Oudh and Rampur cannot be overlooked, as many of them were *sahib-e Diwan* and famous *shairas* of their time. The charming wife of Wajid Ali Shah used Sultan Jahan Mahbub as her *takhallus*,

---

[53] Aftab Jahan, an Urdu poetess of Delhi, used to participate in ladies' *Mushairas* held in Delhi (Kausar and Kabir, *Biographical Dictionary*, 7).

[54] ibid., 494.

[55] ibid., 362. Alam Ara Naz was another famous Mughal princess and poetess of Urdu, who lived for several years after the mutiny. See Kausar and Kabir, *Biographical Dictionary*, 71. See also Sughra Mehndi, *Urdu Adab me Delhi Ki Khawateen ka Hissa* (New Delhi: Urdu Academy, 2006), 35.

[56] Susie Tharu and K. Lalita, *Women Writing in India: 600 BC to the Present* (New Delhi: Oxford University Press, 1991), 391.

[57] There was also Zia-I Ahmadi Begum, who composed lyrics in Urdu, Arabic and Persian (Singh, *Encyclopedia of Women*, Vol. III, 496).

and continued with her literary efforts till her death.[58] Another *sahib-e Diwan* Urdu poetess, Alam Begum, was a Mughal princess.[59] The Begums of Rampur were not far behind either, as one of their most famous princesses, Bahu Begum, the wife of Nawab Yusuf Ali Khan, was an Urdu poetess who used Nazim as her *nom de plume*.[60]

While discussing traditional education, one should not forget the *tawa'ifs* of that time. However, in this context a shift needs to be made vis-à-vis the objective of education. Traditional education had two modes: one was prepared by the male *ashra'f* and dealt with educating their womenfolk to manage their homes properly.[61] The second curriculum was prepared by women themselves, and they decided the kind of education they needed to challenge the male-dominated society.[62] A hidden objective here was enabling women to emerge as powerful rulers. To this end, her curriculum had to be different from that of common women. The core curriculum here included dance, music and literature, instead of budget and elementary books. They were taught these courses by prominent teachers in those fields, and participated in *mushairas* along with their male visitors.[63] Mirza Hadi Ruswa skilfully depicted such a talented character in his famous novel *Umrao Jan-e Ada*, where Ada was an institution by herself. In fact, the *tawa'if* of that time was a very important part of *Oudh* culture, so much so that one could not be considered civilised until he had visited a *tawa'if's* salon.

A close analysis of *Payam-e Yar*, a monthly magazine of the nineteenth century, tells us that prominent *tawa'ifs* of the time regularly sent in their *ghazals* and *qaside* for publication. Interestingly, while *ashra'f* women kept their names hidden, the *tawa'ifs* were eager to preserve their identities as independent women, and often wrote under their pen names along with their real names, such as Ada, Umrao, Dilber and Jan. They always mentioned the names of their towns, especially if they hailed from prominent places like Lucknow, Gorakhpur or Badayun. Most prominent amongst them were Waheed Jan Sahiba of Aligarh,

58 ibid., 343.

59 Kausar and Kabir, *Biographical Dictionary*, 13.

60 ibid., 49.

61 See the lineages of Maulvi Nazir Ahmed and Altaf Husain Hali, and the way they depicted their female characters in their novels *Mirat-ul Urus, Banat-ul Nash* and *Majalis-un Nisa*, to educate *ashraf* women.

62 See Ruswa, *Umrao Jan–e Ada*.

63 Veena Talwar Oldenberg, 'Lifestyle as Resistance: The Case of the Courtesans of Lucknow', *Feminist Studies*, 16: 259–87.

Biggan Jan from Lucknow, Sitari Jan from Gorakhpur, Abbasi Jan Ada of Badayun, Sahib Jan from Ghazipur, Bi Ghafuran Jan of Gorakhpur, Umrao Jan Sahiba of Kanpur, and Bi Abiran Jan Sahiba of Unnao. Their *qasida* and *ghazals* are available in *Payam-e Yar*.

The well-known *tawa'if* Zohra Bai of Lucknow was both a famous *shaira* and a skilled calligrapher in *nastaleek*.[64] Sheerin Jaan, a famous Delhi courtesan who was praised by the great poet Altaf Husain Hali in his biography *Hayat-e Javed*, is credited with having written a *Diwan*, which, unfortunately, is no longer available.[65] Khaksari, too, was not far behind.[66] This is why *tawa'ifs* are said to have helped greatly in developing culture through their contributions to literature.

Muslim Social Reformers and the Question of Female Education

Hamida chamki na thi English se jab begana thi
Ab hai shama-e anjuman pahle chirag-khana thi

Akbar Allahabadi[67]

The year 1857 was crucial in the history of Muslim society. After this, British policy with regard to the Muslims left them far behind in the competitive arena. Soon after, there emerged social reformers who tried to reduce the gap between the past and the present. A wave of new thought took over Muslim society, with several questions being raised over every aspect of their lives. The question of female education also merited space till 1870. It is surprising to see that while these reformers agreed on every question related to social evils, they failed to agree on the subject of women's education. One group, under the leadership of Sir Saiyid Ahmed Khan, was convinced that the level of female education amongst Muslims was satisfactory. Interestingly, Sir Saiyid himself had received his initial education at home, his first teacher being his mother before he was provided with an *ustani*. His ideal was his mother, Begum Aziz-un Nisa, who

[64] Schimmel, *Islamic Society and Culture*, 54.

[65] ibid.

[66] Kausar and Kabir, *Biographical Dictionary*, 162. Although Kabir Qausar identified herself as a courtesan, fiction writer Sughra Mehndi has mentioned her as a *purdanashin shareef* woman of Delhi who lived till 1877; see *Urdu Adab me Delhi ki Khawateen ka Hissa*, 33.

[67] Mehndi, *Urdu Adab*, 8.

ran her family very well, despite having received only traditional education at home.[68] She was the perfect mother who excelled in every domestic field, be it the upbringing of her children, or taking care of the household. Moreover, the social structure of Muslim society ordained that a woman's primary task was to manage her home properly. If this requirement could be fulfilled by traditional education, what then was the need for Western education?

However, a detailed study of the document related to Sir Saiyid shows that he held rather contradictory views about female education. Extremely impressed with the *zenana* school at London during his trip in 1869, he expressed his desire to open such a school in India. While on his journey with Miss Mary Carpenter, he spoke in favour of female education in an interview with her, which can be found in her diary.[69] But when the time came to apply these views, he backed out. Although white, Western ways had influenced him for a while, he soon realised the ground realities prevalent in India. He then argued that the status of *ashra'f* Muslim women, whose level of education was quite satisfactory, was better than their male counterparts.[70] One can question his neglect of *ajlaf* women, who were never considered worthy of his attention. It is obvious that they had no access to education of any kind since they were in no position to hire an *ustani*.

When, at a public deliverance in 1884, the women of Gurudaspur wanted Sir Saiyid's go-ahead on female education, he averted the issue cleverly by stating that their status was better than men, and so there was no need to make special arrangements for girls' education. They should restrict themselves to traditional education because the new education was not appropriate for them.[71] In 1882, he had accepted before the Education Commission that the increasing poverty was the major cause behind the declining level of education among Indian Muslim women. He also asserted that contrary to the prevalent notion, *ashra'f* women were not uneducated. He opined:

---

[68] Hali, *Hayat-e Javed*. See also Minault, *Secluded Scholars*.

[69] K.A. Nizami, *Sir Saiyid Ahmed Khan* (New Delhi: Publishing Division, Ministry of Information and Broadcasting, Government of India, 1959), 55, 62. Referring to Miss Mary Carpenter's efforts to improve the condition of women, he wrote, '... to interest one's self in the education of women, whom God hath made as an helpmate to man in good works, is worthy of every praise. To do good in every way is most laudable; as if the foundation is good results must follow.'

[70] Bhattacharya et al. (eds), *Development of Women's Education in India*, 101.

[71] Shaikh Ismail Panipati, *Saiyid Ahmed Ka Safarnama-e Panjab*, Mohemmad Saiyid Iqbal Ali (ed.), (New Delhi: Educational Publishing House, 1979), 142–45.

> The question of female education much resembles the question of the oriental philosopher who asked whether the egg or hen was first created. Those who hold that women should be educated and civilized prior to men are generally mistaken. The fact is that no satisfactory education can be provided to Muslim females until a large number of Muslim males receive a sound education. The present state of education among Muslim female is, in my opinion, enough for domestic happiness, considering the present social and economic condition of the life of the Muslims in India.[72]

It was not only Sir Saiyid, but most other reformers of the time who professed themselves satisfied with the educational status of women. Slowly, though, they changed their stance over this issue, and the matter became a subject of debate during the 1870s and 1880s. Questions began to be raised on issues related to female education in newspapers and conferences,[73] such as: Why is female education necessary? To whom should it be imparted? What should the curriculum be? The significance surrounding its necessity increased after 1875, when the Mohammedan Anglo Oriental College came into existence. Now the emerging educated Muslim youth had to grapple with a new question: What kind of life partner should he get?

This first generation of educated Muslim men in Aligarh raised their voices in support of women's education, stating that *ashra'f* women should be taught in the same way as their male counterparts. Otherwise, these youth threatened, they might just deviate from tradition and begin marrying outside the *ashra'f* circle. Nawab Hasan Khan Bahadur believed that the contemporary youth wished for a wife who was at the same mental level as himself. However, in reality it was difficult to distinguish between a mistress and her maid when it came to their knowledge; it was only their apparel and features that distinguished one from the other. This was also why the spectre of social danger began confronting *ashra'f* Muslims at this juncture—girls from *ajlaf* Muslim families were now getting an education comparable to that received by *ashra'f* girls.[74] It should be noted that these social reformers, all of whom were of *ashraf* origin, were concerned only about the *ashraf* Muslims and the issues faced by

[72] Bhattacharya et al. (eds), *Development of Women's Education in India*, 102.

[73] Nawab Safi-ud Daula, Hisam-ul Mulk, Md. Saiyid Ali, Hasan Khan Bahadur, in Maroof (Journal), MAO College, Aligarh, Haji Md. and Md. Wahid-uddin Salim (eds), 1 May 1899, 343. See also Syed Mehndi Hasan Khan, Speech No. 79, 28 December 1903, Bombay.

[74] ibid., 344–48.

ashraf women, even though they constituted a very small percentage of the Muslim population.

Although Haji Ismail Khan expressed satisfaction over the existing levels of female education, he felt that there was a dire need for girls' schools. He tried to convince the men of his community of the necessity of a *zenana* school for the moral and mental development of girls. While a number of elite girls were being educated at home, they had to contend with a dearth of able female teachers. This vacuum was being filled by missionary women, but *ashra'f* Muslims were not in favour of allowing these women into their homes. They feared that the women were actually proselytisers disguised as educators. Therefore, Haji Ismail suggested the idea of a *zenana* school. He was also progressive enough to consider opening medical education to girls, an issue that a number of his contemporaries refused to accept.[75]

Most of the reformers of the Aligarh movement centred their concern around *ashra'f* women, discussing only those issues that these women faced. They did not worry about *ajlaf* women. In the meantime, a number of Urdu newspapers and magazines had begun publishing views and counterpoints on why female education was necessary for *ajlaf* women, too.[76] It seems that the growing need for educated wives had forced them to rethink their previous notions on women's education.[77] (This could probably explain why the number of literate females increased in the later Census Reports of India.) On the other hand, since *ajlaf / arzal* Muslims were themselves uneducated, they had never felt the need to raise the matter.

The second, and more difficult, question that they grappled with was the age till which education would be continued. What would be the method of teaching and curriculum? They were unable to fix any age limit on education; it would not be wrong to assume that adult education was in practice, since

[75] The Aligarh Movement: Basic Documents, Haji Md. Ismail Khan, 671–72.

[76] *The Aligarh Institute Gazette*, 18 July 1871, quoted in The Aligarh Movement: Basic Documents, Abstract of a letter from a European lady, 386.

[77] Haji Ismail expressed his fear that the youth would want to marry wives who had been instructed in the same language; and if this intention of theirs was thwarted, they would take wives from other communities, thereby harming the Muslim community (The Aligarh Movement: Basic Documents, 671). See also Minault, *Secluded Scholars*, 215. The goal confronting the men involved in the movement for women's education among Indian Muslims was to create women who would be better wives, better mothers, and better Muslims.

many women who had been denied education in childhood were taught by their husbands after marriage. Several scholars were of the opinion that women should be educated in home management as well as be given vocational education; after all, it was a woman's professional skills that would help her in her misfortune, not her bookish knowledge. A debate related to female education was started in the *Islamic Anjuman*, too, with everyone opining that while women should be educated, the curriculum should make sure that they gained knowledge of both domestic work and handicrafts, as women were not supposed to work outside their homes.[78]

Yet another group, this time comprising Urdu authors and poets, helped to bring the women's question into the limelight. Most prominent amongst them was Maulvi Nazir, who demanded equal treatment for boys and girls. He asked the men of his community whether knowledge was meant to reform, or give rise to greater deviance. If knowledge is seen to corrupt, its spread should be halted.[79] Nazir did not believe that girls should be educated with a view to their taking up a profession; however, he did believe that they should be prepared to earn their living, should the need arise. This was why they needed a home management course, along with vocational knowledge. His idea of what constituted vocational knowledge can be traced to the book *Banat-ul Nash*, where the author provides a detailed account of how girls could learn handicrafts, stitching, sewing and embroidery.[80] In fact, Nazir was the first to present the plan of Wardha education, to which Mahatma Gandhi later attached a broader meaning. In his opinion, both husband and wife ought to be educated for an ideal marriage.

Altaf Husain Hali, too, was in favour of female education. Hali always believed that for progress to take place, one half of our population should not be overlooked and deprived of knowledge. In 1874, he wrote his famous novel *Majalis-un Nisa*, which was part of the school syllabus for decades in Punjab and the United Province. In the book, he raised several burning issues in the form of a conversation, against the backdrop of a women's assembly. His heroine, Atoji, headed this assembly, and inclucated awareness among *ashraf* women

[78] Maulvi Nazir presented his views on vocational education for girls on several occasions during his lecture in Anjuman-e Islam–e Hind, and also provided a pictorial form to his thoughts in *Mirat-ul Uroos* and *Banat-ul Nash*.

[79] Nazir, *Mirat-ul Uroos*.

[80] Nazir Ahmad, *Banat-ul Nash* (New Delhi: Qaumi Council Barae Farog Urdu Zabaan, 2007), 5, 18–19.

through literature and education. If a *tota* and *maina* can increase their worth by remembering words, then why would you depriving your better halves?[81] He believed that all evil customs and superstitions practised in society could be abolished, and awareness brought to the womenfolk. Hali had a different education plan in mind, which also included a fresh course for the new education system. He placed equal emphasis on cooking, home management, washing and sewing, as well as on math, literature, history, geography and religious education.[82]

Several alumni of the Aligarh school tried to draw the attention of the public through their Urdu writings. Prominent among them was Saiyid Iftikhar Bilgrami. In his book *Vaqeel-e Niswa*, he represented himself as an advocate for women's needs, and emphasised the need for female education. He asked whether the union of man and woman completed a person; and if so, then the question as to whether education was required for women is needless as asking whether it is necessary for men.[83]

By the 1890s, this debate amongst reformers led them to think about female education as being essential for the progress of the *Qaum*. Therefore, they also realised the importance of opening schools for girls. On the recommendation of Khawaja Ghulam Saqlain and Qaramat Husain, the sixth session of the Mohammedan Educational Conference of 1891 accepted Resolution No. 2. This resolution accepted that in contemporary times, it was essential to provide the same education to both Muslim men and women. On 17 November 1896, the Central Standing Committee of Aligarh passed Resolution No. 1, under which a separate section for female education was established. Maulvi Karamat Husain was selected as its president. Thus, a department for women (*shoba-e Niswa*) came into existence by 1898.[84]

By the end of the nineteenth century, the stage was set for the opening of the first systematic Women's College (in 1906) in Aligarh, through the efforts of Shaikh Abdullah and his wife Begum Waheed Jahan. After long discussions and efforts by Indian Muslims, it became necessary to discuss possible government initiatives in this regard.

---

[81] Majalis-un Nisa, 98.

[82] ibid.

[83] Saiyid Iftikhar Bilgrami, *Vakeel-e Niswa* (Aligarh: Institute Press, 1907). His book *Talim-e Niswa* won a prize at the select ommittee of *talim –e Niswa* in December 1899.

[84] Husain, *Sir Saiyid aur unka Ahad.*

Formal Education

It is important to mention that after 1858, there was a demonstrable change in the attitudes and policies of the missionaries. Christian missionaries wanted to support the cause of education, but with a difference. Missionaries of the day believed Christianity to be more rational than any other religion; as such, they reasoned that through education, they would be able to teach more people about Christianity.[85] By this time, the missionaries had realised the failure of their approach vis-à-vis the higher-caste Indians, and so turned their attention to the lower castes.

This chapter is concerned with the progress of education among Indian Muslim women in the United Provinces, where the population of Muslims during this period was 14.3 per cent.[86] The Muslim population was spread over both rural and urban areas.[87] Their economic position gradually began declining, corresponding to the decline in the number of Muslims holding land and in government service.[88]

The upsurge of 1857 saw the destruction of several schools that had been opened for girls under the recommendation of the Wood Dispatch of 1854.[89] Schools run by missionaries were also destroyed. After 1858, realising the people's disinclination to send their daughters to such schools, the British administration expressed their concern for the education of the native *zenana*. The local population, who adhered to the system of *purdah*, were averse to sending their daughters outdoors.[90] The administration thus also realised the

---

[85] Sharma, *Christian Missions in North India*, 43, 162. The primary vocation of the missionaries was evangelism; regardless of whether they opened schools, hospitals, or undertook social programmes, conversion of non-Christians remained their sole aim.

[86] Census Report of India, NWP of Agra and Oudh (henceforth CR), 1901, by R. Burn, Government Press, Allahabad, 1902.

[87] CR, 1891, by D.C. Belly, Government Press, Allahabad, 1893.

[88] Francis Robinson's analysis shows that while Muslims in the United Provinces of that period were happy enough, contemporary Muslim scholars, particularly Sir Saiyid Ahmed Khan (in *Asbab-e Baghawat Hind*) and Altaf Husain Hali (*Maddo Jazr-e Islam*), expressed great concern over the deteriorating condition of Muslims.

[89] Bhattacharya et al. (eds), *Development of Women's Education in India*.

[90] Report on Public Instruction in the State of Oudh, 1877. The *purdah* system put an end to all earnest teaching besides shutting down inspections, too, as the Deputy Inspectress could only visit those few schools located in Lucknow or nearby. The closing down of seven schools in the western circle and the opening of three new

need to appoint female teachers. While the government was trying to meet these local challenges, the Christian missionaries opened a few *zenana* schools in the cities.[91] However, local response to such advances was weak because of the people's fear that attendance in these schools would lead to conversion.[92]

The debate on issues related to female education continued for a few years and ultimately, in 1868, government officers decided to open normal *zenana* schools in Lucknow.[93] The main objective of these schools was to provide *zenana* teachers for native girls. A European female inspector was appointed to supervise these schools. The *zenana* school was set up to train female native teachers for posts in other women's schools.[94] Surprisingly, the normal *zenana* schools sometimes had only Muslim students enrolled.[95] In the initial year, the school functioned as an experiment.[96] While enrolment fluctuated, in 1868 the number of girls enrolled in the training school was twenty.[97] In 1881–82, this dropped to only seven who had passed their examination.[98] However, the number soon reached nineteen in 1891.[99]

Another *zenana* school was opened in Faizabad, but this school later divided into two because of a dispute that had arisen among the mistresses. This affected the enrolment of girls.[100] However, despite all shortcomings the school at Faizabad progressed well because of the individual effort put in by Miss Reuthor,

---

ones in the eastern reduced the net loss to four. 'It is hoped that we may gradually make up this loss; but until the problem as to how efficient teachers, male or female can be trained has been solved; it would be premature to extend present operation.'

[91] Bhattacharya et al. (eds), *Development of Women's Education in India*, 131.

[92] *The Aligarh Institute Gazette*, 13 March 1894. In a letter, Haji Md. Ismail disclosed the apprehension of Muslims regarding the missionary agencies working in India.

[93] Home Education, 1868, 31 October, File No. 3–4. A Normal school had been opened in Lucknow with twenty pupils, costing Rest. 120 per mensem; extracted from W. Handford, Esquire, M.A., Director of Public Instruction, Oudh, to the Secretary to the Chief Commissioner of Oudh, No. 678, dated Lucknow, 3 September.

[94] ibid. The Report states that the Inspectress would be given immediate charge of the two normal schools.

[95] Bhattacharya et al. (eds), *Development of Women's Education in India*, 58. At the time, the normal *zenana* school at Lucknow trained only Muslim women.

[96] Home: Education, 678, Lucknow, 3 September. The school was opened as an experiment and accordingly sanctioned in the first instance for one year.

[97] ibid.

[98] Bhattacharya et al. (eds), *Development of Women's Education in India*, 141.

[99] Home: Education, General Table III, 1891.

[100] Bhattacharya et al. (eds), *Development of Women's Education in India*, 58.

who possessed a good knowledge of Urdu.[101] The school in Lucknow, though, had a different experience. Operating at the mercy of the local population, it faced a lot of difficulties at a very early stage. The local people wanted their daughters to go to school in covered palanquins, and demanded that the school not be inspected by male inspectors. Surprisingly, this last demand was also supported by the female teachers of the school.[102] It was soon realised that conveyance was more expensive than the tuitions![103]

While the government's efforts were commendable, the local response in Lucknow was feeble. Even with the provision of covered palanquins, attendance was generally poor.[104] The government alleged that both Hindus and Muslims were deliberately depriving their women of the new education, for they feared that education might emancipate them.[105] As a result, the British government changed its policy and decided to open such schools in the interior parts of the province, that is, in remote villages. It was also assumed that these schools would be cheaper to maintain.[106] At this juncture, Handford expressed astonishment that a sensible native would deprive his daughters of enlightenment on such grounds.[107]

At this time, a communal divide came to dominate women's education in the United Provinces. The Handford Report suggested that a separate national school for Hindus be set up on grounds of religion, as they did not wish to send their daughters to the same school as Muslims.[108] In this way, he linked

---

[101] Home: Education, 678, 3 September 1868.

[102] Home Department: Education, 1868, proceeding 31, October, File No. 3–4. In September 1868, Mr Handford submitted a report stating that the education of girls in Oudh was beset with difficulties. 'Here not only do school mistresses object to male inspection even from behind screen, and of whose condition I can form but the faintest idea.'

[103] ibid.

[104] Home: Education, 1868, proceedings, 31 October, F.N. 3–4, from the Chief Commissioner of Oudh, No. 3843, dated 10 September.

[105] Bhattacharya et al. (eds), *Development of Women's Education in India*, 59.

[106] ibid., 59–61.

[107] Mr Handford stated that he 'really cannot see how any sensible native can object to government opening female school'; however, the greatest outcry and opposition would certainly have been raised by those natives who were not what Mr Handford would term 'sensible', and there was no question that this would certainly retard the movement. Home: Education, Proceeding 1868, 31 October F.N. 3–4, N03843, dated 10 September.

[108] Home: Education, from W. Handford, Esquir, M.A., Director of Public Instruction Oudh, to Secretary to the Chief Commissioner of Oudh, No. 678, dated Lucknow, 3 September 1868.

the question of nationalism with Hindus, while the school for Muslim girls was repeatedly termed the '*zenana* school'. However, despite the government's efforts to establish communally segregated female schools, the enrolment of Hindu women remained low, while that of Muslim women showed an increase.

The normal school did a creditable job of producing native instructresses. These female instructors could now be engaged to teach *purdanasheen* girls who had never been to school,[109] thereby encouraging some Muslim girls from well-to-do *ashra'f* families. These girls required both traditional education and the new education, which until then was considered appropriate only for men. The curriculum had changed; it now included history, geography and elementary math.[110] However, despite these developments, an enquiry committee set up by the government expressed discontent with the result. Although at some schools girls continued to learn the alphabet for two to three years, sometimes they left school while still in the process of learning the alphabet.[111]

It is interesting to see that the girls admitted to such schools were drawn from the lower stratum of Muslim society. Only in Lucknow and Faizabad did *ashra'f* girls find a presence, primarily due to the availability of covered palanquins.[112] In

---

[109] ibid. 'I proposed, in first instance to invite respectable natives to select candidate for the national schools whom they could be willing to admit to their *zenana* to teach their female relatives.'

[110] ibid. 'Expecting the Normal School the studies are confined to reading, writing, sewing and little arithmetic .... On admission they could barely read but the first class can now read and write very fairly, are well acquainted with the geography of Asia, know the fair simple and compound rules in arithmetic and Indian History.'

[111] Bhattacharya et al. (eds), *Development of Women's Education*, 69–70. See also Report of Public Instruction in the State of Oudh for the year 1876.

> I visited a considerable number of girls school last year, many of them, more especially those in villages, are taught by old man of local influence, either *maulvis or pandits* according as pupils are either Mohammedan or Hindu, for the two castes very seldom mix in girls schools as they do in boy's schools. The teacher can teach nothing but reading and writing, and do not understand management after our methods. Sewing or fancy work is of course, quite out of their sphere, by the Deputy and Circle Inspector fears to replace them by better teachers, as it was only by influence possessed by these old man that a school could be conducted at all, and if they were now removed and a stranger put in their place, the school would break up.

[112] Home: Education, from W. Handford, Esquire, M.A., Director of Public Instruction, Oudh, to the Secretary to the Chief Commissioner of Oudh, No. 678, dated Lucknow, 3 September 1868. 'Social status of the pupils; they are principally poor, though in Lucknow and Faizabad belonging to classes who are socially respected. The wealthy hold aloof from movement.'

other cities where this facility was unavailable, only girls from the lower classes (*ajla'f*) were enrolled in schools. Statistics show that in Faizabad, all the girls were from *ashra'f* families, daughters of *Maulvis* and masters, with only twenty girls from the servant class.[113]

Also, after 1870 schools were established in cities other than Lucknow and Faizabad. We have the example of two *zenana* schools, one in Partabgarh in Nawabganj district, managed by the Deputy Inspector of schools, Munshi Mohammad Husain. In 1878, the number of girls attending this school regularly was thirteen.[114] The second school was opened by Munshi Zaqa Ullah in Bulandshahar for widows.[115] By 1875, 100 *zenana* schools had been opened, and of these, eighty-one were under direct government control, sixteen were aided by the government, and three were private.[116] It is surprising to see that enrolment in government schools had dropped by 1875. The Government Report suggested that enrolments dropped because of the death, resignation and transfer of teachers. It also attributed the decline to the arrival of new teachers; Indians did not like sending their daughters to be taught by a teacher who was a stranger.[117] However, a large number of schools were opened by Indians. As a result, after 1875, growing consciousness with regard to female education began developing among *ashra'f* Muslims. Some people from both communities supported the cause of female education,[118] and there were people who preferred to send their daughters to these non-government schools. The Reports of the Education Department of 1876 accepted that the good management of native schools was an important factor in encouraging greater enrolment. At the

[113] ibid. The girls numbered twenty in 1868, and had dropped to sixteen by 1870. See also A. P. Howell, *Education in British India, 1870–71* (Calcutta, 1872).

I may remark here that at Faizabad, where the palanquin expenditure is the most extravagant, 54 of the students are the children of government servants, about 27 belongs to the trading classes, and 26 are the children of private servants. I should say that the majority of these girls ought to be able to walk to school.

[114] Gazetteer of the Province of Oudh, Vol. III, N-Z, Allahabad, NWP and Oudh Government Press, 1878, 136.

[115] *Aligarh Magazine*, Khawateen Number, 2001, Aligarh Muslim University, Aligarh, 33.

[116] Bhattacharya et al. (eds), *Development of Women's Education*, 65.

[117] ibid.

[118] *Oudh Akhbar*, 28 July 1868. Wali-e Rampur had opened a school for native women. See also Home: Education, 1891, Simla Records, Proceedings; February Nos 18–52, No. 28 from W.C. Banett, Esq., Secretary to the government of the NWP of Agra and Oudh. There had been a slight rise in the number of girls in aided schools under private management.

time, the native Urdu school of Mirajganj of Malihabad was declared the best school by the education department. Some literary missions had also become active around this time, and they extended their dynamic ties into the village. These institutes, *maulvis* and *pandits* ran the schools for women. However, the performance of these schools was not satisfactory.[119]

The environment surrounding women's education changed by 1880. Several women discarded the *purdah* and freely participated in prize distribution ceremonies in schools (earlier, prizes were accepted from behind screens), and even appearing without their *purdahs* before the male inspector.[120] By 1876, a need was felt to revise the curriculum for female students. More books in vernacular languages were now to be included in the curriculum. The help of the vernacular society was sought, and the curriculum now included books such as *Mirat-ul Uroos* and *Majalis-un Nisa.*[121]

By the 1880s, the question of women's education had become a burning issue among Muslim scholars.[122] Surprisingly, Muslim girls maintained their presence in government schools in large numbers. A similar increase was recorded in the Islamic *Anjumans*, too. Progressive Urdu writers began a campaign for the education of women.[123] The government invited several prominent Muslim

---

[119] Bhattacharya et al. (eds), *Development of Women's Education*, 65.

[120] ibid. See also Report on Public Instruction in the State of Oudh for the year 1876.

> At the large school in Malihabad the girls were carefully screened from the view of the Deputy Inspector and myself, and no one but the Deputy Inspectress was admitted behind the veil, but as soon as the examination was over, and prizes had been distributed, the girls impatient for their liberty, came out from behind the *'purda'* and passed us without betraying any symptoms of fear. About a year ago, even the Deputy Inspectress, a native lady, was refused admission behind the *'purda'* in some of the school in her circle.

[121] ibid.

> A new programme is drawn up, which it is hoped, when the new books and edition are ready, will not be found either beyond the capacities of the most of the teachers or repulsive to the students. History and Geography in the prospectus are most entirely set aside; but arithmetic and writing are both insisted on, especially the latter.

[122] Most prominent among those who took part in the debate were Nawab Mohsin-ul Mulk, Saiyid Mehndi Hasan Khan, Maulvi Nazir, Altaf Husain Hali, Saiyid Husain Bilgrami, Haji Md. Ismail Khan and Mumtaz Ali. It is noteworthy that most were first-generation students of MAO College or the Delhi School. Urdu newspapers, such as *Oudh Akhbar*, *Oudh Panch* and *Rafiq-e Hind*, also played a pivotal role in spreading awareness of female education.

[123] The *Anjuman Himayat-e Islam* and the Mohammedan Educational Conference raised this issue.

social reformers and educationists to endorse women's education before the education commission. It is astonishing to note that the most progressive leader of Muslims, Sir Saiyid Ahmed Khan, demonstrated his reluctance with regard to the education of women, and expressed doubt over its success. However, despite such misgivings, Muslim women continued to turn to education.

Again, the issue of the curriculum for women was raised by both the government and the reformers. A suggestion was made to retain the same curriculum for both boys and girls. For girls, needlework was added, along with moral education. However, the content of moral education was defined separately for both genders. Indians did not want moral lessons that inculcate boldness and a spirit of leadership to be imparted to women. Women, it was suggested, need remain only virtuous.[124]

In 1888–89, 3,088 Muslim girls were enrolled in primary classes; in the following year, though, the number dropped to 2,669. This was probably because a large number of Muslim girls were enrolled in private schools, and this was not included in the Education Department[125] (see Table 5.1).

Table 5.1: Nunber of Educated Muslim Women in Government Schools

Year	*European and Native Christian*		*Hindus*		*Muslims*	
	Primary	*Secondary*	*Primary*	*Secondary*	*Primary*	*Secondary*
1888–89	916	1,744	5,490	13	3,088	15
1889	1,188	2,275	5,518	17	2,669	18

Source: Home: Education, 1891 (NAI, New Delhi)

In 1890, the enrolment of Muslim girls in the English Secondary School increased to nineteen, and there were 524 girls over 64,479 Muslim boys in the Vernacular Secondary School. At times, the number of Muslim girls in the Vernacular Primary School was 19,045, while the total number of boys was 511,084. In Training School, Muslim girls numbered nineteen. One thousand, two hundred and eight-one Muslim girls were enrolled in elementary teaching in the vernacular language, 8,627 in the teaching of the Quran, and 212 were enrolled in unspecified classes.[126] It is remarkable to see *ashra'f* Muslim girls dominating over both *ajla'f* and Hindus girls (see Table 5.2). It is because of this that *ashra'f* Muslims had been reaping most of the benefits in the United

[124] Bhattacharya et al. (eds), *Development of Women's Education*, 133.

[125] Home: Education, 1891, Simla Records, Proceedings: February, Nos 18–52, No. 28, from W.C. Benett.

[126] Home: Education, 1891, General Table III.

Provinces;[127] therefore, it is clear that the socio-economic factor in Muslim society determined the position of their women, too. Also, marital conditions were favourable among *ashra'f* Muslims, with child marriage being rare.[128] This can perhaps explain the greater number of literate Muslim women among the 15–20 age group (see Table 5.3).

Table 5.2: Number of Muslim Women per 100 Women by Caste

Group and Caste	*Learning*		*English*		*Other Language and Total 1891*	
	1921	*1891*	*1921*	*1891*		
Rajput Muslim	-	0.02	-	-	0.13	100
Julaha	0.28	0.014	0.003	-	0.043	100
Muslim Artisan and Village	-	0.01	0.00	-	0.03	"
Menial	-	0.01	-	-	0.03	"
Bhangi	-	0.14	0.13	-	0.45	"
Non Indian Asiatic Race	3.8					"

Source: CR of 1891, 262; CR of 1921, 87

Table 5.3: Literacy Rate of Women per 100 Literate Women

Age	*Hindu Women*				*Muslim Women*			
	Literate		*English*		*Literate*		*English*	
	1921	*1931*	*1911*	*1931*	*1911*	*1931*	*1911*	*1931*
All Age	51.9	63.2	28.1	33.25	8.7	20.92	3.8	6.21
0–10	55.98	63.44	21.84	33.54	9.7	19.11	3.2	6.6
10–15	55.68	63.9	35.24	36.27	8.97	20.45	3.88	7.49
15–20	64.53	63.87	34.88	36.6	8.45	34.74	4.45	8.88
20 and above	50.19	62.80	25.15	47.38	8.53	20.98	8.53	7.88

Source: CR of 1921, 120; CR of 1931, 150.
Note: All percentages have been drawn by me

[127] They held 35 per cent of the entire government service. Robinson, *Separatism Among Indian Muslims*, 22–23.

[128] Mohammedans of better classes usually married around the ages of seventeen or eighteen, while girls and boys from the poorer classes married earlier, around fourteen. CR of India, 1911, Government Press Allahabad, Allahabad, 1912, 227. The CR of 1901 points out that this was strictly adhered to in the eastern United Province, which is a point worth making, as the lower castes resided mostly in the east. See CR of India, 1901, Allahabad, 1902.

Besides, the *ashra'f* Muslims were more urbanised.[129] Traditional education had been commonly imparted among them for a long time, and it was not long before they took to the new education too.[130] Also, all the social and religious reform movements were active in the western United Province, where most Muslims enjoyed a good socio-economic status.[131] Although two-fifths of Muslim women lived in the western United Province, the large number of Muslim women included in the illiterate category in the Census Report is startling, given that a large number of Muslim women had received traditional education, and knew how to read and write.[132] In 1891, only 0.59 per cent of women were literate, and so *ashra'f* women could not even reach the 1 per cent literacy rate. It was generally acknowledged that no Muslim woman could read or write English, despite there being plenty of evidence showing that they used to write letters in English, too.[133]

Thus, the colonial period presumed a very low literacy rate among women in general, despite a great number of Muslim women being literate. Also, their literacy growth rate was better than that of Muslim men (see Tables 5.4 and 5.5). Although a knowledge of English was not common amongst women in general, more Muslim than Hindu women knew English.

This also shows a regional variation in the literacy rate. In the United Provinces, geographic, economic, and other disparities make it difficult to consider the entire United Province one unit. In the west United Province and central United Province, Muslims belonged to a better social class (either the landed class or related to the service gentry), and were numerically stronger compared to Muslims in eastern United Province, who were mostly poor,

---

[129] CR of India, NWP of Agra and Oudh, 1881, W. White, Allahabad Government Press, Allahabad.

[130] Gail Minault's analysis shows this tendency of *ashra'f* women to be educated at home (Minault, *Secluded Scholars*).

[131] CR of India, 1901.

[132] Education Commission: Report by the NWP and Oudh Provincial Committee and Memorial Address to the Education Commission, Calcutta, 1884. In this report, it was accepted that it was a custom among well-to-do and respected Muslim families to employ tutors to instruct their girls in the Holy Quran, and in elementary theological books written in Urdu. Sometimes a father, or brother, or some other close kinsman taught them to write in Urdu, and occasionally imparted instruction in Persian.

[133] CR of India, NWP of Agra and Oudh, 1891, Allahabad, 1892, 262. During this period, Sir Saiyid too agreed before the Education Commission that there were Muslim girls who had learnt how to write in English.

Table 5.4: Education with Traditional Language

Age Group	*No. out of 10,000 Literate*				*Urdu Only*		*Hindi Only*		*Urdu and Hindi; Knowing Urdu Better*		*Urdu and Hindi; Knowing Hindi Better*		*Other Language*		*No. out of 10,000 Literate in English*		*Female to 10,000 Muslim Males*	
	Total	*Male*	*Female*	*H*	*M*	*H*	*M*	*H*	*M*	*H*	*M*	*H*	*M*	*H*	*M*	*H*	*Literate*	*Lit. in Eng.*
0–10	34	59	7	3	5	-	1	3	-	-	-	-	1	-	-	-	1,081	191
10–15	238	407	31	15	25	1	2	13	-	-	-	-	4	1	-	-	627	33
15–20	417	742	48	29	39	1	5	25	1	1	-	-	3	2	1	1	582	83
20 and above	393	752	33	19	26	1	3	16	1	-	1	1	2	1	-	-	439	67
Total	282	526	27	15	20	1	3	13	1	-	1	1	2	1	-	-	493	69

Source: CR of 1901, 162–63, Subsidiary Table 1.

Table 5.5: Education by Age, Sex and Religion

Religion and Age Period	*No. per Mille who were Literate*			*No. per 10,000 who were Literate in English*		
All Religion	*Person*	*Male*	*Female*	*Person*	*Male*	*Female*
All Ages	42	74	7	44	75	10
5–10	9	14	3	7	9	4
10–15	39	162	9	31.5	47.1	10.9
15–20	57	93	12	76.9	124.7	16.3
20 and above	49	90	7	51.3	90	10
Muslims All Ages	43	74	8	50	92	3.8
5–10	8	12	3	3	6	0.6
10–15	35	54	10	26.7	14.7	3.0
15–20	54	87	14	83.4	14.7	5.7
20 and above	53	94	9	62.3	117.5	3.0
Hindu All Ages	39	70	5	29	53	2
5–10	8	13	3	2	4	5
10–15	37	60	7	21.3	35.7	2.3
15–20	54	89	9	56.3	97.5	4.1
20 and above	46	81	2	33.3	63.1	2.0

Source: CR of 1921, 120.

landless, and belonged to a lower social order.[134] In eastern United Province, social hierarchy was flexible. Government and missionary schools were very popular among the poorer classes. As such, in the western United Province the literacy rate was lower, compared to the east, as the hierarchical nature of their society restricted them from attending school after a certain age. This probably explained why Muslim women of the eastern United Province and Bundelkhand were considered more literate (see Table 5.6).

As far as district-level literacy was concerned, it was greatest in Benares district, where literate Muslim women numbered were 61 per 10,000 in 1901. District Lucknow (fifty-six) came next, followed by Agra (fifty-six) and Allahabad (fifty-five)[135] (see Table 5.7).

[134] CR of India, 1901, 154.

[135] ibid., 154, 120, 173, Subsidiary Table VIII.

Table 5.6: No. of Literate at per Mille (for 1901): Education of Women by Religion and Natural Division

Region	*1901*				*1921*		
	Total	*Male*	*Female*	*H. Female*	*Male*	*Female*	*H. Female*
NWP and Oudh	282	527	27	15	74	8	5
1. Himalaya West	334	552	26	15	100	17	7
2. Sub Him. West	197	358	24	16	59	7	5
3. Ind. Gangetic Plain West	231	420	25	17	65	9	7
4. Ind. Gangetic Plain Central	371	706	36	14	96	9	5
5. Central India Pateu	495	951	39	10	141	13	4
6. Sub Him. East	232	448	11	12	42	4	4
7. Ind. Gangetic Plain East	423	841	41	20	128	15	7
8. East Satpura	335	644	34	21	101	3	5
9. Tehri Garhwal	334	653	13	8	38	-	2
10. Rampur	144	273	14	12	49	5	4

Source: CR of 1901, 165–66, Sub. Table II; CR of 1921, 122.

Table 5.7: Literate at per 10,000 for 19 Cities in 1901

City	*Muslim*	*Hindu*
Agra	96	78
Allahabad	127	236
Bareilly	197	224
Benares	104	260
Cawnpur	136	83
Farukhabad	97	151
Fyzabad	64	98
Gorakhpur	39	286
Hathras	28	32
Jaunpur	53	115
Jhansi	94	95
Koil	33	53
Lucknow	134	110
Meerut	72	27
Marzipan	112	89
Moradabad	71	226
Muttra	29	173
Saharanpur	33	122
Shahjahanpur	189	118

Source: Census Report of India, North Western Province of Agra and Oudh, 1901, Allahabad.

The number of Muslim women who could read and write English came to eighty-nine, even though they accounted for only 14.3 per cent of the entire population.[136] Muslim women were more likely to learn English at a relatively later age. As Muslim women were more inclined towards home education, they often learnt English from their fathers, brothers, husband, or other close male relatives. Sometimes they even hired Christian missionaries or European lady tutors to learn English[137] (see Table 5.8).

Table 5.8

	No. of Literate Women in 100 Women				*Literate in English Per 100 Women*			
	Hindu		*Muslim*		*Hindu*		*Muslim*	
	1921	*1931*	*1921*	*1931*	*1921*	*1931*	*1921*	*1931*
All	52	62.4	8.7	20.1	2.4	3.9	0.33	0.73
0–10	41.7	63.4	8.12	19.1	1.5	2.7	0.22	0.53
10–15	62	64	9	20.5	2.7	4.9	7	1
15–20	64.5	64	8.5	22.2	3.1	7.2	0.38	1.75
20 and above	50.2	62.8	12.6	21	2.23	4.6	0.32	0.72

Source: CR of 1921, 72–74; CR of 1931, 450.

Women were gradually moving towards professional education, along with traditional and formal education. In 1885, the establishment of the Lady Dufferin Fund cleared the way for women to enter medical colleges. While no woman in the province was considered eligible for admission to the MBBS or any other equivalent degree, several women from both communities took two or three-year diploma courses to become midwives, nurses, hospital assistants, and *da'is* at the Agra Medical College and other places. In 1889, eight Muslim women out of nineteen were enrolled in diploma courses. It is important to note that these women (neither Hindu nor Muslim) did not belong to the high castes[138] (see Table 5.9). This was almost certainly because high-caste families

[136] ibid. It was highest for Lucknow (eighty), Agra (fifty-six) and Allahabad (fifty-five).

[137] Haikh Abdullah, *Sawan-e Hayat Beghum Abdullah* (Aligarh, 1951). Beghum Abdullah was taught by her father and a European tutor, and became a staunch advocate of female education.

[138] Annual Report of Dufferin Fund, Vth Annual Report, 1889, 157–59. See also *The Araya Darpan*, January 1894. As a result, it was decided to pass a resolution in favour of women's education at the Mohammedan Educational Conference, 1896.

regarded medicine as a profession that would contaminate their social standing. As such, this profession was considered appropriate only for low-born women or widows.[139]

Table 5.9

Year	*No. Joining the Agra Medical College*		
	Hindu	*Muslim*	*Total*
1885	7	1	19
1886	17	3	42
1887	3	6	21
1888	3	-	9

Source: The Countess of Dufferin's Fund, Vth Annual Report, 157–59.

The efforts put in by the Aligarh Movement in the literacy mission were noteworthy. It was in the 1890s that MAO College produced a number of Muslim graduates. These graduates demanded educated wives, which helped the spread of education among high-caste Indian Muslim women.[140] This could perhaps also explain why the MAO College graduates expressed concern over the ignorance of *ashra'f* women. In her analysis in *The Growth of Education and Political Development in India, 1898–1920* (1974), Aparna Basu stated that Muslims in the Province were a mainly urbanised, non-agricultural community and relatively well-to-do, and were ahead of Hindus in the field of education.[141]

[139] *The Jam-e Uloom*, Moradabad, 28 February 1897.

[140] As a result, it was decided to pass a resolution in favour of women at the Mohammedan Educational Conference, 1896.

[141] Aparna Basu, *The Growth of Education and Political Development in India, 1898–1920* (New Delhi: Oxford University Press, 1974), 150.

CHAPTER 6

Patriarchy and Social Obligation of Indian Muslim Women

Agosh madar voh school hai pahla
Jahan Tarbiat pate hai sare ezaa
Jahan looh sad ape khichta hai naksha
Utarta hai maa ke khayalon ka charba

Altaf Husain Hali[1]

Several myths and stories tell of women's resistance to male-dominated society. In any discussion on gender, aspects of patriarchy and caste hierarchy—particularly in the Indian context—cannot be overlooked. Janaki Nair connected these two factors with the legal rights of Indian women.[2] Patriarchy often perceives women as merely sources of entertainment and child-producing machines.

This chapter explores the diverse shades of the lives of Indian Muslim women. Indian Muslims lead lives that are very similar to Hindus in most respects, especially vis-à-vis customs and living conditions. A number of local customs, not inscribed in the Quran, prevail among Indian Muslim—*chhatti, chilla, manjha, rasm-e mehndi, chauthi, soem;* and some obligations such as *aqiqa, khatna bismillah khawani* and *aameen.*[3] Some *ashra'f* Muslims practised only

[1] Sughra Mehndi, *Urdu Adab men Khawateen Ka Hissa* (New Delhi: Urdu Academy, 2006), 97.

[2] Janaki Nair, *Women and Law in Colonial India* (Bangalore: National School of Indian University, 1996), 59.

[3] *Rasoom-e Hind*, 129; Ashraf Ali Thanvi, *Behisht-e Zewar* (New Delhi: New A. S. Press, 1994), 299–334.

those customs inscribed in the Quran and Sunnah.[4] The dearth of evidence on *ajlaf* and *arzal* girls (save what is available in European accounts and oral history) creates a problem: How are they to be depicted in writing? A number of patriarchal folk songs sung on different occasions reflect how these were celebrated in Muslim families, and what the status of women in society was.

Bara baras beti palna jhulaya ab na jhulaya jae ....

The birth of a girl child has never been considered either a disgrace or a burden in Muslim families,[5] but it is never welcomed as enthusiastically as the birth of a male child. Women would even wear *taweez* and *ganda* in the hope of conceiving a son. The birth of a boy was celebrated with ceremonies like *chatti* and *chilla.* Pathans, especially, placed great emphasis on sons. The famous theatre artiste Zohra Segal[6] spoke about her own patriarchal family and how she had to suffer when her younger brother was born:

> The most dramatic event of this period was the birth of my brother at Dehradun, when I was three years old.[7] The doors of my parent's bedroom were locked and I was wandering around listlessly on the verandah of the bungalow, completely unaware of the situation, when Anna Bua (my mother's nurse and then ours) pounced on me from behind and said, 'It's a boy! Let me break this coconut on your back for being auspicious in having a brother born after you!' I bent down as instructed and heard a coconut lying on the floor, with its milk spilt all over, and back! And then I heard two gun shots and the flapping and shrieking of parrots as they flew away from the guava trees. Later I learnt that the gun salute was an established custom with Pathan at the birth of a son.[8]

---

[4] Gail Minault, *Secluded Scholar: Women's Education and Muslim Social Reform in Colonial India* (New Delhi: Oxford University Press, 1998). See also Abdul Halim Nadvi, *The Musalman* (Lucknow: Islamic Research and Publication, 1977), 19–68; Thanvi, *Behisht-e Zewar,* 308.

[5] The birth of a girl was not considered a burden especially among *sharif* groups.

[6] She was descended from Quas Abdul Rashid, who was supposed to have accepted Islam from the hand of the Prophet Muhammad (PBUH). One of his descendants migrated to India in 1769 and settled in Rampur. They were Barka Zai Rohilla Patha, a branch of the Daulat Zai clan of the Yusuf Zai tribe. See Zohra Segal, *Close-Up* (New Delhi: Women Unlimited, 2010), 14–17.

[7] She was born in April 1912.

[8] Segal, *Close-Up*, 27–28.

On such occasions, women would gather at home, and songs were sung and dances performed to celebrate the birth of a boy. The practice of *neg* was one through which the women of the household expressed their happiness. A number of *sohar* songs reflect how girl children were discriminated against:

Jachcha charh gai atariya kaise sapri
Aee sasuiyaa sowar takan ko mange apna neg
Nega-nega na kar sasu piya gae pardes
Nahi lae mathe bindiya kaise sapri
Jachcha charh ....
Aee jethaniya pipar pisan ko mange apna neg
Nega-nega na kar jethani piya gae pardes
Nahi lae neklasiya kaise sapri
Jachcha charh gae ....
Aee nandiya sohar putan ko mange apna neg
Nega-nega na kar nandi piya gae pardes
Nahi lae kangnava kaise sapri
Jachcha charh gai ....
Aaya devra bansi bajan ke mange apna neg
Nega-nega na kar devar piya gae pardes
Nahi lae hai rupiya kaise sapri[9]

The male child was considered the only real heir in both communities.[10] The famous folk song, '*Hae-hae re lalla jeeo-jeeo re lalla bare hoshiyaar*', illustrates the significance of *lalla* (a baby boy) in a common household. The absence of any registration of female infants in the 0–1 age group can be explained as yet another form of gender discrimination (see Table 6.1).[11] However, we find a large number of registered Muslim women in the age group of 15–40. Also, the sex ratio was favourable where Muslims were concerned;[12] more so, in 1881, than in other communities.[13] Several religious books depict a gender-friendly picture of Muslim society. The nineteenth century saw socio-religious movements grow within both Hindu and Muslim communities; as mentioned

[9] These folk songs have been sung by both Muslim and Hindu women for centuries.

[10] Maulvi Nazir Ahmed wrote about a spoilt male heir in his famous novel *Fasana-e Mobtela* (New Delhi: Qitabi Duniya, 2003 [1888]), 5.

[11] Census Report of India, NWP of Agra and Oudh, 1901, R. Burn (Allahabad: Government Press, 1902).

[12] ibid. The sex ratio stood at 801 per 10,000 for Muslims and 783 for Hindus.

[13] CR of India, NWP of Agra and Oudh, 1881, 73. There were 49.8 males and 52.02 females per 100 population.

earlier, Muslim society has witnessed two major religious reform movements in India: the Wahabi Movement, which gave rise to the purification movement aimed at bringing pure Islam back to India, and the Barelvi movement. While the latter did not raise any gender issue, both published literature for women, as their main concern was with creating an ideal and religious Muslim woman. There was a difference between Wahabi and Barelvi: Wahabi believes in only the Quranic inscription, considering everything beyond the Quran *bidat*, while Barelvi gives space to the Prophetic tradition and the Sufi *khankah*, bringing it closer to Hindustani culture. There is a long tradition amongst Barelvi Muslims of reciting the Milad *shareef* in praise of the Prophet Muhammad; they even published books on Milad, for example *Milad Akbar*, *Milad Gauhar*, *Maulood Saiyedi*, *Saiyeda Bibi ki Kahani*, *Das Bibi ki Kahani* and *Noor Nama*. These books were designed keeping in mind their female readers as, unlike other religious books, their *nazm* and *munajat* are addressed to women. One of the most popular Milad books written by Khawaja Akbar Warisi Merathi depicts a very gender-friendly *munajat*, which shows that Muslims never discriminated between boy and girl children, praying for and welcoming both. The only exception was the Pathan caste, which was more patriarchal in nature than any other Muslim caste; they preferred sons over daughters, as baby boys were considered the *chiragh* (lamp) of the home.

Momino Waqt Rahmat Rab hai ab vo mango jo dil ka matlab hai
Sab ko rabbe ghafoor deta hai hai vo data zaroor deta hai
Yun karo arz ae karam vale hath faila rahe hai raham vale
Hai Ghafoor-ur raheem tera naam bhakhshna hai kareem tera nam.....
Naz hai tujhpe tere bandon ko de muraden murad mandon ko
Dono aalam me abroo dena apne bandon ke aib dhak lena
Joki aulad ke hai khawahish mand de khuda unko dukhtar farzand
Bhar ke paimana shariat de apne mahboob ki muhabbat de[14]

Thus, *aulad* includes both the son and the daughter as the heir apparent. An *ashra'f* girl was to be instructed by the elders of the family after attaining *balug* (puberty) when the general practice was to confine a girl child in the age group of 7–9 at home.[15] Girls from the lower socio-economic order, who had to

[14] Khawaja Akbar Warisi, *Milad Akbar* (Delhi: Farid Book Depot, Mata Mahal, n.d.). It is believed to be one of the oldest books for Milad, and it could always be found in the book collections of *shareef* Muslim families, so that the women of their households could learn Urdu and the Milad practice. I, too, learnt Urdu from Milad Akbar.

[15] ibid.

contribute to their families' livelihood, were free from these cultural constraints.[16] For centuries, these girls were expected to take on economic responsibilities while *ashra'f* girls were expected to safeguard family customs and values. After attaining puberty, the latter were confined within the house, and given lessons in etiquette and manners.[17] *Purdah* was observed, and some *ashra'f* families did not give their women's clothes to the washerman, fearing the touch of the *namahram.*[18] Women's names could not be mentioned on the cover pages of books and magazines; instead, they went by *tahzeeb-e niswa* and *khatoon.*[19]

The late nineteenth century was a transitional period for Muslims in India; now under British rule, they came into direct contact with Europeans. One section of Muslims expressed intense rancor towards the British, and resisted the spread of Western influence,[20] believing that it would lead women away from a virtuous life and turn them as capricious as their European counterparts.[21] Therefore, several new restrictions were imposed on women. This was perhaps why Sir Saiyid Ahmed Khan did not permit his daughter-in-law to meet the wives of British Judges and Collectors; and, despite being a staunch supporter of Western education, his belief in the practice of *purdah* meant he was against female education.[22]

---

[16] Shahid Amin (ed.), *A Concise Encyclopedia of North Indian Peasant Life* (New Delhi: Manohar, 2006). See also William Crook, *The North Western Provinces of India: Their History, Ethnology and Administration* (Delhi: Low Price Publication, 2003 [1987]), 229–30. If her husband was an artisan, she provided him with material assistance. In a weaver's family the women cleaned the thread or arranged the web; in the case of potters, she collected and mixed the clay. In every instance, it was the woman who carried the manufactured goods for sale at the nearest village fair or market.

[17] Maulvi Nazir's novel and Altaf Husain Hali's *Majalis-un Nisa* were chiefly motivated by this objective: of turning a girl from a *sharif* family into a polite and polished woman. See the contrast between Akbari Begam of *Banat-un nas* and the heroine of *Mirat-ul Urus.*

[18] Naved Anjum (ed.), *Aligarh Magazine, Khawateen Number* (Aligarh: AMU, 2001), 30.

[19] ibid. When Sir Saiyid was asked to name the woman editor of the forthcoming journal for women, he hesitated, on the name of any other woman instead he chose to name it, *Tahzeeb-e Niswa,* viz., women's culture.

[20] The Wahabi Movement was launched against *Dar-ul Harb.*

[21] Early Mohammedan conference proceedings expressed this fear of Muslims.

[22] Nawab Mohsin-ul Mulk, Speech No. 79, 499. He claimed that 90 per cent of the students of Aligarh was in favour of *purdah.* See also Akhbar-e Scientific Society, 186.

It will be unjust to say that women were mere domestic creatures confined to their homes; rather, Crook confirms Mrs Hasan's statement that Muslim women wielded enough power in domestic matters.[23] Maulvi Nazir's famous novel *Mirat-ul Uroos* clearly shows that in India, even women who keep *purdah* wield significant influence in the affairs of the household. It will not be an exaggeration to say that they were the controlling forces in a family, particularly women from *ashra'f* families. There is a lot of evidence to support this statement; take, for instance, Begum Aziz-un Nisa, who played a significant role within the family, along with other outside activities. Her father, Meer Mutaqqi, would often take her advice on official matters. Umme Safiya and Abidi Begum's contributions in both family matters and public life are also considerable.[24] Indeed, caste and class were key factors in determining their position, both at home and outside. The *ashra'f* Muslims were against their women stepping outside the home,[25] but imposed no further restrictions. A woman was always free to work for her family or for the welfare of the society, as long as she did not cross cultural barriers. In a normal Muslim family, the eldest woman was in charge of all family matters. Some elderly village women would use their influence to settle local village issues by playing the role of arbitrator in, say, domestic disputes, and their decision was obeyed by all.[26]

However, lower-class *ajlaf* women, despite their access to public spaces, were deprived of many privileges. Their ignorance meant that they could not claim the Quranic rights, and could be easily subjugated by everyday violence.[27] References of domestic violence are rife among this section of women, and it was perhaps their ignorance that led them to not seek legal redress in matters of dowry, maintenance rights, and protection against domestic violence However, contemporary literature paints a different picture—as these women hailed from the uneducated, ignorant and lower economic strata, most of them became involved in immoral activities. The use of magical arts, charms, spells

[23] Crook, *The North Western Provinces of India,* 230–31. Indeed, women from landed and wealthy families held significant positions both inside and outside; there were, for instance, Azizun Nisa Begam, Safiya Begam, and Abidi Beghum alias Bi Amma.

[24] See *Mirat-ul Uroos*, *Banat-ul Nash*, and *Majalis-un Nisa.*

[25] Minault, *Secluded Scholar*, 235–39; Thanvi, *Behisht-e Zewar*. See also *Aligarh Magzine,* 2001, 30.

[26] This practice was rampant in many north Indian villages till a few decades ago, although now no one brooks any outside interference in family matters.

[27] This concept is backed by contemporary vernacular literature and accounts of travellers.

and amulets was rampant, as they believed new misfortunes and adversities would befall them otherwise.[28] In his survey of the Eastern United Province, Crook found that Muslim peasant women also believed in deities such as *sahja bi, bare pir, Imam Husain, Mian Sahib, Panch Peer, Gazi Mian Satnami, Malka Phoolmati, Kalka, Muhammad Sahib,* etc.[29] Both Hindu and Muslim peasant women believed in visiting shrines and seeking the advice of *pir-mursheed.*[30] They even participated in *'urs'* processions. Many women made vows at these shrines, especially if they failed to conceive a child.[31] They also wore *taweez* and *ganda* to conceive male children, the only real heir for both communities.[32] It was difficult to distinguish between lower-class Hindu and Muslim women as both practised the same rituals and traditions.

Dress Code

It is assumed that a Muslim woman can be recognised from her attire and style of living. However, this distinction was possible only among upper-class women. They often wore *pyjama, kurta* and a *dupatta*, unlike the women from a lower stratum, who wore either a sari or *ghaghra choli.*[33] At the time, Muslim women of Lucknow had begun experimenting with dress designing and fashion. Sharar was of the opinion that no change was noticeable among the Hindus, while it was the Muslims who introduced stitched clothing:

> When they came to India, Muslim women wore wide loose Persian pyjama which gathered and fastened round the ankles. Later the hems become narrow and leg tight at the extremities but the body remained loose.[34]

Clothing and other adornments depended on the class and locality to which the women belonged; for instance, in predominantly Muslim localities, women

---

[28] Sheikh Ismail Panipati (ed.), *Akhbar-e Scientific Society,* 16 April 1876, 188–93.

[29] CR of 1901, 93–94. See also CR of 1891, 176.

[30] Minault, *Secluded Scholar*, 16. See Barbara Daly Metcalf, *Perfecting Women* (New Delhi: Oxford University Press, 2002), 36. See also Altaf Husain Hali, *Hayat-e Javed* (New Delhi: Taraqqi Urdu Board, 1979).

[31] CR of 1901, 94.

[32] Maulvi Nazir Ahmed, *Fasana-e Mobtela* (New Delhi: Kitabi Duniya, 2003 [1888]), 5.

[33] Amin, *A Concise Encyclopaedia*, 103.

[34] Abdul Halim Sharar, *Lucknow: The Last Phase of Oriental Culture* (New Delhi: Oxford University Press, 1994), 180–81.

wore typically 'Muslim' clothes and vice versa. In the villages, women (especially those from the lower caste) wore either saris or *ghaghra choli*.[35] European women also wrote about how north Indian women distinguished themselves from women living in southern India, who usually wore saris. Servants in elite families wore old clothes cast off by their mistresses. For a long time, local influence determined the dress code, leading Muslim social reformers to raise a hue and cry over Muslim women losing their cultural identity by wearing saris. Additionally, the sari was perceived as sensuous,[36] and was therefore prohibited in Islam, which emphasised 'proper clothing' where women were concerned. The *ulema* in particular lamented the spread of the sari.[37]

Lucknow soon replaced Delhi as the hub of fashion. Sharar provides a detailed account of the footwear favoured by Lucknawi women. *Ghatela* shoes were their favourite, followed by *tat bani* (brocaded) shoes.[38] Muslim women were always fond of jewellery. As Sharar pointed out:

> In most provinces in India, clumsy heavy jewelry is more commonly worn as being more valuable, and this desire for heavy jewelry is increasing in the rural parts of India ... when noble ladies came from Delhi to Lucknow they wore the jewelry that was common throughout India. In recent times it became the fashion for elite ladies to wear simple dresses without decoration and to content themselves with one or two pieces of jewelry which were light and delicate but valuable.[39]

Muslim women favoured the *kil* instead of the *nath*, which was considered the symbol of *suhag*,[40] although the *nath* remained in use during wedding ceremonies. Muslims across castes, classes and regions believe that a *Nikah* can be solemnised only by wearing a *nath*, which cannot be taken off for the next three days (there, however, is no Quranic inscription available with regard to this custom). This *nath* ceremony is very popular among courtesans, who term it *nath utrana*, that is, to lose one's virginity.

---

[35] The accounts of European women travellers highlights this contrast, especially through their photography.

[36] Nawab Mohsin-ul Mulk raised this issue while delivering a lecture on 22 October 1883, 30. See also Sharar, *Lucknow*, 181.

[37] Thanvi, *Behisht-e Zewar*, 168–81.

[38] Sharar, *Lucknow*, 179.

[39] ibid., 183.

[40] ibid., 184.

Marriage Customs

Among Muslims, marriage is considered a civil contract rather than a religious sacrament. Sometimes marriages are contracted before puberty, but are generally consummated after reaching puberty.[41] Several non-Islamic customs form an integral part of Muslim marriages. *Manjha* and *mehndi* were celebrated in Muslim families, despite the several *fatwa*s against these non-Islamic customs. Maulana Ashraf Ali Thanvi strictly forbade performing the *manjha* and *mehndi rasm*, where women gather together and express their emotions through music and dance. These were rare occasions, as it was strictly prohibited for *ashra'f* Muslim women to sing or dance. Women of the higher class were not allowed to participate in literary gatherings or musical concerts unless these were family gatherings, where a few women would play the *dhol* and some would sing traditional songs. In a Muslim family, the custom of *Maulood Shareef* was used to begin any significant work, like *aqiqa*, a marriage, or the *Haj*. The *Milad sharif* would then be recited in memory of Prophet Hazrat Muhammad (PBUH). Many Muslim girls learn Urdu through reciting the Maulud Book.[42] A *manjha* custom began with the *Milad sharif*, after which women rubbed yellow paste (*uptan*) on each other. The prospective bride was confined to a dark room for the next week to ten days. Every day, a number of women gathered to sing and dance at *mahfil*s where no men were allowed. The *mahfil* would always begin with five religious songs, also known as *pir-buzurgain* in some places. In my family, the ceremony began with a few customary songs, which are believed to have been passed down through generations. I learnt this song from my elders and have sung it on many wedding occasions:

Bagh me tooti bole maina bole Bismillah
sara alam parh utha Qalma Rasul Allah
Arsh-e Azam se jora aaya Dupatte pe Qalma likha
Banno tum Shauq se pahno tumhe Maizar Mubarak ho
Bagh me ...
Arsh-e Azam se Jhumka aaya, Teeke pe Qalma likha
Banno tum shauq se pahno ki tumhe zhumar mubarak ho

The families of the bride and the groom held contrasting sentiments. Marriage is always a joyous occasion for the groom's family while the bride's

[41] Census Report of India, NWP of Agra and Oudh, 1881, 78.

[42] I too learnt Urdu from *Milad Akbar*. The *Milad Akbar* and *Milad Gauhar* have been integral parts of every Muslim household since they were first printed.

family would be enveloped in an atmosphere of gloom. *Malin* is the most celebrated person for the groom; at the same time, *kahar* would be placed on every lip in the bride's home.

Nai malan mere naushe ke brabar lana sehra
Sehre ka jab waqt hua abba miyan khare hue
Amma bi ne sar aankho se lagaya sehra ....

Tying the knot on the *sehra* is said to be the most joyous moment in one's life. Different occasions called for different songs.

Shuru sansar se reet chali aee kal banno apni thi aj hui paraee
Teeka jo ayaa vo bhi sawa lakh ka, jhumar ke beech likhi hai judaee
Kal banno apni thi aj hui paraee ...
Jhumka jo ayaa vo bhi sawa lakh ka, jhale ke beech me likhi hai judaee
Kal banno apni thi ...
Kangan jo ayaa vo bhi sawa lakh ka, churi ke beech me likhi hai judaee
Kal banno ....
Nikles jo ayaa vo bhi sawa lakh ka, laket ke beech me likhi hai judaee
Kal ...
Tora jo ayaa vo bhi sawa lakh ka, payal ke beech me likhi hai judaee
Aj banno apni ....
Shuru sansar se reet chali aye, kal banno apni thi aj hui paraee

This traditional song highlights the pomposity of the Muslim marriage system. Weddings imposed a lot of pressure on the girl's parents, as the bride's attire was considered incomplete without a lot of jewellery. A girl was considered *paraya dhan* by her family from her birth, as she would eventually belong to the groom's family. Women, the true custodians of culture and tradition, expressed their helplessness through songs. Indeed, for centuries Amir Khusro's famous wedding song remained a part of many north Indian weddings:

Kahe ko behaya vides o lakhiya babul mere
Ham to hai babul ahira ki gaiyya jidhar hanke hank jab
O lakhiya babul ...
Ham to hai babul dhobian ki ladiya jidhar ladeb lad jab
O lakhiya babul ...
Ham to hai babul bela chameliya mahke mahak rahe
O lakhiya babul ....
Maiyaa ke kokh me do jan utre ek bahin aur ek bhaee

O lakhiya babul ....
Bhaiyya ke likhe babul apni mahliya hamko likhe pardes
O lakhiya babul ...
Ek ban dake, dusar ban, teesre me lagi peas
O lakhiya babul ...
Ek boond paniya pilado mere bhaiyya ab to aa gae hai vides
O lakhiya babul ...
Mahal ke samne se dola jo nikla bhaiyya ne khaee pachar
O lakhiya babul ...
Sab kuch diyo babul kandha pichliya na diyo sas nand tana de
O lakhiya babul mere ...

Through the ages, a woman has been considered akin to cattle, with no desire of her own, and forced to migrate to *vides* (foreign country). Interestingly, in the pre-colonial period *vides* meant moving from one village to another. As *paraya dhan*, a woman is considered a burden. The famous folk song '*Barah baras beti paalna jhulaya, ab na jhulaya jae*' depicts an interesting picture of a woman's life. Marriage was viewed as the ultimate objective for women; it therefore became necessary for them to leave their natal homes at some point in their lives, regardless of whether they were married or not. During this time, celibacy was also more commonly practised among Muslims, and there were more self-reliant women among Muslims than among Hindus. However, reports often linked the practice of celibacy with the widespread prevalence of prostitution amongst Muslims, since the majority of single women hailed from the prostitute class. As most of them believed in Islam and were single, all single women were stereotyped as prostitutes and as Muslim.[43]

Weddings are considered auspicious, especially amongst women. Indeed, this is one of the few occasions when women were given the chance to step outside their homes and interact with women outside their families. *Ashra'f'* women were given several occasions to celebrate, despite their strict confinement. *Domni*s and *Mirasin*s were the only performing artists allowed at women's gatherings. They would traditionally sing *sohla*s and *gali*, accompanied by the *dhol-manjeera*.[44] Elite families usually organised ostentatious festive occasions at their homes. While women were not allowed into the *mardana* section, they

[43] Census Report, 1881, 80.

[44] Madhu Trivedi, *The Making of the Awadh Culture* (2010), 109; see also Thanvi, *Behishte-e Zewar*, 316.

could enjoy the festivities from the *zenana.*[45] The *Deoband* school of thought strictly condemned the entertainment provided by *Domnis* and *Mirasins*, calling this practice un-Islamic.[46] Ashraf Ali Thanvi dedicated his *Behisht-e Zewar* to these deviant Muslim women. This book became so popular that it became a traditional wedding gift for a new bride.[47] The intention was to help the bride understand the true nature of Islam and remove ignorance from her mind, so she could become the perfect wife. Thanvi had clearly initiated a crusade against the prevailing 'evil customs' amongst Indian Muslim women. Interestingly, it was only women who were held responsible for every superstition and barbaric custom that had entered Muslim life over time.[48] Thus, an imaginary picture of the ideal Muslim woman emerged, while the significance of local customs was ignored. A surplus of religious and *adab* literature was also projecting a patriarchal Muslim society, encouraging several restrictions on women. Among the magazines was *Islah,* a nineteenth-century monthly, where issues of polygamy were discussed within the narrow framework of Islamic theology. This magazine even favoured the custom of polygamy, citing as reasons for its endorsement the Quranic provision, along with the 'laws of nature'. *Islah* argued that since a man can remain virile up to 100 years, he has the right to leave his wife once she has crossed the age of forty-five or fifty and go to [the market] to marry [buy] a much younger wife, with whom he can cohabit happily. Does the Quran really state that all middle-aged wives should be replaced with new, younger ones?

Unfortunately, many social reformers were inspired by these *fatwa*s given out by the *Deoband* school of thought. However, the Aligarh school of thought adopted a more liberal attitude towards women. The initial meeting of the Mohammedan Educational Conference stated clearly its intention to refrain from religious matters.[49] Aligarh's first generation advocated female education, so that the next generation would not be deprived of educated wives.[50]

45 Amrit Lal Nagar, *Ye Kothevaliyan* (Allahabad: Hindi Sahitya Sammelan Library). See also Sharar, *Lucknow*, 186, 192.

46 Thanvi, *Behishte-e Zewar*, 296.

47 Metcalf, *Perfecting Women*.

48 Thanvi, *Behishte-e Zewar*, 50.

49 *Lecturon ka Majmua,* speech of Nawab Mohsin-ul Mulk, where he suggested refraining from religious issues (p. 494).

50 Mohammadan Anglo Oriental Educational Conference Report, 11, 27–30 December 1896, Meerut, 244–45.

Fundamentalists, on the other hand, demanded the strict imposition of *shariat* law. This orthodox group raised only those issues that would protect their patriarchal interest.[51] Maulvi Nazir projected a patriarchal picture of Muslim society through a father's letter to his newly-wed daughter:

> The creation of woman was merely to insure the happiness of man, and it is woman's function to keep man happy. It is greatly to be regretted that so few women in the world fulfil this task. God had given to a man somewhat higher status than to woman not only by his command, for he has also given men's bodies greater physical strength, and to their mental faculties a greater perspicuity. All the control of the world's affair is affected by men. They are workers who earn money by their toil, from time to time to their best advantage. A family is like a boat, and the man in it like a sailor. If there is no sailor in the boat, it will either founder in the waves, or be dashed to be pieces against the shore. If there is no man in the family capable of managing it, every kind of mischief may be apprehended.[52]

Several Muslims in India were influenced by the *Barelvi* sect, which emphasised a composite culture built through the amalgamation of Islamic law with Indian traditions, that is, *ganga-jumni tahzeeb*. Nevertheless, the question of the 'perfect wife' remained a burning issue for both liberals and orthodox Muslims—while Aligarh's liberals dreamt of educated and cultured wives, the orthodox dreamt of a purified Islamic family. However, the concerns of both groups lay with *ashra'f* women alone. As far as social reformers were concerned, women should be at the same mental level as their men, understand their feelings as well as manage the home, and share their sorrows and joys. However, the problem lay in finding such a life partner, since in India, the bride and groom were not supposed to meet before their marriage, regardless of their own feelings in the matter.[53] As Nawab Mohsin said, he had no regret championing the European system of courtship; Europeans had happy marriages not only because their courtships, but also because of the like-mindedness of both husband and wife.[54]

---

51 See Thanvi, *Behisht-e Zewar*, and the journal *Islah*.

52 Nazir Ahmad, *The Bride's Mirror*, C. E. Ward (trans.), (New Delhi: Permanent Black, 2004), 62.

53 *Majmua Lecture va Speech,* Nawab Mohsin-ul Mulk, 22 October 1883, 28.

54 ibid.

No *ashra'f* wanted to marry their children outside their kin groups, making it convenient for girls and boys to get to know each other before marriage.[55] This was perhaps why conjugal issues were rare in *ashra'f* families; marriages were usually fixed at the ages of six or seven, and took place after attaining puberty.[56]

The age of marriage boys was between nineteen to twenty, and for girls, between fourteen to fifteen.[57] However, high-caste Muslims often delayed their daughters' marriages till they had crossed the age of twenty.[58] Marriages also took place within caste groups. Inter-caste marriages were considered harmful to the social order and surprisingly, even Muslim social reformers and the Ulema were not in favour of them, preferring to protect the caste hierarchy of the Indian social order instead. Thanvi, too, emphasised marriages within the caste circle. Furthermore, he provided a detailed account of who one could marry.[59] Lower-caste women were considered suitable as concubines and mistresses, but were rarely given the status of a legal wife. Post 1857, it was a period of transition for Indo-European relationships as well, particularly with Muslims. Malcolm Speirs reveals how the British were taking their political rivalry a step further by maintaining their own *harems*. However, almost no *ashra'f* Muslim had given their daughter to the British in marriage, and most of their female partners were concubines with no legal status.[60] These women were mostly slave girls, with whom it was easy to develop relationships. Also, the events of 1857 had warned the British against developing intimate relationships with Indian women.

Malcolm Speirs' account raises a big question: Why were all the concubines and wives of British officers Muslim? Was this because they wanted to subjugate their primary political rival? Several instances of inter-racial marriage were available, but they usually did not succeed due to the cultural differences. Nawab

---

[55] The tight, cross-cousin marriage alliances maintained by the purest gentry also ensured that 'blood' and lineage continued to be important determinants in politics and social life. C. A. Bayly, *Rulers, Townsmen and Bazaars: North Indian Society in the Age of British Expansion* (Oxford University Press, 2009), 352. See also the *shazra* of an *ashra'f* Muslim family in Munshi Abdul Ali, *Alfaiz al Zari, Sham-e Oudh* (Lucknow, 1901), 18.

[56] CR of 1901.

[57] CR of 1891, 248.

[58] The study of some elite women shows that they would get married at a relatively later age. Kabir Qausar and Inamul Kabir, *Biographical Dictionary of Prominent Muslim Ladies* (New Delhi: Light and Life Publisher, 1982).

[59] Thanvi, *Behisht-e Zewar*, 193–94.

[60] Malcolm Speirs, *The Wasikadars of Oudh* (New Delhi, Rupa and Co.), 68.

Mehdi Hasan's marriage to a European woman was written about in vernacular newspapers; she converted to Islam and adopted her husband's culture for twelve years, but later reverted to her original religion without breaking her marital ties with her husband.[61] Through such marital ties, some people tried to enhance their social status.[62] Social reformers, though, continued to remain concerned with the increasing ostentation of the marriage ceremony, which placed a huge burden on the bride's parents. Nawab Mohsin-ul Mulk and Ashraf Ali Thanvi both declared this custom un-Islamic, stating that Muslims should avoid extravagance and unnecessary ceremonies. As Mohsin said in a lecture:

> The rituals of marriage are very inappropriate. The first prerequisite of marriage, that is, the consent of both the parties, cannot be taken. Neither the man nor the woman can see each other. The basis of Nikah rests on an imaginary being. Very often, the man and the woman are not happy with the marriage, but do not utter a word due to shame and fear. The man rejects his wife in his heart despite accepting her verbally, and the woman sheds a flood of tears at her precarious condition.
>
> .... In addition, the wasteful expenditure during marriages, the distribution of food, and the gathering of common folk like a flock of sheep and feeding them, are all senseless practices .... Shame for a woman means it is better to die rather than speak to her husband before any relative. However old she might become, she cannot take charge of the household as long as the parents are alive. If by mistake she pronounce her husband's name, the *Nikah* stands dissolved.[63]

Lakhs of rupees would be spent on lavish weddings in *ashra'f/*elite families.[64] Poor people had to take loans at a high rate of interest, often mortgaging their property in the process (the financial consequence in the form of property litigation will be discussed in the next chapter). Marcus Fuller presented an amazing picture of *mahr:*

> In well to do communities, it is fixed at from one thousand to fifteen hundred rupees; but to make it impossible to divorce her we have heard of the sum being put at very fanciful figure. We read of one case where it was set at twenty six

[61] *Oudh Akhbar,* 6 October 1892, 20 October 1892, 28 October 1892, 3 November 1892.

[62] Nawab Mehdi Hasan was accused of improving his position in the government through the marriage he contracted. In the pre-Mutiny period, the British did the same; they entered into marital relations with elite Muslim families.

[63] Nawab Mohsin-ul Mulk, 28.

[64] Ali, *Sham-e Oudh,* 32–33.

thousand rupees; and the other day we heard of a young clerk on a salary of ten rupees per month signing an agreement to a mahr of three lakhs of rupees.[65]

Poor Muslims were the worst affected by this ostentation and found it difficult to marry off their daughters. As a result, these girls often had to marry a much older *duhaja* or *tihaja*.[66] The Deoband School repeatedly expressed its anguish over extravagant marriages and declared them un-Islamic. People soon began following these *fatwa*s and began organised simple marriage ceremonies instead, particularly in the Western United Province.[67] Reformists followed suit; Maulvi Nazir gave his daughters a share in property and some cash.[68] Nazir talked about the evil custom of dowry in his novels, and also supported the move to put aside some share in property for girls.

Issues of Polygamy, Divorce and Iqrarnama

Muslims are generally alleged to be polygamous by nature. They often defend themselves by saying that contrary to popular perception, this was not an exclusive feature of their culture. E. Westermark pointed out in *History of Human Marriage* (1894) that polygamy was permitted by most ancient people, and even by several civilised nations and tribes desirous for a male child to continue their family line.[69]

This issue is debatable to this day. *Naturees*[70] stated that the sex ratio had proved that the number of men was greater than that of women, thereby making it clear that one man could marry only one woman.[71] On the other hand, fundamentalists referred to the studies of Dr Tailor, Dr Carling and Dr

[65] Mrs. Marcus Fuller in Eunice de Souza (ed.), *Pardah: An Anthology* (New Delhi: Oxford University Press, 2004), 75-76.

[66] Also, at some places it became a custom to not give their daughter in marriage until a suitable bride price had been paid. *The nasim-e Agra*, 15 October 1890.

[67] Thanvi, *Behisht-e Zewar*.

[68] Zeenat Basheer, *Nazir Ahmad ke Navilon me Nusvai Kirdar* (Hyderabad: Iliyas Traders and Publishers and Book Sellers, 1991), 57.

[69] Quoted in *The Aligarh Magazine*, *Rashid Shaz*, AMU, Aligarh, 1984, 103. See also *Rasoom-e Hind*, 254–55.

[70] Sir Saiyid Ahmad Khan was called *naturee* by contemporary ulema, and all his followers have been remembered as thus.

[71] *Islah*, 5, Jild 1, Mohammad Ghulam Husain (ed.), Saiyid Ali Haider, 1315 (H), 139–40.

Began, who propounded the theory of co-habitation as an objective behind marriage. According to them, men could remain virile from seventy to 100 years, but for women, a similar situation could not extend beyond fifty to fifty-five years. Armed with this theory, the orthodox group argued that if a man were to marry only one woman at a time, a long period of his valuable life would go waste.[72] Although Muslims were permitted to keep four wives at a time, they were required to treat all the wives equally.[73] Since it was not possible to treat each wife equally and justly, as per the command given in the Quran ('if ye fear that ye shall not be able to deal justly with the orphans, marry women of your choice, two, or three, or four; but if ye fear that ye shall not be able to deal justly [with them], then only one, or that which your right hand posses. That will be more suitable, to prevent you from doing injustice': Quran, 4:3), most reformers condemned it.[74] *Risala-e Anjuman-e-Panjab* stated: "At home, man is like a heart of a body. Just as one heart is not sufficient to take concern of two bodies, in that manner two homes do not manage with one man."[75]

However, wealthy people—and sometimes even a few poor people—did marry twice or thrice in India. Usually, though, the common Muslim married only once.[76] Moreover, Muslims of the United Province hailed from the landed class, and the practice of polygamy was common amongst talluqdars and zamindars. Generally, they had at least two or three wives and/or mistresses. But this practice was prevalent among Hindus and Anglo-Indians as well. An interesting picture emerges in Malcolm Speirs' work on Anglo-Indian history, where he talks about the latter's fondness for keeping big *harems* like the *nawabs*.[77] The author is one of the descendants of Sultan Marrium Begum, who had a European connection and was also known as Firangi Begum. She was one of King Ghaziuddin Haider's favourite wives, and was entitled to a royal *wasika* of Rs 2,500 per month. Contemporary records pertaining to the Board of Revenue and the Indian Law Report show that all the cases apropos women's rights with regard to property dispute, claims for dowry, money, and

72 ibid.

73 The Quran clearly states that if a man cannot perform *adal* (justice), he should not take yet another wife.

74 *Rasoom-e Hind*, Sir Rishta-e Talim, Panjab, 1868, 254 55.

75 *Risala Anjuman-e Panjab, 1869–70*, 152.

76 *Rasoom-e Hind*, 254–55.

77 See the court cases of Joseph Short's descendants in Malcolm Speirs, *The Wasikadars of Awadh* (New Delhi: Rupa and Company, 2008). For his family tree, see p. 2.

maintenance were connected with those of the co-wives of the deceased, who had all been left with nothing. These widows were forced to file petitions against each other, or against the legal heir now in possession of the property. This practice was common among the landed class of both Hindus and Muslims, as well as Europeans and Anglo-Indians.

Some columnists tried to justify polygamy by linking it with widow remarriage.[78] Maulvi Nazir highlighted this custom in his famous novel, *Fasana-e Mubtela*. Interestingly, a few years after it was published, he took a second wife, despite his advancing years.[79] In addition, he had his son remarry after his first daughter-in-law failed to bear a child. It is significant that his wife, Umme Safiya, did not attend her son's second marriage.[80] Thus, if women were considered sources of entertainment for fundamentalists, they were looked upon as child-producing machines for the so-called reformists. If she failed to fulfill her obligations, she would inevitably be replaced.

The fact that co-wives never got along is well-documented in literature. Royal women, too, were not without their jealousies and quarrels.[81] However, the Nawabs of Oudh often tried to treat their several wives justly, especially with regard to finance. Every legal wife of the Nawab was given a fixed monthly allowance and a share in immovable property.[82] In the case of divorce, she had her dower money and proper maintenance to fall back on.[83] The Begums of Oudh were always financially strong, which was why the British could not overlook their significance.

Hypothetically, if a couple could not live together amicably, they could divorce; however, in reality, Muslims often avoided doing so. Divorce was considered a stigma amongst the *ashra'f*, as was widow remarriage. Both the *Ulema* and the reformers were against divorce.[84] The sanctity of marriage was emphasised in *adab* literature, too. Thus, the flexibility provided in Islam was hardly ever exercised by Muslims. This is how the mother of Muhammad Aqil (a character in *Mirat-ul Uroos*) expressed her astonishment at her son's decision to not leave his mother, but leave his wife instead: 'Son, you do not know what

78 *Oudh Panch*, 15 January 1892, 4.

79 Zeenat Basheer, *Nazir Ahmad ke Navilon me Nusvai Kirdar*, 38.

80 ibid., 39.

81 Sheikh Tasadduq Husain, *Beghmat-e Oudh* (Lucknow, 1956), 260.

82 ibid.

83 ibid., 243, 263. Some wives of the Nawab had opted for divorce when Wajid Ali Shah was exiled to Calcutta.

84 Thanvi, *Behisht-e Zewar*, 205.

it is you are saying. Are wives ever divorced in respectable families? It is with her that you will have to spend the whole of your life.'[85]

Although it was difficult for Muhammad Qamil to adjust to his short-tempered wife Akbari Khanam, the author does not endorse the option of separation or divorce. While he was keen to portray an ideal wife as one who is submissive to her husband, he also tried to emphasise the duty of a husband to maintain the sacred relationship of marriage. Through his character, Nazir preached:

> God has given to men a nature like that of tigers; whoever tries to tame them by force or domineering will find it impossible. A very simple receipt for taming them is being agreeable and submissive; and every silly woman assertion of her own authority makes a great mistake. She is sowing the seeds of strife from the very beginning, and, though she may not think so at first, strife will inevitably be the ultimate result. My advice to you my dear Asghari, is that you should make a point of treating your husband with respect, even in your conversation and demeanour.[86]

The author's attempt was to convey the importance of adjustment, even in adverse situations, as only through this can a marriage be saved. And saving a marriage should be the ultimate objective of a couple although, admittedly, the onus lay more on the woman. It is believed that a Muslim husband can declare '*talaq*' at any time. The truth is that *talaq* was more common in European society than among Indian Muslims.[87]

In Islam, the provision of *mahr* and maintenance is primarily to safeguard women's interest, as it is believed to discourage divorce and protect women financially.[88] However, the true concept and nature of dower was apparent in the Allahabad High Court's decision in the 1888 case of Abdul Qadir v. Salima, where Justice Mahmud delivered a historical judgement. Also, the families of both the bride and the groom considered *mahr* part of their family honour.[89] Sometimes the *mahr* amounted to more than the total worth of the groom's estate, and could never be paid in the husband's lifetime. It could be as little as

[85] Nazir Ahmad, *The Bride's Mirror*, C. E. Ward (trans.), (New Delhi: Permanent Black, 2004), 39.

[86] ibid., 63. This was a father's letter to his newly-wed daughter, Asghari.

[87] *Tahzeeb-e Akhlaq*, Jild 1, No. 41. 266–69.

[88] M. Afzal Wani, *The Islamic Law on Maintenance of Women, Children, Parents and Others* (Kashmir: Upright Study Home, 1995).

[89] Nadvi, *The Musalman*, 32–33.

Rs 500, or extend to lakhs of rupees.[90] Divorce, considered a slur on respectable families, was sometimes practised amongst low-caste Muslims, although the husband rarely paid the *mahr* on his own; in fact, he would constantly look for ways not to pay.[91] Since Islam absolved the husband of any liability after the expiration of *iddat*, it was easy for men to claim that they had divorced their wives much earlier.[92] Sometimes the husband tried to claim bankruptcy in an attempt to not pay maintenance.[93] In such situations, women had to turn to the law.

Muslim marriage is considered a contract. Justice Mahmood cites the classic exposition: 'Marriage among the Mohammedan is not a sacrament, but purely a civil contract and though solemnized generally with recitation of certain verses from the Quran ... Mohammedan law does not prescribe by service peculiar to the occasion'.[94] Under Muslim Law, marriage is purely a civil contract, and therefore the terms of the *iqrarnama* must be construed in the same way as the provisions of any other contract. In those days, several landholding families would fix large amounts as mahr, along with an *iqrarnama* (an agreement between the husband and the wife). What is most interesting about this agreement is that it would often be in favour of the bride, with the groom required to sign several obligations such as *kharch-e pandan/mewa khori*, and several other demands besides. This custom was practised especially in Oudh and Delhi.

In the pre-colonial and late colonial periods, polygamy was practised among both the Hindu and the Muslim elites. The common people, though, preferred to marry only once.[95] As the Muslims of UP and Delhi hailed from the landed class and service gentry,[96] this practice was more common in north

---

[90] This conclusion was drawn after a perusal of all the India Law Reports of the time, with regard to dower cases.

[91] Nadvi, *The Musalman*, 32–33. Thanvi. *Behisht-e Zewar*, 194–98, 334.

[92] Mahbuban v. Fakir Baksh, ILR, All. XV, 1893.

[93] ibid.

[94] Shahid Akhtar, *Muslim Law Digest*(Allahabad: Premium Publication Co., 1999), 17.

[95] Sir Rishta Talim, *Rasoom-e Hind* (Panjab, 1868), 254–55. Islam permits four wives at a time, on condition that they would all be treated equally. Since this was clearly not possible, most social reformers condemned the practice.

[96] Francis Robinson, *Separatism among Muslims of India* (New Delhi: Oxford University Press, 1993). See also Firdous Azmat Siddiqui, 'Colonial Report on Census and its Reflection on Indian Muslim Women', *Islam and Muslim Societies*, Nadim Hasnain (ed,) (New Delhi: Serial Publications, 2005), 158.

India, especially amongst *talluqdars* and zamindars (regardless of their religion and caste), who generally had between two and four wives, along with several concubines. Keeping in mind the real possibility of divorce, these elite Muslims used to draw up an *iqrarnama*, elaborating the provision of maintenance. This agreement would get precedence over sacred law. Since divorce is considered undesirable in *ashra'f* families, their agreements had conditions that made divorce and polygamy almost impossible, in an attempt to safeguard the rights of the woman.[97] Surprisingly, this agreement favoured the bride, since it was invariably primed at the initiative of her parents. The socio-economic status of the bride's family also determined the extent of their influence. *Iqrarnama* is acceptable under Islamic law under some condition, as Afzal Wani elaborates, and it aided a wife to secure a valid agreement stating that her husband would provide maintenance, should the need arise.[98] However, given that both elite Muslims and Hindus practised polygamy, the groom did not always accept the *iqarnama*. Generally, the bride's parents emphasised three conditions:

(*i*) The groom could not marry again.
(*ii*) If the bride does not want to live with her in-laws, her husband cannot force her to. In addition, if she were to return to her natal home, he would provide her with maintenance.
(*iii*) After marriage, the groom would have to stay with his in-laws.

A wife could provide stipulations against ill-treatment by her husband and disagreements between the spouses, as was the case during Maulvi Nazir's (1833–1912) marriage.[99] Sir Sayyid Ahmed Khan's father, Mir Mutaqqi, was also a *khanadamad*.[100] As a surprised Minault stated, in a society where wives customarily went to live with their husband's families, Sayyid Ahmed's father, a religious mystic, was willing to have the responsibility for his family rest with his wife's father, a high-ranking official in the Mughal court. This trend was common during the nineteenth century, after which grooms began considering the practice an insult, and even refused the maintenance claims made by their

[97] Mrs. Marcus Fuller in Eunice de Souza (ed.), *Purdah: An Anthology* (New Delhi: Oxford University Press, 2004), 74.

[98] M. Afzal Wani, *The Islamic Law on Maintenance of Women Children, Parents and other Relatives* (New Delhi: Qazi Publisher and Distributors, 1995), 61. See also Verma, *Commentaries on Mohammedan Law*, 8th edn (Allahabad: Law Publisher [India] Private Limited, 2004), 334.

[99] Zeenat Basheer, *Hayat-e Nazir* (Hyderabad), 30–31.

[100] Gail Minault, *Secluded Scholars* (New Delhi: Oxford University Press, 1998), 14.

brides. In such cases, the court often ruled in favour of the wife, especially when she was in possession of the *iqrarnama.* In one case, the wife entered into an agreement whereby her husband would provide her with separate maintenance while she continued living in her parents' home. The court held that the wife could secure such an agreement, should she be unable to get along with another wife. Yet another custom prevailed among the elite *ashra'f* of Oudh and parts of north India—parents would agree upon a huge amount in the name of *mewakhori* or *kharch-i pan.*[101] This *iqrarnama* would be fixed before the marriage ceremony, and according to the terms of this agreement, the husband was liable for the expenses of *mewakhori* or *pankhori* for all his life. The court held that an agreement to pay *kharcha-e pandan* is not opposed to public policy, and is payable even if the wife refuses to return to the husband.[102] If the husbands tried to escape their liability, the wives were free to approach the court to claim their right, citing the agreement.[103] An *iqrarnama* stating that the mother-in law would provide the allowance for *mewakhori* could also be enforced.[104]

Thus, through the *iqrarnama*, the socio-economic interests of women could be secured. However, this custom eventually disappeared, apparently because of the declining socio-economic condition of Muslims at large. The partition of India played its own role. Recent studies have shown that Muslim women of the nineteenth century were educated,[105] more in pace with their times, and aware of their rights. Now, though, priorities have changed; Muslims these days are more concerned with their cultural identity. Their focus on their 'minority' status has resulted in the subjugation of their women. A woman wishing to get married using the old custom of *iqrarnama* would probably remain unmarried her whole life. Also, the increasing demand for capable grooms and easy accessibility of suitable brides has further distorted another age-old custom, the *paigham bhejna*, which used to be sent by the groom. Now, though, this responsibility falls on the bride's parents. It is believed that desperation fuelled the *iqrarnama—jiski shadi kahi na ho rahi ho vahi iqrarnama manzoor karega*—further contributing to the decline of this custom.

---

[101] Tasadduq Husain, *Begmat-e Oudh*,.

[102] Ali Akbar v. Fatima Begum, ILR, 32, All. 410. Quoted in Verma, *Commentary*, 335.

[103] Khaja Muhammad v. Husain Begum, ILR, 32, All, 410, quoted in Wani, *The Islamic Law*, 61.

[104] Sikander Ara v. Husain Ara, AIR, 1936, Oudh 196, 197, quoted in Verma, *Commentary*, 335.

[105] At the time, education referred to creative skill and awareness, along with some traditional education. A woman endowed with these qualities was considered perfect.

Widowhood and Widow Remarriage

Widow remarriage has never been looked down upon in Islam; nor has it ever been held in contempt in any custom. Enforced widowhood and the prohibition of widow remarriage were the two burning issues of the late nineteenth century; Indian Muslim women had suffered the consequences of these evil customs, along with their Hindu counterparts. In 1862, Sir Wiliam Hay McNaghten stated: 'Second marriages, after the death of the husband first espoused are wholly unknown to the Hindu law; though in practice, among the inferior caste families, nothing is so common.'[106] Janki Nair termed this traditional practice (prevalent mostly among high-caste Hindus) 'a living death'.[107] However, enforced widowhood was rampant not only amongst Hindus; it was also practised to a large extent amongst Muslims.[108]

Muslims have preferred to distance themselves from this practice, declaring that the Quran clearly states, *'ankehul aiyaama minkum'*.[109] The question therefore arises: Why was this sacred command, obeyed in other Islamic countries, violated in the Indian subcontinent?[110] The condition of Muslim widows need to be highlighted; why did colonial discursive writing overlook such an important issue? Did they intend to divert the Indian Muslim's attention from real issues? Why did the Muslims themselves accept this reality? Why was the Widow Remarriage Act named the 'Hindu Remarriage Act, 1856'?

The Hindu social structure exerted a lot of influence on Indian Muslims.[111] *Ashra'f* Muslims, who considered it appropriate to adopt the high caste Hindu culture, or Brahmanical culture, were similar to high-caste Hindus, whereas *ajlaf* Muslims were influenced more by lower-caste Hindus, rather than by Muslims of noble birth. The treatment of widows is generally accepted as one of the worst outcomes of this intermingling between Hindu and Muslim

---

[106] Janaki Nair, *Women and Law in Colonial India* (New Delhi: Kali for Women, 1996), 59.

[107] ibid.

[108] Contemporary vernacular literature, as well as data available in census reports proves that the belief that widow remarriage was practised amongst *ashra'f* Muslims was wrong.

[109] This means 'remarry your widows'.

[110] This question had been raised in Maulvi Nazir's *Aiyama.*

[111] Nadvi, *The Musalman*, 6. Nadvi states that Indian Muslims have, on the other hand, adopted numerous customs that are used where necessary to identify their indigenous origins. Maulvi Nazir, too, blamed Hindu culture, stating on several occasions that Indian Muslims were imitating Hindu in every respect.

cultures. Social reformers and Urdu litterateurs Maulvi Nazir Ahmad and Maulana Ashraf Ali Thanvi were of the opinion that the custom of enforced widowhood was due to Hindu influence.[112] Maulvi Nazir said in the Preface to his famous novel *Aiyaama*:

> Religiously, there is clear command for Muslims to re-marry their widows, what's more, in Arab countries this issue has been performed liberally until now. And not considered a vice in a slightest but in India, Muslim has adopted this evil custom with imitation of their co-brothers Hindus. As well as they regarded it as a dishonor and disgrace on to their family name to re-marry widows.[113]

Altaf Husain Hali, too, delineated a pitiful picture of a young widow in his famous elegy *Munajat-e Bewa*. A distressed widow complained to her God about the pain she had suffered:

> Cast away by kin and strangers, Load on both, in laws and home
> Sacred inside with many lesions, more than words can state, express
> Every hour I burn and smoulder, widowed life, how will it pass?[114]

What is astonishing is the way female European travellers ignored this issue, even those who professed to be staunch supporters of the female cause. Mary Francis Billington, for instance, expressed her satisfaction apropos Muslim widows. In spite of a touching appeal made by a young widow in Hali's *Munajat-e Bewa* and an account of adolescent widowhood in Maulvi Nazir's *Aiyama*, Billington's statement about Muslim widows shows how contradictory assumptions were rife with regard to Indian Muslims.

> In the case of young widows all reasonable effort is made by her family to find her another husband, and this fact should not be forgotten in any attempt to appreciate the degree in which the prohibition of widow re-marriage presses upon the population.[115]

---

112 Thanvi, *Behisht-e Zewar*, 338. See the Preface of Nazir's novel *Aiyama*.

113 Bilgrami Saiyid Iftikhar, *Hayat-ul Nazir* (1912), 295. He referred the Preface to *Aiyama*.

114 Altaf Husian Hali, *Hali Panipati ki Nazmen* (Panchkoola: Haryana Urdu Academy, 2008), 1–45.

115 Mary Francis Billington, *Women of India* (New Delhi: NAI, 1894), 120.

This statement is substantiated in English fiction, too,[116] fostered no doubt by the relatively courteous conduct of Muslim families towards their widows and the sacred command in Quranic verses.[117] The Census Report also insisted that Muslims were liberal when it came to widow remarriage; they went so far as to connect it with the burgeoning population, believing that since Islam provides a space for widow remarriage, it results in more children being born.[118] In the last two decades of the nineteenth century, the number of married Muslim women in the age group of 15–40 was high, further strengthening this belief. What is more problematic is that English literature also depicted Muslim women as sexually vibrant.

In 1891, Nazir wrote his famous novel *Aiyama* (an Arabic word meaning 'widow'). Speaking about the basic need for marriage, he stated that a widow's existence is considered as much a danger in Muslim families as it is among Hindus:

> *Bura Dastoor beja bat na hanjar shewa hai*
> *Bari khauf aur khatar ki jae jis ghar me bewa hai*[119]

Although a few *ashra'f* families accepted the remarriage of young widows, they traditionally never paid much attention to it. This was partly compelled by their imitation of the dominant Hindu culture, and partly because of issues arising from the inheritance rights of widows. The custom was to ask widows whether they wanted to remarry; often, despite their longing for remarriage, widows would be forced to refuse, fearing the disgrace this would bring to their families. At times, women who had loved their husbands deeply found it difficult to remarry soon after their death.[120] Nazir Ahmad raised the question: Was their refusal believable?[121] Through Azadi Begum, Nazir showed how, for the

---

[116] The English story *Firoza* also emphasised the trend of remarriage among Muslims. The young widow Firoza was remarried to her brother-in-law; in contrast, *Sati* talked about how Hindu widows were pushed into nervous breakdowns by their enforced widowhood.

[117] This is because Muslims widows were never forced to reside in seclusion or shave their heads, both common Hindu customs.

[118] C.R. of 1881, 1891 and 1901.

[119] Bilgrami, *Hayat-ul Nazir*, 295.

[120] As Azadi Begham says, how can a widow dare to think about remarriage while living in a society that never approved of it?

[121] *Aiyama*.

sake of their honour, *ashra'f* Muslims forced their widows to lead difficult and miserable lives. At the end of the story, Azadi Begum informs a male gathering about the pathetic condition of widows: 'Which desire was in this world that I hesitate to die? I am damned if I know I will be remitted from these difficulties if once dying.'[122]

This was a very progressive novel, particularly in a society where even the clothes of women were not given to the washermen. This was a challenging to attempt to incite the most marginalised section of society to speak out. Nazir was rightly convinced that without changing the mindset of men, reform could not be ushered into a traditional society. However, the participation of women was equally necessary if both communities of India had to do away with the pains of widowhood.[123] If the false picture presented in British discursive writings was true, the number of Muslim widows should have been numerically low; census reports and vernacular literature, though, tell a different story. Also, if all Muslims were following their sacred law strictly, why was the percentage of Muslim widows so close to their Hindu counterparts? Nazir's opinion about the excess of widows in Muslim society was:

> Since the wife is ... younger than her husband, ... men passed away much earlier leaving his wife a widow. Another reason: man is supposed to be too weak to tolerate the difficulties of loneliness. *Aur marne vale ka qafan tak maila nahi hone paya ki unka iman danvadol hone lagta hai aur na keun ho marne vale ke sath mara to nahi jata.*[124]

In 1881, the number of Muslim widows stood at 4,64,175 (12.52 per cent of the Muslim population and 1.62 per cent of the whole), while the number of Hindu widows stood at 31,20,273 (13 per cent of the Hindu population and 11.25 per cent of the whole).[125] It is important to note that Hindus accounted for 86.4 per cent of the total population, whereas Muslims formed only 13.37 per cent of the entire population. A marginal difference of 0.5 per cent was visible at the provincial level. Besides, the sex ratio of Muslims was 994.3, as compared to 946.64 among Hindus. Thus, given the number of females in their population, the percentage of widows among Hindus and Muslims was 26.53 and 25.1 per

122 Bilgrami, *Hayat-ul Nazir*, 297.

123 If any *ashra'f* widow dared to remarry, she was socially boycotted in her community and never allowed to enter any respectable family (Minault, *Secluded Scholars*, 41).

124 Bilgrami, *Hayat-ul Nazir*, 296.

125 CR of 1881, 82.

cent, respectively.[126] The male : female ratio for both communities was 48.62 : 51.38 and 50.09 : 49.91, respectively. Therefore, the average percentage of Muslim widows was greater than the number of their womenfolk, despite the Census Report's repeated assertions that widow remarriage meant there were to few Muslim widows.[127] They even tried to draw parallels with English society, stating that the increasing number of widows was due to the increase in the number of marriages, and not enforced widowhood.[128]

The number of widows per 1,000 population was greater than the number of widowers, and even greater than contemporary British widows in England.[129] Table 6.2 shows that this difference in the 10–30 age group started declining slowly, and spiked in the age group of fifty.[130] It was clear that women were reluctant to marry after a particular age. Also, the comparatively liberal attitude of Muslim families meant that widows tended to live longer.[131]

Colonial discursive writing ignored caste variations, local influence, and land settlement, all of which were key factors in Muslim lives. Why were there more Muslim widows in Central United Province? Why was Benares division the most affected? Why had the practice of enforced widowhood increased among *ashra'f* Muslims, and in rural areas? Before answering these questions, it is important to examine the social structure of Muslims.

All high castes practised enforced widowhood except for a few elite in the Rampur, Oudh and Bhopal estates, where widow remarriages did take place in the royal *zenana*. As stated earlier, the issue of widow remarriage was linked with family honour,[132] especially among the *Saiyid* and *Pathan* castes. The *bhangi* and *julaha* castes were the least affected,[133] especially in the Benares division, where they formed a majority.[134] In addition, rural Muslims were more

---

[126] ibid., 80.

[127] CR of 1891, 249. See also CR of 1881, 91.

[128] CR of 1891, 249.

[129] ibid. The somewhat higher proportion of Muslim widows as compared with English figures is probably due to the greater possibility offered to an English widow to remarry.

[130] ibid., 250.

[131] CR of 1891, 182. According to the census reports, chances of survival for both boys and girls were better amongst Muslims.

[132] Bilgrami, *Hayat-un Nazir*, 295.

[133] CR of 1891, 250.

[134] Provincial Gazetteer of India, Vol. II, 128. *Julahas* constituted 28,000, Shaikhs 26,000 and Pathans 10,000 out of the whole population.

affected.[135] As social mobility became a big part of Muslim life from the last two decade of the nineteenth century, claims registered by upper castes increasingly came to light from the early twentieth century. The new wealthy caste of Muslims had begun imitating the conduct of high-caste people in an attempt to raise their social status commensurate to their educational and economic achievements. The prevalent culture of Benares was strictly Brahmanical, and they believed in enforced widowhood; it is quite possible that this culture affected the Muslims of Benares of all castes.

The colonial government, though, adhered to their conventional understanding of Muslims living in India—that customs not cited in the Holy Quran could not be a part of Muslim society. The Quran clearly instructs remarrying widowed daughters; therefore, in the British view, enforced widowhood had to be confined only to Hindus. They overlooked the influence of local factors like caste and regional variation.

It is clear why enforced widowhood was widespread in those areas where Islamisation was not diluted by local influences, such as Bundelkhand, Benares and Mirzapur divisions.[136] However, why were Allahabad and Lucknow divisions affected equally, especially in age group of 15–40? Muslims in these regions hailed either from the landed class or from high castes.[137] The landed class tended to discourage widow remarriage so they could prevent any division in land and moveable property.[138] But why did the *Shia* sect do so, given that *Imamia* law does not give a widow any share in immovable property, especially if she were childless?[139] For centuries women used to consolidate their positions

[135] *Rasoom-e Hind*, 255.

[136] CR of 1901, 143.

[137] Provincial Gazetteer of India, Vol. II, 5, 24, 28, 35–36, 42, 53, 67. In central UP, the dominant castes were Shaikh, Saiyid and Pathan.

[138] The Contemporary Indian Law report reflects this increasing trend; a number of Muslim widows were constantly asked whether they were the legal wives of the deceased.

[139] Fazl Rab v. Khatoon Bibi, ILR, 1892, Vol. XV. The pleader, Abdul Majid, contended that under the *Shia* Law governing the case, a childless wife was not entitled to any share in the immoveable property. During the hearing, Justice Mahmood gave a detailed account of the *Imamia* Law of Inheritance, referring to several authentic original Arabic works. One such, the *Mushalik-ul Afham*, says,

> The substance of what may be deduced from the Nusus, (authorities) is this that, there is no consanguinity between her and other heirs, and she is no more than an intruder upon them, that is, a mere stranger, It may happen that she afterwards

in the household by providing the family with a (male) heir, thereby sheltering under caste hierarchy and patriarchy, both of which forbade widows to re-marry Since the Muslims of Central United Province comprised 15.5 per cent of the whole population (of the United Provinces) and 8.5 per cent of the Eastern United Province, this big chunk affected the average of the entire province.[139]

Although the percentage of Muslim widows was never satisfactory, a slow decline could be seen after 1890. The percentage of Hindu widows, though, remained the same. A close analysis of three decennial government reports shows that the percentage of Muslim widows had dropped from 16.1 per cent (1881) to 14.8 per cent (1901), while that of Hindu widows had risen slightly to 0.1 per cent (see Table 6.I). As far as the age of marriage was concerned, it had dropped to 0.3 per cent, although Hindu women maintained their growth at 0.2 per cent. Thus, by 1901, Muslim widows were only 0.4 per cent behind Hindu widows. While Muslims constituted one-sixth of the population, their widows accounted for one-eighth of the whole population. The decrease in the percentage of widows was due to the favourable sex ratio; however, their average had increased.

Muslim Social Reformers and Widow Remarriage

Why was enforced widowhood considered problematic in the Muslim social reform agenda ? What was Muslim social reformers' attitude to dealing with these issues? Since the prohibition of widow remarriage, several new social issues had come into being: Indian widows had been forced to wear only white, and kept away from auspicious occasions, especially weddings. If they dared to participate, they were subjected to social boycott.[140] They were to refrain from worldly pleasures, and as a result, widows either suffered nervous breakdowns or depressions, or indulged in illicit relationships. Several willingly chose prostitution as way of life.[141] In 1830, it was reported that prohibition of widow

---

marries a stranger who is an enemy and adversary of her husband and she makes the stranger live in his house and allows him possession of his iqar and thus causes great grief and sorrow to the other heirs, therefore the almighty God provided that she should be debarred from the dwelling houses and iqar and should be compelled to receive the price thereof, which is equelent [sic] to the things themselves.

The Sharah Kabir, however, says a woman does not inherit anything out of *iqar*, and gets only the price of the buildings, trees and plants.

[140] Indian Journal of Gender Studies, 6 (2), 1999, 512.

[141] *Azad*, 30 March 1886.

remarriage was the main factor behind the high rates of infanticide.[142] This was why Sir Saiyid Ahmed Khan decided to attack this vice: 'Perhaps the power of appetite and fulfillment of indispensability is controllable near to them, because they perceives to this power in control in their opinion that God has entrusted to every man and women with His mystery.'[143]

In addition, vernacular newspapers and Urdu literature drew people's attention to the miserable condition of widows. They wondered how Indians could accept their women indulging in immoral activities instead of giving them permission to remarry. As *Azad* stated:

> The custom of sati was really not as cruel as compulsory widowhood. All was over in a few short minutes with the women who burnt herself to death in the funeral pyre of her dead husband, but under the later institution widow have to endure life long miseries.[144]

This was why they demanded government interference in such matters. The protests launched by Urdu newspapers led to many endorsing polygamy by taking a widow as a second or a third wife, defying Maulvi Nazir's image of a husband and wife:

> as two wheels of one cart, rather columnist imagined this cart as a *rath, tamtam* and train or as a railway engine that runs with four wheels. In this way, a man could marry with three women of whom one should necessarily be a virgin and other two, widows.[145]

Concomitantly, some Hindi newspapers began writing against widow remarriage. They argued that as this was a religious sanction, it had to be protected. Some European scholars, too, supported this viewpoint, saying: 'Hindu physicians hold that women visited by more than one man suffer in health, and that the children born of such women are also weak. The prohibition by Hindu religion of the re-marriage of widow is based on this belief.[146]

Muslim social reformers vehemently attacked this prohibition, blaming it squarely on the Hindus. Through his *Akhbar-e Scientific Society*, Sir Saiyid

[142] Nair, *Women and Law in Colonial India,* 59–60.

[143] Sheikh Ismail Panipati, *Maqalat-e Sir Saiyid, Akhbar-e Scientific Society,* Aligarh, March 31, 1876. 200–202, Vol. 13, Majalis-e Taraqqi Adab, Lahore.

[144] *Azad, Opcit.*

[145] *Oudh Panch,* No. 8, 25 February 1892, 7.

[146] *The Subodh Sindhu (khandwa),* 17 February 1886, 161.

Ahmad drew the attention of common people to every social issue. Since enforced widowhood was practised by both Hindus and Muslims, he addressed both communities: 'The one vice which originates in the re-marriage of widows, if be considered, appears not only to go against the shariat, but rather it breaches their worldly honour. The truth is that it even breaches humanity.'[147]

So both social reformers and the *ulema* used the *shariat* as a tool to draw the attention of common people to this moral weakness. Nawab Mohsin-ul Mulk and Ashraf Ali Thanvi led the reformers, accompanied by the *ulema*, who declared this custom un-Islamic.[148] In his *Behisht-e Zewar*, Thanvi expressed his deep concern for Muslim widows, and over Muslim ignorance, which led to this unfortunate *ashra'f* custom. He, too, blamed Hindu customs and traditions, apart from economic considerations (in fact, he was the first to connect enforced widowhood with economic factors). In UP, economic considerations played an important part because one-fifth of the land was held by Muslims. Besides, Islamic law provides legitimacy to female inheritance, both with regard to moveable and immoveable property. In addition, the new judicial system offered widows a platform from which to exercise their rights. Since all personal law had been codified, female inheritance rights could no longer be overlooked. It was natural for a hierarchal and patriarchal society to try and keep their property from being handed over to a stranger or an outsider, and this could perhaps explain the great number of cases regarding the recovery of dower money in the lower and upper courts. However, the British too exempted the *talluqdar* of Oudh from the personal law of inheritance, because of which widows were compelled to claim their inheritance rights on both moveable and immoveable property in lieu of dower money (for details, see Chapter 9).[149]

A few elite Muslim or royal families never followed such customs and traditions, as they did not have to face people's reactions, or confront any social boycott. In fact, royal and some educated Muslim families allowed their daughters to remarry twice, or even thrice.[150] These elite women were aware of

---

[147] Panipati, *Maqalat-e Sir Saiyid.*

[148] Nawab Mohsin-ul Mulk, *Lecturon ka Majmua*, 29, 22 October 1883. Thanvi, *Behisht-e Zewar*, 338–39.

[149] However, the British Law of Inheritance does not recognise female inheritance.

[150] The daughters of Nawab Yusuf Ali Khan of Rampur provide the best example of this trend. Firoz-un Nisa married twice, while Abbasi Begam married thrice after her husbands had passed away See Nagendra Kumar Singh, *Encyclopaedia of Indian Women*, Vol. III, 2001, 426. See also Kabir Kausar and Inamul Kabir, *Biographical Dictionary of Prominent Muslim Ladies* (New Delhi: Light and Life Publisher, 1982), 4.

their Quranic rights, and therefore nobody could challenge their inheritance rights easily. This was why the British could not afford to overlook the *Begums* of Oudh, and accounts for why legal disputes relating to the property rights of women were increasing.

Clearly, it was middle-class *ashra'f* and landed-class women who were affected by enforced widowhood.[151] On this issue, Muslim and Hindu society mirrored each other; however, the condition of Muslim widows was better as they had enough to eat, did not need to shave their heads, sleep on the floor, or turn vegetarian. To an extent, the women were themselves responsible for their condition—most were unaware of the *shariat* or their rights. As Gail Minault said, *ashra'f* women tended to recite the *Quran* mechanically, without much understanding. Maulvi Nazir and Ashraf Ali Thanvi bemoaned the state of affairs and despaired of ever getting widows remarried.[152] This was why Azadi Begum, heroine of Nazir's novel, asked men to note the wretched condition of widows and take the initiative in social matters, because she believed that without their intervention, no social revolution could be possible. However, it would be unjust to say that all women remained silent about social issues; some elite women fought for the cause of women. Aziz-un Nisa Begam, the mother of Sir Saiyid Ahmad, for example, convinced several widows to remarry, and provided them all with assistance.[153]

Muslim Women, Public Spaces and Insecurity

The increase in vernacular newspapers provided a space to air both public resentment and gender discourse in civil society. Debates especially raged over the ever increasing rate of violence against women, questioning the British government's claim that they were delivering Indians from a feudal and barbaric system of law. This violence gave Muslims further reasons to confine their women indoors, and impose several restrictions upon them. Simultaneously, European travellers began raising a hue and cry over this confinement of women,

151 Thanvi, *Behisht-e Zewar*. See also *Rasoom-e Hind*. Abul Hasan Nadvi's stated that during the reign of Muhammad Shah (1719–48), the nobility began treating the remarriage of widows with contempt and disrespect. Second marriages were seen as an affront to the family honour, and as an act of infidelity on the part of the widows (Nadvi, *The Musalman*, 53).

152 Through *Aiyama*, Maulvi Nazir elaborated the prevalent custom of enforced widowhood.

153 Hali, *Hayat-e Javed*.

especially in the *zenanas*, which they likened to a prison. However, they too avoided long routes while travelling, despite the fact that means of conveyance were being developed further with each day. By the 1880s, train travel was no longer safe for women, not least because of the increasing racial tyranny in the coaches, which was fast attracting the attention of people. Interestingly, waiting rooms for women had been built in every station; strangely enough, though, native women who adhered to strict *purdah* were not permitted inside these waiting rooms. European officers were badly behaved—if any veiled women tried to enter the waiting rooms, they were not above using physical violence to throw them out.[154] Soon afterwards, the *Najm-ul Akhbar* reported:

> Natives are subjected [to] too much humiliation in railway travel. Nothing could be more unreasonable than to assign a separate waiting room to European ladies, who are accustomed to appear in public but to require native ladies who lived behind screen to wait in the ordinary shade.[155]

The Oudh Criminal Justice Report (1885) also expressed concern over the increasing criminalisation of the province.[156] Criminality was rampant to such a degree that women could be waylaid and assaulted by ruffians on the street.[157] However, there were more acquittals than convictions (see Table 6.1). The police were believed to be responsible for the insecurity that women were living under.[158] A significant number of Europeans had been convicted of heinous crimes such as rape.

To top it all, the Pascal Railway guard case provoked countrywide resentment against the racist tactics employed by the British.[159] Fearful of the increasing violence, *sharif* Muslims became obsessed with the *purdah*. Indeed, rape cases were rarely reported to the police because *sharif* Muslims, fearing disgrace,

---

[154] *Delhi Panch* (Lahore), 30 December 1885. See also *Najm-ul Akhbar*, 24, 1886.

[155] *Najm-ul Akhbar* (Etawa), 24 February 1886.

[156] Home: Judicial, Proceedings, November 1885, File No. 221–22.

[157] *The Cawnpore Gazette*, 23 October 1891. On the evening of 20 October one Mumtaz Begam and others were waylaid and beaten with sticks by ruffians near the parade ground in Kanpur.

[158] Home: Judicial, Proceedings, November 1885, File No. 221–22.

[159] A native woman named Kamia, who was travelling to Meerut from Aligarh on a passenger train, was raped on the way by Mr Pascal, the railway guard. *The Akhbar-e Alam* (Meerut), 21 August 1888 was surprised to notice that the railway guard was released by the sessions judge of Meerut on a security bond of Rs 250.

never lodged complaints.[160] Some women who dared to do so never received justice, especially if the rapist was European.[161] Given this state of affairs, natives demanded a female guard for women's coaches.[162] Following the example set by the Oudh and Rohilkhand line, the East Indian and Panjab North Western Railway authorities provided reserved accommodation for native women in railway carriages.[163]

In matters of law and order, if the culprit was found to be Indian, punishment could be very harsh. A European culprit, on the other hand, was freed on a financial bond, regardless of whether he had raped a woman or confined her against her will.[164] Some princely states were also cruel, as the *Rohilkhand Panch* reported:

> The prince summoned the woman whom he keeps as a mistress and her husband before him. The woman had been warned to tell the prince in the presence of her husband that the latter had divorced her. But when she arrived and was questioned, she denied that her husband had divorced her. The prince was enraged at her denial cowhided the man had him burnt with red hot iron sent him back to jail and ordered him to be given only one chatak of flour during the day and night. The woman was also beaten by the prince.[165]

In those days, prisoners serving life sentences were imprisoned in Port Blair. Muslim women, too, were confined on a large scale, either for being directly involved in a crime, or—as was usually the case—for aiding and abetting their husbands in a criminal act.[166] Mary Francis Billington gave a detail account of such 'criminal' women. In her survey of jails in Agra and elsewhere, she concluded that most of the women had been imprisoned for petty crimes such as the theft of a handful of rice, or for disposing of goods stolen by her husband. The main motivation behind their criminal activities was extreme poverty,[167] as all the convicted women hailed from lower economic and caste groups.[168] Sometimes, women were also involved in heinous crimes such as

---

[160] *The Mulk-e Shuhda* (Lahore), 6 December 1886.

[161] Kamia initiated criminal proceedings against Pascal, but he had already been released.

[162] *The Najm-ul Akhbar,* 16 February 1890.

[163] *Azad,* 16 March 1886.

[164] *The Nasim-e Agra,* 30 October 1887.

[165] *The Rohilkhand Panch,* 24 October 1886.

[166] Billington, *Women of India*, 242.

[167] *Al-Rashid,* (Allahabad), 11 January 1897.

[168] Billington accepted that women from nomadic groups were more involved in criminal activities.

murder, motivated either by a property dispute, or inter-marital relationships.[169] The British government, though, dealt with such criminals harshly in order to create fear among the common people. The case of a female Muslim water carrier was reported in *Sitara-e Hind* (12 February 1894): mistaking her own son for her brother, she had killed him with the intention of inheriting all his property. After her arrest, she was forced to wear a thick iron ring in her nose and private parts. The District Magistrate carried her from village to village to frighten the people, and she received five stripes with a cane everyday.[170] Several Muslim women were also held at Port Blair.[171] While severe punishment for heinous crimes had never been condemned, the natives did complain of racial discrimination. Amir Jahan's case provoked a lot of resentment among people, who spoke about how royal women were ill-treated by European officers who, blinded by their racial pride, were always ready to disgrace respectable natives.[172] The *Halat-e-Hind* observes:

> Nothing could be more tyrannical than Mr. Cobb's conduct. European Magistrates are ready to disgrace even one's mother and sisters. If any European ladies have occasion to appear before native magistrate or judges, they are always treated with respect. On the other hand European officers do not hesitate to ill treat most respectable ladies of ex-royal families.[173]

Interestingly, an ex-royal lady had been summoned by the court, fined and punished, while several European officers who had taken native women hostage and physically abused them were never convicted. The prison system was also questioned. Since there was no female wing in jails, female prisoners had to face untoward hardships.[174]

---

[169] *Oudh Akhbar, Jild 10,* 25 February 1868. One Musammat Nooran (Faqir) had a relationship with Buta Faqir. She eventually poisoned her husband.

[170] *Sitara-e Hind,* 12 February 1894.

[171] Home: Judicial, Port Blair, 4–5 October, Ref. No. B. See also Home: Port Blair, 18–19 January, Part B, Home: Port Blair, December, 158–59, Part B, Home: Port Blair, August, 75–76, Part B.

[172] *The Nairang,* 16 February 1891. *Halat-e Hind,* February 1891.

[173] *The Halat-e Hind,* February 1891. However, the *Oudh Punch* justified her conviction, terming her a wilful woman.

[174] However, Billington professed herself satisfied with the living conditions of female prisoners in India.

Table 6.1: Births by Religions, Registered for 1891–1900

Year	*Hindu*			*Muslim*			*Total*	
	Male	*Female*	*%*	*Male*	*Female*	*%*	*Male*	*Female*
1891	7,04,508	6,39,662		1,10,481	98,093	13.24	8,18,759	7,41,129
1892	7,65,833	6,96,510		1,20,097	1,06,437	13.2	8,89,814	8,06,613
1893	8,64,335	7,91,612		1,35,727	1,21,923	13.3	10,03,852	9,16,979
1894	8,38,335	7,67,229		1,31,721	1,17,918	13.3	9,73,597	8,88,438
1895	7,29,747	6,69,964		1,21,651	1,10,515	14.1	8,54,203	7,83,032
1896	7,42,792	6,84,315		1,20,153	1,08,529	15.1	8,65,417	7,94,970
1897	6,52,806	6,00,249		1,06,233	96,219	13.8	7,60,836	6,98,111
1898	7,84,863	7,27,299		1,23,195	1.13,124	13.4	9,09,746	8,41,979
1899	10,05,991	9,38,053		1,60,214	1,47,502	13.6	11,68,209	10,87,418
1900	8,42,264	7,85,017		1,35,859	1,25,610	13.8	9,79,859	9,12,319

Source: CR of 1901, Subsidiary Table VI, 128.

Table 6.2: Number of Married Women in Each Age Group

Age	*Hindu*			*Muslim*		
	Number	*% at Own Population*	*% at Total Population*	*Number*	*% at Own Population*	*% at Total Population*
0–10	6,38,861.5	1.6	1.34	78,079.99	1.16	0.16
10–15	2,44,9647.4	6.02	5.14	3,07,608.25	4.57	0.64
15–40	1,40,54,954	34.54	29.5	22,94,609.5	34.1	4.81
40 and Over	6,429,307.2	15.8	13.5	7,52,529.6	11.2	1.6
All Ages	2,131,4374	52.4	44.7	3,432,827.3	50.99	7.2

Source: CR of 1901, 138.

Table 6.3: Marriageable Age of Girls in 0–15 Age Group at per 1,000

Age	*All religion*			*Hindu*			*Muslim*		
	1901	*1891*	*1881*	*1901*	*1891*	*1881*	*1901*	*1891*	*1881*
0–5	9	6	51	9	6	53	8	6	35
5–10	110	99	11	115	104	-	82	73	-
10–15				562	594	569	419	456	428

Source: CR of 1921, 105.

Table 6.4: Number of Married Women at per Mille Based on CR of 1921

Religion and Natural Division	*Age Group*		
	0–5	*5–10*	*10–15*
United Province			
Hindu	7	107	520
Muslim	6	72	379
Himalaya West			
Hindu	1	61	542
Muslim	4	79	373
Sub-Himalaya West			
Hindu	2	85	492
Muslim	5	67	348
Indo-Gangetic Plain West			
Hindu	3	46	480
Muslim	4	44	333
Indo-Gangetic Plain Central			
Hindu	10	148	535
Muslim	7	82	346
Central India Plateau			
Hindu	9	141	626
Muslim	11	73	448
East Satpura			
Hindu	9	156	576
Muslim	13	111	467
Sub-Himalaya East			
Hindu	9	98	454
Muslim	6	99	496
Indo-Gangetic East			
Hindu	9	157	603
Muslim	8	97	452

Source: CR of 1921, Subsidiary Table II, 106–7.

Table 6.5: Marriageable Age for Selected Caste

Caste	*Age Group*	
	0–5	*5–12*
Shaikh	6	86
Pathan	11	95
Nai	10	123
Saiyid	8	53
Julaha	11	171
Teli	18	183
Bhangi	12	150

Source: CR of 1921, 110–11.

Note: Due to a paucity of accurate data, Tables 6.4 and 6.5 are based on the Census Report of 1921.

Table 6.6: Number of Women by Civil Condition and Main Age Group/100

Age	*All religion*			*Hindu*			*Muslim*		
	1901	*1891*	*1881*	*1901*	*1891*	*1881*	*1901*	*1891*	*1881*
				Unmarried					
0–10	24.2	25.8	24.8	20	25.8	24.7	25.2	26.3	25.2
10–15	4.8	4.3	4.3	4.5	4.2	4.2	6.2	5.0	5.7
15–40	1.5	0.8	0.8	1.4	0.7	0.7	2.3	1.6	1.65
40 and Over	0.3	0.1	0.1	0.3	0.11	0.11	0.5	0.3	0.32
All Ages	30.8	30.1	30.1	30.2	30.2	30.3	4.2	33.3	32.9
				Married					
0–10	1.5	1.38	1.3	1.6	1.44	1.4	1.2	1.03	0.91
10–15	5.8	5.4	5.5	6.0	5.6	5.7	4.6	4.3	4.3
15–40	34.5	35.5	35.7	34.54	35.5	35.8	34.1	35.1	34.9
40 and Over	10.4	10.3	10.3	10.3	10.2	10.2	11.2	10.9	10.9
All Ages	52.2	52.5	52.7	52.4	52.7	53.1	32.1	51.0	51.4
				Widowed					
0–10	0.05	0.03	0.02	0.06	0.03	0.02	0.04	0.03	0.02
10–15	0.13	0.10	0.11	0.13	0.10	0.12	0.06	0.06	0.07
15–40	3.9	3.55	3.8	4.08	3.7	3.9	2.84	2.74	3.13
40 and Over	12.9	13.1	13.2	13.2	13.2	13.2	11.9	12.5	12.9
All Ages	17.0	16.8	17.1	17.43	16.9	17.3	14.8	15.3	16.1

Source: CR of 1901, 141.

Table 6.7: No. of Widows per 1,000 Males

Division	*All Ages*	*0–10*	*10–15*	*15–40*	*40 and Over*
0. NWP and Oudh	2,377	2,216	1,295	1,543	2,731
1. Himalaya West	1,336	800	1,338	682	1,905
2. Sub-Him. West	2,098	2,830	1,585	1,381	2,424
3. Ind. Gang. Pl. West.	2032	1,380	1,414	1,278	2,358
4. Ind. Gang. Pl. Cent	2,709	2,393	1,633	1,760	3,066
5. Cent. India Plateau	3,603	1,455	2,400	2,630	4,129
6. East Satpura	3,005	250	1,462	2,262	3,904
7. Sub-Him. East	2,663	2,943	687	1,674	3,236
8. Ind. Gang. Pl. East	3,214	3,026	1,931	2,588	3,469
Muslim					

Contd.

Contd.

0. NWP and Oudh	2,400	1,463	1,435	1,827	2,677
1. Himalaya West	2,930	3,327	3,270	2,117	3,322
2. Sub-Him.West	1,917	1,409	1,194	1,310	2,230
3. Ind. Gang. Pl. West	1,818	1,245	1,534	1,384	2,000
4. Ind. Gang. Pl. Cent.	2,470	746	1,124	2,840	2,779
5. Cent. India Plateau	3,228	2,912	1,475	2,662	3,593
6. East Satpura	3,789	2,318	2,002	3,061	4,265
7. Sub-Him. East	2,935	2,934	1,594	2,138	3,349
8. Ind. Gang. Pl. East	3,197	3,378	1,651	2,555	3,552
All Religion					

Source: CR of 1901, 143.

Table 6.8

Age	*Hindu*			*Muslim*		
	Number of Widows	*% Age at its Own Population*	*% Age at Total Population*	*Number of Widows*	*% Age at its Own Population*	*% Age at Total Population*
0–10	24,415	0.06	0.051	2,692.4	0.04	0.01
10–15	52,899.4	1.3	0.11	6,058	0.1	0.01
15–40	16,60226.2	4.1	3.5	1,91161.4	2.84	0.4
40 and	53,55043.2	13.2	11.23	7,98300.6	11.9	1.67
Over All Ages	70,92583.9	17.43	14.87	9,98212.3	14.83	2.09

Source: CR of 1901, 138.

Table 6.9: No. of Widows at 10,000 Per Caste

Caste	*0–9*	*10–14*	*15–39*	*40 and Over*	*Total*	*Total Women*	*% Age of Each Caste*	*Sex Ratio*
Rajput Hindu	2	6	237	732	977	4,600	21	920
Muslim	2	3	166	653	824	4,901	16.2	920.2
Julaha Muslim	2	3	95	535	635	4,945	12.8	989
Hindu Artisan Village menials	2	4	144	559	709	4,894	14.5	978.8
Muslim	1	4	109	539	653	4,901	13.3	980.2
Bhangi Muslim	-	2	138	544	684	4,949	13.8	989.8
Non Indian Asiatic	1	2	155	698	856	4,895	17.5	979
Pathan	1	3	163	714	881	4,867	18.1	973.4
Sheikh	1	2	147	677	827	4,893	16.9	978.6
Saiyid	1	2	176	745	924	4,963	18.6	992.6

Source: CR of 1891, 250.

Table 6.10: No. of Widows Per 1,000 Widowers in Each Age Group

Religion	*0–9*	*10–19*	*20–29*	*30–39*	*40–49*	*50 and Over*
Hindu	1,364	1,354	1,479	1,976	2,663	2,880
Muslim	1,228	1,158	1,199	1,724	2,720	2,991

Source: CR of 1891, 249–50.

Table 6.11: Major Crime Rates

Class of Offence	*Acquittal*	*Convicted*	*% of Conviction*
Kidnapping	87	58	39.72
Rape	52	27	31.4
Marital Dispute	805	183	17.87
Assault	2,878	674	18.69

Source: Oudh Criminal Justice Report, Home Department: Judicial, 1885.

Appendix 1

Munajat-e Bewa

Altaf Husain Hali

Ai sab se aual aur akhir- jaha tahan hazir va nazir
Soch me dil bahlane vala- bipta me yad ane vala
Ai atkal aur dhean se bahar- dhean se aur pahchan se bahar
Aqal se koi pa nahi sakta- bhed tere huqmon me hai kea-kea
Ek ko tune shad kia hai- ek ke dil ko dag dia hai
Kheti ek ki hai lahrati- ek ka har dam khoon sukhati
Hal garz dunia ka yahi hai- gam pahle aur bad khushi hai
Ranj ka hai dunia ko gila kea- tohfa yahi mle dekh hai yahan ka
Yan nahi banti ranj sahe bin- ranj nahi sab ek se lekin
Tuhi kar insaf a mere maula- kaun hai jo beaas hai jeeta
Khawah dukhi hai khawah sukhi hai- jo hai ek ummid usko bandhi hai
Khetiyan jinki khari hai sookhi- as vo bandhe baithe hain munh ki
Ek hai us ummid pe jeeta- ab hui beti ab hua beta
Par nahi uth sakti vo hai musibat- aegi na jiske bad rahat
Shad ho us rahgeer ka kea dil- marke kategi jiski manzil
Un ujro kokal pare keon kar- ghar na basega jinka janam bhar
Aain bahut dunia me baharei aish ki ghar-ghar pari pukaren
Pare bahut bagon me jhoole-dhak bahut jangal me phoole
Gain aur aeen chandni raten- bares khulin bahut barsaten
Par na khuli hargiz na khulegi-vo kali jo murjhaee thi dil ki

As hi ka yan nam hai duniya- jab na rahi ye hi to raha kea
Huqm se tere par nahi chara- karvi meethi sab hai gawara
Tujhse kahin kar bhagna chahen- bandhi charo khoot ki rahen
Tu mare aur navaze- pari hun mai tere darvaze
Tujhi ko apna chahti hun mai- tujhse nahi to aur kis se kahun main
Laundi teri dukhyari- darvaze ki teri bhikhari
Maut ki khawah jan ki dushman- jan pe apni ap ajiran
Apne parae ki dhutkari- maike aur sasral pe bhari
Beyah ke dam paee na lene- lene ko yan par gae dene
Ek khushi ne gam ye dikhae- ek hansi ne gul ye khilae
Ro nahi sakti tang hun yahan tak- aur roun to roun kahan tak
Din bheyanak aur rat darawani- yun guzri ye sari jawani
Bahne aur saheliyan meri- sath kit hi jo kheliya meri
Bol na saki ji khol ke mujh se- khush na huin has bol ke mujh se
Sab aeein rod ho ke gain vo- jab gain be kul ho ke gain
Kali khuli dil kin a kisi par- ghul gai jan andar hi andar
Dukh ke chup na jana kisi ne- jan ko phunka dil ki lagi ne
Qaum me vo khushiya beyahon ki- shahar me vo dhoomen sahon ki
Nahvaron ka ae din ana- aur sab ka teohar manana
Aur chet va fagun ki hawaen- vo sawan bhadon ki ghataen
Vo garmi ki chandni raten- vo armano bhari barsaten
Kis se kahun kis tayr se katen- khair kati jis taur se katen
Gaya dekar chand dikhaee- chand hua par eid na aee
Na badli par hui na barkha- badal garja aur menh na barsa
Ret me zarre dekh chamakte- daur pari mai jheel samajh ke

A deen aur duniya ke malik- raja aur praja ke malik
Purab, pakshim, dakhin aur uttar- bakhshish teri am hai ghar-ghar
Sab par khula hai dar rahmat ka- baras raha hai menh neamat ka
Sab ko tere inam the shamil- mai hi na thi inam ke qabil
Agar kuch ata bant me meri- sab kuch tha sarkar me teri
Thi na kami kuch tere ghar men- noon ko tarsi main sanbhar me
Pahron ye sochti hun ji me- aee thi keon is nagri me main
Rahi akeli bhari sabha me- peasi rahi bhari ganga men
Qismat ne jab munh na mora- admiyon ka ho gaya tora
Bap au bhaee chacha aur bhateeje- sab rakhti hunt ere qaram se
Nahi pati ek bhi aisa- jisko ho meri jan ki parwa
Tere siwa a raham ke bani- kaun sune ye ram kahani
Koi nahi lagoo ab mera- bap na bhee sas na sasra

Die to sab rote hain ghar ke- rone nahi dete ji bharke
Hanse to hansna aib hai hamko- keon kar ilahi kate gam ko

Sonch me mere sara ghar hai- mere chalan pe sab ki nazar hai
Mehndi maine lagani chori—patti maine jamani chori
Kapre mahinon me hun badalti- itr mai bhool kar hun nai malti
Surma nahi ankhon me lagati- bal nahi barson main gundhwati
Do do chand nahi sar ko dhoti- atharon kanghi nahi hoti
Kan me patte hath me kangan- pahan chuki sab jab this suhagan
Ap ko yan tak maine mitaya- par duniya ko sabr na aya
Ham ne hai eke k ko ghera- jab dekho tab ziqr hai mera

A amber ke chamakte taron- a ghar ke dar va divaron
A jani pahchani raton- tanhaee ki daravani raton
Ek din is gandi duniya se- jana hai malik ke age
Jab vahan pooch ho merit teri- tum sab deejio gawahi meri
Mai neki ka dam nahi bharti- paki ka dawa nahi karti
Par ye khuda se darke hun kahti- munh pea e bin ye nahi rahti
Khawah buri thi khawah bhali thi mai- bat se apne nahi tali mai
Sath na qaum va des ka chora- aur na khuda kea had ko tora
A iman ke rakhne vale- a niat ke parakhne vale
Mai nahi rakhti kam kisi se- chahti hun insaf tujhi se
Huqm par chalti agar tere mai- chain se karti umr basar mai
Lekin hat pearon ki yahio thi- marzi gamkhawaron ki yahi thi
Apne baron ki reet na chote- qaum ki bandhi rasam na tute
Jan kisi ki jae to jae- an me apni farq na ae
Tujh pe ye raushan a mere maula- waqt ye kaisa mujh pe para
Rakhne the hamle mujhe dil ke- tha mujhe jeena khak me mil ke
Sanbhale jan thi jati- jan bachae aan thi jati
Par karne the sat samandar- huqm ye tha han paon na ho maila
Charon khoont tha phaila- huqm ye tha paon na ho maila
Jan na samjha jan ko apni- dia na jane an ko apni
Jane achche aur bur eke bhedi- khote ke aur khare ke bhedi
Bhed dilon ke jaan ne vale- pap aur punya ko chan ne vale
Aib aur gun sab tujhpe hai raushan- pap aur punya sab tujhpe hai raushan
Munh aur aankhen,hath aur bazoo- jin jin pet ha mujhe qaboo
Sab ko badi se maine bachaya- sab ko khudi se maine hataya
Rok keaur yun tham ke aapa- maine ye kanta apna randapa
Dhoop thi tez aur ret thi tapti- machli thi ek usme tarapti
Rooh na machli kit hi nikalti- aur munh sar se dhoop thi talti
Rahe magar us bat ka dana- maine kaha na dil ka mana
Manana dil ka kam tha mera- aur thamana kam that era
Saza de agar dil ki khata pet u- main razi hun teri raza par

Apni to khair jaisi guzri guzar gai- ab dhean hai to iska ki
A gam khawar hare k bekas ke- hami har ajiz bekas ke
Hai apne ajiz bandon par- pear tera man bap se barhkar
Jis ne lagi mai tujh ko pukara- samne tere hath pasara
Fira na khali is chaukhat se- gaya na peasa is panghat se
Ghar basne ki as na rahi- sari umr judaee sahi
Hai vo bala jo sahi na jae- bipta hai jo kahi na jae
Qadar uski ya tu pahchane- ya jis pe guzri hai v jane
A khavind khudavandon ke- malik khudavand aur bandon ke
Vasta apni khudavandi ka- sadqa apni khudavandi ka
Tu ye kisi ko dag na deejio- kisi ko bevaris mat keejio
Jis dukhiya par pare ye bipta- kar use peband zamin ka
Ya aurat ko pahle bula le- ya dono ko sath utha le

Chup ki dad

Altaf Husain Hali

A maon bahno, betion, dunia ki zeenat tum se hai
Mulkon ki basti ho tumhi qaumon ki izzat tumse hai
Tum ghar ki ho shahzadian, shahron ki ho abadiyan
Tum gamgeen dilon ki shadiyan, dukh such me rahat tum se hai
Tum ho to izzat hai watan, tum bin hai veeran chaman
Ho des ya pardes, jeene ki haladat tum se hai
Neki kit um tasveer ho, ifat kit um tadveer ho
Ho deen kit um pasban, iman salamat tumse hai
Fitrat tumari hai haya, teenat me hai mahr va wafa
Ghutti me hai sabr va raza. Insane iburat tumse hai
Mardon me sut vale jo the sut baithe vo apna jane kab ka kho
Duniya me a sutvantiyon! Le de kea b sut tumse hai
Mowannis ho khavindo kit um,gam khawar farzandon ki tum
Tum bin hai ghar viran sab, ghar bhar ki sab barkat tumse hai
Tum as ho bimar ki, dhadhas ho tum bekar ki
Daulat ho tum nadir ki, israt me ishrat tumse hai
Ati ho aksar be talab dunia me jab ati ho tum par mohini se apni yan ghar bhar pe cha jati ho tum
Maike me sare ghar kit hi tum malik va mukhtar tum
Par sare kunbe ki rahi bachpan se khidmatgar tum
Man-bap ke hukmon pe putli ki tarah firti rahi
Gham khawar bapon ki rahi, maon ki tab-e dart um
Din bhar pakana rendhna, seena, pirona, tankna
Baithi na ghar bap k khali kabhi zanhar tum

Raton ko chote bhai bahno ki khair uth-uth ke li
Bachcha koi sote me roya aur hui bedar tum
Sasral me pahunchi to van ek dusra dekha jahan
Ja utri goya des se pardes me ekbar tum
Van fiqr thi tum har dam yan nakhush na ho tumse koi
Apne se ranjish ke kabhi pao na tum van asaar tum
Badle na shauhar ki nazar, sasre ka dil maila na ho
Ankhon me sas aur nand ki khatko na misl khar tum
Pala gar buron se pare, bad khu ho sab chote bare
Chatoon pe mail ane na do, go dil me ho bezar tum
Gham ko ghalat karti raho, sasral me hans bolke
Sharbat ke ghunto ki tarah piti raho khoon-e jigar

Shadi ke bad ek-ek ko thi arzoo aulad ki
Tum fans gai janjal me khalik ne jab aulad di
Dardon ke dukh tumne sahe, jape ki jheli sakhtiyan
Jab maut ka chakha maza tab tumko ye daulat mili
Maike me aur sasral me sab ki hui dil bagh-bagh
Ghar me ujala to hua par tupe bipta par gai
Khana pahanna orhna apna gai sab bhool tum
Bachon ke dhandhe me thi apni na kuch sudh-budh
Tab tak bhi samjho khair thi jab tak bhale change the sab
Par samna afat ka tha gar ho gaya manda koi
Sooli pe din katne lage raton ki neend ur gai
Ek-ek baras ki ho gai ek-ek pal ek-ek ghari
Bachon ki sewa me thi guzre hai jaise das baras
Qadar uski janega vahi dam par jiske ho un bani
Ki hai muhim jo tumne sar, mardon ko uski kea khabar
Jane parai peer vo jiski fate jiski boaee ho fati
Tha palna aulad ka mardon ke bute se siva
Akhir ye a dukhyario khidmat tumaro sar pari
Paida agar hoti na tum bera na hota ye par ye
Cheekh uthne do din me agar mardon pe parta bar ye

Letin khabar aulad ki maen na agar chutpan me yan
Khali kabhi ka nasl se adam ki ho jata jahan
Ye gosht ka ek lothra parwan charhta kis tarah
Chati se liptae na hardam rakhti bache ko man
Voh deen aur duniya ke maslah jinke vaez va pand se
Zulmat me batil ki hawa duniya me noor haq ayan
Vo ilm va hiqmat ke bani jinki tahkikat se
Zahir hue alam me israre zameen va asman

Afsos duniya me tumpe bahut hue zulm va jafa
Haq talfiyan tumne sahi be mahriyan jheli sada
Aksar tumare qatl pe qaumon ne bandhi hai kamar
Den taki tumko yak qalam khud looh, hasti se mita
Gari gait um muddaton mitti me jeeti jagti
Hami tumara tha magar koi jaz zat khuda
Zinda sada chalti rahi tum murda khavindon ke sath
Aur chain se alam raha ye sab tamasha dekhta
Beyahi gai us waqt jab beyah se waqif na thin
Jo umr bhar ka ahad tha vo kachche dhge se bandha
Beyaha tumhe ma bap ne a bezaban us tarah
Jaise kisi taqseer pe mujrim ko dete hai saza
Guzri ummid va beem me jab tak raha baqi suhag
Bewa hui to fir umr bhar chain qismat me na tha
Tum sakht se sakht imtehan deti rahi lekin raega
Keen tumne jane tak fida kahlaeen fir bhi bewafa
Go sabr ka tumko apne na kuch mila inam yan
Par jo farishte se na ho sake kar gai vo kam tum yan

Ki tumne is darul mahan me jis tahmul se guzar
Zeba hai ki kahe tume fakhre nabi noohe basher
Jo sang dil sefak peyase the tumare khoon ke
Unki to hai berahmiyan mashhoor alam me magar
Tumne to chain apne kharidaron se bhi paya na kuch
Shauhar ho usme ya pidar, ya ho biradar ya pisar
Ulfat tumari kar gai ghar dil me jis bedeed ke
Vo badguman tumse raha a badnaseebon umr bhar
Go nek mard aksar tumare nam ke ashiq rahe
Par nek ho ya bad, rahe sab mutaffiq us rae par
Jab tak jio tum ilm va Danish se raho marhoom yahan
Aee ho jaisi be khabar vaisi hi jao bekhababar
Tum us tarah majmool aur gumnam duniya me raho
Ho tumko duniya kin a duniya ko ho tumari khabar
Jo ilm mardon ke lie samjha gaya ab-e hayat
Thahra tumare lie vo zahar halahal sar basar
Ata hai waqt insaf ka nazdeek hai yaum-ul hisab
Duniya ko dena hoga un haq talfiyon ka wan jawab

Guzre the jag tumpar ki hamdardi na thi tumse kahin
Tha munharif tumse falak, bargushta thi tumse zameen
Duniya ke data aur hakeem us khaf se larzan the sab
Tum par mubada ilm ki par jae parchaeen kahin

Aisa na ho mard aur aurat me baqi na farq
Taleem pake admi banna tume zeba nahi
Yahan tak tumari haju ke gae gae duniya me rag
Tumko bhi duniya ki kahan ka a gaya akhir yaqeen
Ilm va hunar se rafta rafta ho gain mayoos tum
Samjha liya dil ko ki ham ilm ke qabil na the
Jo zillaten lazim hain duniya me jahalat ke lie
Samjha na tumko ek din mardon ne qabil bat ke
Tum bewafa kahlaeen lekin laundiyan banke rahin
Akhir tumari chup dilon me ahal dil ke chup gai
Sach hai ki chup ki dad akhir be mile rahti nahi
Bare zamana neend ke maron ko laya hosh me
Aya tumare sabr pe daryae rahmat josh men

Naubat tumari haq rasi bat muddat ke aee hai
Insaf ne dhundhli si ek apni jhalak dhikhlaee hai
Go hai tumare hamion ko mushkilon ka samna
Par hal hare k mushkil unhi duniya me hoti aee hai
Atke hain rore chalti gari me sada sachchaee ke
Par fatah jab paee hai sachchaee ne akhir paee hai
A bezabanon ki zabanon, bebason ke bazuon
Taleem nuswa ki muhim jo tumko jo ab pesh aee hai
Ye marhal aya hai tumse pahle jin qaumon ko pesh
Manzil pe gari unki isteqlal ne pahunchaee hai
Hai raee bhi parbat agar dil me nahi azam-e durust
Par than li jab ji me fir parbat bhi ho to raee hai
Ye jeet bhi kea kam hai khud haq hai tumari pusht par
Jo haq pe munh aya hai akhir usne munh ki khaee hai
Jo haq ke janib dar hain bas unke bere par hai
Bhopal ki janib se ye hatif ki awaz aee hai
Hai jo muhim dar pesh dast ghaib hai usme nihan
Taed haq ka hai nishan imdad-e Sultan Jahan

CHAPTER 7

Cultural Clash: From *Tawa'if* to *Kasbi*

Pahle dil lete hai voh ya pahle jan ahle dard
Dekhie karte hain keunkar imtehan ahle dard
Kaun kahta hai nahi hai qadardan ahle dard
Dard dil dag jigar hai meharban ahle dard
Ranj va gham dard va alam aah va Fagaan va qurb va qalaq
Ajkal to hain yahi bas meharban ahle dard
Dono hathon se kaleja tham ke baithen huzoor
Shauq sunne ka agar hai dastan ahle dard
Qissa ranj va alam sun-sun kar ro dega har ek
Zikr jab saaqi ka hoga darmayan ahle dard[1]

Sitari Jan Saqin Tawa'if Saqin Baska Jila Ghazipur

Would my friends take first my heart or my life
Let's see what tests they put me through, what strife
Who can ever claim they care not for me
They inflict sufferings on my heart, scars on my soul
Grief, sorrows, pains, sufferings, cravings and yearnings,
These alone are my friends these days, my companions
My friend! hold your heart with both your hands
If you are inclined to hear the tale of my afflictions
These tales of woes would bring tears into every eye
Whenever the mention of saqi would be made in midst of friends.

(Tr. into English by Nishat Zaidi)

This is not merely a verse; it symbolises the pain of the dying culture of the *tawa'if*. Etymologically, *tawa'if* is the plural of the Arabic word *taifa*, meaning 'band' or 'group' but the word *tawa'if*, used as a singular in Urdu,

[1] Muhammad Nisar Husain Nisar (ed.), *Payam-e Yar*, Vol. XVI (Lucknow: Qaumi Press, 1898), 13.

means 'prostitute'. The common and derogatory word for prostitute in Urdu is '*randi*'. There are different types of *tawa'ifs*: those who were 'kept' on a permanent basis by a man and might eventually have married him, and those who led an itinerant life, moving from city to city.[2] In some cities, especially Lucknow, the *tawa'if* occupied a relatively respectable position in society and was admired for her sophistication and culture.[3] The elite of the town would send their sons to the *tawa'if*s residence to be educated in manners and letters. Dr W. Crook, in an article on Indian prostitution in Hasting's *Encyclopedia of Religion and Ethics*, remarked that in that period, prostitutes were tolerated in India to an extent unparalleled in any other part of the world.[4] Also, British discursive writing often alleged that prostitution has existed in India from time immemorial.[5]

If prostitution had always been rampant in India, then why did the number of prostitutes show a declining trend? Their numbers dropped from 26,915 to 22,472 between 1881–91, and the total decline recorded was 4,500.[6] The number of dancers, prostitutes and procurers were at 11,423, 11,005 and 644, respectively.[7] Gradually, these numbers too dropped to 21,787 by 1901 (0.3 per cent of the entire Muslim population), and out of this, the total number of males was 7,302.[8] Interestingly, all the prostitutes had been registered under the professional class of Muslims. Most were single, and the males in this group were either illegitimate children, or procurers. The other male auxiliaries of the establishment—like doormen, touts and pimps—were often relatives of the chief courtesan, and they provided the much-needed male support and security. Here, a question arises: Why was the British government so keen to register prostitutes under a separate category? Did they want to keep a check on the latter, or was there some other hidden objective that led them to provide prostitutes with a space in colonial census reports? Why were the highly cultured salons degraded

---

2 Veena Talwar Oldenberg, 1997, 'Lifestyle as a Resistance: The Case of the Courtesans of Lucknow', in Violette Graft (ed.), *Lucknow: Memories of a City* (New Delhi: Oxford University Press, 2997), 136–43.

3 Abdul Haleem Sharar, *Lukhnow: The Last Phase of Oriental Culture* (New Delhi: Oxford University Press, 1994), 192.

4 S. M. Edwards, *Crime in British India* (New Delhi: ABC Publishing House, 1983).

5 ibid.

6 C.R. of 1881, 81.

7 ibid.

8 C.R. of 1901, 254–55, Subsidiary Table I.

to mere flesh trade? Before going into further details, it is necessary to look at the social structure of the world of *tawa'ifs*.

The world of the *tawa'if* was as hierarchical as the society of which it was a part. Indeed these women were divided into two groups, in much the same way as Indian society, viz., *tawa'if*, and *randi* or *kasbi khangi*. Unlike Indian society, though, this division was based on talent and profession, and not on birth. It would not be an exaggeration to say that the status of *tawa'ifs* was akin to that of nawabs and feudal rulers; they had the same lavish lifestyle and on occasion, even issued challenges to the local nawabs.[9] As Vikram Sampath (2010: 21) said,

> The community (tawaif) also had a rigid social hierarchy. One had to be born to a tawaif and claim a lineage to be accepted as a tawaif. Girls who were kidnapped were never inducted into the performing space of a tawaif. They were consigned to flesh trade. Thus a clear distinction between tawaif and prostitutes was always made in society.

These skilled courtesans entertained only the elite; they visited no houses other than the big mansions of the nawabs and taluqdars. People used to visit their salons on their own;[10] indeed, a man was not considered polished until he had visited these salons,[11] as in those days salons provided social etiquette as well as literary gatherings. Sometimes, young boys from *shari'f* families were sent to the salons, accompanied by an elderly person, to learn etiquette and manners. Munir Bai, the famous courtesan and president of the Music-Artist Union of *Deredar* Tawa'if, recalled their glory days and lamented the degrading status of her *qaum*:

> Sir, as far as award was concerned, there were many nobles who used to throw notes and coins at us. At that time we used to keep our honour and were respected. Even very affluent people used to make us sit beside them. Chaudharayan used to arrange *darbars* at her house. Honourable people used to go there to learn etiquette and manners. Now people consider us as belonging to *Bagchavali Gali* ....[12]

---

[9] David Mathews (trans.), *Umrao Jan-e Ada* (New Delhi: Rupa and Co., 1996), 39.

[10] A close analysis of *Umrao Jan-e Ada* brings out a very interesting picture of this trend.

[11] Sharar, *Lukhnow*, 192.

[12] Amrit Lal Nagar, *Ye Kothe Valiyan* (Allahabad: Hindi Sahitya Sammelan Library), 109.

Tawaif Culture: *Umrao-Jan-e Ada* as a Woman of Power

Mirza Hadi Ruswa painted an interesting picture of this hierarchical society in his famous novel, *Umrao Jan-e Ada.* A well-educated, polished and classy courtesan of Lucknow, Amiran (who came to be known as Umrao Jan-e Ada) appeared to be a helpless, delicate girl at the mercy of an exploitative society, who was drawn into the profession of prostitution. With the help of her classical talent, she rebelled against society and carved out an identity of her own. The novel tells the story of a woman's journey from Amiran to Umrao, and from Umrao to Umrao Jan. Eventually, she established herself as an eminent poetess and courtesan, Umrao Jan-e Ada. She took on 'ada' as a *takhallus* for the literary world. Her debates on social issues and literature with famous litterateurs are proof of the vociferous challenge she presented to the male-dominated world of literature. 'Ada' soon became the talk of the town. As she claimed:

> My ability to sing dirges was well known, and no one knew more of the finer points of the art than I. Even the greatest master does not dare to open their mouths in my presence, and it was for this reason that I gained access to the court of nawab Malika Qausar. King himself praised my nauha khawani. Every Muharram, I received much attention from royal circles. I also excelled in the art of the elegy, and in the evening, after having performed my lamentation in the imambara, I was obliged to stay at the place door until two in the morning.[13]

Umrao Jan broke away from the traditional image of the prostitute; skilled in the arts, she perhaps wanted to be counted as an equal among 'respectable' people. *Umrao Jan* also shows the double standards men adopted towards women, whom they considered commodities whose only job was to entertain men. Indeed, a *tawa'if* could be a partner—in some cases a life partner—but she could never achieve the status of wife, despite all her inherent talents. An interesting observation: if a man desired intellectual stimulation, he would visit a salon;[14] but when he needed advice regarding family matters, he would discuss it with his uneducated wife. Thus, men had double parameters for the public and the domestic woman. Although Ruswa asserted in his preface to

---

[13] Ruswa Mirza Hadi, *Umrao Jan-e Ada*, 107. See also the translation by David Mathews, 69.

[14] See the tragic life history of renowned singer, dancer and poetess, Gauhar Jaan. She was cheated time and again by her many male partners, and never realized her dream of attaining the respectable status of wife. Vikram Sampath, *My Name is Gauhar Jaan* (New Delhi: Rupa & Co., 2010).

Umrao Jan-e Ada that the work was the outcome of his regular visits to the salon and interaction with courtesans, several scholars argue that the book is mere fiction. However, there is evidence of the existence of Umrao Jan Sahiba 'Dilbar' Saqin Unnao, Muqeem Kanpur. She was a famous courtesan whose verses were published in *Payam-e Yar, a* monthly magazine. Coincidently, she was also a resident of Kanpur, where Umrao Jan-e Ada was supposed to have lived for a few years. She seemed very skilled in her composition of ghazals:

Ik na ik ki voh jan lete hai- jab voh teer va Kaman lete hain
Shiqwa zor pe voh kahte hain- ham tera imtehan lete hain
Hoti hai vo laqeer paththar ki- dil me voh jo kuch than lete hain
Ye haya vasal me ki sartapa- voh dulaee ki taan lete hain
Badle angashtari ke ham tumse- dagh dil ka nishan lete hai
Dil ko dete hai ham use dilbar- jinko ham khoob jan lete hain[15]

When he picks up arrows and the bow
Death of someone is writ anyhow;
And if anyone complains, they argue,
'I am only testing you'
Whenever they set their heart on something,
It turns out to be writing on the stone
In place of finger ring, I exchange with you
Signs of wounds inflicted on my heart
I lend my heart to that sweetheart!
Whom I get to recognize very well!
(*English translation by Nishat Zaidi*)

Ruswa's assertion can also be corroborated by other sources. Malka Jan and Gauhar Jan, eminent courtesans of the time, had lifestyles that resembled Umrao Jan's. Malka Jan was born Allen Victoria Heming in 1857 to Anglo-Indian parents, and married Armenian engineer Robert Yeoward. In 1873, they had a baby girl, Eileen Engilina, who was baptised into Christianity. Victoria's love for music and dance soon became a bone of contention between her and her husband, and they divorced in 1879. Alone and helpless, Mrs. Yeward left the city with her daughter with the help of an admirer, Khursheed. They went to Benaras, where she struggled to earn a livelihood for the next two years. Finally, she found a patron in Benares, began learning music, dance and poetry, and settled down there from 1881 onwards. She embraced Islam and

[15] *Payam-e Yar*, 8 (March), 1890, 23.

took the name Malka Jan; she even renamed her little daughter Gauhar Jan. In 1883, they moved to Calcutta in the hope of gaining patronage from the exiled nawab of Oudh, Wajid Ali Shah. It was here that the fame and fortune of both mother and daughter grew. Most prostitutes and courtesans practised Islam in British India.[16]

The courtesans lived in a particular area of the city, under the supervision of the *chaudhrayan*. Areas like Chauk (Lucknow), Dal Ki Mandi (Benaras), and Hira Mandi (Lahore) were famous. The *chaudhrayan* played an important role: she was responsible for the management of every salon, including the finances, and for recruiting beautiful and skilled girls. Her share, as Oldenberg calculates, was close to 43.75 per cent (almost 7 aana out of 16) of every courtesan's earnings.[17] The extent of the financial exploitation prevalent can only be imagined. The remaining share did not belong to the *tawa'if*, though; a long list of middlemen had to be paid first. Renowned courtesans took only a few years to familiarize themselves with the manipulative ways of the salon world, and removed themselves from the *chaudhrayan*'s clutches as soon as they could. It is said that a famous courtesan's fee for one night equalled the daily revenue of the king of Kashi.[18]

Traditionally, most *tawa'ifs* were familiar with this exploitative system since prostitution was largely a hereditary profession.[19] They preferred to be known as *deredar tawa'ifs* instead of *qasbi* or *randi*, whom they held in contempt. They did not even like being called Bai and Jan, choosing to be addressed by that respectable term, *begum*. When Nagar asked them why, the famous courtesan Nasim Ara said:

> O Sir! In these days, this world [has] become a gallows for us. Otherwise we are not the kind of people to indulge in filthy work. That work is done here in *Chawalvali* lane. Sir, we are noble, we used to perform singing and dancing for many generations. We do not associate with everyone. And we are not amongst them who, without any acquaintance, sells herself just because of money .... We do not do this work in our house, we are deredar.[20]

---

[16] Nagendra Kumar Singh, *Encyclopedia of Indian Women*, Vols I–III (2001); Nagar, *Ye Kothe Valiyan*, 198–99.

[17] Veena Talwar Oldenberg, *The Making of Colonial Lucknow, 1856–77*, in *Lucknow Omnibus*, (New Delhi: Oxford University Press, 2001).

[18] Sampath, *My Name is Gauhar Jaan*, 16.

[19] ibid. See also Nagar, *Ye Kothe Valiyan*, 92.

[20] Nagar, *Ye Kothe Valiyan*, 92.

Boasting that the *deredar tawa'if* was the highest *qaum* among all Muslim *tawa'ifs*, she added, 'Sir, Deredar tawaif keeps honour like noble women. And reason of it since they are made to learn etiquette and manners. It can not be found in trafficked women.'[21]

This is why there was little evidence of forceful abduction among *deredar tawa'ifs*.[22] Although the leading character in *Umrao Jan-e Ada* was an abducted girl, Umrao Jan herself accepted that abduction was not the norm in big salons. Most prostitutes there chose the profession willingly.[23] Every salon had its own music band and master for the girls,[24] who were expected to learn the arts and feminine wiles from infancy, in some cases from ages as young as six.[25] Nasim Aara reveals a classic picture of the glorious years of *tawa'if* culture and the meaning of *talim-tahzeeb*:

> Etiquette and manners, that entire thing is considered necessary for noble association. O Sir! From this time to hundred or two hundred years ago there was a custom that from very infant age girls used to make learn marksmanship, riding, poetry, dancing, sewing-stitching and chess etc. When a girl's education used to finish then they used to be sent according to one's approach and talent. She used to give her first performance at the *mahfil* of kings, Talluqdar and zamindar, then used to be offered to any noble. If she was liked and accepted, then our girls used to receive land and property from them, whatever their capacity. That girl used to stay at that particular noble's keeping for [her] whole life. They used to fix a monthly salary for the girl's relatives too. And after his death, his heir used to give this amount.[26]

These *tawa'ifs* learnt the arts of singing, dancing, classical languages and poetry from renowned *ustads* and teachers of the time. Umrao Jan talked about her training at Khanum's house:

> After I had mastered the scales, my ustad began with fragments of melody. He taught extremely methodically, and every note of the raga had to be learned by

[21] Nagar, *Ye Kothe Valiyan*, 97.

[22] Oldenburg, *The Making of Colonial Lucknow*.

[23] Nagar, *Ye Kothe Valiwan*.

[24] W. Wakefield, *Our Life and Travels in India* (London: Low, Searle and Rivington, 1878), 34. See also Kameshwar Nath, *Kashi ki Sangeet Parampara (Sangeet Jagat ko Kashi Ka Yogdan)* (Lucknow: Bharat Book Centre, 1997).

[25] Oldenburg, *The Making of Colonial Lucknow*, 134–37. See also Nagar, *Ye Kothe Valiyan*, 94.

[26] Nagar, *Ye Kothe Valiyan*, 94.

heart and produced exactly by the voice. You could never get away with flattening a sharp, or going slightly off pitch. And I had the habit of asking questions. At first the Ustad (may he be spared his shame in the grave!) would hedge.[27]

They would boast about their *ustads* and the cities from which they hailed. They were proud to be known as the *shagirds* of renowned *ustads*, and never forgot to mention their names; for instance, Janab Atar Badauni is referred to in some verses of Abbasi Jan Ada *Tawa'ifs Qasida*. Hina Sahiba Hina and Shagird Bi Jadu Sandelvi are other names worthy of note.

Bat usne hai kab mani meri- roti hai mujhpar pur Armani meri
Yad Gesu ka asar hai bal-bal- kam na ho ya rab pareshani meri
Shaeri par e Ada Qurban hun- Sun rahe hain ghazal khawani meri[28]
Abbasi Jan Ada, tawaif Badauni Shagird Janab Atar Badauni

When has he lent ears to my words?
My wishful heart weeps at my helplessness
Each hair of my body is overwhelmed
By the memory of her tresses
O God let my sorrows never wane
O Ada! I am besotted with your poetry
The entire world listens to my Ghazal recitation.
(*English translation by Nishat Zaidi*)

Kabhi ham bhule se jo nala karenge-to vo hashr pe hashr barpa karenge
Gham va aas va hasrat ka majma hai kaisa-ye kea qabr ashik pe maila karenge
Kahani ke pairae me ham unko ai dil-ham afsana-e gham sunaya karenge
Naseeb isme hame izzat ho ki zillat-ye dil jab talak hai tamanna karenge[29]
Hina Sahiba Hina, Shagird Bi Jadu Sandelvi

If I err to complain ever
Doomsday on a doomsday he sure will conjure
Why this gathering of sorrows, hope, wishes
Are these out to sully the grave of the lover
I will narrate my heart's agonies O heart
In the form of a story, a tale.
Whether I earn honour or disgrace in this, I do not care
As long as I have heart in my bosom, I will desire.
(*English translation by Nishat Zaidi*)

[27] Mathew (trans.), *Umrao Jan-e Ada*, 22.
[28] *Payam-e Yar*, XVI (January), 1898, 14.
[29] *Payam-e Yar*, XVII, June 1896, 19.

Famous courtesan Bari Malka Jaan received lessons in classical Persian from Husain Ahmad Asghar and Qadar Husain, while Hakim Banno Sahib 'Hilal' was appointed to teach her Urdu.[30]

Kasbi and Khangi

Prostitute fall under two other categories—*Kasbi* and *Khangi*—neither of which refers to any special talent or skill except selling their virtue.[31] *Kasbi*s worked openly in brothels while *khangi*s, who desired to keep their identities secret, mostly had clandestine relationships. Generally, *khangi*s hailed from poor *shari'f* families and remained veiled. They were clearly forced to become prostitutes because of extreme poverty.[32] The nineteenth century was a period of deindustrialization, and many Muslim families met their daily needs by knitting, stitching, embroidery, and some *dastkari* work, all of which were adversely affected by the ushering in of industrialization.[33] This crippled people, especially the women from lower economic strata, who found it difficult to make ends meet. There were castes that considered prostitution a hereditary occupation, for instance the Nat, Bhand and Mirasi communities, where women worked in the flesh trade openly while the men acted as their pimps. They were also known as the *Paturiya* community. Why did prostitution become a problem only in the late nineteenth century, after 1857, when it had been prevalent for a long time? Did the colonial presence make it more problematic? These issues continue to be relevant and debatable.

The European Encounter with Prostitutes

Male European migration to India increased from the eighteenth century onwards. Naturally, these men desperately needed female companionship. Given these circumstances, upper-class Europeans and their subordinates contracted inter-racial marriages with members of the influential local community. These marriages mostly proved temporary because of the huge cultural difference between the brides and the grooms; soon after the men returned home, they

30 *My Name is Gauhar Jaan,* 17.

31 Oldenburg, *The Making of Colonial Lucknow*, 135. In addition, contemporary vernacular newspapers also spoke about the lower-class *randi.*

32 Oldenberg, *The Making of Colonial Lucknow*; Nagar, *Ye Kothe Valiyan.*

33 Mushirul Hasan, *From Pluralism to Separatism: Qasba in Colonial Oudh* (New Delhi: Oxford University Press, 2004), 42–43.

terminated the contracts. In all such cases, these brown 'memsahibs' retired with either maintenance or a pension. The year 1857 was a turning point in Indo-European matrimonial relationships. After the great upsurge, inter-racial marriages were discouraged and female migration from England and other European countries began on a large scale.[34] European women, mostly from the upper or elite classes (long sea voyages were beyond the financial capacity of lower-class women) found in India the perfect site for seeking husbands.

Around the same time, prostitution became a problem for the British at home too, with venereal diseases taking a terrible toll. A serious debate began amongst British officials concerning the security of their soldiers; after lengthy deliberations, two causes were identified: extreme poverty, which forced women into prostitution, and the enforced celibacy that soldiers were subjected to. The presence of an increasing number of European prostitutes was also noticed, both at home and in the Indian subcontinent, alarming British morals even further. Given this situation, the British government decided to allow their soldiers to marry. Interestingly, India was exempted from this concession,[35] but the Indian colony did come under the Contagious Diseases Act of 1864. Under this Act, every prostitute had to undergo a medical check-up at the Lock Hospital to discover whether they were disease-free, so that only healthy women could be procured for the military cantonment.[36] Thus, state-sponsored prostitution had begun in British India, accompanied by the recruitment of '*lalbibi*' in the military. As the *Awadh Panch* remarked, 'Sequence reached up to this degree that government orders to provide flour, pulse, wood, grass for their military thither ask for to provide a pubescent and so-so prostitute.'[37]

People soon began seeking tenders. The *Awadh Akhbar* focused on just such a shameful application of a man who called himself '*bulbul-e hind*', and provided a detailed account of his skills as a procurer:

> White sahibs will bang their heads hither and thither for people (female) and government will have to face. O sir! See how they can understand right and wrong in their adolescence. Hence a restraint for them is incumbent over government such a tie of commensality like that manner, tehsildar and magistrate

---

[34] Indrani Sen, *Women and Empire* (New Delhi: Orient BlackSwan, 2002).

[35] William Acton, *Prostitution Considered in its Moral, Social and Sanitary Aspects* (London: Frank Cass, 1870), 187–233.

[36] *Oudh Akhbar*, 26 May 1868. This is why several newspapers raised questions about their registration in government records, which resulted in a loss in tax collection.

[37] *Oudh Panch*, 45, 10 November 1892, Lucknow.

> of the cantonment is responsible for the procurement of beautiful prostitutes like he is for eggs, chicken and milk. Then why is the government concerned about their comfort for which it is responsible? After all, the soldiers are ready to lay down their lives for the government. Therefore, it is necessary to procure prostitutes and settle a brothel for those gallant enough. Since government officers have no experience in this field, it is thereby humbly request of Your Highness to allow this petitioner to serve. Bulbul-e Hind—Maroof Mian Lucknow.[38]

Again, the question arises: Why did the number of prostitutes drop rapidly despite the British government encouraging their procurement?[39] It was soon found that they either avoided registering themselves in the government records, or fled to other places.[40] The Venereal Disease Act and Income Tax Act added to the reason. The government's major sources of income were revenue tax (which Indians were familiar with) and income tax (which was new to them). These did not pose as great a problem to courtesans, who owned immoveable property, as they did to the low-ranking prostitutes, who earned just enough to fall into the tax bracket. Rampant venereal diseases also forced the British to change their policy towards prostitutes. The British were determined to tax prostitutes and force them to undergo medical check-ups; on the other hand, prostitutes were busy searching for ways to escape. Once a week, every *kasbi* had to go for a medical check-up, and the police were supposed to confirm that they were disease-free.[41] There had long been a nexus between prostitutes and the government, which included ties between the procurer, the *chaudhrayan*, the local police, and the doctor. Some elite courtesans, though, considered this a direct attack on their reputations.[42] The events of 1857 had obviously changed the fate of both *tawa'if*s and *randi*s and increased government determination to control them because, as stated in the preceding chapters, a large number of these women had assisted the mutineers and worked as scouts during the rebellion.[43]

---

38 *Oudh Panch*, 47, 24 November 1892.

39 *The Bharat Bandhu* (Aligarh), 15 June 1888. The newspaper expressed great concern over the British policy of procurement. See also *Subodh Sindhu*, 23 May 1888.

40 *Oudh Akhbar*, 26 May 1868.

41 ibid. See also Oldenburg, *The Making of Colonial Lucknow*, 140.

42 Oldenburg, *The Making of Colonial Lucknow*.

43 Singh, *Encyclopedia of Indian Women*, Vol. I, 101; Vinayak Damodar Savarkar, *Indian War of Independence* (Bombay: Phoenix Publications, 1857), 227.

Public Debate on Prostitution

The countrywide agitation against prostitution attracted the attention of the vernacular press, which focused on three issues: the Venereal Diseases Act, the imposition of income tax, and the resentment of the common people, which raised issues of safety and security of the prostitutes.

In the 1860s, the British government had to deal with the fact that soldiers were dying in greater numbers; indeed, as Veena Oldenberg says, causalities resulting from venereal diseases were greater than causalities in war. Drastic measures therefore became necessary, and the British government found itself facing two options: banning prostitution, or making medical arrangements at the Lock hospitals. Since the former option was untenable—military expenses would increase hugely if every soldier was permitted to bring his wife to India; prostitution was the cheapest way to meet a soldier's needs. Therefore, it was incumbent on the British to ensure that prostitutes remained healthy. In this context, Act XIV, 1868, was enforced in the Indian subcontinent too. Prostitutes, however, did not welcome this move, and began fleeing from one city to another. Since the police were now authorized to control every brothel, several prostitutes argued that they now had an opportunity to detain those elite prostitutes whom they otherwise could never afford.[44] This increasing immigration became a matter of great concern for the Deputy Collector of Kanpur.

Simultaneously, the rise in murder cases involving prostitutes drew the attention of newspapers, and led to growing insecurity amongst prostitutes. In most of the cases, the police were found to be the perpetrators.[45] The prostitutes soon realized that it would be safer to live together in one place to prevent such incidents from occurring.[46] This perhaps explains why elite courtesans posted guards at their doors and why strangers were not allowed to visit them frequently. While lower-class prostitutes were also fearful, they could not afford expensive security. Public resentment against brothels was fast mounting, and demands were made that brothels be banned in the main city and be vacated as soon as possible. Since the common people had never welcomed brothels in residential areas, it forced prostitutes to settle in the outskirts of the city, making them even more vulnerable. These circumstances endangered their lives and provided opportunities for corrupt policemen, who were found guilty of robbery and murder far more than the women's clients.

---

[44] Oldenberg, *The Making of Colonial Lucknow*, 141.

[45] *Oudh Akhbar*, 30 June 1868; 4 August 1868.

[46] Report on the Native Newspaper of NWP of Agra and Oudh, 1891, 27.

Courtesans of Oudh were mostly prosperous, and owned several moveable and immoveable properties from which they earned a sizable income, apart from their income from *mujras* and *mahfils*.[47] That was a time when a *tawa'if* could earn Rs 100 to 1,000,000 a night, whereas a low-ranking *randi* could earn only Rs 5.[48] A male labourer charged Rs 10, but a female was paid only Rs 5 per month.[49] Naturally, this was considered the easiest means of earning more money. Generally, elite courtesans entertained only kings, nawabs and wealthy people, earning millions in cash and several precious ornaments besides.[50] If anyone desired to keep a courtesan, he became responsible for all her expenses, including paying her a monthly allowance for the rest of her life.[51] Monthly allowances often ranged from Rs 1,000 to 3,000.[52] However, the offspring born of such unions could not claim paternity rights.[53] What is surprising, though, is that there was no cultural clash amongst them where religion was concerned. The salons followed the rule of matriarchy: if the mother believed in Islam and the father was Hindu, the children had to necessarily adopt their mother's religion in the maternal home; however, when they visited their father, the Hindu religion had to be followed. Additionally, a daughter born to such a woman had to compulsorily adopt her mother's profession, viz., prostitution.[54] Thus, hereditary prostitution was rampant among these *deredar tawa'ifs*, which was why a large number of *kanchan tawa'ifs* traced their ancestry back to the Sharqi kingdom.[55]

A large section of Muslim women was forced into prostitution to earn a livelihood. Increasing industrialization and mechanization had economically crippled the people dependent on small industries and handicrafts. Perhaps this was why the Benaras locality where *julahas* lived became the main centre for *kasbi* recruitment.[56] Concurrently, *khangi* brothels were emerging fast

---

[47] Oldenberg, *The Making of Colonial Lucknow*, 134; Sharar, *Lukhnow*, 196.

[48] Oldenberg, *The Making of Colonial Lucknow*, 138.

[49] Wakefield, *Our Life and Travels in India*, 203–4.

[50] The Parikhana of Wajid Ali Shah and Nagar's encounters with courtesans show how they had flourished under the royal patronage of the Princely states.

[51] Nagar, *Ye Kothe Valiyan*, 94, 140–41.

[52] Tasadduq Husain, *Begmat-e Oudh*. It was Wajid Ali Shah who fixed this amount for his wives and *mutaee bibis*.

[53] Nagar. *Ye Kothe Valiyan*, 246–47.

[54] ibid.

[55] ibid.

[56] ibid.

in Lucknow. The prohibition on widow remarriage also provided a fillip to prostitution.

This was why the British government alleged that all Hindu women of 'loose-character' accepted Islam.[57] They also realized that prostitutes should be brought under the income tax provision. This became an issue of debate in the vernacular newspapers and stirred up resentment among the common people. Some newspapers were of the opinion that if the government made prostitution taxable, it would increase tax collection as well as check the mobility of such women.[58] They also demanded an increase in the duty on liquor, as this was believed to be the main cause behind prostitution.[59] *Nasim-e Agra* expressed great concern, stating that it was cruel of the government to not exempt dancing girls. The government levied a tax of 2.5 per cent on the prostitutes' income; however, given that the income was shared between several middlemen, in reality it came to around 50 per cent of the total.[60] *Akhbar-e Aam* and *Nasim-e Agra* both wrote in defence of dancing girls and prostitutes, and expressed their annoyance over the method of income tax assessment in Agra. They also argued that it would provide corrupt officers with opportunities to ask for bribes.[61] Some clever courtesans either kept two sets of accounts, one to show income tax officers and another for themselves, or usually evaded paying tax by bribing the officials.[62]

Surprisingly, one section of prostitutes began demanding equal rights for themselves. They argued that if they had to pay taxes like respectable citizens, the government, on its part, should stop treating them like criminals and demanding details of their movements.[63] However, some others were of the belief that since prostitutes were rich, they should be forced to pay tax. Badr-e Munir, a famous courtesan of the time, who obtained Rs 50,000 in eight months from her patron, Asghar Ali of Badaun, was deemed taxable by Azad,[64] as there was a repeated complaint that government officers were biased when it came to collecting income tax. They could be very harsh while dealing with common people; but

57 CR of 1881, 80; CR of 1891, 180.

58 *The Azad (Lucknow)*, 26 January 1886. See also *The Akhbar-e Alam (Meerut)*, 8 June 1886.

59 *The Rai-ul Akhbar (Benares)*, 1 February 1886.

60 *The Nasim-e Agra*, 30 May 1886.

61 ibid., 30 June 1886.

62 Oldenberg, *The Making of Colonial Lucknow*.

63 *The Nasim-e Agra*, 30 June 1886.

64 *The Azad*, 1 June 1886.

vis-à-vis prostitutes, they had a very different attitude. People suspected this was either because they were their clients, or because they stood to benefit by some other means. Therefore, it was suggested that in the interests of fairness, the District Magistrate himself deal with such cases as well as investigate which government officers and common people visited these women.[65] A moral policing of sorts was believed to be the best way to regulate prostitutes. In fact, several instances show that government officers were in the habit of keeping prostitutes as mistress; furthermore, these prostitutes were treated very cruelly, even being kept imprisoned and pawned at home by European officers,[66] who did not hesitate to even go to the courts and police stations to assert their claim over the prostitutes.[67] Courtesans and prostitutes were clearly considered little more than commodities in the hands of the Europeans, who always swung the cases their way. Europeans even objected on a large scale to *Friends of India* when it shifted the focus on such shameful acts, for which it had to later apologize.[68]

The early nineteenth century belonged to kings and nawabs who extended their patronage to this system. With the decline of monarchy, the *tawa'ifs* began losing their rich patronage, and had to confront a new ruling class that had neither the interest nor the understanding to appreciate their culture.[69] So while the British considered them morally 'evil', they nevertheless encouraged the flesh trade.[70] It is notable that in contemporary England, prostitution had a very different meaning; in Europe, its significance lay in only the physical aspect, while in India, social and cultural aspects were highlighted along with the physical.

Some prostitutes were selected for the cantonment while the others were treated strictly. There was no sympathy or admiration for their art and academic skills, as the British did not understand their language or their culture. It was only natural, then, that the women became increasingly more frustrated. The dual policy of the British vis-à-vis prostitution was considered a threat and a slur on Christianity by the monks, who puzzled over how the government

---

65 *The Najm-ul Akhbar*, 24 March 1890, 195.

66 *The Nasim-e Agra*, 30 October 1887.

67 *The Colonel (Moradabad)*, 16 January 1894, 43.

68 Sen, *Women and Empire*.

69 Oldenberg, *The Making of Colonial Lucknow*, 138.

70 It is noticeable how, at the time, vernacular newspapers demonstrated great resentment over the government's procurement policy for single soldiers. *The Prayag Samachar* (Allahabad), 18 June 1888, 382. Also see *The Bharat Bandhu* (Aligarh), 15 June 1888, 383; *The Mihir Nimroz* (Bijnor), 28 June 1888; and *The Almora Akhbar*, 16 July 1888.

could boast about the moral and religious superiority of Christianity while permitting brothels to run under government protection. In fact, Indians themselves condemned such a policy. Strangely enough, eminent Muslim social reformer Maulvi Zaqaullah expressed his support for the recruitment of *lal bibi*s at the military cantonment in *Rafiq-e Hind.* He hoped this would discourage European soldiers from looking at *shari'f* women.[71] Perhaps Zaqa Ullah's attitude towards social issues was biased and narrow, and made no allowance for women from the lower socio-economic strata. As a matter of fact, the Aligarh school of thought was never interested in understanding the problems faced by common Muslims; instead, they were solely concerned with *shari'f* Muslims. Since prostitutes came from either low castes or very poor households,[72] it is not surprising that some greedy and unscrupulous people actively appealed to the government for contracts as government procurers. This encouraged even greater human trafficking.

As a result, the British government brushed aside issues of morality and ordered the recruitment of beautiful and healthy women for the military cantonment.[73] At the same time, European chaplains expressed their annoyance over this issue.[74] Some Muslim columnists, too, raised questions on the issue of '*zana*' (sexual relationship outside of marriage) and tried to co-relate it with the paternity rights of children, because the refusal to grant the offspring of prostitutes paternity rights was considered a barefaced violation of children's rights.[75] The supply of prostitutes to the British cantonment became a burning issue in vernacular newspapers like the *Subodh Sindhu* and *Bharat Bandhu.* According to the *Bharat Bandhu*, prostitutes had been at the military cantonment for a long time; now, though, if any prostitute was found affected with a venereal disease, she was immediately referred to the Lock Hospital.[76] It also expressed annoyance at the Venereal Diseases Act, under which the European soldier's interests were protected, rather than those of the women from *shari'f* families. When the Act was repealed in Parliament, they expressed their happiness and obligation to Mr MacLaren for his efforts.[77]

---

[71] *Oudh Panch*, 45, 10 November 1892, 24 November 1892.

[72] Nagar's analysis shows that poverty had forced many *shari'f* women to turn to this profession.

[73] *Oudh Panch*, 10 November 1892.

[74] *Oudh Panch*, 24 November 1892, No. 47, 1.

[75] *Oudh Panch*, 17 November 1892, No. 46, 2.

[76] *The Bharat Bandhu*, 15 June 1888. Also see *Subodh Sindhu*, 23 May 1888.

[77] *The Bharat Bandhu*, 13 July 1888.

The common people, who professed themselves inconvenienced by the lifestyle of these prostitutes, demanded that they be kept away from the main city. They argued that prostitutes were spoiling the environment.[78] Despite the glorious past of these courtesans and dancing girls, a number of cities expressed concern over the increase in their numbers. The question arises: Was public concern directed against prostitution, or were they agitated about the declining morality amongst courtesans, who were once considered the teachers of etiquette and manners?[79] The people of Benares demanded that prostitutes be evacuated from Dal ki Mandi and relocated to some remote place.[80] *Nasim-e Hind* apprehensively reflected on the increasing number of prostitutes at Nawabganj (Allahabad), a centre known for its courtesans and prostitutes.[81] The people of Meerut, Faizabad, Moradabad and Etawa also pondered this issue.[82] Surprisingly, the people of Sitapur expressed no concern, even though Paturiya village was the main centre for hereditary prostitution—the women of the *Gaur Thakur* class had been involved in prostitution for over a century (as claimed by most courtesans interviewed by Amrit Lal Nagar).[83] It is striking that despite the mass conversions, the people here remained silent. Either public resentment was weak, or patronage of this system was strong enough to subdue all protest. Indeed, these courtesans had an honorary position in Indian society and were known for their culture;[84] their contribution to music could not be denied.[85]

Cultural and Creative Aspects

Since music and dance come more naturally to women, the salons doubled as learning institutes too. As Abdul Halim Sharar says,

---

[78] *The Nurul Anwar (Cawnpore)*, 1 November 1890.

[79] *The Paryag Mitra (Allahabad)*, 29 April 1894.

[80] *The Rafi-ul Akhbar (Benares)*, 28 June 1886.

[81] *The Nasim-I Hind*, (Fatehpur), 8 April 1894.

[82] *The Najm-ul Akhbar (Fatehpur)*, 24 March 1890. Also see *The Amir-ul Akhbar (Merrutt)*, 1 April 1890; *Hamdard (Fyzabad)*, 1 September 1890. See also Report on Native Newspaper, 1891, 27.

[83] Nagar, *Ye Kothe Valiyan*, 124, 127.

[84] Sharar, *Lukhnow*, 196.

[85] Wakefield, *Our Life and Travels in India*, 340–41. Also see VeenaTalwar Oldenburg, 'Lifestyle as Resistance: The Case of the Courtesans of Lucknow,' in Violette Graft (ed.), *Lucknow: Memories of a City* (Oxford: Oxford University Press, 1997), 136–43. Courtesans were an important link in the development of Hindustani music.

> Dance instruction is in the hands of men and they are the masters of this art. However, men could never have achieved the widespread popularity that the art attained. Dancing is more natural to women and they display their grace in art.[86]

The contribution of courtesans to *kathak, battana, thumri, khayal, ghazal* and *tappa* is memorable.[87] The Benares and Lucknow *gharana*s were famous for the development of Hindustani classical music. Courtesans all over India dreamed of learning music from these eminent musicians. The daughters of these musicians also gained popularity, the most prominent among them being Zeba-un Nisa of Benaras Gharana, whose son often said that every thing he knew had been learnt from his mother.

These courtesans were not only skilled in music and dance, but they were also well-versed in composition, as the monthly magazine *Payam-e Yar* reveals. A number of courtesans from Gorakhpur, Ghazipur, Benaras, Allahabad, Lucknow, Kanpur, Unnao, Badaun, Shahjahanpur, Sandila, Aligarh, Aara, Darbhanga, Calcutta, Delhi and Gurgaon sent their *ghazal*s and *qasida*s regularly to the magazine, using pen names along with the name of the city they belonged to. A few were frequent contributors, and the most talented among them were Sitari Jan and Bigan Jan. Sharar has praised the literary skills of the courtesans Mushtari and Zohra, who were not only poetesses, but also accomplished vocalists and dancers.[88] In his opinion, Jaddan Bai was the most famous dancer of her time. These courtesans had, of course, never gone to any English schools, receiving instruction from the traditional Hindustani *ustad* instead. Their academic soundness belies all claims of the rationality of the British educational system. They are the best examples of the *ustad-shagird* tradition, which continued for generations.

> *Is qadar furqat ne lagar kar dia- Shakal yaron ne na pahchani meri*
> *Dar hai fir paida na ho tufaan-e nooh- Zor par hai ashak afsaani meri*[89]
> *Sahab Jan Baqi, Tawaif, Gorsara Parghana Zamania, Jila Ghazipur*

> Separation has made me so frail
> In recognizing me, my friends fail

[86] Sharar, *Lukhnow,* 145. See also Zarina Bhatty, 'Status of Muslim Women in India', in *Indian Women: From Purda to Modernity* (New Delhi: Radiant Publishers, 1990), 105.

[87] ibid. Also *see Kashi ki Sangeet Paramparaen*, 134, 152; and Oldenburg, 'Lifestyle as Resistance', 136–43.

[88] Sharar, *Lukhnow,* 145–46.

[89] *Payam-e Yar*, XVI (January), 1898, 14.

I fear another storm like one that hit Noah
At peak is my tears' trail.
(*English translation by Nishat Zaidi*)

Kea kahun saudaiyon me hun- a kaminde zulf mai tere griftaron me hun
Bakhsh dega shafie mahshar ke sadqe me khuda- talibe rahmat hun a Zahra griftaron me hun[90]
Bi Zahra Bai Sahiba, Zahra, Sakin Jodhpur, Mulazim Riyasat Darbhanga, Shagird Nayyar

What can I say, I am amongst lovers
O tresses' noose, I am one of thy prisoners
God will forgive me in favour of doomsday's rescuer
I am an aspirer of benevolence,
O Zehra! I am one of the prisoners.
(*Translated from the Urdu by Nishat Zaidi*)

It is not clear whether this Zohra bai was the same Zohra whom Sharar admired so deeply. It is possible that the Zohra referred to here was the Zohra Bai of Lucknow, since in those days, there was no fixed place for a *tawa'if*. They were somewhat like nomads, moving from one place to another, depending on the patronage offered.

Kisi zulf par dil fida ho raha hai- Griftar ranj-o bala ho raha hai
Kisi but ko khauf-e khuda ho raha hai- mera aj vaeda vafa ho raha hai
Mujhe hure jannat ki khawahish nahi hai- mera dil tumhi pe fida ho raha hai
Tere vassal ke jisme rahte the arman- vo dil aj matam sada ho raha hai
Raqibon ko mere aj khushi ho rahi hai-khafa mujhse vo dilruba ho raha hai
Khafa ho gae mujhse tum jabse sahib- mera dil bhi mujhse khafa ho raha hai
Laagate ho munh dukhtar raz ko zahir- ye haq me tumhare bura ho raha hai
Lagana kisi ka nahi dil se achcha- zamane ka rang ab bura ho raha hai
Shab-e gham ki baten jo sunae unko- vo samjhe ki mera gila ho raha hai
Vo apni zafaon pe nadim hue hai- nae sire se ahde vafa ho raha hai[91]
Sitari Jan

My heart is falling in love with someone's tresses
It is getting trapped in sorrows, distresses
Some idol is becoming God fearing
Getting fulfilled are my promises
My heart is falling in love with you

[90] *Payam-e Yar*, VI (August), 1888, 15.
[91] *Payam-e Yar*, VXI (January), 1898, 14.

I care not for houries in paradise
The heart that treasures thy union's desire
Today the same heart is doleful; it laments
Today my foes are drawing pleasure
For unhappy with me is my lover
Ever since O sahib you are miffed with me
My heart too is not my friend any longer
It is not wise to endear anyone
The ways of the world are changing colours
When I retold the miseries of the night of separation
He thought I was expressing my grievances
He feels embarrassed at his infidelities
His devotion in love is finding new horizons.
(*Translated from the Urdu by Nishat Zaidi*)

Bat sun o dushman jani meri- kar lahar pe fateha khawani meri
Fir usi bedard pe marne laga- vae ghaflat vae nadani meri[92]
Bigan Jan, Bigan, Tawaif Laukhnow Varad Patodi, Jila Gurgaon

Listen to me O enemy of my life!
Prepare to say prayers on my grave.
My heart has fallen for that merciless once again
I pity my ignorance, my ways inane.
Bigan Jan
(*Translated from the Urdu by Nishat Zaidi*)

Rashak Aina hai hairani meri- vahshat afzan hai pareshani meri
Hai kisi aina ru ka dil ko dhean- kah rahi hai saf hairani meri
Khoon-e dil peeta hun ham khata hun mai- khub tum karte ho mehmani meri
Unki shokhi vassal me kahti hai ye- a haya tu kar nigahbani mari
Bat karne pe vo hote hai khafa- unse ab bolun to nadani meri
Apne is ashiftapan pe hun nisar- zulfen jana bhi hai diwani meri
Sher parhte hai vo meri qabr pe- ho rahi hai fateha khawani meri
Hun vo awara ki saqi bad-e murg- qabr pe roi pareshani meri[93]
Sitari Jan, Ghazipur, az Benares

My amazement is mirror's envy
My anguish is causing anxiety

[92] *Payam-e Yar*, XVI (January), 1898, 16–17.
[93] *Payam-e Yar*, XVI, 17. *Kashi ki Sangeet Parampara*, 134, 152. See also Oldenburg, 'Lifestyle as Resistance', 136–43.

My heart is smitten by some translucent soul
My wonder betrays this clearly
I eat up my sufferings, conceal my grief
So admirable is your hospitality
His playfulness in the night of union declares
Protect me now my modesty!
He is irked when I talk to him
Speaking to him would now be such an idiocy;
I am proud of my charm, my playfulness,
Even my lover's tresses are entranced with me;
They recite poetry on my grave
These are prayers on my death, my elegy.
O Saqi! I am such a vagabond that after my death,
Wails at my grave my misery.

Sitari Jan
(*English translation by Nishat Zaidi*)

Almost all famous courtesans of the time were masters of *thumri*. The word '*thumri*' is derived from the Hindustani word '*thumakna*', which means an attractive gait (as explained by Gauhar Jan's biographer).[94] The growth of *thumri* was initially linked with another sister art, Kathak, the classical dance form of north India that originated in the Indo-Gangetic belt. King Wajid Ali Shah's reign is considered the golden period for the development of these arts. He produced lavish dance dramas and lyrics, and wrote excellent *thumri*s and *dadra*s under the pen name 'Aktar Piya'. The most famous among his compositions is:

Babul mora naihar chuto hi jae,
chaar kahar mil duliyaan mangao
apna bigana chuto hi jae

O! Father! I forsake all my relationships in my maternal home. Four bearers bear my palanquin and take me to my beloved's home.[95]

Both Malka Jan and her famous daughter, Gauhar Jan, excelled in thumri composition and ghazals. Malka Jan even has a published diwan *Makhzan–e Ulfat-e Malika* (1886), which covered a wide range of topics, from spirituality and philosophy, to sensuality, unrequited love, pessimism, betrayal and romance.

[94] Sampath, *My Name is Gauhar Jaan*, 102.
[95] Sampath, *My Name is Gauhar Jaan*, 107.

Through her composition, she also seeks forgiveness from God for sins she may have committed. One of her finest *thumris* reads:

Mero Mar lio chain, akhian rasili waaki
Mori aali woh baanki chitwan, batyan karat peari-peari
Moorakh nipat anari baat chalet bholi bholi
Boli tholi kimag mag thak thak mohe muskaa de
Dagar chalet nit garaave baari basi
Vaako Krishna bhes hum unhi par tan man Malka taj dein

His eyes, full of elixir, have captured my mind. Being naïve and immature, I have been swayed away by his sweet talk and make some innocent conversation with him. As we walk the path, he tries to embrace me. But even if this attractive captor is not the original Krishna an imposter, Malka would still submit her body and mind to him.[96]

A few of her couplets speak of the secular atmosphere in salons:

Nikal aayee dair va haram se Malka
Kare zikr Sheikh va Brahmin kisi ka

What does Malka have to do with matters of religion?
Are not those better served in the hands of the Sheikh and Brahmin?

Malka aata hai ab tauba ka zamana nazdeek;
Wasl ke lutf utha leejie apni qasam se pahle

Oh! Malka your days are numbered and your end is nearing. Enjoy the indulgences of the world soon so that you can take an oath to abstain from sin thereafter and atone for the acts of omission committed by you all your life.[97]

If the mother was a famous litterateur, the daughter was not too far behind. She was born Victoria Hemming on 26 June 1873 in Azamgarh to Anglo-Indian parents. When she was six, her parents separated, and her mother, influenced by her new partner Khursheed, converted to Islam and took up dancing and singing to earn a livelihood. She was tutored by an eminent musician of Benaras, Pandit Bechoo Mishra. The mother-daughter duo soon became the talk of the town. Malka Jan was called Bari Malka to distinguish her from the other, well-known Malka Jan, while Victoria was renamed Gauhar Jan. In 1883, they migrated to Calcutta, where Malka Jan began accompanying little Gauhar to *mujras*. Very

[96] ibid., 284–85.
[97] ibid., 300.

soon, their fame had spread all over the city. During one performance, young Gauhar's talent caught the attention of famous musician Bindadin Maharaj, who offered to take her on as his pupil. Bindadin was one of the most important figures in the development of *thumri.* Gauhar had to travel to his hometown, Lucknow, every now and then to continue her lessons. Another famous singer, Zohra Bai of Agra, was also a student of his. Gauhar learnt Bengali songs from Bamacharan Bhattacharya. Like her mother, she began composing songs under various pen names, like Hamdam and Gauhar Piya. No self-respecting *Mahfilen* was considered complete without her presence. Gauhar Jan's famous composition was *Ras ke Bhare Tore Naina*:

> *Arey pathik giridhari sun itni kahio ter*
> *Dig jhar layi radhika ab brij bhoolat pher*
> *Aa ja sanvariya tohe garva laga loon*
> *Ras ke bhare tore nain, saanvariya*
> *Ras ke bhare tore nain*
> *Jehi chitwat tehi bas kari rakhat*
> *Naahi pare moika chain saanvariya*
> *Ras ke bhare tore nain*

O traveller just tell Girdhari (Krishna) when you see him that Radha has run out of tears, when he would come back to Brij. Come to my Saanvariya, let me embrace you. Your eyes full with elixir. O Krishna your image is in my heart and I can find no peace.[98]

Every king, petty and important, nawab, and wealthy person would vie with each other to be the first to call a famous courtesan to events held at his home. They would even bet everything they possessed.[99] Courtesans of the time thus earned both money and fame under the royal patronage of these connoisseurs. In addition, these patrons took a personal interest in the development of music and art. King Wazid Ali Shah even established a separate department, which he named 'Parikhana'. Parikhana was a music school which recruited beautiful and skilled girls. The king's many *mutai* wives hailed from this Parikhana.[100] Often, after earning enough money, some courtesans would leave this profession

---

98 ibid., 283.

99 Nagar, *Ye Kothe Valiyan,* 140–41.

100 Tasadduq Husain, *Begmat-e Oudh,* 241, 43–44, 48, 53, 57, 59, 66. See also G. D. Bhatnagar, *Oudh Under Wajid Ali Shah* (Varanasi, 1968).

and set up households of their own.[101] This was known as *Ghar Parna* in the language of the brothel, and took the place of marital life.

Sharar spoke about a few famous Lucknawi courtesans, prominent among whom were Kanchan and Chunawali, who were considered the queens of the market. However, Sharar referred to Kanchan as a mere harlot, whose main profession was selling her virtue.[102] Surprisingly, after a few decades this category of *tawa'ifs*, emphasizing their *got* and qaum, claimed to represent the highest class of all *deredar tawa'ifs*,[103] Social mobility had clearly entered this group, too. When the famous Hindi litterateur Amrit Lal Nagar met several prostitutes and courtesans of bygone days while writing his book, *Ye Kothe Valiyan,* he wondered why a large chunk of prostitutes hailed from the *Jugela Gaur Thakur* caste, and why most of them believed in Islam (thus echoing the British allegation that all 'loose' Hindu women embraced Islam).[104] But as both Veena Oldenburg and Nagar both show, these salons provided the best example of Hindustani composite culture and a matriarchal society. A Muslim woman was free to marry a Hindu, just as a Hindu woman was free to marry a Muslim. They appeared to believe only in *biradari*, and their *biradari* derived from sisterhood and womanhood. The birth of a girl was always welcomed in a brothel, while baby boys were often met with gloom.

Bhartendu Harish Chandra's correspondence with famous courtesan Husna shows that he was a regular visitor to the salon. He once converted the courtesan Malka from Islam to Hinduism, and re-named her Mallika. This act was not considered appropriate by the orthodox Hindus of his time, who forced him to abdicate his *Chaudhrahat* post in the Agrawal community. This also led to common saying to be associate with Bhartendu: '*Vo bhai ka sath na deen jo yawani ko Hindu keen*'.[105] This saying also highlights the intolerance prevalent among the Hindu community. Here, a question arises: Why was Bhartendu so eager to convert women? Was he looking to purify this group? This question unfortunately remains unanswered because of a dearth of other sources, especially *Devnagri* literature, and the limitations of my research, which is confined to Urdu and English literature. Also, this was a time when India was facing a language divide: Urdu was identified with Muslims and there was a natural demand for a Hindu language. Hindi seemed to meet this need.

[101] Tasadduq Husain, *Begmat-e Oudh.*

[102] Sharar, *Lukhnow,* 146; Nagar, *Ye Kothe Valiyan,* 93.

[103] Nagar, *Ye Kothe Valiyan,* 92, 97, 112, 119, 123.

[104] ibid., 124, 129, 127, 165.

[105] *Kashi ki Sangeet Paramparaen*, 136.

Furthermore, it is not clear why the British were keen to register all prostitutes as dancing girls, categorized under 'professional class' in the Muslim community.[106] The fact is, prostitutes often embraced Islam to safeguard their property for their children. Hindu Law gave no property rights to women, and so prostitutes, in an attempt to provide some rights to their illegitimate children, sometimes converted to Islam.[107] It is only in Islam that the maternity claim is recognized, thereby providing even illegitimate children with rights. Government statistics also considered all prostitutes to be Muslim.[108] They were also registered as owners of property and taxed accordingly.

The year 1857 also witnessed the beginning of a cultural decline. By the end of the century, there were no more *mujra*s, *mahfil*s or *mushaira*s, which were once considered an essential part of Oudh culture. Historian Mushirul Hasan connects this decline with the declining status of *qasba* culture. Once this took place, *qasba*s proved unequal to the task of distributing goods and services, wealth and pleasure. The *shair*, the *bhand*, the *qawaal*, the *mirasi* and *mirasin*, the *zankha* (eunuch), and the *tawa'if* disappeared from the *qasba* landscape. In a real sense, the *tawa'if*s of the nineteenth century were the queens of the literary world, passionate as they were about music, dance and *ghazal*s. It would be apt to conclude this chapter with these lines:

Bat usne hai kab mani meri-roti hai mujhpar purarmani meri
Yad-e gesu ka asar hai bal-bal-kam na ho ya rab pareshani meri
Shaeri pe e Ada qurban hun-sun rahe hai vo ghazalkhawani meri
Abbasi Jan Ada

[106] The British often registered them as dancing girls. See Wakefield, *Our Life and Travels in India*, 340–41.

[107] In the Allahabad case, Justice Mahmood delivered a historical judgement when he stated that while paternity could be disclaimed, maternity could never be.

[108] CR of 1901, 255, Subsidiary Table I.

CHAPTER 8

Law, Land and Muslim Women: The Economic Situation

Traditionally, the position accorded to women is gauged either by that of their husbands or the status of their families; they do not possess a separate identity of their own. Few women from the upper classes were economically independent; most women were reliant on their husbands or other male members of their family.[1] In fact, almost all religious scriptures affirm women's economic dependence on men. The second largest chapter of the Quran states:

> Men are the protectors and maintainers of women, because Allah has given the more (strength) than the other, and because they support them from their means. Therefore the righteous women are devoutly obedient, and guard in (the husband's) absence what Allah would have them guard.[2]

From time immemorial, women belonging to lower social orders had contributed to their means of subsistence, and therefore appeared free from unnecessary restraint. Since for centuries the Indian economy has been based on agriculture, a large portion of its population was directly or indirectly dependant on land. Among the female population, about 59.3 per cent of women belonged to the agriculture class; however, only 4.8 per cent owned their land.[3]

---

[1] Mary Francis Billington, *Women in India* (London: Chapman and Hall, 1895), 22. It is supposedly against the character of the true Hindu or Mohammedan woman to desire to be independent of men.

[2] Quran, 4:34.

[3] *Census Report of India*, NWP of Agra and Oudh, 1881, E. White, Government Press, Allahabad, 1882, 112.

This chapter explores the economic condition of Indian Muslim women and the extent to which they enjoyed property rights. To properly understand their economic condition, it looks at Indian Muslim women of two classes, viz., the landed class and the occupational class. Since one-fifth of the land in the United Provinces belonged to Muslims, it is essential to investigate the colonial land system before investigating the condition of peasant women. During the colonial period, the main source of income was land revenue, and so the British were concerned with introducing a new land system from the beginning of their rule. As a result, the number of claimants for ownership on land increased.[4] Thus, land in the United Provinces was divided into three categories during colonial rule: acquired land, ceded land and conquered land.

Owing to the huge regional variation in the province, it became difficult to bring the whole province under one land settlement. Therefore, the British introduced two popular systems of land settlement here—*mahalwari* and *zamindari*—and land settlement thus varied with reference to circumstances and place. In the meantime, wary of further tension after the great uprising of 1857, the British began a desperate search for a loyal group, which led to the emergence of a new landed class, following the pattern of the medieval British feudal system. They naturally defended the interests of this loyal group for the sake of their colonial empire. In addition, they did not want any fragmentation of land, and so to 'preserve' the name and grandeur of the *taluqdar* of Oudh, they exempted the latter from the personal law of inheritance.[5] The Quran, though, is very clear about property rights for both men and women; in its fourth chapter, 'Sura Nisa', it is clearly laid down: 'From what is left by parents and those nearest related, there is a share for men and a share for women, whether the property be small or large—a determine share.'[6] Despite this, the British rejected the property rights of Indian Muslim women under the Oudh Taluqdari Act of 1877. It is interesting to see how hard they worked to codify law according to religion—as the Hindu Civil Code and the Mohammedan Civil Code—although agriculture was exempt from personal law.

---

[4] J. Krishnamurthy (ed.), *Women in Colonial India: Essays on Survival, Work and the State* (New Delhi: Oxford University Press, 1989), 123–24. C. Kozlowski, 'Muslim Women and Control of Property in North India', *Indian Economic and Social History Review*, 24 (2), 1987: 163–81.

[5] Kozlowski, 'Muslim Women and Control of Property'.

[6] Quran, 4:7.

Women and Landownership

Papers related to the Board of Revenue and the Indian Law Report demonstrate that the British could not abolish women's ownership rights to land entirely. Around the same time, women had begun seeking ways to maintain their ownership rights over immoveable property. Muslim women tried their best to keep a hold over land; while they succeeded to some extent, they were not given their property rights as stated in the Shariat Act. Sometimes they claimed their rights either as dower right,[7] or as maintenance right,[8] or as guardians of their minor sons.[9] Perhaps this can explain why the landed class used to fix huge amounts as *mahr*, which varied from a thousand to lakhs of rupees.[10] It was very common to hear a marital family claim that a bride's *mahr* was '*fatimi mahr*'.[11] *Fatimi mahar* was believed to be 500 *Dinar* (in gold), which carried far greater value than the Indian rupee. Another way for a woman to safeguard her possessions was to proclaim herself the sole manager and guardian of her minor or lunatic son, or even an incapacitated husband.[12] In these situations, gender bias was clearly very pervasive in both Hindu and Muslim communities, and to question a woman's capacity to manage her property and estate was to demean her.[13] British interference (as the Court of Wards) increased as traditionally practised law began disappearing. Women were now considered incompetent

---

[7] Amani Begam v. Md. Karim Khan, ILR, Alld., Vol. XVI, 225. In this case, the judge contended that their (widows') possession appeared perfectly lawful as they were the heirs of their deceased husbands according to Mohammadan Law, and the creditors of their dower.

[8] Mahbuban v. Fakir Baksh, ILR, Alld., Vol. XV, 1893.

[9] Saiyid Mazhar Husain v. Bodha Bibi, ILR, Alld., 1894; see also Board of Revenue Records, Bundle No. 62, Box No. 93, Sl. No. 1, File No. 200, 1878, Regional Archive (henceforth RA), Allahabad, Petition of Must Haidari Begham, mother of Ibu Ali *Zamindar mauzah* Rasoolpur, Sakhmora Pargana Karari.

[10] S. Abdul Hasan Nadvi, *The Musalman* (Lucknow: Islamic Research and Publication, 1977).

[11] Chunni Bibi v. Shams-un Nisa, ILR, Vol. XVII, 1895.

[12] Fazl Rab v. Khatun Bibi and others, ILR, Alld. Vol. XV, 1893. In this case, a basic question was raised: Is a wife of a lunatic his legal heir; and does she therefore fall under the prohibition contained in the proviso to s. 10 of Act No. XXXV of 1858?

[13] Masuma Bibi vs. the Collector of Ballia, ILR, Alld., 1894.

with regard to managing property; instead, they were given a monthly allowance in lieu of property or land.[14]

Some women retained indirect control over land that came under the mahalwari system. Shariat law protected female inheritance in those parts that did not come under the Oudh Taluqdari Act of 1877.[15] Nevertheless, it is surprising to see women from taluqdari regions maintaining their hold over immoveable property; so it cannot be said that women had been entirely deprived of their inheritance rights in these regions either. It is remarkable how wonderfully Chaudharain Sahib-un Nisa, Bibi Bechun Nisa and Bibi Ilahi Khanam managed their estates in male-dominated taluqdari regions of Oudh.[16]

After establishing peace, the British began to identify those landowners from whom they could collect huge revenues. In their haste to safeguard their economic interests, they overlooked some established tenets in the case of influential women. Under their policy of 'rewarding obedience and punishing rebellion', the British had seized the lands of those who had participated in the mutiny, and rewarded those who had remained loyal even under dire circumstances.[17] Since it was assumed that Muslims were more prone to rebellion, they were the first targets of British rage. This was why the Muslim community—particularly those from regions affected greatly by the mutiny—wrote more petitions than others for ownership of land. Interestingly, most of them were women petitioners, pleading to the British to have mercy on their helpless and impoverished condition (brought on by widowhood, among other

[14] Bundle No. 140, Box No. 194, Sl. No. 6, File No. 26, Must Wahidatun Nisa Estate, Fatehpur, 1894, RA, Allahabad.

[15] Records of Board of Revenue and ILR, Alld. show that women had continued holding land despite the several hurdles in their way.

[16] *Gazetteer of the Province of Oudh*, Vol. III-N to Z, North Western Provinces and Oudh Government Press, Allahabad, 1878, 63, 332, 436.

[17] Records of the Board of Revenue from 1858 onwards show this trend among Muslims—particularly among widows—of appealing on a large scale to the Board of Revenue for recovery of their seized property. Deprt.-Judicial, Bundle No. 35, Box No. 57, Sl. No. 6, File No. 9, R.A., Alld. In her petition, Must Bano, widow of Mohsin Ali, prayed for the release of her late husband's property, which had been confiscated in the rebellion. Her plea was rejected on the grounds that Masum Ali had been the chief assistant of Maulvi Liaqat Ali, and his widow had other sources of income. Besides, she lived with her mother-in-law, who possessed ample means, and she also had several other relatives in the city. Her share had been distributed among deserving persons who had remained loyal under dire circumstances.

reasons). This shows that Muslim women were well aware of their rights; and perhaps they had also become too impoverished to support themselves. They seemed conscious of British atrocities, and lodged their protest through petitions.[18] It is equally possible that some of these women's male relatives were using them as scapegoats, since much sympathy could be gained if one wrote petitions in a woman's name. It is surprising to see the women of Chail pargana of Allahabad division out-numbering women in other parts of this division—were they more conscious of their rights, or the most deprived in the suppression that followed the revolt? Interestingly, the 'benevolent' British government rejected such claims over and over again.[19]

Despite these hurdles, Muslim women retained their control over their *mahal* and *seer* land.[20] A close analysis of Wahidat-un Nisa's estate in Fatehpur pargana shows that some landowning women had no difficulty in paying the government revenue. Wahidat-un had four shares in a mahal and the total area of her estate was 405/3/15 (r/a/p), which collected 950/9/0 (r/a/p) of the exact revenue demand. At the time, the total debt of this estate was Rs 242 with an interest of 46/11/0 (r/a/p), as well as Rs 150 of *takavi* debt. This was why the estate was kept under the Court of Management from 1892 to 1894 (See Table 1–3). But due to surplus revenue collection and payment of debt, the Board of Revenue released this estate in 1895.[21] At the time, Sultanpur district was mainly a taluqdari district, and hence the *zamindari*, *pattidari* and *Bhayyachari* systems of land settlement prevailed among the people of Sultanpur. Bibi Ilahi Khanam was the best-known woman taluqdar of Sultanpur; she occupied forty-seven demarcated villages and three *patti* villages in Ditto Pali (See Table 4).[22] All women of the landed class belonged to ashraf families. Most preferred to manage their estates through male relatives, since they were denied free access outside their homes.[23]

---

[18] Bundle No. 36, Box No. 58, Sl. No. 14, File No. 30, 1861, R.A., Allahabad. See also, Criminal Records, Basta No. 6, File No. 7; in this case a *tawa'if's* house situated in Dariabad locality of Allahabad had been seized because of her direct involvement in the mutiny.

[19] File No. 104, Bundle No. 135, Box No. 189, 1873, Dept. – Board of Revenue, Regional Archive, Alld.

[20] Niaz Ullah Khan v. Nazir Begam, ILR, Alld., 1893.

[21] Bundle No. 140, Box No. 194, Sl. No. 6, File No. 26, Must Wahidatun Nisa Estate Fatehpur, 1894, Allahabad.

[22] ibid., 436.

[23] Mariam Bibi v. Sakina and others, ILR, Alld., Vol. XIV, 1892.

Table 8.1: Government Demand for the Revenue Year 1894–95 of Must. Wahidatun Nisa's Estate, Fatehpur

Item	*Government Demand*			*Payment*			*Balance*
For year of report	*Rs*	*A.*	*P.*	*Rs*	*A.*	*P.*	*Rs A. P.*
1. Land revenue on the roll.	495	14	8	495	14	8	Nil
2. Do not on the roll.	-	-	-	-	-	-	
3. 12% cess	59	7	10	59	7	10	
4. Patwaris rate	19	12	0	19	19	0	
Total	575	2	6	575	2	6	

Source: Dept: Board of Revenue, Bundle No. 140, Box No. 194, Sl. No. 6, File No. 26, 1894, RA, Alld.

Table 8.2: Collection detail of the Revenue of Wahidatun Nisa

Receipts	*Actual Receipt of Previous Year*			*Year under Report* *Estimated Receipts*			*Actual Receipts*		
	Rs.	*a.*	*p.*	*Rs.*	*a.*	*p.*	*Rs.*	*a.*	*p.*
Opening cash balance	280	12	11	256	1	2	256	1	2
1. Cash rents	867	12	7	877	-	-	767	-	9
2. Sayar	50	11	5	30	-	-	32	8	11
3. Manual dues	23	5	4	23	-	-	37	14	8
4. Patwari's cess	8	11	8	8	3	-	7	12	7
Miscellaneous	70	6	9	64	8	-	61	11	3
Total annual income	1020	15	9	1002	11	-	907	0	2
Grand Total	1301	12	8	1258	12	2	1163	1	4

Source: Depart: Board of Revenue, 1894, Bundle No. 140, Box No. 194, Sl. No. 6, File No. 26. RA, Alld.

Table 8.3

Items	*Demand*						*Collection*						*Balance*		
	Previous Year			*Year under Report*			*Previous Year*			*Year under Report*			*Recoverable*		
	Rs	*a*	*p.*	*Rs*	*a.*	*p.*	*Rs*	*a.*	*p.*	*Rs*	*a.*	*p.*	*Rs*	*a.*	*p.*
Cash rent	867	12	7	885	5	2	867	12	7	767	-	9	118	4	5
Sayar	50	11	5	42	4	1	50	11	5	32	8	11	9	11	2
Manorial due	23	5	4	37	14	8	23	5	4	37	14	8	-	-	-
Patwari's cess	8	11	8	8	11	6	8	11	8	7	12	7	-	14	11
Total	950	9	0	974	3	5	950	9	0	845	4	11	128	14	6

Source: Dept: Board of Revenue, Bundle No. 140, Box No. 194, Sl. No. 6, File No. 26, 1894, AR, Alld.

Table 8.4: Estate of Bibi Ilahi Khanam of Sultanpur

No. in list I under Act I of 1869	*Name of taluqdar*	*Name of estate*	*No. of demarcated village*		*Revised revenue*					
228	Bibi Ilahi	Maniarpur	whole patti		*Of each estate*			*Of each Taluqdar*		
	Khan	Ditto Pali	47	2	*Rs.*	*a*	*p*	*Rs.*	*a*	*p*
			25	3	13,193	4	0	40,385	9	9
					11,407	15	0	34,601	15	0

Source: Gazetteer of the Province of Oudh, Vol. III, N–Z, North Western Province & Oudh Government, Allahabad, 226.

Law of Pre-emption

At that time, it was not easy for a woman to hold immoveable property directly; one had to confront several hardships to stake a real claim over joint property. That was why they would sell their shares by violating the *shufaa* (law of pre-emption) of the *Hanafi* sect, or mortgage their share to fulfil their daily needs. These sale deeds were usually verbal, and therefore their legitimacy was often in question.[24] According to *shufa*, if one has a joint immoveable property, another shareholder (nos 1 or 2) cannot sell it outside their kinship circle without the permission of shareholder No. 3, who has the right to challenge this sale deed under the Islamic Law of *Shufa*, which gives him the right to retain his property in the face of outside intrusion. The intention behind pre-emption is to prevent the introduction of a stranger into one's home, and to eventually bring the property under one owner.[25] Due to this, women had to face several confrontations when they claimed a pattidari share.

A woman named Aziz-un Nisa had a share in pattidari land, but it was declared that she should not be considered a co-owner, as under British law, women could not own property independently.[26] They could only manage the property on behalf of their minor sons. She was stated to have lost her rights; but if she had no share in the village remaining to her, how were her profits estimated at Rs 129?[27]

[24] Begams and others v. Md. Yaqub and others, ILR, Alld., 1894.

[25] M. Hidayatullah and Arshad Hidayat Ullah, *Mulla's Principles of Mahomedan Law*, 19th edn (New Delhi: Lexis Nexis Butterworths, 2005), 203.

[26] Bundle No. 95, Box No. 140, Sl. No. 2, File No. 260, 1876, Deprt.- Board of Revenue, Regional Archive, Alld.

[27] ibid.

Another way to disown women's rights over property was to question their reproductive abilities and fecundity. If a woman could conceive a child, she was considered eligible to claim her right in her husband's share of the property. It was necessary for a widow to have a child if she were to retain her possession over the immovable property of her deceased husband (this condition was applicable only to the *Immamia* sect of Muslims).[28] Consequently, in such a patriarchal society, a woman was often considered little more than a child-bearing machine.

Most men belonging to the landed class were either polygamous or had several mistresses. They also had many heirs, both legitimate and illegitimate, which resulted in serious battles over the ownership of land.[29] Although neither mistresses nor illegitimate sons had the right to disown a legal heir, some of them were somehow able to convince the landlords to create a deed in their names. This deed had a special importance in Islamic Law, and it perhaps became a quick way to disown a legal female heir.[30] In most cases, the disowned heirs were either daughters or their grandsons (see Appendix for the deed of Basharat Ali).[31] Thus, in this patriarchal system, giving full recognition to female heirs was frowned upon.

It would be appropriate to mention the dispute over Amir Ali's estate of Pargana Karari. His only legitimate male heir was Ibu Ali, his grandson from a daughter.[32] Amir Ali also had two mistresses, Must. Bodhni (Gareria qaum)

---

28 Fazl Rab v. Khatun Bibi and others, ILR, Alld., Vol. XV, 1893. It was contested by Justice Mahmood that the wife, regardless of whether she was childless, is one of the husband's heirs. The history of Mohammadan jurisprudence explains why absolutely no distinction is made between a wife with a child and a childless wife among *Sunni* Mohammadans, while a great distinction is made in this respect among the *Shia* creed. The next question to consider is also a matter of importance, namely the exact period in which, for purposes of administering *Shia* law, it should be decided that a young woman such as Must. *Zainab*, be declared barren or childless.

29 Liaqat Ali v. Karim-un Nisa, ILR, Alld., 1893. Vol. XV. It was held that a Mohammadan could not, by acknowledging as his son, render legitimate a child whose mother he could not marry at the time of his birth because of her being the wife of another person.

30 Hidayatullah and Hidayat ullah, *Mulla's Principle on Mahomedan Law*, 112.

31 Murtazai Bibi and others v. Jumna Bibi and other, ILR, Alld., 1891, Vol. XIII. In this case, the plaintiff Jumna Bibi's share was refused as the common ancestor had made a deed in 1848, according to which she was not to be considered a co-sharer of the property. This was because the plaintiff could have no claim to the inheritance so long as there were living male descendants of Basharat Ali.

32 An heir was often considered to be a son's child. Therefore, a grandson from a daughter was often discouraged, since his mother was not considered a complete heir.

and Nasiban (Bharbhuja qaum), both of whom had borne Amir Ali male children. However, since both hailed from the lower social order and had no claims to legitimacy, Amir Ali's relatives did not accept or recognise them as co-sharers along with their grandson from daughter's side (Ibu Ali), a Saiyid. Thus, the hierarchal caste system of the *ashra'f* was also a factor in the additional difficulties suffered by lower-caste women, who could not raise their social status by marriage, although their male child could be recognised as an heir in some cases. Does this not show that lower-class women were important only when they produced male heirs, especially in cases where a man's upper-caste wives had failed to do so?[33]

Amir Ali attached too much significance to these male children; he even gave them his surname, Saiyid. He divided his entire estate in his lifetime into two, and gave an 8-aana share to Ibu Ali and an 8-aana each to both minor sons, whose guardians were their mothers.[34] However, Ibu Ali never accepted this deed, and so a prolonged dispute arose amongst them that also witnessed the increasing interference of the Court of Wards.[35] Thus, it was very difficult for a woman claimant to retain possession over immoveable property in the presence of other male co-sharers. It was also clear that a lower-caste woman could only be a male-child bearing machine, but never a wife. Another aspect of this case is that it shows a daughter could not be considered the full owner of immoveable property. It was clearly the aspiration for a male heir that led Amir Ali to keep two mistresses. He would not have given so much importance to these sons if his legal wife had given birth to one.

The second kind of land was ceded or conquered land. These were annexed to the British territory through wars and pacts. The Bundelkhand region was important in this regard. After annexing this area, the British government had either fixed some compensation for landowners in lieu of their land, or assigned them a hereditary pension.[36] After 1858, Muslim widows constantly

---

33 From another angle, it seems unfortunate that illegitimate sons were considered a better option than daughters in a landed family. This son preference was the basic cause behind the daughter's deprivation of property.

34 Bundle No. 62, Box No. 93, Sl. No. 1, File No. 46, 1878, Dept. - Board of Revenue, Regional Archive, Allahabad.

35 ibid. See also Saiyid Mazhar Husain v. Bodha Bibi. See how long this case (Amir Ali's estate of *pargana* karari) had continued—till the 1890s.

36 At that time, several appeals had come to the Board of Revenue for mutation of names of those with hereditary pension. File No. 46, Bundle No. 138, 137, 1875, Dept. Board of Revenue, RA, Alld. See also File No. 84, Bundle No. 138, Box No.

complained that their pensions had been reduced, and that they considered the reduced amount insufficient for their daily requirements. Begum Mumtaz Mahal, widow of the late Nawab Nusrat Jang of Farukhabad, made her protest public when her pension was reduced to Rs 100 and Rs 50 for the begum and her daughter, respectively, from the Rs 1,000 per month that had been granted to her father-in-law, Nawab Nasir Jang.[37] Later, even that allowance was withdrawn; the explanation given was that her son-in law was wealthy. The Begum, on the contrary, asserted that her son-in-law was bankrupt, and that he had mortgaged all his property.[38] Around the same time, Nawab Begum, mother of Nawab Ally Bahadur, also filed a petition for a promised stipend.[39] She complained that the British government had agreed to pay a remuneration of Rs 400,000 to her late husband in lieu of the Bundelkhand province, the major portion of its share having been allotted to her son. But after peace had been restored, the British agreed to pay a pension of only Rs 250. The pensioner could not make ends meet on such a small amount, and lost her home. She was compelled to live in a rented house in unhealthy surroundings, in a narrow lane in the Tajganj locality of Agra.[40] She further stated that the house she occupied before the mutiny was confiscated, along with Ally Bahadur's other properties. That house remained unoccupied, and she prayed that orders be issued permitting her to re-occupy it, or that she be directed to occupy some other house.

The second complaint was related to those people who had participated in the mutiny, for which transgression their property had been seized. In some cases, entire parganas had been declared confiscated property. This was why there were more women petitioners from Chail pargana. These women appealed relentlessly on the grounds of their widowhood and poverty. Interestingly, they also made many attempts to prove both themselves and their husbands innocent, but most of the appeals were rejected on the grounds of confiscation and the Limitation Act of 1858.[41] In most cases these women petitioned from 1870 onwards,

192, 1875, continuation of pension of Farokhbad district. See also File No. 154, 1894, Arrears of pension due and mutation of name of Fakhrul Islam in place of Karim-un Nisa. See also Bundle No. 57, Box No. 87, Sl. No. 16, File No. 22, 1882.

[37] Home Depart: Public, 1862, Port B, Proceeding 5 March, Nos 37–38, National Archive (henceforth NA), New Delhi.

[38] ibid.

[39] Home Deprt; Public, 1862, Port-B, Proceeding 5 March, Nos 39–40, NA, New Delhi.

[40] ibid., 6 November 1861.

[41] File No. 30, Bundle No. 36, Box No. 58, Sl. No. 14, 1861,

thereby coming automatically under the Limitation Act of 1858, which allows only twelve years to file a suit. Every so often, the British government rejected the suits, stating that the land in question had been awarded to another, or that it had been seized for official purposes, and therefore could not be returned.[42]

At that time, the Begums of Oudh were monetarily strong, and independent. The Nawabs of Oudh traditionally allotted a monthly allowance to their Begums, and in some cases also gave them the rights to immoveable property.[43] This was why the British could not overlook their significance in the politics of the Oudh region. The British, too, assigned allowances to some elite women and provided pensions to some widows.[44]

To sum up, all these landed women hailed from *ashra'f* society. No evidence can be found of lower-caste women owning large pieces of land. Most women belonging to the lower social orders were either engaged in agricultural work, or involved in their ancestral professions. Census Reports show them as part of the labour class, or as skilled professionals. After the arrival of the British, the boundaries between professional castes had begun to blur, and one caste could no longer monopolise a profession. Middle-class Muslim families were in the throes of poverty, and it was therefore the need of the hour for them to adopt traditional professions that required skill rather than bookish knowledge.[45]

In the colonial economy, working women came under the occupational class, which was divided into two groups: domestic workers and women skilled in some profession (for instance, sewing, stitching and embroidery). Domestic workers used to work for European and elite Muslim families as maid servants. During this period, European women were emerging as memsahibs and women imperialists. Their responsibility was to manage the home, just as the men

---

[42] File No. 9, Bundle No. 35, Box No. 57, Sl. No. 6. See also File No. 29, Bundle No. 36, Box No. 58, Sl. No. 1, 1861. See also File No. 104, Bundle No. 135, Box No. 189, 1873, Dept. Board of Revenue, RA, Alld.

[43] Sheikh Tasadduq Husain, *Begmat-e Oudh* (Lucknow: Kitab Nagar, 1956).

[44] Home Deprt; Public, 29 July 1859, File No. 23, a letter from Secretary to Government of India. See also Kabir Kausar and Inamul Kabir, *Biographical Dictionary of Prominent Muslim Ladies* (New Delhi: Light and Life Publishers, 1982), 39. A daughter of Bahadur Shah Zafar, an able lady, was assigned a *wazifa* by the British government after AD 1857, when it was established that she had not participated in the war against the British.

[45] Muslim social reformers of the time lamented the declining economic condition of Muslims, and suggested that they adopt and learn other professions instead of sticking to their traditional jobs.

managed the colonial empire.[46] Indeed, the British had become used to the same luxurious lives as their predecessors, the Nawabs and the Mughals. Since their eating habits were similar to Muslims, they preferred Muslim servants to others, particularly as cooks or *ayahs*.[47] They required a large number of servants, both male and female, for various categories: attendants, hair dressers, tailors, ayahs, *mehtranis* and cooks. These were always some indispensable female workers in a European family.

Of these female servants, the ayah was considered the most important because she was responsible for raising a child. As Indira Ghosh points out, the main point of contact between English women in India and Indians themselves were the servants—indispensable for tourists and memsahibs alike. Only women were considered fit for the position of ayah, and these ayahs were paid less than their male counterparts. Her salary ranged from Rs 5–8 per month, while most domestic servants were paid between Rs 8–12 per month.[48] Her primary task was to look after the European children.[49] Her secondary tasks included sewing, hairdressing, and assisting English women with their toilette. In the hierarchy of servants, the *mehtarani* was ranked the lowest. The filthy nature of her work meant that she was not allowed to enter other parts of the house and was paid

---

[46] Indrani Sen, *Women and Empire* (New Delhi: Orient BlackSwan, 2002), 9–10.

[47] As Emma Roberts says:

> It is generally considered essential for the ayah to be a Musalman woman, as none but a low Hindu would take the office; and it may safely be averted, that not one respectable woman out of a hundred is to be found in this class. The single circumstances of her mingling unveiled with the males domestics, is sufficient to show that she has lost all claim to reputation; she has seldom any good quality left, excepting honesty, ... the Musalman *ayah* is usually found the lesser evil of the two, and when she happens to be clever and active, she is a treasure beyond price (quoted in Indira Ghosh [ed.], *Memsahibs Abroad: Writings by Women Travellers in Nineteenth Century India* [New Delhi: Oxford University Press, 1998], 192–93).

[48] W. Wakefield, *Our Life and Travels in India* (London: Sampson Low, Marston, Searle and Rivington, 1898), 203–4. Also see the quote from Fanny Park, in Ghosh, *Memsahibs Abroad*, 185–86.

[49] Where mothers are unable to nurse their own children, a native women are *dhye*, as she is called, is usually selected for the office, European being difficult to procure; these are expensive and troublesome appendages to a family; they demand high wages on account of the sacrifices which they affect to make of their usual habits, and the necessity of purchasing their reinstatement to caste, forfeited by the pollution they have contracted, a prejudice which the Musalman have acquired from their Hindu associates (Ghosh, *Memsahibs Abroad*, 195).

very little—only Rs 2 per month (Rs 2 less than her male counterparts).[50] It is a point of concern that the British actively encouraged gender prejudice, especially where wages were concerned.

However, it was clear that some kind of workers' union was fast coming into existence ever since a vernacular newspaper had reported instances of female sweepers threatening to go on strike in the absence of an adequate allowance. The British government was held responsible for this situation because the municipal corporation had not fixed any particular salary for these workers. As a result, the workers were dependent on the public, and it was the common people who had to suffer when they went on strike.[51]

Although Muslims were fast becoming crippled by financial difficulties, they did not change their style of living. They continued to hire many servants and lead lavish lives, even though this just increased their mounting debts and forced them to mortgage their property.[52] This explains the reason behind the vast number of Muslims mortgagers.

Most professional women took up their ancestral occupations. These women's skills lay in professions like knitting, sewing and embroidery. Poverty had even forced some *ashra'f* women to work. Many social reformers and *ulema* had also asked their womenfolk to learn handicrafts and other professions so they could look after their children in times of dire need.[53] The Urdu novelist Maulvi Nazir and the eminent Urdu poet Hali had emphasised the importance of vocational education.[54]

In 1881, 36.2 per cent of women were contributing to the ancestral occupations of their husbands. It is noteworthy that at the time, domestic work was not considered an occupation since the women were already taking care of the household. These women either assisted their husbands in their work, or worked as weavers. Overlooking their actual production (as their work was considered part of their husbands' work, and never independently valued on its own), they were increasingly being recognised under the agriculture and the

---

50 Wakefield, *Our Life and* Travels, 203–4.

51 *The Akhbar-e Islam* (Agra), 30 August 1894, 375. Report on Vernacular Newspaper of NWP of Agra and Oudh.

52 The luxurious lifestyle of the Urdu poet Ghalib was a fine example. He, too, had to sell his home.

53 Ashraf Ali Thanvi, *Behisht-e Zewar* (New Delhi: New A. S. Press, 1994), 578.

54 Maulvi Nazir Ahmad's *Mirat-ul Urus* and *Banat-ul Nash* and Hali's *Majalis-un Nisa* dealt with the issue of the declining condition of Muslims, and provided the womenfolk with advice on how to uplift the status of Muslim society.

weaver categories. Hence, 59.3 per cent of women formed part of the agricultural class among the professional women.[55] By the 1890s, the definition of 'domestic worker' was extended to new occupations, handled predominantly by women, like *chikan* and *kamdani* embroidery, net work (mostly *kamarband*), baskets made of *munj*, fan-making, vermicelli (*siwain*) making, sewing, stitching and knitting (a late accomplishment), spinning, and cotton cleaning.

Muslim women were the only ones engaged in sewing. This was because Hindus were presumed to wear clothing that required little in the way of embroidery and stitching, and so did not feel the need to learn sewing.[56] It was mostly *ashra'f* women who were involved in domestic sewing; however, they refused to admit to doing it to earn money. This was especially common among Lucknavi women.[57]

Compared to men, women were more involved in field labour. A few occupations recognised women's contribution, for instance grain parching, oil pressing, weaving and spinning of wool and cotton, basket making, and general manual labour. However, their presence was negligible in the technical professions.[58]

Sharar provided a detailed account of Lucknavi Muslim professionals. Muslim shoemakers crafted only *ghatela* and *kafash* shoes, considering it beneath their dignity to make any other.[59] The Industrial Revolution had brought about a change in the old professions, and machines were fast replacing the old *charkhas*. Elite Muslim women had once thought of spinning as pleasing work, but now Lucknavi women had begun to consider it a disgrace, and were adopting sewing and embroidery as a profession instead.[60] It was believed that Muslim women were naturally fond of sewing, embroidery, *chikankari*, and gold and silver wire embroidery,[61] one reason why Muslim-dominated areas were famous for their

[55] CR of 1881, 101, 103, 112.

[56] Bernard Cohn, 'Colonialism and its Forms of Knowledge: The British in India', in *Bernard Cohn Omnibus* (New Delhi: Oxford University Press, 2009), 130–31.

[57] CR of 1891, D. C. Bailly, Government Press, Allahabad, 1894, 327.

[58] CR of 1901, R. Burn, Government Press, Allahabad, 266.

[59] Abdul Halim Sharar, *Lucknow: The Last Phase of Oriental Culture* (New Delhi: Oxford University Press, 1994), 179.

[60] ibid., 192.

[61] Ghosh, *Memsahibs Abroad*, 151; *The Imperial Gazetteer of India—The Indian Empire, Economic*, Vol. III (Oxford: Clarendon Press, 1908), 202–22. At the time, Sikandrabad in Bulandshahar district, Mau in Azamgarh, Mahmudnagar in Lucknow, Jais in Rai Bareli, Tanda in Faizabad, and Benares were famous for their plain, striped and

handicrafts. *Chikankari* refers to the delicate embroidery traditionally prepared on white muslin cloth by women. This embroidery was believed to have been brought by the Mughals from Persia, although stories of its origin in the zenanas of the Oudh and Lucknow courts abound. *Taipchi, bakhia, phanda* and *murri* are the names of some of the stitches used for embroidery, which seem to play with light and shade. Mary Francis Billington, too, accepted embroidery as the purview of poor Muslims.[62] She states:

> From Dacca still a considerable trade is done with Jadda and Bushire in worked cotton or mixes silk and cotton clothes for Mohammadan wear. Though sketchy in design, and rough in execution, many of these pieces are decoratively effective, but better perhaps is not to be expected for the low rates, which are paid for them. It is done almost exclusively by the women of poor though respectable Mohammadan families, and is rather a curious instance of the 'pocket money' wage as I am assured that only a rupees to a rupee and a half a month is given for it, which is accepted, much as the worker at home assured for her bread and butter by father and husband under sell the necessitous wage-earner merely to obtain enough to buy the finery she covets.[63]

Agra and Delhi were famous for their fine gold and silver metal work on clothes.[64] Agra was well-known across the country for its quilts,[65] and it was mostly Muslim women who were engaged in making them. In fact, women from the lower economic stratum adopted these traditional professions to earn money, while some upper-class women did it to fulfil their surplus requirements, or during their leisure hours. Sharar lamented how men were indulging only in merry making, while all responsibility of livelihood fell on women's shoulders.

In their moments of leisure, Muslim women from big families passed their time with *domnis* or supervised maidservants in their household chores.[66] A few women were engaged in government and private jobs. This was the time when the British system of work was being introduced in the Indian

flowered muslin, while Lucknow was the one famous centre in the United Provinces for its *chikan* work. Massive (*zardoji*) embroidery was well produced in Delhi, Agra and Benares. The *kamdani* work was connected with Lucknavi women.

62 Billington, *Women in India*, 200.

63 ibid.

64 ibid., 197–98.

65 Charles Raikes, *Notes on the Revolt in the NWP of India* (London: Longman & Roberts, 1858).

66 Sharar, *Lucknow*.

administration. However, there was no evidence of either Indian or European women performing administrative services, although mutiny records uncover evidence of women who performed well in administrative posts, particularly during the uprising. It seems that the need of the hour allowed them to demonstrate their administrative skills.

As Indrani Sen argues, marriage and motherhood were identified as the central goals for middle-class women.[67] Moreover, part of the strategy to confine women to domestic life included denying them access to higher education, the argument being that medical studies had clearly indicated the harmful effects of excessive study on female menstrual cycles, which in turn affected a woman's ability to conceive.[68] In the 1860s, the question of women's health was cited to establish how incapable women were for the roles of empire-builders or administrators: 'Not one girl in a hundred would be able to work up the subjects required for an Indian Civil Service examination in the way which boys do.'[69] How, then, could this be expected of Indian women, who were *purda nashin?* It was therefore natural for Indian women to opt for teaching and nursing as their professions, much like their European counterparts. At the time, the Lucknow Normal School had trained seventeen Muslim girls who could impart formal education to students.[70] Surprisingly, despite these trained teachers, no women were considered suitable when the Abdullah Girls School was established in 1906, and the Abdullah couple had to hire a Muslim woman from Delhi. So where had these trained girls gone? Were they torn between their professional duties and their tradition? What prevented sharif women from earning their living? Indeed, the presence of *ustanis* was common among sharif Muslims (for details, see Chapter Five). In the field of medicine, no native women had an MBBS; instead, they were initiated into nursing and midwifery courses.[71] The Female Dufferin Fund had presented such women with a platform. While in the beginning nearly all working nurses and midwives hailed from the lower social orders, upper-caste women from both communities gradually entered this field,[72] although they had to face the disapproval of their families, a disapproval

[67] Indrani Sen, *Women and Empire* (Hyderabad: Orient BlackSwan, 2002), 3.

[68] M. Burrows, '*Female Education*', *Quarterly Review*, 126, 1869; quoted in Sen, *Women and Empire*, 3.

[69] ibid. Also see Elizabeth Sewell, *Principles of Education* (London, 1865), quoted in Sen, *Women and Empire*, 3.

[70] Home: Education, Handfort Report, 1868.

[71] Billington, *Women in India,* 100.

[72] ibid., 120.

that in some instances extended to brutal killings.[73] Nurses and midwives were paid wages that ranged between Rs 8–12 per month.[74]

Appendix

The Will of Basharat Ali, made in 1848

Let it be known that this property, together with its income, has been assigned to my heirs, for maintenance and for protection and perpetuation of '*riasat*' and not for any sort of transfer; but the way for the management is that one person be the owner and manager of the whole and the rest be his dependents and sharers in the profits in cash to the extent of their fixed shares without division of any land, for by division power will be diminished and the '*riasat*' will be reduced to small parts. Then there will be neither the perpetuation of '*riasat*' nor the perpetuation of honour, and then the distinction of my family will be lost. Therefore the powers of my management of villages and domestic affairs, payment of revenue, and defending the claim of adversaries to the '*riasat*', &c., i.e., of all matters in connection with the protection, authority, and proprietorship have been conferred upon Kurban Ali just as I have. He shall not been interfered with therein by any one else. It is incumbent on him also that by honestly acknowledging and giving effect to this deed he should assign this '*riasat*' to one of his legitimate and rightful issue after his death, and he, the latter, should also do the same after his death, i.e., should assign this '*riasat*' in regular succession, subject to these customs, so that God willing, this '*riasat*' may be preserved in my family generation after generation. It should also be binding that so long as there may be any male issue of any share this right should never be conferred upon any daughter or the issue of daughter. But it is allowed to fix something in cash for maintenance for life as I have done, in case of insufficient livelihood. The document, with all its conditions, should be in force after my death; both against my heirs and the property left by me, and every one should consider it binding on him to carry it into effect. Until my death my power will remain as it is.

---

73 *The Arya Darpan (Shahjahanpur)*, January 1894. A young Brahman girl named Shama, employed as a compounder and dresser at the Shahjahanpur Dufferin Hospital, was murdered by her father and uncle.

74 *The Arya Darpan*, Vth Annual Report, 157.

CHAPTER 9

Muslim Women's Response to the New Judicial System

This chapter tries to understand and analyse the impact of the British judicial system on the rights of Indian Muslim women in the late nineteenth century. Examining the problems faced by Indian Muslim women, it looks at the positive and negative aspects of the British judicial system, as well as the response of the Muslim community to it. Bernard Cohn stated, 'It cannot be denied that in India the laws that exist today grew out of a colonial legal system, with its bipolarity of authority and norms that derived from the indigenous and the colonial systems.'[1] This chapter will also focus on the development of the Indian legal system, and its impact on women.

Several of the problems that Indian Muslim women faced arose from the British perception of Indian Muslims. Taking all Muslims all over the world as one monolithic category, the British assumed that Indian Muslims were similar to those they had come in contact with in Europe and other Arab countries. They were unclear about who a Musalman really was.[2] The British referred to Muslims as 'Moors' because of the language the latter used. The word 'Moor' was considered pidgin, or, as Gilchrist thought of it, as barbarian gabble.[3] Another British fallacy was assuming that Indian Muslims could be understood from the Holy Books, and that religious dogmas were the Muslims' only concern. The *Hedaya*, translated by Hamilton from Arabic into Persian, and then into

[1] Bernard Cohn, 'An Anthropologist Among Historians', in *Bernard Cohn Omnibus* (New Delhi: Oxford University Press, 2009), 615.

[2] Jivan Khan v. Habib, AIR, 1933, Lah.; Shahid Akhtar, *Muslim Law Digest*, (Allahabad: Publication Co., 1999).

[3] Bernard Cohn, *Colonialism and its forms of Knowledge*, (New Delhi: Oxford University Press, 2009), 30–40.

English, was regarded as the Bible of the British judiciary where Muslim law was concerned.[4]

In order to provide a moral basis to their rule in India, the British focused on the uncivilised nature and backwardness of Indian society.[5] As Muslims were a part of that same society, the British decided that their purpose should be to infuse rationality into what they considered the inherent irrationality of Islam. To prove this, the British examined the administrative policy of the Mughals and emphasised the despotic nature of their legal system. The East India Company servant, Alexander Dow, prefaced his translation of Ferishta's *History of Hindustan* (1770–72) by saying:

> The History now given to the public, present us with a striking picture of the deplorable condition of a people subjected to arbitrary sway; and of the instability of empire itself, when it is founded neither on law, nor upon the opinions and attachment of mankind .... In a government like that of India, public spirit is never seen, and loyalty a thing is unknown. The people permit themselves to be transferred from one tyrant to another, without murdering; and individuals look with unconcern upon the miseries of others, if they are capable to screen themselves from the general misfortune. This however is the picture of Hindostan in bad times, and under the worst kings. As arbitrary government can inflict the most sudden miseries, so, when in the hand of good men, it can administer the most expeditious relief to the subject. We accordingly find in this history, that the misfortunes of half an age of tyranny are removed in a few years, under the mild administration of a virtuous prince.[6]

The British felt that to come to a proper understanding of Indian law and polity, it was necessary to divide Indian administrative policy into a Hindu era, a Muslim era, and a Modern era (the British period). Since the British had replaced the Muslims, it was not surprising that they focused on only the negative aspects of Muslim rule.[7] In the latter half of the eighteenth century,

---

[4] Md. Anis Ansari and Arshad Masood (eds), *Aligarh Law Journal*, V (Aligarh: AMU, 1973), 70.

[5] ibid.

[6] Quoted in Cohn, *An Anthropologist Among Historians*, 62–63.

[7] It was the British who classified the history of India according to religion, that is, Hindu era, Muslim era and British era, the British period being considered the Modern period of Indian history. Unfortunately, we continue to follow this classification even today. They envisioned the Vedic period as the mot enlightened, and the Muslim invasion as the source of all evil. According to the British, it was their

the British began perceiving the people living in the Indian subcontinent as a uniform category.[8] The only variation was that of religion. They believed that no written system of law existed in India,[9] and so the task of the codification of law was begun.[10] Hindus were placed under the Hindu Civil Code while Muslims came under the Mohammedan Civil Code.[11] The British introduced the tier system in the judicial sphere—the Court of First Instance was at the lowest level, after which were the Lower Appellate Courts, the High Court, and finally came the Privy Council, the highest court of appeal. In pre-British times, judicial pronouncements took a more flexible approach, through the interpretation of local customs and traditions. Although it is true that in those days sacred books formed the basis of judicial decisions, several decisions were largely determined by local customs and traditions.

Complexities arose in the British judicial system due to their determination to develop a uniform civil code. It was inevitable that this would create problems, as local variations were determined by local customs and traditions.[12] The British therefore applied stricter rules,[13] which they derived from the traditional system of law, where priority was accorded to local customs, traditions and values, and minor disputes were resolved through an arbitrator. The sacred books were also used, but only in a secondary capacity, and for local problems. At this time, justice was both cheap and equal, and rich and poor alike could appeal for justice in these courts of law. A new professional class, called 'pleaders', was created.[14] After this, though, both defendants and plaintiffs came to face severe

benevolent government that brought civilisation to India. By labelling the Muslim period a 'dark era', Hindus were provoked into highlighting their own glorious past.

[8] Janaki Nair, *Women and Law in Colonial India* (Bangalore: National School of Indian University, 1996), 19. All idol worshippers fell under the Hindu category, and those who were bearded and ate beef were considered Muslim, without any distinction between them.

[9] Cohn, *Colonialism and its Forms of Knowledge*, 64.

[10] Planning Commission, *Social Legislation: Its Role in Social Welfare* (New Delhi: Planning Commission, Government of India, 1956).

[11] Cohn, *Colonialism and its Forms of Knowledge*, 74.

[12] J. K. Krishnamurty, *Women in Colonial India: Essays on Survival, Work and the State* (New Delhi: Oxford University Press, 1989), 126.

[13] ibid.

[14] *Mulk-e Shuhda* (Lahore), 18 January 1894. A cow named India is held by the horns and tail by two people, named the plaintiff and the defendant, while two others (the government and the pleader) are busy milking her.

difficulties,[15] as cases before the court began to pile up because of the lengthy debates involved, and were not resolved quickly enough. This posed a greater problem for the female litigant. Indeed, this court culture had an intricate, traditional system of law, to which women were more accustomed. A close study of the Indian Law Report (ILR) informs us that the majority of women litigants came from the landed class and wealthy families. Surprisingly, Muslim women from the lower classes never approached the courts. While this could be taken to mean that lower-class Muslim women had no problems, what is more probable is that they could not approach the court due to poverty and/or ignorance. Poverty was certainly a deciding factor as in the new legal system, both the plaintiff and the defendant had to pay the pleader a hefty fee.

Yet another problem confronted Indian Muslim women. Adhering as they did to the norms of strict *purdah*, it was difficult for them to approach the court frequently.[16] They could only file a suit with the help of close male relatives, who often cheated them.[17] In several instances, the court considered a woman unfit to be the guardian of her minor son or lunatic husband. In the Fazl Rab v. Khatun Bibi case, for example, it was contended that Musammat Zainab, by reason of being a *purdanashin* lady and the wife of a lunatic, and as such one of his heirs, was unfit and legally ineligible for guardianship of the person or the property of the said lunatic.[18] Also, as women were necessarily accustomed to traditions and customs, they had no knowledge of the language in which the court transacted its proceedings. The technicalities of law could only be understood through the pleader, and once again, this posed a problem.[19]

Presuming that there were no laws in India, the British decided to introduce their own laws and institutions into the vacuum. Warren Hastings, however, protested this proposal to introduce British law, stating that Indian circumstances were not appropriate for such a change, given that Hindus were accustomed to only oral traditions. He argued that British law was too technical, too complicated, and totally unsuited to the Indian context. Hindus were in possession of laws that had continued unchanged from time immemorial; and

---

[15] ibid., 24 May 1894. Many illustrate the dispensation of justice by the Civil Court through the fable of the monkey, who, while pretending to make equal divisions, gradually eats everything up, leaving the cat and the mouse to return home with nothing.

[16] *Akhbar-e Am (Lahore)*, 8 December 1894.

[17] ibid.

[18] ILR, Alld., XV, 1893, 31.

[19] Mariam Bai v. Sakina and others, ILR, Alld., XIV, 1892, 182.

therefore, there was no need to impose new laws.[20] In this way, a communal seed was sown in the context of the need for new laws. At the same time, it was also propagated that people had been deprived of justice in the pre-British period, since 'justice' at that time had been predicated purely on the will of the emperor. A number of failures of the pre-British judicial system was then detailed, and the British stated that justice had been dependent not upon the rule of law, but upon the rule of men, who could be influenced by money, status and connections in the exercise of their office of judge.[21]

The problems faced by Indian Muslim women were peculiar to their group, determined as they were by local traditions and the nature of familial relationships. A British judge was generally unable to understand such unique problems, to the detriment of these poor women. Earlier, British judges had been confronted with problems of language, when they realised that mere knowledge of Persian, Arabic or Sanskrit was not enough to grant them command over Indian people. In seventeenth-century India, the British understood that Persian, as the language of the court, was the most crucial of them all. That was when the process of learning the classical languages of India began.

Warren Hastings stated:

> To the Persian language as being the medium of all political intercourse the first place ought to be assigned in the studies of the pupils; and as much of the Arabic as is necessary to show the principles of its construction and the variations which the sense of the radical words derives from its inflections, to complete their knowledge of the Persian, which in its modern dialect ought to be studied to perfection, and is requisite to all the civil servants of the company, as it may also prove of equal use to the military officers of all the Presidencies.[22]

The British were in desperate need of translators and interpreters. As it was not advisable to depend on native translators, they soon began to learn the classical languages for themselves. As a result, a number of books related to the Hindu *Shastra* and Muslim *Shariat* were published. William Jones proposed a digest of Hindu and Muslim laws, taken from the best available sources, which could then be translated into English, providing European judges with the knowledge necessary to check native interpreters.[23] These translations of

[20] Cohn, *Colonialism and its Forms of Knowledge*, 65–66.

[21] ibid., 65.

[22] Cohn, *Colonialism and its Form of Knowledge*, 24.

[23] ibid., 29.

translations created new difficulties in the judicial system. Justice Mahmood expressed his anger in the famous historical judgement in the Jafri Begum v. Amir Muhammad Khan case:

> One reason why I refrain from doing so is, that one of the greatest difficulties in the courts established in British India is the paucity of text books upon Muhammadan Law written in English which are sufficiently accurate to be safe guides in the administration of those branches of that law which, by section 24 of the Bengal Civil Courts Act VI of 1871 are bound to administer. The only means of information consists of books of reference which are either incomprehensive compilation or abbreviated translations, and in some cases, translation of translations. Another difficulty is that the language of the highest court in India is not the language of the people, and consequently the vast majority of the advocates who appears in those courts are not likely to refer to the original Arabic authorities. For these reasons, I confess, I fully expected that the judgment of the court would have been reserved in such a case.[24]

In this context, we also note that the British system of law in India was more sympathetic to the interests of men. While the *Shariat* observed rights for women in land, the British were more inclined to declare inheritance of property in land to the men. An example is the Fazl Rab v. Khatun Bibi case, where the technical term 'the legal heir' was questioned by Justice Mahmood. The word 'heir' was understood to pertain to the masculine gender, and the enactment which provided that the 'word importing the masculine gender shall be taken to include female' was unavailable to ascertain whether a wife or a mother, who under Mohammedan (henceforth, I will refer to Mohammedan law as Muslim law, although the Indian Law Report prefers the former term[25]) law was entitled to inherit, was included in the term 'heir'. The last part of Section 23 of the enactment possibly involved the necessity of a different interpretation, although the section is far from clear on this point. The peculiar use of the word 'legal' *before* the word 'heir' in the proviso enhanced the difficulty, leaving room for the suggestion that while drafting that enactment, the legislature was thinking more about the terminology of English laws of inheritance of real property, rather

[24] ILR, Alld., VII, 826.

[25] Terming all followers of Islam 'Mohammedan' would imply that they were all followers of Prophet Muhammad; but terming them Muslim and followers of Islam would also include those Muslims who believe in all the Prophets, including those of the Jews, Christians and Zoroastrians. In this context, Muslims believe lastly in the Prophet of Islam, Prophet Muhammad.

than the exigencies of native personal laws of inheritance, such as the Hindu and Muslim laws.[26] In this case, the question was whether Zainab, a childless widow, was entitled to a share in her lunatic husband's *zamindari*/landed estate. The British rationalised this as an effort to preserve the sanctity of land. They argued that it was better to prevent the fragmentation of landed property.[27]

The next section examines three kinds of rights related to women: Property Rights, Dower and Maintenance Right, and Conjugal Bliss.

Property Rights of Women

The Holy Qura'n contains several verses dealing with women's right to property. In the fourth chapter, titled 'Sura Nisa', it was asserted that women were entitled to inherit a portion of their parents' or husbands' wealth and property. Many Muslims who were among the *taluqdars* of Oudh had special exemption from 'Quranic' rules of inheritance. The special code governing *taluqdari* succession bound both Muslims and non-Muslims to accept male primogeniture as the basis of inheritance.[28] Women received, at best, a cash allowance, but their Quranic rights were denied. Many women were deprived of their inheritance in the name of Act XV of the 1877 (Limitation Act), Art. 179 (2).[29]

In pre-British times, the relationship of women and land was determined by local customs and traditions.[30] British Rule changed the traditional relationship between land and people when the government, considering land to be one unit, tried to identify the owner. Under these circumstances, land became a commodity and its significance increased. Several cases were reported of women, who were co-sharers in landed property, losing their rights of ownership to land. The British government enacted the Transfer of Property Act IV of 1882,[31] which secured land for the landlords and *Sahookars* in the event of a default in the payment of land revenue. Thus, men used the provision of this Act to disown their female relatives. Generally, a male owner declared himself bankrupt and mortgaged his property. As his bankruptcy continued, the property in question could be transferred under the Act. The rights of female co-sharers were overlooked, as they were unable to give the women the amount due within

26 ILR, Alld., XV, 35.

27 Nair, *Women and Law in Colonial India*, 183.

28 Krishnamurty, *Women in Colonial India,* 127

29 Hakim-un Nisa v. Deo Narain, ILR, Alld., XIII, 1891.

30 Nair, *Women and Law in Colonial India*, 64–68.

31 Anandi Ram and others v. Dur Najaf Ali Begum, ILR, Alld., 1890.

the time specified under the Act of Limitation. Given this situation, landed property was gradually transferred from mortgagor to mortgagee against the payment of a meagre amount.[32] Court proceedings were tiresome and expensive. There were instances where female plaintiffs had to sell a portion of their share to provide funds for the purpose of litigation. Female heirs were also considered unacceptable in several cases. At times, they were resisted by their in-laws, relatives, and others, on the grounds that the woman was not the widow of the concerned person.[33] The court, too, appeared to have little sympathy for female litigants,[34] and instances of contradictory decisions being delivered by different courts abound.[35] Sometimes, the courts themselves questioned earlier court orders on grounds of jurisdiction. There were cases where the court reserved judgement, particularly in those dealing with women as heirs of property. Women were denied the right to collect rent from their *seer* land.[36]

Women could receive rights as co-sharers of property through their children. It thus became normal practice to prove that a woman was incapable of bearing children. In the Fazl Rab v. Musammat Khatun Bibi case, Justice Mahmood was surprised at a young wife being declared barren, especially when she had given birth to a child (who had unfortunately died two years previously). Therefore, it could not be denied that she was still capable of bearing children.[37] A common practice under Shia law was an attempt to disinherit the wife (the legal heir) of a lunatic from the property, especially if she was childless.[38] In the case cited above, the defence lawyer argued that under Shia law (which governed the case), a childless wife was not entitled to any share in her husband's immoveable property. However, in the present case there was no allegation or proof that the lunatic possessed any immoveable property, and therefore there was no illegality in appointing Musammat Zainab the guardian of her lunatic husband. This contention was met with the allegation that Zainab had had a child by the lunatic husband, and therefore could not be called 'childless' within the framework of the Shia law of inheritance.

[32] Mahabir Singh and others v. Saira Bibi and others, ILR, Alld., 1895.

[33] Murtazai Bibi v. Jumna Bibi, ILR, Alld., XIII, 1891, 261.

[34] It was often observed that in the traditional system of law, local jurists, like the pandit/maulvi, showed some concern towards the widow or destitute wife. Now, though, the scenario had changed, with everything depending on witnesses, power and money.

[35] ILR, Alld., XII, Hikmat Ali V. Wali-un Nisa.

[36] Mirza Anand Ram v. Masuma Begum, ILR, Alld., XIII, 1891, 364.

[37] Fazl Rab v.Khatun Bibi, ILR, Alld., XV, 1893, 34.

[38] ibid.

It is surprising how many differences cropped up in Shia theology while dealing with this case. Justice Mahmood referred to as many as ten contrary doctrines in the Shia rules of inheritance, citing an original textbook written in Arabic. He also questioned the translation from Arabic to English. After going through all the original Arabic texts, Justice Mahmood concluded the case by stating:

> I have been at pains not only to quote these numerous texts from the Shia law, but also to take care that they are properly translated into English. It is obvious from these texts, and it would simply involve my judgement being a volume of a book instead of what I want it to be, a simple statement of what the law is, if I were to show that these texts leave absolutely no doubt in my mind that the law which governs the present case, shows one deniable fact, that the wife, be she a mother or childless, is one of the heirs of her husband. The history of Muhammadan jurisprudence explains why, while among the Sunni Muhammadans absolutely no distinction is made between a wife who has children and childless wife, a great distinction is made in Shia creed in this respect. I do not intend to go into the history of how the difference between the Sunni and Shia creed has arisen, but it is simple enough for everyone who reads the history of Muhammadan Jurisprudence to show that because Ayesha, the childless widow of the prophet, was childless and never had a child, therefore the dissensions which arose upon the death of the prophet created difficulties with which we have to deal.[39]
>
> This being my view of the Shia law, the next question to consider is also a matter of importance, namely, the question what is the exact period at which, for the purposes of administering the Shia law, we ought to decide that a young woman, such as Zainab is, should be declared to be barren or childless. I hold it true upon the very authority that exists, nor can the Shia law to declare that a woman in the position of Zainab, respondent, is totally devoid of any right of inheritance from her unfortunate lunatic husband, Muhammad Sadik. Absolutely no such authority exists, nor can the Shia law contemplate such a thing, because if it did it would be considering itself. What it does contemplate is that for the purpose of considering whether or not a widow or a wife who is childless is entitled to take part or share in the estate of her deceased husband, one has to see whether she gave birth to a child and if she did, if the child is alive at the time when the husband dies. This is the Shia law, and it is consistent with the principle upon which it proceeds. The inheritance to the estate of a Shia, as well as a Sunni, opens upon the death of porosities, namely, the person whose estate is in question. In this case the childless wife of her husband, Musammat Zainab, being still alive it is impossible to say whether or not she is childless in the sense of being childless at the time when her husband Muhammad Sadik

[39] Fazl Rab V. Khatun Bibi, 44-45.

> may die. It is impossible legally for Muhammad Sadik to know whether or not his wife would be an inheritor not only of his personal or moveable estate but also of his real estate. Nobody knows this without the help of prophesy, but I have to consider the matter as it now stands, and I have no doubt that under the Shia law upon the text which I have quoted Musammat Zainab, respond it, is one of the heirs of her lunatic husband, Muhammad Sadik, with whom we are concerned.'[40]

The government declared that women were kept away from shares. However, this was a time when many women did claim profits in certain *mahal*s.[41] There were cases where women had to prove their title in the bond of auction sale, where the mortgagee purchased the debt secured by him.[42] The government enacted the law of 'pre-emption', and a person would now claim ownership through the '*wajib-ul arz*'. Once again, this posed a problem for women, as they could only claim their rights through male relatives. Women received their rights through the Transfer of Property Act and Mortgage Sale Deed.[43] The sale deed held by the male proprietor was declared null and void through the CPCs 311.[44]

A wide gulf exists between the Shia and Sunni laws of inheritance. According to Shia law, female inheritance is allowed through the maternal line as well; Sunni law, however, does not allow this.[45] Women approached the courts several times to receive their partition right in property.[46] They filed petitions requesting the cancellation of sale deeds. This plea generally related to technical irregularities.[47] Under these circumstances witnesses played an important role, and in several instances actually changed the direction of the case.[48] Women also

[40] ibid., 45-46.

[41] Niaz ullah v. Nazir Begum, ILR, Alld., XV, 1893.

[42] Karim-un Nisa v. Phul Chand, ILR, Alld., XV, 1893.

[43] Begum and others v. Md. Yaqub, ILR, Alld., XV, 1893.

[44] Umrao-un Nisa v. Md. Ali Khan, ILR, Alld., XII, 1890.

[45] Hayat-un Nisa v. Md. Ali Khan, ILR, Alld., 1890. The right of the defendant to the inheritance, clear enough in Sunni law, was disputed by the daughters of Wazir-un Nisa's maternal uncle, on the grounds that the latter belonged to *Imamia* law. This meant that as the nearest kin of the deceased, the inheritance belonged to them.

[46] Hiqmat Ali v. Wali-un Nisa, ILR, Alld., XII, 1890.

[47] Taqaddus Fatima and others v. Baldeo Das, ILR, Alld., XII, 1890.

[48] Mariam Bibi v. Sakina, ILR, Alld., XV, 1893. This case serves as an example of how, with the help of two witnesses who were also close relatives of the defendant, a fraudulent deed was prepared, disowning a legal heir from his property.

claimed possession of shares in immovable property and '*mesne* profits'.[49] They claimed their tenancy rights, but did not receive it due to technical loopholes.[50] It was common to keep women away from their property, stating that they could not manage it properly because of their ignorance.[51]

Dower and Maintenance Rights

The second question before the court was how to deal with *mahr* (dower) cases and maintenance rights. Under Muslim law, 'mahr' refers to a sum of money or other property that the wife is entitled to receive from the husband in the event of her marriage.[52] In India, it was usual for the husband to seek ways to secure this *mahr* in the name of the *Shari'ah*.[53] Several aristocratic families settled large sums of money commensurate to their family honour, which was usually far in excess of the total value of their estates. Thus, these large sums were never paid in their lifetimes.[54] Since the main rationale behind *mahr* is to protect the wife against divorce, it was considered a mark of respect towards the woman.[55] Problems such as these were brought before the court. Aware of this problem, the British government codified the Law of Maintenance under CPC.[56] However, the Act had an unintended consequence: men began escaping their liabilities, aided by certain procedures enumerated in the law. The law allowed a man to be relieved of his liability if he could show his incapacity to pay. Several men therefore declared themselves financially bankrupt.[57] The Act also raised the issue of what the minimum[58] or maximum amount of

[49] Fatima Bibi v. Abdul Majid, ILR, Alld., XIV, 1892.

[50] Haidari Begum v. Nathu, ILR, Alld., XVII, 1895. In this case, notice of the determination of tenancy under s. 106 of Act IV of 1882 was in question.

[51] Masuma Bibi v. The Collector of Ballia, ILR, Alld., VII, 1885.

[52] B. R. Verma, *Commentaries on Mohammadan Law*, 8e (Allahabad: Law Publisher [India] Pvt Ltd, 2004), 156.

[53] Saiyid Abul Hasan Ali Nadvi, *The Musalman* (Lucknow: Islamic Research and Publication, 1977), 33.

[54] Sughra Bibi v. Masuma Bibi, ILR, Alld., II, 1877.

[55] Abdul Kadır v. Salima, ILR, Alld., VIII.

[56] Afzal Wani, *The Islamic Law on Maintenance of Women & Children, Parents and other Relatives* (Kashmir: Upright Study Home, 1995), 99–101.

[57] Mahbuban v. Fakir Baksh, ILR, Alld., XV, 1893. Usually, husbands would claim that they were not in a sufficient enough position to maintain their wives.

[58] Sughra Bibi v. Masuma Bibi, ILR, Alld., II, 1877.

mahr[59] should be. The dower amount was usually fixed through an oral contract, which was considered valid. There was also no limit to either the maximum or the minimum amount, although early Hanafi lawyers had fixed 10 *dirham* as the minimum while the Maliki considered an even smaller sum acceptable.[60] Justice Ameer Ali observed in his Mohemmadan Law treatise:

> In India, for example among the upper middle class, the amount of dower ranges from Rs. 4,000 to 40,000. In Bihar the latter is generally speaking, the customary dower; in lower Bengal, there is no custom. Among the lower classes, the mahr varies from Rs. 50 to 400. In princely families, the dower consists of several lakhs.[61]

In 1876, the Oudh Laws Act came into existence to redress the injustice that the children of a Mohemmadan had to face because of the oppressive dower amounts fixed by the bride's family. Section 5 of this Act gave the court the power to fix a reasonable amount as *mahr*, after taking into consideration the economic condition of the husband and the status of the wife.[62] Contemporary records reveal that it was an accepted practice amongst middle and upper middle-class Muslims to fix huge amounts as *mahr*, which ranged from thousands to lakhs of rupees. Interestingly, *mahr* was to protect women from divorce and polygamy, and safeguard their rights. Maulvi Nazir Ahmad's marriage was a case in point—he apparently signed a pre-nuptial bond which inscribed Rs 11,000 as the *mahr* amount.[63] At that time it was a huge sum of money, something that Muslims today would never agree to.[64]

---

59 M. Mujeeb, *Islamic Influence on Indian Society* (Meerut: Meenakshi Prakashan, 1972). It was obligatory for the husband to pay, or bind himself to pay, the *mahr* to the bride before the marriage. The amount depended on the social status of the family.

60 Verma, *Commentaries on Mohemmadan Law*, 161.

61 Quoted in Verma, *Commentaries on Mohemmadan Law*, 162.

62 ibid.

63 Zeenat Bashir, *Nazir ke Navilon me Nuswai Qirdar* (Hyderabad: Ilias Traders and Publishers and Book Sellers, 1991), 30–31.

64 In the twenty-first century, Muslims speak of *fatimi mahr*, that is, Rs 500. This amount used to be converted from dirhams. The example of *mahr* makes clear that religions provide space for the status of women, too; this status depends upon their education, beauty, and social class. In the latter half of the nineteenth century, Umme Safiya's (the wife of Maulvi Nazir) *mahr* was Rs 11,000. In 2008, my own *mahr* was Rs 14,000. I was also not part of the discussion during which the amount the fixed. It is clear that Muslim women of that time were more protected than they are today. In those days, they lived by custom, while today they have to assert their own rights.

A perusal of the ILR makes clear that the court had accepted the dower right of the wife as the husband's debt, and considered his property analogous to being mortgaged till her dower debt was paid.[65] In fact, it was common in Muslim society for a divorced wife to never receive her *mahr* during her husband's lifetime, or even after his death, as other co-sharers usually deprived her of her property in lieu of her dower debt.[66] Examples abound of women finding themselves unable to retain ownership of their deceased husbands' property in lieu of their dower. Under such circumstances, she either sold her share or converted it to a deed, a decision often questioned by the other co-sharers.[67] Another major question before the court was whether a wife had the right to obtain the property of her deceased husband in lieu of her dower without the consent of the other co-sharers.[68] The court could come to no uniform decision on the matter, providing contradictory decisions that were sometimes positive,[69] and sometimes not.[70]

The third problem had to do with maintenance rights. Should a wife be given maintenance rights after divorce?[71] While Muslim law extended the duty of maintenance to a considerable degree, it was based on the principle that all persons were bound to maintain their poor relations at all times.[72] So why were women being deprived of their maintenance rights in the name of the expiration of *iddat*? What happened to the humanitarian grounds of the British legal system?

Conjugal Bliss

This question usually arises only among the poorer sections of the Muslim population. Can the sacred marital tie be snapped only on monetary grounds?[73] The court's concern was that marriage among Muslims was not a sacrament,

[65] Azizullah Khan v. Ahmad Ali Khan, ILR, Alld.

[66] Amini Begum v. Md. Karim, ILR, Alld., 1894.

[67] ILR, Alld., VII, Jamaitun Nisa v Lutfunnisa, 1885, 606. In this case, the defendant contended that she was in possession of the property until the dower debt had been paid, and that her possession could not be disturbed so long as the debt remained unpaid.

[68] ibid.

[69] ibid.

[70] Amanat-un Nisa v. Babirun.

[71] Mahbuban v. Fakir Baksh.,ILR, Alld., 1893.

[72] Paras Diwan and Piyush Diwan, *Muslim Law on Maintainence in India* (New Delhi: Deep and Deep Publication), 72.

[73] *Aligarh Law Journal*, V, 69.

but a civil contract. It was analogous to a sale, with the dower being the price for connubial intercourse; therefore, the right of co-habitation would not accrue till the dower had been paid. Justice Mahmood used law and logic to defeat the sale price; he demonstrated that the right of dower and the right of co-habitation were independent of each other, and came into existence simultaneously, as marriage provided the right of co-habitation not only in favour of the husband, but also in favour of the wife.[74]

Yet another question was whether the wife could be forced to return to a violent husband.[75] A Muslim husband could not ill-treat his wife because the tenets of criminal law offered the wife personal security (which matrimonial law did not). In several cases, it was also ruled that maternity could not be disclaimed.[76]

Therefore, one may say that on the one hand, women were not encouraged to fight for their property rights; but on the other hand, where marital issues were concerned, her rights had been protected. An awareness of their own rights was steadily becoming more apparent, especially among north Indian Muslim women. The establishment of new laws had encouraged them to venture outdoors. Natives were also demanding the appointment of female judges in courts,[77] a further indication of women's growing awareness of their legal rights. Around this time, female European travellers expressed appreciation of the way the legal status of Muslim women had been secured in the *shariat*. Sir Saiyid and social reformers like Maulvi Mumtaz Ali boasted about the *huquq-e niswa*, and how Islam gave several rights to their women, in contrast to women belonging to Christian, Jewish and other religious faiths, who had no rights and had to have their identities and rights merged with those of their husbands'.

Child Marriage and Age of Consent Bill

Social reform was one of the primary platforms on which the gender question was debated in the late nineteenth century. The abolition of sati, the Widow Remarriage Act of 1856, and the Age of Consent Bill of 1891 were included in this series of debates. The great uprising of 1857 had warned the British to not interfere in social or religious matters that could lead to tension, and they

---

[74] ibid.,70–71.

[75] ibid., 72.

[76] Liaqat Ali and others v. Karim-un Nisa and others, ILR, Alld., XV, 1893, 396. See also Allahdad Khan v. Ismail Khan, ILR, Alld., X, 289.

[77] *The Akhbar-e Am* (Lahore), 8 December 1894.

remained firm in their resolve to stay away from these issues.[78] The latter half of the nineteenth century witnessed much social reform.[79] However, during the codification of law, the British realised that Hindus had no systematic code of law. As stated earlier, the British looked at sacred religious texts to formulate a Hindu Civil Code and a Mohammedan Civil Code. During the process, they introduced several modifications, which the Muslims always protested.[80]

I will now focus on the traditional aspects of Muslim society. The Age of Consent Bill was the most hotly debated issue of the late nineteenth and early twentieth century, and provoked countrywide protests.[81] Social reformers led the debate: Hindu reformers fiercely criticised every evil custom that had entered their society over time, and expected the government to abolish or reform these through legislation.[82] Some orthodox groups, however, considered government legislation unnecessary interference in religious matters, and raised their voices against it.[83] During this period, European travellers and British officials had launched an attack on the traditional education system and the low status of women in society. While Hindus did not oppose the new education system, they were enraged by the gender issue, and linked it to religious issues. This was probably because both the ruler and the ruled were part of patriarchal societies that could concede women's free will only up to a point.[84]

Muslim women had to contend with different problems. They were concerned about the social reform agenda, but only within the limitations of their confinement. Muslims had alienated themselves from many of these issues; some of the practices under discussion were not prevalent in the Muslim community, while the Quran provided multiple answers to some other questions.[85] They felt no need to modify the *Shariat*. As a result, the Mohammadan Civil Code was applied only in matters of marriage, divorce, and family disputes.[86]

---

[78] S. A. Natrajan, *Century of Social Reform in India* (Bombay: Ashia Publishing House, 1962), 71.

[79] ibid.

[80] Indira Jaisingh (ed.), *Justice for Women* (Mapusa, Goa: The Other India Press, 1996), 3.

[81] Charls Heimsath, *Indian Nationalism and Hindu Social Reform* (Bombay: Princeton University Press, 1964), 161–74.

[82] ibid., 9–27

[83] ibid., 163–65, see also Natrajan, *Century of Social Reform in India,* 66–67.

[84] *Bharat Bandhu* (Aligarh), 1 July1887, 152.

[85] *Najm-ul Akhbar* (Etawa), 24 February 1891, 152.

[86] Jaisingh, *Justice for Women*, 3.

The widespread prevalence of child marriage in the 1870s drew the attention of social reformers. In 1872, the Native Marriage Act came into existence, under which the marriageable age was fixed at fourteen years,[87] providing some measure of relief to a significant problem. The Muslim community, however, did not welcome the Act, regarding it as religious interference.[88] They claimed that since marital rights could not be consummated before puberty, there was no need to replace the *Shariat* with any new law.[89]

Sir Saiyid Ahmad Khan was also uncomfortable with legislative reform, especially with regard to the issue of child marriage. He suggested that the government refrain from legislating on social issues, because that could provide grounds for revolt. He was of the opinion that there could be no one marriageable age that both communities would find agreeable, and therefore legislation would merely amount to unnecessary interference in personal matters.[90] This view led to allegations that Sir Saiyid and his followers ignored problems concerning common people, raising only those issues that were related to *ashra'f* society. Since child marriage was rampant only among *ajlaf* Muslims, it was these communities (located mainly in the eastern part of the province) that were in need of social reform.[91] It was in this context that 'The Durdi' of 'Ispahan' wrote to 'Azad' (in Lucknow), stating that the so-called leaders of Muslims were not really their well-wishers after all.[92] In the late 1880s, the Rukmabai case engendered widespread protests across the country.[93] Both Hindus and Muslims believed that the Age of Consent Bill would make Indian women capricious, much like European women.[94] It would curtail the right of restitution of cohabitation with the wife, and would destroy Indian society.[95]

---

87 Natrajan, *Century of Social Reform in India,* 49.

88 *The Najm-ul Akhbar* (Etawa), 8 February 1891, 101, commented that there was no justification for the government to meddle in religious and social matters.

89 ibid.

90 Sheikh Ismail Panipati (ed.), *Akhbar-e Scientific Society*, 13, 12 May 1876, 514–18.

91 CR, of 1911, E. H. Blunt, Allahabad, 1912, 230

92 *Azad* (Lukhnow), 23 November 1894.

93 *The Namj-ul Akhbar,* 8 April 1887. Several newspapers questioned the right of restitution of marriage; Section 260 was also in debate. See *The Bharat Bandhu,* 1 July 1887; *Azad,* 5 August 1887.

94 *The Bharat Bandhu* protested the proposed abolition of imprisonment in the execution of a decree for the restitution of conjugal rights, because fear of imprisonment often induced women to continue living with their husbands (29 July 1887).

95 *The Nairang* (Agra), 19 February 1891.

Muslim women married only after attaining puberty. The provision of this Bill increased the minimum age of marriage from ten to twelve years. Since girls in India did not attain puberty before the age specified in the Age of Consent Bill,[96] Muslims generally did *not* get their daughters married prematurely. Thus, they felt that the Bill did not apply to them, and was a superfluous intervention in their personal matters. They also feared that Muslims would be affected more than Hindus as the latter could provide horoscopes declaring a suitable age of marriage, which Muslims were not privy to.[97] They viewed the Bill as a form of tyranny, unleashed by corrupt police officers and magistrates. Innocent people would be punished, and women would be confronted with new problems, for instance, a woman's husband could be imprisoned for seven years. Who, then, would look after her? This Bill would certainly complicate the social order in India, where girls often become mothers by the age twelve.[98]

Most Muslims objected strongly to some of the provisions laid out in the Bill.[99] This was only natural in a feudal and hierarchal society that could not tolerate the thought of women's liberty beyond a point. The Bill prohibited any male below the age of twelve to marry; failure to comply would result in seven years' imprisonment. While the Bill did not forbid early marriage, it forbade the couple to cohabit even after they had reached puberty. This was also not feasible, as it was unlikely that a married couple would live in the same house and yet refrain from sexual intercourse.[100] It was this that led Indians to demand a clear distinction between rape and cohabitation.[101] Despite the widespread protests, the Age of Consent Bill was passed in the Legislative Assembly on 19 March 1891.[102] Muslim women were not part of the ruling; however, the Criminal Procedure Code was applicable to all. Nawab Ehsan Ullah, a Muslim representative in the Legislative Assembly, expressed his support for the Bill, much to the annoyance of several other Muslims. Several columnists writing in vernacular newspapers voiced their concern about how Nawab Ehsan Ullah could be considered the sole representative of the Muslim community.[103] *The*

[96] *The Najm-ul Akhbar*, 8 February 1891.

[97] ibid.

[98] ibid.

[99] *The Hindustani* (Lucknow), 14 February 1891.

[100] *The Najm-ul Akhbar*, 8 February 1891.

[101] *The Nairang*, 19 February 1891.

[102] Heimsath, *Indian Nationalism*, 173.

[103] *The Hindustani*, 14 February 1891. See also *Najm-ul Akhbar*, 8 February and 24 February 1891.

Azad and the *Muhazzib* were the only two newspapers to conduct an enquiry into the Bill; but they disapproved of the Hindu custom of child marriage and wanted the Bill to be amended considerably before being passed.[104]

From then onwards, child marriage became a significant topic of discussion in vernacular newspapers. *Nazmul Akhbar* wrote that child marriage was rare among Muslims. On those rare occasions when such marriages took place, the young couple was not allowed to cohabit till they reached puberty. Given these circumstances, Sir Andrew Scoble's bill could not be considered anything but an undesirable intrusion into the religious concerns of Muslims.[105] Shaikh Kamil's case was referred to,[106] which proved that people had begun using fake medical reports to escape its strict provisions. So at the end of the day, the Bill had no actual effect on either the Hindus or the Muslims. In addition, statistics show a decline in child marriage among Muslims for the entire province as a unit (see Table 9.1).

Table 9.1: Number of Married Women in Each Age Group

Age	*Hindu*			*Muslim*		
	Number	*% at its own population*	*% at total population*	*Number*	*% at its own population*	*% at total population*
0–10	6,38,861.5	1.6	1.34	7,80,79.99	1.16	0.16
10–15	2,449,647.4	6.02	5.14	3,076,08.25	4.57	0.64
15–40	14,054,954	34.54	29.5	2,294,609.5	34.1	4.81
40 and over	64,293,07.2	15.8	13.5	7,525,29.6	11.2	1.6
all ages	21,314,374	52.4	44.7	3,432,827.3	50.99	7.2

Source: CR of 1901.

The conventional belief is that Muslims habitually alienated themselves from real issues. The fact that local customs and traditions were always prioritised over the *Shariat* was conveniently ignored.[107] However, Muslims of the United Province could be understood only with reference to regional variations, viz., the Eastern United Province, Central United Province and Western United Province. Social and economic positions, and land settlements were the factors

104 *The Hindustani*, 14 February 1891.

105 *The Najm-ul Akhbar*, 24 February 1891.

106 Sheikh Kamil hailed from Krishan Nagar. His father-in-law falsely accused him of raping his daughter, the motive behind his allegations being to get Kamil imprisoned, and then marry his daughter to another man in return for more money. However, medical reports declared her to be over the age of twelve (*The Nairang*, 17 August 1891).

107 Jaisingh, *Justice for Women*, 3.

affecting inhabitants the most. Muslims in the Eastern United Province were mostly landless and low-born.[108] In the Central United Province, conditions were varied, while cash allowance was practised in the Western United Province. Muslims in the Western region came from the landed class or the service gentry class, and were more urbanised.[109]

The amount of money taken on as debt on the occasion of a daughter's wedding is remarkable. Marriage ceremonies in India have always been expensive for both communities, and the Reports of the Banking Committee and Revenue Committee demonstrate the rapid increase in indebtedness. Contemporary literature also throws light on how a poor father is often forced to marry his daughter to a far older bridegroom just for the sake of money.[110] Faced with these circumstances, both communities used to get their daughters married at an early age.[111] Muslims in the Eastern United Province, who were poorer than their counterparts in the West, were more prone to child marriage. Table 9.2 shows that child marriage was not in evidence in those areas where well-to-do Muslim families resided; and as two-fifths of the entire Muslim population lived in the Western United Province and were well-off economically,[112] child marriage was absent among them.

Table 9.2: Age of Marriage for Girls in 0–15 Age Group at per 1,000

Age	*All religion*			*Hindu*			*Muslim*		
	1901	*1891*	*1881*	*1901*	*1891*	*1881*	*1901*	*1891*	*1881*
0–5	9	6	51	9	6	53	8	6	35
5–10	110	99	11	115	104	-	82	73	-
10–15				562	594	569	419	456	428

Source: CR of 1921.

[108] All the census reports of the time mention this condition. See also Firdous Azmat Siddiqui, 'Colonial Report on Census and its Reflection on Indian Muslim Women', in Nadeem Hasnain (ed.), *Islam and Muslim Societies* (New Delhi: Serial Publications, 2005), 155.

[109] ibid.

[110] *The Nasim-e Agra,* 15 October 1890. Premchand's novels and Nazir's *Aiyaam'a* also speak about this practice. See Firdous Azmat Siddiqui, 'Unnisvin Sadi Ke Utrardh Men Muslim Vidhvaon Ki Isthiti', in A. K. Sinha (ed.), *Perspective of Indian History* (New Delhi: Anamika Publications, 2002), 359.

[111] *The Najm-ul Akhbar,* 8 April 1887. Indeed, this practice was prevalent in both communities in India, with children becoming betrothed in infancy, and sometimes even before their birth.

[112] CR of 1901. See also Siddiqui, 'Colonial Report on Census'.

Caste variation at the local level was also considerable. The data and sources available provide very little evidence of child marriage among *ashra'f* Muslims,[113] while it was widely prevalent among *ajlaf* and *arzal* Muslims, probably due to the incomplete 'Islamisation' of this group. Their customs and traditions remained the same as their 'co-brothers', and religion did not play as pivotal a role.[114] Most social reformers of the time hailed from *ashra'f* society, which perhaps explains why Muslim social reformers refrained from participating either for or against these issues. The proportion of married children under the age of twelve gives us some idea about the age of marriage favoured by different Muslim communities: the Saiyid community (53); Kayasth (60); Bhuinhara (70); Shaikh (86); and Jats (87). Late marriages seem to be closely connected to school-going girls, and to those castes with a high proportion of literate women (see Table 9.3).[115] Colonial discursive writing blamed the Muslim invasion for such evil customs, citing the Nesfield theory in support of their allegation.[116] All statistics provided in the Census Reports prove that the Age of Consent Bill turned into a dead letter. Opinions vary, though; with changing circumstances, Muslims realised that the legislation did not pose a problem only for the Hindus. Orthodox groups among both communities continued with their protest.

Table 9.3: Number of Married Women per Mille

Religion and Natural Division	*Age Group*		
	0–5	*5–10*	*10–15*
United Province			
Hindu	7	107	520
Muslim	6	72	379
Himalaya West			
Hindu	1	61	542
Muslim	4	79	373
Sub-Himalaya West			
Hindu	2	85	492

[113] CR of 1891, 246.

[114] ibid.

[115] C. of 1921, 103.

[116] CR of 1911, 225. Child marriage was considered a means to save girls from inter-tribal marriages and marriage by capture.

Religion and Natural Division	*Age Group*		
	0–5	*5–10*	*10–15*
Muslim	5	67	348
Indo-Gangetic Plain West			
Hindu	3	46	480
Muslim	4	44	333
Indo-Gangetic Plain Central			
Hindu	10	148	535
Muslim	7	82	346
Central India Plateau			
Hindu	9	141	626
Muslim	11	73	448
East Satpura			
Hindu	9	156	576
Muslim	13	111	467
Sub-Himalaya East			
Hindu	9	98	454
Muslim	6	99	496
Indo-Gangetic East			
Hindu	9	157	603
Muslim	8	97	452

Source: CR of 1921, Subsidiary Table II, 106–07

Table 9.4: Marriageable Age for Select Castes

Caste	*Age Group*	
	0–5	*5–12*
Shaikh	6	86
Pathan	11	95
Nai	10	123
Saiyid	8	53
Julaha	11	171
Teli	18	183
Bhangi	12	150

Source: CR of 1921, 110–11.

Note: Due to the paucity of accurate data, Tables 9.3 and 9.4 are based on the Census Report of 1921.

Table 9.5: Number of Women by Civil Condition and Main Age Group / 100

Age	*All religion*			*Hindu*			*Muslim*		
	1901	*1891*	*1881*	*1901*	*1891*	*1881*	*1901*	*1891*	*1881*
				Unmarried					
0–10	24.2	25.8	24.8	20	25.8	24.7	25.2	26.3	25.2
10–15	4.8	4.3	4.3	4.5	4.2	4.2	6.2	5.0	5.7
15–40	1.5	0.8	0.8	1.4	0.7	0.7	2.3	1.6	1.65
40 and over	0.3	0.1	0.1	0.3	0.11	0.11	0.5	0.3	0.32
All ages	30.8	30.1	30.1	30.2	30.2	30.3	4.2	33.3	32.9
				Married					
0–10	1.5	1.38	1.3	1.6	1.44	1.4	1.2	1.03	0.91
10–15	5.8	5.4	5.5	6.0	5.6	5.7	4.6	4.3	4.3
15–40	34.5	35.5	35.7	34.54	35.5	35.8	34.1	35.1	34.9
40 and over	10.4	10.3	10.3	10.3	10.2	10.2	11.2	10.9	10.9
All ages	52.2	52.5	52.7	52.4	52.7	53.1	32.1	51.0	51.4
				Widowed					
0–10	0.05	0.03	0.02	0.06	0.03	0.02	0.04	0.03	0.02
10–15	0.13	0.10	0.11	0.13	0.10	0.12	0.06	0.06	0.07
15–40	3.9	3.55	3.8	4.08	3.7	3.9	2.84	2.74	3.13
40 and over	12.9	13.1	13.2	13.2	13.2	13.2	11.9	12.5	12.9
All ages	17.0	16.8	17.1	17.43	16.9	17.3	14.8	15.3	16.1

Conclusion

This book highlights the real efforts made by both middle-class Muslim women and marginalised women to break out of several Victorian ideas and actions on the part of their menfolk, who sought to re-create the woman as an ideal mother, an ideal daughter, and an ideal wife. These three phases were considered necessary stages in the life-cycle of women, and those women who did not fall within this parameter were considered 'bad' or deviant.

This book has also tried to contest the prevalent belief that Indian Muslim women were backward and deprived of all rights as per the Muslim Laws, in both their natal and marital families. During the course of my research, I came to the conclusion that Indian Muslim women were actually determined to progress in the fields of education and literacy achievement, or even in matters concerning the ownership of property, despite being victimised by traditional values and customs, much like their Hindu counterparts. Also, while it is commonly assumed that Indian Muslim women were denied several rights, the fact remains that they did exercise several rights which accrued to them through either their natal or their marital families.

Further, it is erroneous to assume that Indian Muslim women were untouched by the social reform movement in India. From the early stages of the movement, the reformists focused on the condition of women, but only within the paradigm of their patriarchal interests. These reformers might have seemed extremely progressive, especially in matters in which they had a direct interest, for example, on the subject of education. However, this was mostly because they needed educated wives! This was why it was considered necessary for women to be privy to the new education—so that they could become 'good housewives'. This education in no way encompassed higher education, which was considered appropriate only for men. Those issues that did not impact directly on the interests of men were overlooked. Since higher education led to a broadening and liberation of mental horizons, along with providing some opportunities for freedom, it could explain why men chose to remain silent on this matter, instead encouraging traditional knowledge along with some Western thought.

They seemed to alienate themselves from real, mainstream issues concerning women as well, for instance, major issues such as widowhood (and widow remarriage) and child marriage, which inflamed the nineteenth century. Although some attempts were made to address the issue of enforced widowhood, it is amusing to note that according to the reformers, the solution lay either in polygamy, or in denying its prevalence. It is perhaps this attitude of Muslim social reformers that led the British to conclude that Muslims were polygamous and they frequently practised widow remarriage, thereby making them more fertile than Hindus, who were (in contrast) perceived as monogamous. The prohibition of widow remarriage was considered an obligation and an essential part of Hindu life. This generalisation ensured that the social reform agenda for Indian Muslim women did not extend beyond education. However, education provided Indian Muslim women with the impetus to review their socio-economic condition, raising several questions about the patriarchal nature of Muslim society in the process. Muslim women were among the first women in north India to claim their rights and form organisations to enforce their demands. The increasing number of women's magazines and the *Anjuman Khawateen-e Islam* strengthened the idea of progressiveness of Muslim women in India.

Glossary

Aayah: Maid, babysitter

Adab: Manner, behaviour

Aali: From the upper caste/class

Adal: Justice

Ahl-e Kitab: Those believing in the four sacred Books—Injeel, Jaboor, Tauret and Quran

Allah hafiz: Goodbye in Arabic. Literal meaning is: 'be in God's protection'

Annadata: Giver of food

Aqiqa: To shave a new-born child's head as part of religious ritual; an offering is made at the same time, through the sacrifice of goats—one goat for girls, and two for boys

Arzal: Those converted from untouchable Hindu castes

Ashraf: Socially high-born Muslims; migrant Muslims, particularly those who claimed origin from Arab or other Middle East countries

Azlaf: Those converted from the indigenous people. They were also known as *nau Muslim*

Babu: Clerk

Basant: A festival to welcome the autumn season

Bhand: A dancer community

Bidah: Innovation. In special terms, it means carrying out actions that displease Allah and His messenger.

Biradari: Brotherhood/sisterhood

Begum: Your highness, feminine form of Turkish title Beg: it refers wife or daughter of Beg

Bharbhunja: Nut baker

Bhishti: Water carrier

Bibi: Wives, daughter and sister, generally used for Indian Muslim women

Bismillāh ḳhawānī: A religious ceremony marking the beginning of reading the Quran when a child is four years, four months, and ten days old

Burqā: A loose garment that cover a woman from head to toe

Chaudharain: Madam

Chaklakhana: Brothel

Chandu: Opium

Chapatti: Bread

Chatti: Six days after childbirth

Chauthi: Third and fourth day of the marriage ceremony, when the bride and groom's families visit each other

Chaudhrayan: Head of the salon

Cheek: Airy bamboo curtain, normally used in old-fashioned Indian households

Chilla: Forty days after childbirth

Choli: Blouse, top

Churihain: Woman bangle seller

Dal: Pulses

Dalan: Veranda

Darbar: Court

Dar-ul Harb: Abode of non-Muslims, such areas that are governed by non-Muslims

Dastkaari: Handicraft

Deredar: Professions performed over generations

Dhobin: Washer woman

Dhol: Drum

Dholli: A woman included as the second, third or fourth wife

Dirham: Currency used in Arab countries

Domnis: Female member of untouchable castes, whose profession is singing and dancing in a lewd manner during weddings

Duhaja: Someone who has been married at least once

Dupatta: A two and half metr long and 1 metre wide scarf

Faqiran: Female beggar

Fatwa: Religious injunction issued, keeping in mind the Quran and Prophetic tradition

Gali: Abuse

Ganda: Black knotted thread used as an amulet

Ghaghra: Long skirt

Gharana: Music school

Ghazal: Poetry

Gumnam: Unknown

Hanafi: Followers of Imam Abu Hanifa

Harem: Women's section in a royal family

Hasb: Economic and social status

Hindustani zuban: A mix of the Hindi and Urdu languages

Huquq-e Niswa: Women's right

Iddat: Waiting period (four months, ten days) mandatory for a wife after divorce, or after a husband's death

Imambara: A symbolic grave of the martyrs of Qarbala

Imamia sect: Shia

Iqrarnama: Agreement

Jachcha: A woman who has recently given birth

Jhilmil: Curtain

Jihad: Religious war. This term is used particularly for Muslims waging war against non-Muslims, protest against evils.

Khandan: Big family; generally used for the extended Indian family

Khanadamad: A man who stays with his in-laws

Khangi: Veiled prostitute

Khankah: Building design for the Sufi brotherhood. A spiritual retreat and place for character reformation.

Kharch: Expense

Kharcha-e pandan: Pocket money

Khatna: Circumcision

Khudahafiz: Good-bye in Persian

Kil: Nose pin

Kameen: Low status

Kasbi: Low-ranking prostitute

Kunjra: Vegetable seller

Kurta: Shirt

Lalbibi: Prostitute

Lathi: Bamboo Stick

Madarsa: A medieval non-formal school

Mahal: The word Mahalwari is derived from the term Mahal, referring to a neighbourhood or a quarter. Under this system, the unit for revenue settlement is the village.

Mahfil: Auspicious gathering

Mahr: Maintenance

Maliki: Followers of Abu Abdullah, Malik bin Anas, the great scholar of Fiqh

Mānjhā: Women's seclusion for one week (although the time period is flexible) just before marriage

Malkin: Mistress

Manjira: A kind of drum

Maulvi: Religious master

Mayub: Bad

Mehtarani: Female sweeper

Mardaana: The domain of men

Masnad: Round, long pillow

Memsahib: White women

Mesne: Profits which have accrued during a dispute over land ownership. If it is determined that the party using the land was not the legal owner, the true owner could sue for some or all of the profits made in the interim by the illegal tenant.

Mewa khori: Pocket money

Milad shareef: Religious gathering of Muslims in the memory of Prophet Muhammad (PBUH). On these occasions, they deliver religious lectures and recite poems in praise of the Prophet.

Mirasi: Male singer

Mirasin: Female singer

Mohulla: Locality

Mujra: Performances by courtesans, involving singing and dancing

Mushaira: A gathering of poets

Mutaee Bibi: A wife in a temporary marriage; this is valid in the Shia sect

Nain: Female barber

Nasb: By virtue of birth

Nasbi: By birth status

Nawab: Feudal

Nath: Nose ring

Naturees: Unbeliever

Nau: New

Nauha khawani: Sad elegy sung in commemoration of the martyrs of Qarbala

Neg: Token money or jewellery given and taken at auspicious occasions. These are mostly given to women and sons-in-law.

Nikah: Muslim marriage ceremony

Paigham bhejna: Send an offer for marriage

Paji: Demoralised, low born

Palkis: Palanquin

Pallu: Mantle; the part of the *dupatta* that is left loose and floating

Panbharan: Female water carrier

Pargana: District

Purdah: Veil

Purdanashin: Veiled woman

Parja: Common man/woman; in villages, *parja* is referred to lower-class people who provide services to the upper class. Its literal meaning is the ruled, or common people.

Pyjama: Trousers

Qaum: Community

Qasbi: Low-ranking prostitute

Qasba: Town

Qasida: Verse

Qawwal: A community of singers who sing while clapping their hands. Indeed, *qawwali* often refers to music competitions between two groups of *qawwal*s.

Randi: Prostitute

Rath: Chariot

Riasat: Princely state

Risaldar: High-ranking soldiers in the later Mughal period

Sabha: Meeting

Saltanat: Kingdom

Sati: A Hindu woman who immolates herself on the funeral pyre of her husband

Seer land: Land assigned for personal use, as allotted by the landlord

Shaer: Poet

Shagird: Pupil

Shariat: Quranic injunction

Sharafat: Gentleness

Shariat: Islamic law

Sharif: Gentle

Shastra: Knowledge based on principles that are held to be timeless.

Shia: A group of Muslims who believe only in the Prophet Muhammad and Ali, son-in-law of the Prophet, as *khalifa* (religious and political supreme), and reject the other three khalifa: Abu Baqr Siddique, Umar Farooq and Usman

Shirq: Un-Islamic custom not authenticated by the Quran and the Sunnah

Sohar: Baby shower, song sung at the birth of a child

Soem: A custom practised on the third day after a death

Suhag: Marriage symbol worn by women

Sunni: One who believes in Islam and the Prophet Muhammad and his four companions as khalifa, including Ali, Abu Baqr, Usman and Farooque.

Sunnah: Following the Prophetic tradition

Swarn: Hindus born in the top three social castes, Brahmin, Kshatriya, Vaishya

Tahzeeb: Culture

Tak: Walled arch

Takhallus: Nom de plume

Taleem: Education

Talliqdar: Big landlord

Talaq: Divorce

Tameez: Manners

Tamtam: A kind of chariot

Tauhid: Belief in the oneness of God

Tawaif: Courtesan

Tawiz: Amulet

Tihaja: One who has been married at least twice before

Thumri: Composition

Urs: Annual celebration of a saint's birth

Ulema: Religious master of the Muslims

Umma: One who believes in Islam across all castes, sects and ethnicity

Uptan: Turmeric paste

Ustaad: Master

Wajib-ul Arz: The exclusion of strangers from a village. Under the law of *Wajib ul arz*, before a co-sharer fixes a price, the owner has the right to whatever price he can command from an outsider.

Wazifa: Scholarship

Yawani: Muslim woman

Zamindar: Landlord

Zenana: Feminine, women's domain

Bibliography

Government Records and Printed Documents

1. Board of Revenue Records, Regional Archive (RA), Allahabad.
2. *Census Report of North Western Province of Agra and Oudh* (henceforth CR), 1881, compiled by Edmund White, Allahabad, NAI, New Delhi.
3. CR, 1891, D. C. Bailey, Allahabad, 1894, NAI, New Delhi.
4. CR, 1901, R. Burn, Allahabad, 1902, NAI, New Delhi.
5. CR, 1911, E. A. H. Blunt, Allahabad, 1912, AU Central Library, Allahabad.
6. CR, 1921, E. H. H. Edye, Allahabad, 1921, State Archive, Lucknow.
7. Criminal Records, RA, Allahabad.
8. Depart.: Judicial, Sub.: Female Medical Education, 1889, Bundle 161, Box No. 224, Sl. No. 13, File No. 166.
9. *Gazetteer of the Province of Oudh*, Vol. III N–Z, North Western Provinces and Oudh Government Press, Allahabad, 1878.
10. Home Department: Sanitary, September 1890, Nos. 24–25.
11. Home: Education, 1868.
12. Home: Judicial, Proceedings, Nov. 1885, File No. 2122.
13. Home Department: Public, 1862, Port B, Proceeding 5 March, Nos. 37–38, NAI, New Delhi.
14. Home Department: Public, 1859, RA, Allahabad.
15. *Indian Law Report* (ILR), Allahabad, Vols. II, VII, X, XII, XIII, XIV, XV, XVI, XVII.
16. Mutiny Papers, Collected from NAI, New Delhi.
17. Port Blair Proceedings, December 1886 to 1990, NAI, New Delhi.
18. *Social Legislation: Its Role in Social Welfare*, 1956, The Planning Commission, Government of India, New Delhi.
19. *The Gazetteer of India*, Vol. II, History and Culture, 1973, Ministry of Education & Social Welfare, New Delhi.

20. *The Imperial Gazetteer of India: The Indian Empire*, Vol. 1 (Oxford: Clarendon Press, 1907).
21. *The Imperial Gazetteer of India: The Indian Empire*, Vol. IV, Administrative, Published under the authority of His Majesty's Secretary of State for India in Council, (Oxford: Clarendon Press, 1909).
22. *The Imperial Gazetteer of India: The Indian Empire*, Economic, Vol-III (Oxford: Clarendon Press, 1908), AU Central Library, Allahabad.
23. The Countess of Dufrin Fund: Vth Annual Report, 1890, NAI, New Delhi.

Primary Sources

Action, William, *Prostitution: Its Moral, Social and Sanitary Aspects* (London: Frank CASS), Collected from All India Women's Conference, New Delhi.

Ahmad, Maulvi Basheer Uddin (ed.), *Lecturon ka Majmua: Maulvi Hafiz Nazeer Ahmad, Jild-1,* Collected from AU Central Library, 1918.

Ahmad, Nazir, *The Brides Mirror*, G. E. Ward (trans.), (New Delhi: Permanent Black, 2004).

Ali, Munshi Abdul, *Alfaiz al Zari, Sham-e oudh* (Lucknow, 1901).

Bart, Sir Richard Temple, *Men and Events of My Time in India* (Delhi: B. R. Publishing Company, 1882).

Bilgrami, Saiyid Iftikhar Alam, *Vakeel-e Nuswa* (Aligarh: Institute Press, 1907).

————, *Hayaat-un Nazir* (1912).

Bilington, Mary Francis, *Women of India* (1894), Collected from NAI, New Delhi.

Copper, Elizabeth, *Women Custom and Folklore, Harem and the Purda* (London: T. Fisher Unwin Ltd, 1915).

Crook, William, *The North Western Provinces of India: Their History, Ethnology and Administration* (Delhi: Low Price Publication, Vth edn, 1897).

Hali, Altaf Husain, *Hayat-e Javed* (New Delhi: Taraqqi Urdu Board, 1979).

Harris, Lady James P., *A Lady's Diary of the Siege of Lucknow: April 15, 1857 to January 3, 1858* (New Delhi: Asian Education Service, 2006).

Hasan, Mrs. Meer, *An Observation on Musalman of India*, Vol. 1 (London, 1832).

Homes, T. R. E., *Story of the Indian Mutiny* (London: H. Allen & Co., 1888).

Howards, William and Russell Howards, *My Indian Mutiny Diary,* Michel Edwards (ed.), (London: Cassell & Co. Ltd., 1957).

Hull, E. C. P., *Europeans in India* (New Delhi: Asian Educational Services, 2004).

Khan, Sir Saiyid Ahmed, *Asbab-e Baghawat Hind,* Abu Layis Siddiqui (ed.), (Karachi: Urdu Academy, 1976).

Majmua Lectures va Speech, Nawab Mohsin –ul Mulk Saiyiid Mehndi Ali Khan (Aligarh: Madrasat-ul Uloom; Lahore: Nawal Kishor Printing Press, 1904).

Mill, John Stuart, *Striyon ki Pradheenta* (Hindi translation by Rajkamal Prakashan, 2002 [1867]).

Minault, Gail (trans.), *Voices of Silence* (New Delhi: Chanakya Publication, 1986).

Mohemmadan Educational Conference Report, Aligarh, AMU, 1896.

Panipati, Sheikh Ismail (ed.), *Maqalat-e Sir Saiyid*, Vol. 13 (Aligarh: Akhbar-e Scientific Society, 1876).

Raikes, Charles, *Notes on the Revolt in the NWP of India* (London: Longman & Roberts, 1858).

Rasoom-e Hind, Sir Rishta-e Taleem (Panjab, 1868).

Russel, William Howard, *My Diary in India in the Year 1858–59* (London: George Routledge & Sons).

Sarwar, Mohemmad (ed.), *Ap Beeti- Meri Zindagi Ke Pachas Sal: Majameen Mohemmad Ali* (Delhi: Maqtab Jamia, 1927).

Siddiqui, Atique (ed.), *1857 Akhbar aur Dastavez* (Delhi: Urdu Bazar, 1966).

Tassy, Gracin De, *Muslim Festivals in India,* M. Waseem (trans. and ed.), (New Delhi: Oxford University Press, 1997).

Thanvi, Ashraf Ali, *Behisht-e Zewar* (New Delhi: New A. S. Press, 1994).

Wakefield, W., *Our Life and Travels in India* (London, 1878).

Journals

Aligarh Magzine: Khawateen Number, Naved Anjum (ed.), (Aligarh: AMU, 2001).

Aligarh Law Journal, Mahmood Number, Vol. V, Md. Anis Ansari (ed.), (Aligarh: AMU).

Ashat-us Sunnate Nabuat, Jild 11, 1888, Abu Sayeed (ed.), (Lahore; Aligarh: AMU).

Indian Journal of Gender Studies (New Delhi: Sage Publications).

Islah, Mohammad Ghulam Husain (ed.), Saiyid Ali Haider, 1315 (H), No. V, Jild I.

Maroof, Haji Mohemmad Ismail Khan and Md. Wasi Uddin Salim (eds), 1 May 1899 (Aligarh: MAO College).

Payam-e Yar, Nisar Husain (ed.), Lukhnow, 1877 onwards, Maulana Azad Libraray, AMU, Aligarh.

Risala- e Anjuman-e Panjab, 1869–70.

Social Reformer: Tahzeeb-e Akhlaq, No. 41, 1281 H.

Newspapers

Collection of vernacular newspapers from the 'Report on Native Newspaper of NWP of Agra and Oudh', NAI, New Delhi: *Akhbar-e Alam (Meerutt), AL- Rashid (Allahabad), Azad (Lukhnow), Delhi Punch (Lahore), Sitara-e Hind, Subodh Sindhu, The Almora Akhbar, The Amir-ul Akhbar (Meerutt), The Halat-e Hind, The Colonel, (Moradabad), The Hamdard (Fyzabad), The Nurul Anwar (Cawnpore), The Paryag Mitra (Allahabad), The Paryag Samachar (Allahabad), The Mihir Nimroz (Bijnour), The Nasim-e Agra, The Najmul Akhbar (Etawah), The Nasim-e Hind (Fatehpur), The Bharat Bandhu (Aligarh), The Nairang (Agra), The Hindustani (Lukhnow), The Rafi-*

ul Akhbar (Benares), The Sajjan Kirti Sudhakar, The Jam-e Uloom (Moradabad), The Roznamah (Lukhnow), The Cawnpore Gazzett, The Mulk-e Shuhda (Lahore), The Rohilkhand Punch.

Oudh Akhbar (Lukhnow), Jild 10, 1868; also No. 47, 1892, Maulana Azad Library, AMU.

Oudh Panch (Lukhnow), No. 45, 1892, Maulana Azad Library, AMU.

Fiction

Ahmed, Maulvi Nazir:
- *Aiyama, 1891*
- *Banat-ul Nas, AU Central Library*
- *Fasana-e Mubtala* (New Delhi: Kitabi Duniya, 2003)
- *Ibn ul Waqt* (Qaumi Urdu Council Addition, 2005).
- *Mirat-ul Uroos* (Lucknow: Uttar Pradesh Urdu Academy; Aligarh: AMU)
- *Taubat-un Nasooh* (Qaumi Urdu Council Addition, 2005).

Hali, Altaf Husain:

Majalis-un Nisa
- Munajat-e Bewa
- Chup-ki Dad

Ruswa, Mirza Hadi, *Umrao Jan-e Ada* (New Delhi: Lerity Art Press, Pataudi House, 1991).

Secondary Sources

Abdullah, Shaikh, *Sawan-e Hayat-e Beghum Abdullah* (Aligarh, 1956).

Ahmed, Qayamuddin, *Wahabi Movement in India* (Calcutta, 1966).

Ahmad, Aziz, *Studies in Islamic Culture in Indian Environment* (Oxford: Clarendon Press, 1969).

Ahmad, Imtiaz (ed.), *Modernization and Social Change among Muslims in India* (New Delhi: Manohar, 1983).

Ahmad, Rafiuddin, 'The Bengal Muslims 1871–1906: A Quest of Identity', in *India's Muslims Omnibus* (New Delhi: Oxford University Press, 2008).

Agarwal, C. M., *Nari: Facet of Indian Womanhood* (New Delhi: Indian Publisher Distributer, 2000).

Akhtar, Shahid, *Muslim Law Digest* (Allahabad: Premium Publication Co., 1999).

Ali, Azra Asghar, *The Emergence of Feminism among Indian Muslim Women: 1920–1947* (New Delhi: Oxford University Press, 2000).

Ali, Md. Saiyid Iqbal, *Saiyid Ahmed Khan ka Safarnama-e Panjab* (Delhi: Educational Publishing House, 1979).

Angol, Padma, *The Emergence of Feminism in India, 1850–1920* (USA: Ashgate, 2005).

Anjum, Mohini (ed.), *Muslim Women in India* (New Delhi: Radiant Publishers, 1992).

Anwar, Ali, *Masawat Ki Jang* (New Delhi: Vani Prakashan, 2001).

Amin, Shahid (ed.), *A Concise Encyclopedia of North Indian Peasant Life* (New Delhi: Manohar, 2006).

Azhar, Mirza Ali, *King Wajid Ali Shah of Oudh* (Karachi: Royal Books and Company, 1982).

Basheer, Zeenat, *Nazeer Ahmed ke Navilon me Nusvae Kirdar* (Hyderabad: Iliyas Traders Publishers and Book Sellers, 1991).

Basu, Aparna, *The Growth of Education and Political Development in India: 1898–1920.*

Begum, Rehmani, *Sir Sayed Ahmad Khan: The Politics of Education Reform* (VANGUARD).

Bhatnagar, G. D., *Oudh under Wajid Ali Shah* (Varansi, 1968).

Bhatacharya, Sabyasachi, Joseph Bara, Chinna Rao Yagati and B. M. Sankhdhar (eds), *Development of Women's Education: 1850–1920* (New Delhi: Krishna Publication and Distributers, 2001).

Brijbhushan, Jamila, *Muslim Women: In Purda and Out of it* (New Delhi: Vikas Publishing House).

Dalrymple, William, *The Last Mughal: The Fail of a Dynasty Delhi, 1857* (New Delhi: Penguin Viking, 2006).

David, Saul, *The Indian Mutiny: 1857* (Viking).

Diwan, Paras and Piyush Diwan, *Muslim Law on Maintenance in India* (New Delhi: Deep and Deep Publication).

Edwards, S. M., *Crime in British India* (New Delhi: ABC Publishing House, 1983).

Naggendra Kumar Singh (ed.), *Encyclopedia of Indian Women*, Vol. I–III, 2001.

Engineer, Asghar Ali, *Islam and Muslims: A Critical Reassessment* (Jaipur: Printwell Publishers).

Forbes, Geraldine, *Women in Modern India: The New Cambridge History of India* (Cambridge University Press, 1998).

Ghosh, Indira, *Women Travelers in India: The Power of Female Gaze*, (New Delhi: Oxford University Press, 1998a).

__________, *Memsahib Abroad: Writing By Women Travellers in 19th Century India* (New Delhi: Oxford University Press, 1998b).

Graff, Voilette (ed.), *Lucknow: Memories of a City* (Oxford University Press, 1997).

Gupta, Pratul Chandra, *Nana Sahib and the Rising at Cawnpore* (Oxford: Clarendon Press, 1963).

Hasan, Mushirul, *A Moral Reckoning* (New Delhi: Oxford University Press, 2009).

__________, *From Pluralism to Separatism: Qasbas in Colonial Awadh* (New Delhi: Oxford University Press, 2004).

Heimsath, Charles H. *Indian Nationalism & Hindu Social Reform* (Bombay: Oxford University Press, 1964).

Hibbert, Christopher, *The Great Mutiny: India 1857* (London: Penguin Books, 1980).

Hodges, Sarah (ed.), *Reproductive Health in India: History, Politics and Controversies* (Hyderabad: Orient Black Swan, 2006).

Husain, Tassadduq, *Begmat-e Oudh* (Lucknow: Kitab Nagar, 1956).

Jaffery, Patricia, *Frogs in Well: Indian Women in Purda* (New Delhi: Manohar, 2000).

Jain, Devaki (ed.), *Indian Women* (New Delhi: Publication Division, Ministry of Information and Broadcasting, Government of India).

Jaisingh, Indira (ed.), *Justice for Women* (Goa: The Other India Press, 1996).

Joardar, B., *Prostitution in India* (New Delhi: Inter India Publications, 1986).

Joshi, P. C. (ed.), *Rebbelion 1857* (New Delhi: National Book Trust India, 2007).

Jones, V. R. and Beven, *Women in Islam* (Lucknow: The Lukhnow Publishing House, 1941).

Joshi, S. T., *A Documentary History of Prejudice against Women* (Promtheus Books, 2006).

Kausar, Kabir and Inamul Kabir, *Biographical Dictionary of Prominent Muslim Ladies* (New Delhi: Light and Life Publishers, 1982).

Khan, Gulfishan, *Indian Muslim Perceptions of the West during 18th Century* (Karachi: Oxford University Press, 1998).

Khan, Iftikhar Alam, *Sir Saiyid Ahmad Khan* (New Delhi: Urdu Academy, 2008).

Kinsley, Davis, *The Population of India and Pakistan* (New Jersey, 1951).

Krishnamurty, J. K. (ed.), *Women in Colonial India: Essays on Survival, Work and the State* (New Delhi: Oxford University Press, 1989).

Lateef, Shahida, *Muslim Women in India: Political and Private Realities: 1890–1980s* (New Delhi: Kali for Women, 1990).

Lown, Judy, *Women and Industrialisation: Gender at Work in 19th Century England* (UK: Polity Press, 1990).

MacMillan, Margaret, *Women of the Raj* (London: Thames and Hudson, 1980).

Mehndi, Sughra, *Urdu Adab men Khawateen Ka Hissa,* (New Delhi: Urdu Academy, 2006).

Metcalf, Barbara Daly, *Perfecting Women* (New Delhi: Oxford University Press, 2002).

__________, 'Islamic Revival in British India. Deoband 1860–1900', in *India's Muslims* (New Delhi: Oxford University Press, 2008).

Metcalf, Barbara Daly and Thomas R. Metcalf, *A Concise History of Modern India* (New Delhi: Cambridge University Press, 2008).

Minault, Gail, *Secluded Scholar: Women's Education and Muslim Social Reform in Colonial India* (New Delhi: Oxford University Press, 1998).

Mishra, Kameshwar Nath, *Kashi ki Sangeet Parampara (Sangeet Jagat ko Kashi Ka Yogdan)* (Lucknow: Bharat Book Centre, 1997).

Mohanty, Manoranjan (ed.), *Class, Caste and Gender* (New Delhi: Sage Publications, 2004).

Mohemmad, Shan (ed.), *The Aligarh Movement: Basic Documents: 1864–1894* (Meenakshi Prakashan, 1978).

Mujeeb, M. *The Indian Muslims* (London: George Allen and Unwin, 1967).

Mumtaz, Khawar and Farida Shaheed (eds), *Women of Pakistan: Two Steps Forward, One Step Back* (London and New Jersey: Zed Books Ltd., 1987).

Nadvi, S. Abdul Hasan, *The Musalman* (Lucknow: Islamic Research and Publication, 1977).

Nagar, Amrit Lal, *Ye Kothe Waliyan,* Collected from Hindi Sahitya Sammelan Library, Allahabad.

Nair, Janki, *Women and Law in Colonial India* (Bangalore: National School of Indian University, 1996).

Nanda, B. R. (ed.), *Indian Women: From Purda to Modernity* (New Delhi: Radiant Publishers, 1990).

Natrajan, S., *A Century of Muslim Social Reform in India* (Bombay: Ashia Publishing House, 1962).

Nizami, Khawaja Hasan, *1857 Ki Kahaniyan*, Jagdeesh Chandra (trans.), (New Delhi: National Book Trust, 2008).

Nizami, K. A., *Saiyid Ahmed Khan* (New Delhi: Ministry of Information & Broadcasting, Government of India, 1959).

———, *1857 Ki Tarikh-e Roznamcha* (Delhi: Nadwat-ul Musnafeen, 1958).

Papanek, Hanna and Gail Minault (eds), *Separate World: Studies of Purdah in South Asia* (New Delhi: Chanakya Publications, 1982).

Qureshi, Ishrat Ali (ed.), *Proceedings of Seminar on Educational needs of Indian Muslims and the Role of Aligarh Movement* (Aligarh: The Duty Society, AMU, 1993).

Reves, Peter, *Landlords and Governments in Uttar Pradesh: A Study of their Relations until Zamindari Abolition* (Oxford University Press, 1991).

Robinson, Francis, *Separatism among Muslims of India* (New Delhi: Oxford University Press, 1993).

———, *Farangi Mahall and Islamic Culture* (New Delhi: Permanent Black, 2005).

Roy, Shibani, *Status of Muslim Women in North India* (Delhi: B. R. Publishing Corporation, 1979).

Ruswa, Mirza Hadi, *Umrao Jaan e Ada,* David Mathews (trans.), (New Delhi: Rupa & Co., 1996).

Said, Edward, *Orientalism* (Penguin Books).

Sarkar, Mahua, *Visible Histories Disappearing Women: Producing Muslim Womanhood in late Colonial Bengal* (New Delhi: Zubaan, 2008).

Schimel, Annemarie, *Islamic Society and Culture: A 19th Century Anthropology of Poetess* Collected from G. B. Pant Social Science Institute, Allahabad.

Sen, Indrani, *Women and Empire* (New Delhi: Orient BlackSwan, 2002).

Segal, Zohra, *Memoirs of a Life on Stage and Screen: Close-Up* (New Delhi: Women Unlimited, 2010).

Sharar, Abdul Haleem, *Lukhnow: The Last Phase of Oriental Culture* (New Delhi: Oxford University Press, 1994).

Sharma, Raj Bahadur, *Christian Mission in North India: 1813–1913* (New Delhi: Mittal Publication, 1988).

Srivastava, Sushil, *Disputed Mosque* (New Delhi: Sage Publications, 1991).

Souza, Eunice De (ed.), *Pardah: An Anthology* (New Delhi: Oxford University Press, 2004).

Tharu, Susie and K. Lalita, *Women Writing in India* (New Delhi: Oxford University Press, 1991).

Trivedi, Madhu, *The Making of the Awadh Culture* (New Delhi: Primus Books, 2010).

Verma's Commentaries on Mohemmadan Law, 8th edn, (Allahabad: Law Publisher [India] Private Ltd., 2004).

Wani, M. Afzal, *The Islamic Law on Maintenance of Women & Children, Parents and other Relatives* (Kashmir: Upright Study Home, 1995).

———, *The Islamic Institution of Mahr* (Kashmir: Upright Study Home).

Ward, Andrew, *Our Bones are Scattered: The Cawnpore Massacres and the Indian Mutiny* (New York: A John Macrrae Book, Henry Holt & Co., 1996).

Zaman, Md. Shafiquz, *Problems of Minorities in India* (Hyderabad: Booklink Corporation, 2001).

Index

Abbasi Begum, 139n
Abbasi Jan Ada, 162
Abidi Begum, 114
Abul Qasim Mohtesim, 86
Ajlaf, 3, 4, 10
    nau Muslims, 4, 7, 9, 11, 92
Afroz Begum, 61n,
Aftab Jahan, 87n
Agra, 105, 177, 194
Agra Medical College, 52, 53, 107
Aiyama, 133
Akbari Begum, 87
Akbar Allahabadi, 89
Akhbar-e Scientific Society, 18, 138
Alam Begum, 88
Aligarh, 18, 50, 91, 121
    Aligarh Movement, xxvii, 19, 20, 29, 30, 34, 92, 108
    Aligarh first generation, 120
Allahabad, xiv, 3, 50, 60, 68, 105, 136, 184
    Allahabad zenana Hospital, 53
Allahdad Fatima, 83n
Allen Victoria Heming, 159
Altaf Husain Hali, xxiin, 18 n, 21, 22, 23, 27, 28, 57n, 82n, 93, 109, 132, 140n
    his concern towards social evils of society, 24
    his laments for ashraf Muslims decline, 28, 47
Amrit Lal Nagar, 160, 161, 178
Amroha, 49n
Anjuman Khawateen-e Hind, 72
Anjuman Rafatiya, xvi n
Anglo-Indian, 126
Anthony Seldon, xiii
Arabic, 9, 30, 38, 81, 87, 201, 205
Arzal, xi, 6, 11, 92
    low born Muslim, 3, 4
    untouchable Muslims, 7, 8
    praja caste, 8
    conversion of low born Hindu and wandering caste, 10
    their ignorance of Islamic tenets, 10
Ashraf, 3, 4, 7, 10
    Perso-Islamic culture, 10n
    ashraf culture, 10n
    ashrafization, 14
Ashraf Ali Thanvi, 50, 117, 120, 123, 132, 139, 140
Ashrafun Nisa, 84
Ayah, 191n
Ayesha Jalal, 56
Azamgarh, 60, 176
Azim Ullah Khan, 66
Azkar-e Khawateen, 87
Aziz un Nisa, xxii, 22, 114, 140
Aziz-un Nisa, 186

Badayun, 88
Bahadur Shah Zafar, 55, 56n, 64

Bahistan-e Naz, 86
Bahraich, 49n
Bahu Begum, 88
Banat ul Nas, 93
Barah Saiyid, 22
Bareli, 3
  Barelvi, 3, 112
Bashir Ahmad, 25
Begmat Ke Aansu, 62
Beghum Hazrat Mahal, 59
Begum of Bhopal, 42
Begum Mumtaz Mahal, 189
Begum of Oudh, 87, 126, 140
Begum of Rampur, 88
Begum Shah Jahan, 42
Behisht-e zewar, 50 n, 120, 139
Benaras, 60, 135, 136, 159, 167, 176, 194n
Bengal, 38
Bhartendu Harish Chandra, 178
Bhopal, 135
Bibi Allah Bandi, xviii
Bibi Bechun Nisa, 183
Bibi Nasir-un Nisa, 51
Bihar, 12n
Bijnour, 25,
Bi Nawab Begum Sahiba, 85
British, xxvi, 38
  class, race and ethnicity, 41n,
British perception about Islam and Muslim, 37n, 38, 41, 197, 198
  Muslim abductors, 37
  Britsih observation on social custom, 39
  powerful purdah, 42
  interracial marriages, xiii, 42n, 68, 69, 122
  Colonel Gardner's marriage, xiii
  British divisive policy, 4 n, 43, 198
  demand for separate accommodation on the ground of religion, 52
  demand for separate national school for Hindus, 97
  British policy regarding prostitution, 169, 170
  British system of Law, 202
Bulandshahar, 29, 61
Bundelkhand, 136, 189

Calcutta, 160, 176
Chail, 71, 184, 189
Chaudharain Sahib-un Nisa, 183
Child Marriage and Age of Consent debate, 210
  widespread prevalence of child marriage, 212
  Nawab Ehsan Ullah support to Age of Consent Bill, 213
  debate in Legislative Assembly, 213
  Sheikh Kamil's case, 214
  marriageable age in various caste of Muslims, 216
Christianity, 2, 42
Christopher Hibbert, 61n
Chup ki Dad, 24, 151
Codification of Law, 199
  flexibility in traditional law, 199
  complexities of British Judicial system, 199
  Warren Hasting views on traditional Indian law, 200, 201
  Indian Law Report, 200
  Hindu Shastra, 201
  Muslim Shariat, 201
Colonial feminism, vi
  colonial historiography, xvi
Common social structure of Hindu-Muslim, xxv
  ganga-jamuni tahzeeb, xxviii, 121
  composite culture, 14, 121, 178
  Hindustani culture, 112,
Contagious Disease Act, 69
Court culture, xix
  shift of court culture from Delhi to Lukhnow, xix

Dacca, 194
Dar-ul Uloom, 18, 32
Dehradun, 110
Delhi, v, xxiii, 20, 23, 25, 54, 60, 60, 62, 82, 87n, 89, 116, 194
 cultural hub, v
Delhi College, 29
Deoband, 20, 32
 Deobandi, 3, 120, 124
Dower and Maintenance Rights, 207
 mahr, 207
 Fatimi Mahr, 208n
Dufferin Medical Fund, 50, 52, 107,

East India Company, XII, xxi
East-West intermingling, xiii, xxviii
 interaction between women of the East and West, xiiin
 Rudyard Kipling, xiii
English, 30, 83, 205
Etawa, xvi, 22, 171
European account about 1857, 65
 John Shepherd, 65
 Keith Young, 65
 John Fitchet, 66
 Mrs Sneyd, 67
European Missionaries, xxi, 49, 107
 missionary school, 105
 missionary concern, vii
 Christian missionaries, 78, 79, 80, 95, 96
 European lady tutor, 107
European 126, 169
 European Scholar, 38
 European Traveler 41n, 50, 132, 140, 210
 European men, 43
 European women, xiii, xxix, 50, 116
 European account, xxi
 European's happy marriage, 121
 Indo-European relationship, 122
 European Judges, 201

Faiz Ali, 63
Faizabad, 60, 96, 98, 99
Fanny Park, xvi, 36n
Farukhabad, 61, 64
Fasana-e Mubtala, 25, 126
Fatehpur, 184
Feminism in South Asia, xi,
Firangi Mahal, 3, 125
Firoz-un Nisa, 139n
Flora Annie Steel, 43

Gauhar Jan, 159
Gender discrimination for inheritance right, 182
Ghazipur, 18, 155, 172
Gopamau, xviii
Gorakhpur, 88
Gudri ka Lal, 87
Gujar, 61, 62
 Gujar women, xiv,
Gurudaspur, 90

Haji Ismail Khan, 73, 79n, 92
Hamilton, 197
Handicraft, 193, 194
Hasina Begum, 86
Hayat-e Javed, xxii, xxiii n, 18 n, xxv n
Heart, 23
Hedaya, 29, 197
Hina Sahiba, 162
Hindi newspaper, 138
Hindu, Hindu myth, 37
 Hindu women, x, xxvi, 37, 43, 45, 78
 Hindu prostitute conversion issue, 47
 Hindu Brahmin, 57
 influence of Hindu culture, xxviii
 Hindu custom, xxviii
 social discrimination inherent in Hindu society, 11
 unveiled Hindu women, 2
 Hindu social reformer, 79
 question of nationalism with Hindus, 98

social intermingling between Hindu and Muslim, 131
Hindu influence, 132
dominant culture of Hindu, 133
Hindustani Zubaan, 22,
Hira Mandi, 160
Hirman, xx
Huquq-e Niswa, 32, 210,
Husain Begum Umrao, 55,
Hyderabad, xx

Ibrat-un Nisa, 64
Indian Law Report, 200
Fazle Rab vs. Khatun Bibi, 200
Mariam Bai vs. Sakina and others, 200n
Murtazai Bibi vs Jamuna Bibi, 204n
Mirza Anand Ram vs. Masuma Begum, 204n
Mariam Bibi vs. Sakina, 206
Hayat-un Nisa vs. Md. Ali Khan, 206n
Sughra Bibi vs. Masuma Bibi, 207n
Abdul Qadir vs. Salima, 207n
Mahbuban vs Fakir Bakhsh, 207n
Amini Begum vs. Md. Karim, 209n
Jamaitun nisa vs. Lutfun Nisa, 209n
Liaqat Ali vs Karimun Nisa, 210n
Allahdad Khan vs. ismail Khan, 210n
Iqrarnama, xxv, 128, 129
mewakhori, 130, kharch-e pandan, 130
Islam, 2, 42
inferiority of Islam, vi
backwardness of Islam, vii
true nature of Islam, xxviii
important sects of Islam, 3
Islamization, 14
Dar-ul Harb, 77

Jagjeet Singh, 37
Jamila, 62
Jaunpur, 3
Justice Amir Ali, 208
Justice Mahmood, 29, 127, 128, 136n, 202, 205

Kalidas, 37
Kanpur, 60, 159, 166
Kapoorthala, 37
Khadijatun Nisa, 87
Khairabad, xx
Khawaja Akbar Warsi Merathi, 112
Khawaja Hasan Nizami, 56n, 59n, 64n
Khawaja Ghulam Saqlain, 94,
King Ghaziuddin Haider, 125
Koel, 63
Kusum kumari, 51

Lock Hospital, 164, 166, 170
Lahore, 160
Lukhnow, xx, 3, 49n, 60, 84, 86, 88, 98, 99, 105, 115, 116, 136, 156, 158, 168, 173, 194
Lukhnow Zenana Hospital, 51

Mahabharata, 37
Majalis un Nisa, 24, 82n, 93, 100
Malihabad, 100
Malka Jan, 159
Marriage custom, 117, 118, 119, 123
inter caste marriage, 122
divorce, 128, 129
divorce as a stigma, 126
Malka Jan, 160, 176
Marry Francis Billington, 36n, 39n, 132, 142, 194
Mary Kempson, 32
Maulana Muhammad Ahsan, 32
Maulana Qasim Nanautvi, 9 n,
Maulvi Liaqat Ali, xiv
Meerut, 60, 15
Meer Taqi Meer, 4, 13
Milad Shareef, 112, 117
Mirajganj, 100

Mirat ul Uroos, 8, 26, 80, 100, 114
Mirzapur, xvi n, 136
Mirza Sultan, 63
Miss Mary Carpenter, 90
Mohammadan Anglo Oriental College, 20, 73, 91
Moor, 197
Moradabad, 63
Mrs. Meer Hasan, XIII, xvi, xvii, xxii, xxiii, xxiv, xxvi
 polygamy as a plague
Muhammadi Begum, 32, 33, 74, 85, 87
Muharram, 158
Mughal dynasty, 55, 56
Mughal Princes, xix, 61, 82
 Kasifa Sultan, 61
 Nawab Khas Mahal, 61n
 Sarfaraj Begum, 61n
 Nawab Noor Mahal, 62n
 Qulsoom Zamani Begum, 61, 62n, 63
 Hafiz Sultan, 62n
Muslim social reformer, 20, 211
 Muslims hostility towards English Education, 18, 79
 need for English education, 19
 social background of Muslim Social Reformer, 21
 issue of fertility among Muslim, 39, 40
 Census Report Observation on Muslim, 39
 cultural identity of Muslims, vi, Muslim's identity, 2
 Muslims as a separatist, x
 Hindu-Muslim Polarization, x
 declining culture of Muslim society, xxix
 Muslim of Bengal, 1
 social mobility among Muslim, 13
 caste identity of Muslim, 13
Musaddas, 27,
Mumtaz Ali, 21, 32, 73, 74
 his social concern, 33
Munajat-e Bewa, 24, 132, 148
Munshi Muhammad Husain, 99
Mushtari, 172
Muslim as a monolithic category, x, xxvii, 1, 22, 35, 43, 15, 199
Muzaffarnagar, 61

Nargis Nazar, 62
Natiqua Begum, 83
Nazar Sajjad, 87
Nazir Ahmad, xxv, 8, 18, 21, 25, 26, 27, 29, 33, 57, 72, 80, 82, 93, 120, 124, 126, 129, 132, 133, 134, 138, 140,
Nawab Akhtar Mahal, 76
Nawab Mehdi Hasan Mohsin ul Mulk, 21, 22, 34, 73, his views on female education, 22, 121, 123, 127, 139
Nawab Khas Mahal, 61n
Nawab Nasir Jang, 189
Nawab Yusuf Ali Khan, 88, 139n

Oral history, xiii
Origin of social stratification among Muslims, 4, 5
 nasbi birth, 4, 11, hasbi birth, 11
 profession as a criteria for caste identity, 6
 caste discrimination among Muslims, 7, 8, 10
Oudh, 3, 130, 135, 139, 142, 160, 194
 Oudhi culture, xix, 179

Panipat, 23
Partabgarh, 99
Payam-e yar, 86n, 88
Persian, xix, xxii, 30, 38, 81, 86, 87, 201
 classical Persian, 163
Polygamy, 120, 124, 125, 128, 129
Prophet Muhammad, 2, 112
 Prophetic tradition, 112
Professional women, 191, 193
 monthly announce, 191

Property rights of women, 203
  Shia Law of Inhertance, 204, 205
  Musammat Zainab, 200, 204, 205
  shia-sunni legal differences related to inheritance, 205
  Sunni Law, 206n
  Imamia Law, 206n
  Wajib-ul arz, 206
  impact of Transfer of Property Act and Mortgage Sale Deed on women's inheritance, 206,
Purdah, xix, xx, xxi
  purdah system connection with caste, 16
  purdahnashin, 78, 98

Qamaruddin Kaleem, xx, 86
Qaramat Husain, 94
Qateel, 4
Qulsoom Zamani Begum, 56n, 61, 62n

Rahimi, 61
Ramayan, 37
Rampur, 61, 65, 83, 87, 135, 139
Rani Luxmi Bai, 59
Ritual and custom, 115
Rohilkhand, 142
Roqaiyya Sakhawat Husain, 74, 84
Rudranshu Mukharji, 56

Sahib Jan Baqi, 172
Saharanpur, 3
Saiyid Ahmad Shaheed, 30, 31
Saiyid Husain Madani, 13,
Saiyid Iftikhar Bilgrami, 73
Saiyid Mubarak Shah, 65
Saiyid Salar Masood, 49n,
Rebellious women of 1857, 64
  Saqina Begum, 64
  Husaini Khanum, 66
  Adla, 66
  elite courtesans, 70
  roti as a symbol of revolt, xiv

Sanskrit, 201
Sarfraj Begum, 61n
Shah Ismail, 31
Shah Mina, 49n
Shah Wali Ullah, 9, 30
Shams-un Nisa Sharm, xx
Sheikh Abdullaha, 21, 94
Sheikh Saddo, 49n
Sir Saiyid Ahmed Khan, xxii, 18, 19, 20, 21, 26, 32, 49, 57n, 74, 79, 101, 112, 138
  his crusade against social evils, 18, 19, 49
  his views on polygamy, 20
  his views on female education, 22, 90
  His views on child marriage, 212
Sir Lepel Grifin, 37
Shirq, xxv
Sitapur, 171
Sitari Jan, 155, 173
Scientific Society, 18
Sultanpur, 184
Superstition of Indian Famialy, 49
Suraiya Barhi Begum, 87

Tahzeeb-e Ekhlaq, 20, 21, 22, 41n
Tagzeeb-e Niswa, 32, 74, 85
Tatya Tope, 66
Taubat un Nasooh, 26
Tawaif, xix, xx, 155
  mujra, xxii
  Sheerin Jaan, xxii, 89
  Jinna, xxii, Muneer Jan, 157
  Malka Jan, 160
  bari Malka, 163
  Nasim Ara, 160, 161
  Gauhar Jan, 160, 175, 176
  Badre Muneer, 168
  culture of courtesan, xxix
  etiquette and manners, 157
  issue of conversion, 159, 176, 178
  deredar tawaif, 161, 167

Kasbi, 163
Khangi, 163
European prostitute, 164
security concern of European soldiers, 164
economic status of courtesan, 167, 168
impact of Industrialization, 167
cultural aspects, 172
Tilanga, 62
Traditional education system, 81
its curriculum, 82

Umme Safiya, 82n, 114, 126, 208n,
Umrao Begum Abida, 86
Umrao Jan Sahiba, 159
Unnao, 159
Urdu, 81, 87, 93, 97, 117, 155, 178
Urdu Literature, xix, 23
Urdu novel, 87
Urdu newspaper, 81n, 92
Urdu Poet, 24, 47
Urdu Poetess, xx, 88, 89
Urdu as a marker of identity, 81n
Hindi newspaper, 81n
Ustani, 82, 83, 90

Venereal Disease, 70, 164, 170
Vilaeti Begum, xiii
Vinayak Damodar Sawarkar, 68
Violence against women, 140
increasing racial tyranny, 141
Vocational education, 192

Wahabi Movement, 30, 56, 112
Waheed Jahan, 94
Waheed Jan Sahiba, 88
Wahidatun Nisa, 184
Wajid Ali Shah, 160, 175, 177
Weavers migration, 16
Western Education, 32, 79, 80
hostility with western medicine, 50
Widowhood, 24
Hindu Widow, xxvi, 24, 46
widow remarriage, 31, 32, 41, 43, 46, 126, 131, 133
widows suffering aftermath of mutiny, 62
young widows, xxii
prohibition of widow remarriage, xxviii
enforced widowhood, 132, 136
inheritance rights of widows, 133
Hindu widow, 137
economic factor of enforced widowhood, 139
widow's inheritance issue, 187
William Crook, 3 n, 156
Willium Jones, 201
W.W.Hunter, 58

Zaka Ullah, 28, 29, 83, 99, 170
Zeb-un Nisa, 172,
Zeenat Begum Ibrat, 87
Zeenat Mahal, 59
Zenana, xiii, xxi, xxiii 50, 78
purdah, 50
royal zenana, xvi
zenana as a part of both elite Hindu and Muslim, xix
zenana madarsa, 83
Zia-I Ahmadi Begum, 87n,
Zohra Segal, 63, 110
Zohra Bai, 89, 172, 173, 177